Cultural Issues in End-of-Life Decision Making

EDITORS

Kathryn L. Braun
James H. Pietsch
Patricia L. Blanchette

Sage Publications, Inc.
International Educational and Professional Publisher
Thousand Oaks ■ London ■ New Delhi

For information:

Sage Publications, Inc.
2455 Teller Road
Thousand Oaks, California 91320
E-mail: order@sagepub.com

Sage Publications Ltd.
6 Bonhill Street
London EC2A 4PU
United Kingdom

Sage Publications India Pvt. Ltd.
M-32 Market
Greater Kailash I
New Delhi 110 048 India

Printed in the United States of America

Library of Congress Cataloging-in-Publication Data

Main entry under title:

Cultural issues in end-of-life decision making / edited by
    Kathryn L. Braun, James H. Pietsch, and Patricia L. Blanchette.
      p. cm.
    Includes bibliographical references (p.) and index.
    ISBN 0-7619-1216-9 (cloth: alk. paper)
    ISBN 0-7619-1217-7 (pbk.: alk. paper)
    1. Death—Social aspects—United States. 2. Terminal care—United
States—Cross-cultural studies. 3. Minorities—Medical care—United
States. I. Braun, Kathryn. II. Pietsch, James H. III. Blanchette, Patricia L.
    HQ1073.5.U6 C85 2000
    306.9—dc21   99-00673

00   01   02   03   04   05   06   7   6   5   4   3   2   1

Acquiring Editor:	Jim Brace-Thompson
Editorial Assistant:	Anna Howland
Production Editor:	Wendy Westgate
Editorial Assistant:	Cindy Bear
Typesetter/Designer:	Marion Warren
Indexer:	Jeanne Busemeyer
Cover Designer:	Michelle Lee

Cultural Issues in End-of-Life Decision Making

Contents

Preface   ix
Joanne Lynn

Acknowledgments   xii

■ *Introduction*

1. **An Introduction to Culture and Its Influence
   on End-of-Life Decision Making**   **1**
   Kathryn L. Braun, James H. Pietsch, and Patricia L. Blanchette

■ *Part 1*
   **The Medical, Legal, and Ethical
   Context of Death and Dying**   **11**

2. **Physical Aspects of Dying**   **13**
   Julie A. Patterson Fago

3. **Cognitive Changes That Affect Capacity
   and End-of-Life Decisions**   **23**
   Ronald A. Martino

4. **Autonomy, Advance Directives, and the
   Patient Self-Determination Act**   **37**
   James H. Pietsch and Kathryn L. Braun

5. Ethical Considerations and Court Involvement
in End-of-Life Decision Making 55
Marshall B. Kapp

■ *Part* 2
**Ethnic Perspectives on
End-of-Life Decision Making** 69

6. Cultural and Religious Issues for African Americans 71
Charles P. Mouton

7. Advance Directives and End-of-Life Care:
The Hispanic Perspective 83
Melissa A. Talamantes, Celina Gomez, and Kathryn L. Braun

8. Cultural Issues in End-of-Life Decision Making
Among Asians and Pacific Islanders in the United States 101
Gwen Yeo and Nancy Hikoyeda

9. End-of-Life Decision Making in American
Indian and Alaska Native Cultures 127
Nancy Westlake Van Winkle

■ *Part* 3
**Religious Perspectives on
End-of-Life Decision Making** 145

10. Christian Perspectives on End-of-Life
Decision Making: Faith in a Community 147
Mary Rowell

11. Catholic Perspectives on Euthanasia and Assisted
Suicide: The Human Person and the Quest for Meaning 165
Marc R. Alexander

12. Jewish Perspectives on End-of-Life Decision Making 181
William Kavesh

13. Muslim Perspectives Regarding Death, Dying,
and End-of-Life Decision Making 199
Hamid Abdul Hai and Asad Husain

14. **Buddhist Issues in End-of-Life Decision Making**   213
    Ronald Y. Nakasone

■ *Part 4*
End-of-Life Issues in Institutional Cultures
and for Special Populations   229

15. **Issues in End-of-Life Decision Making in the**
    Hospital and Nursing Home Culture   231
    Charon A. Pierson

16. **End-of-Life Issues in the Military Culture**   249
    Patricia W. Nishimoto and Ross E. Newmann

17. **End-of-Life Issues in the HIV/AIDS Community**   265
    Russel Ogden

18. **End-of-Life Issues: A Disabilities Perspective**   285
    Tom Koch

■ *Implications*

19. **Talking to Patients About Death and Dying: Improving**
    Communication Across Cultures   305
    Shari L. Kogan, Patricia L. Blanchette, and Kamal Masaki

Author Index   327

Subject Index   339

About the Contributors   349

Preface

JOANNE LYNN

*D*ying in America has changed. During the early 1900s, most people died rather quickly and unexpectedly—at an average age of 47 years. Now, Americans average over 77 years of age at the time of death, and our deaths are preceded by years of gradually worsening disease and disability. It has taken some time for us to start making changes in society so that services are available to match the changes in dying. We also have started a process of encouraging people to take charge and make decisions. We even have defended the authority of the very sick to have their preferences implemented. Recently, we have begun to learn how to talk of slow courses to death, to deal with uncertainty, and to rearrange finances to match people's needs. Yet, much more needs to be done.

Some of what is needed involves straightforward improvement in medical care. For example, some people still suffer without adequate pain relief, whereas others travel in and out of hospitals with no recognition of delirium. Our laws and regulations are much more likely to censure a physician for overprescribing narcotic drugs than for ignoring pain. Many practitioners do not know how to stop a ventilator or how to set up a patient-controlled analgesia pump. Education of doctors and nurses gives little attention to dying. Sadly, except for cancer pain, research on the care of the dying has been almost nonexistent.

Yet, the dying process itself has become the province of medical care. Most Americans die in hospitals, and another large group die in nursing homes. Regulators of the rhythm of life are medical and nursing staff, and unfortunately, opportunities for family togetherness and spiritual peace are routinely overlooked. Poetry, metaphors, and stories exist to make sense of human experience when it overwhelms us, but these have little natural place in modern health care settings.

Present shortcomings can be improved and, indeed, many in health care now aim to find out how. A key opportunity for improvement occurs when dying people have the time to make plans and control a good deal of what happens at the end of life. Because illnesses that now dominate the causes of death—cancer, heart disease, stroke, and dementia—are relatively slow and predictable, patients and families who are affected can plan ahead and shape the course of living near death. We are just learning how to proceed with planning care in advance and how to improve on standard "living will" forms.

However, a manifestation of our society's unfamiliarity with these issues is that we have very little sensitivity to the different ways in which people perceive dying and planning for death. Of course, there are substantial variations simply on the basis of individual preferences and patterns. But there also are relatively predictable variations based on culture and history. Those variations are important in themselves because they allow people within those cultures to make coherent sense of their mortality and suffering. Variation also serves to illuminate what is essential and what is changeable in the human understanding of our finitude. Persons from one culture often learn a great deal when considering how others have made sense of relationships, illness, disability, and death.

This book aims to help us begin to make sense of the differences that arise among groups of people bound together with a common history. Chapters in this volume form a primer on the rituals and history of a range of important groups comprising parts of the American citizenry. Practitioners will find these explanations helpful in understanding patients and families, whereas administrators will find useful guidance in adapting facilities and practices. Also, policymakers often consider laws and regulations only from the perspective of the dominant American culture. Consideration of the types of insights given here would help to ensure appropriate flexibility so that policies may serve those people from nondominant cultural backgrounds as well.

Also provided are short overviews of the ethics, law, communication strategies, and clinical practices that shape the dominant culture. Explanations elsewhere of how "one is supposed to think" about advance directives seem oddly rational and devoid of passion in that we seemingly speak of medicine and law without dealing much with the emotional and spiritual aspects of human suffering and dying. However, the wonderfully metaphorical and historically rooted perspectives provided here from lesser known cultures are powerful and welcome antidotes.

Admittedly, writers warn us many times not to assume much about a specific person on the basis of identification as part of a certain cultural group, and this admonition is well taken to heart. Variation within groups often is as extreme as variation among groups. Nevertheless, by understanding even a fraction of the histories, cultural assumptions, and languages of various cultural groups, practitioners can better serve the increasing diversity of America's populations.

There is a serious need for more research on which to base cross-cultural comparisons. It is a difficult task, requiring more than the usual interview or chart review for reasonable completeness and insight, and in this light, very little research has been done on end-of-life understandings, rituals, and conceptualizations across cultural groups. However, this book brings together the results of that work with a good deal of insight from the experienced authors of each chapter.

This book has long been needed. It helps to start a continuous process of coming to terms with our diversity, even while our society also is trying to come to better terms with our mortality.

Acknowledgments

As with any book, the compilation of this volume took the efforts of many individuals. Many thanks, first, go to the professionals from across North America who agreed to contribute chapters. Their willingness to participate in this project and their patience with its pace of completion are greatly appreciated. At the University of Hawaii, we are indebted to Carol Matsumiya and Kim Sugawa-Fujinaga, of the Center on Aging at the School of Public Health, who coordinated mailings, proofed and edited documents, identified missing references, and otherwise provided moral support to the editors. Thanks also go to Virginia M. Tanji, School of Public Health librarian, for assistance with searches and references. Third, we thank Sage Publications for its support of this effort. Our primary contacts, Daniel Ruth and Jim Brace-Thompson, were especially helpful in guiding us through the process. Finally, we thank our families and friends for their support of this project.

Chapter 1

An Introduction to Culture and Its Influence on End-of-Life Decision Making

KATHRYN L. BRAUN
JAMES H. PIETSCH
PATRICIA L. BLANCHETTE

For most, the mystery of death and dying continues to defy the imagination. What is seen of death is the finality of the physical body. But what is believed about the meaning of death, how it should be faced, and what happens after physical death varies by culture and its associated religion (DeSpelder & Strickland, 1992; Johnson & McGee, 1991).

For example, when we lose a loved one, our culture helps to explain why this death has occurred at this time and in this way. We look to our culture for advice on how to act when a death occurs, how to express grief, and how to remember the person who has died. We find comfort in the rituals that the culture prescribes when a death occurs, and culture presents a structure within which death takes on meaning (DeSpelder & Strickland, 1992; Johnson & McGee, 1991).

Complicating the mystery of death, however, is the collision of medical, legal, and ethical issues that affects the experience of death at the dawn of the 21st century. Although scientific progress has led to previously unimagined cures and the possibility of prolonging human life beyond natural limits, the result sometimes is a painful, uncomfortable, or burdensome process to an inevitable end, often with a loss of control and dignity. There is a notion that the modern death can be planned for and that these actions will improve its timing and meaningfulness. At the same time, death has become invisible and unfamiliar because it has been delegated to professionals and occurs most frequently in health care facilities rather than at home. Thus, although we are encouraged to plan for death, we have little familiarity with it (DeSpelder & Strickland, 1992). These intersecting phenomena raise a number of questions:

- How do we face modern death in a modern time?
- What guidelines do cultural and religious traditions offer for making decisions about treatment preferences, surrogate decision makers, organ donation, and so forth?
- How does an organizational culture, such as that of a hospital, affect dying?
- Have the experiences of specific groups of individuals, such as people with HIV/AIDS and people with disabilities, influenced their views of death and dying?
- How are cultures and religions adapting (or not) as they are called to offer guidance for the more complicated and prolonged death experienced today?

■ CULTURE AND PLURALISM

Culture, in its broadest sense, refers to the worldview, values, norms, and behavior guidelines shared by a group of individuals (Brislin, 1993). When asked to think about a culture, we often think about a group of people, often with the same racial background, who share a language, a religious orientation, feelings about family, and a perspective on how life should be approached. Traditionally, the word *culture* is associated with specific ethnic groups (e.g., Japanese culture). However, it also can be applied to specific religious groups (e.g., Jewish culture), specific regional groups (e.g., culture of the U.S. South), specific institutions (e.g., military culture), and specific interest groups (e.g., culture of people living with AIDS). Each of these groups has explicit or implicit rules of conduct and a language that includes a specific set of symbols and perhaps acronyms associated with the group.

The United States is a nation in which individuals from a multitude of countries and traditions reside. Although the earlier conceptualization of U.S. society was of a "melting pot," this theory of assimilation is being rejected

(Locke, 1992). Instead, we see a call for the appreciation and celebration of the diversity of cultures within the country. Thus, the United States truly is becoming a more multicultural or pluralistic society. A pluralistic society is one in which "members of diverse ethnic, racial, religious, or social groups maintain an autonomous participation in and development of their traditional culture or special interest within the confines of a common civilization," and the basic definition of pluralism is "a theory that there are more than one or more than two kinds of ultimate reality" (Merriam-Webster, 1998, p. 896). Accordingly, there is more than one "truth" about how people can understand life and structure responses to it.

This acknowledgment of multiple truths requires that a society do more than allow multiple cultures to exist side by side in harmony (Loustaunau & Sobo, 1997). Members of a truly pluralistic society also must learn enough about different cultures to help individuals within them to help define the issues and the criteria for their resolution.

■ HOW THE DOMINANT CULTURE INFLUENCES END-OF-LIFE CARE

Even within the ideal of a pluralistic society, there still exists a dominant U.S. culture. The themes of the dominant U.S. culture, identified by Williams (1970), are listed in Table 1.1. These themes have influenced the development of the U.S. legal and medical systems as they structure the dying experience. For example, the value of individual autonomy is seen in laws that require a patient's informed consent for treatment and that allow an individual to specify in advance of incapacitation the type of treatment he or she would want. These values are reflected in the view of death as a "failure" of science and human will to assert mastery over the environment. Dominant values of materialism and secularism might have worked to shorten traditional ceremonies and sanctioned grieving periods when someone dies.

Looking more closely at the U.S. health care system, Kaufman (1998) proposed four major influences on death and dying: (a) that medicine (rather than ethnic culture, religion, or family) has become the dominant framework for understanding old age and death; (b) that technology is allowed to determine end-of-life events; (c) that players are unclear about, and often have competing goals for, end-of-life care; and (d) that few people are knowledgeable about the available technology and the implications of technology-related decisions or are prepared for the level of participation in decision making that is demanded

TABLE 1.1. Themes of the Dominant U.S. Culture: 1970

Achievement and success
Activity and work
Humanitarian motives
Moral orientation
Efficiency and practicality
Progress
Material comfort and consumerism
Equality
Freedom
External conformity
Science and secular rationality
Nationalism and patriotism
Democracy
Individual personality and autonomy
Racism and related group superiority

SOURCE: Adapted from Williams (1970).

of them. Thus, it is especially within the culture of the U.S. medical system, as it influences death and dying, that "clashes" with nondominant cultures become pronounced (Loustaunau & Sobo, 1997).

From this perspective, it makes sense to talk about subcultures (nondominant cultures within a dominant culture) and the categorization of a person as traditional (functioning well within the subculture but not well within the dominant culture), bicultural (functioning equally well in both the subculture and the dominant culture), or acculturated (having given up practices of the subculture in favor of the dominant culture). In fact, much of what we have learned about how other cultures face death and dying has been stimulated by cross-cultural clashes within hospitals and clinics, some of which are referred to ethics committees (Koenig, 1997).

■ OUR VIEW OF CULTURAL INFLUENCES AT LIFE'S END

It is our view that many Americans are not simply a product of one or two cultures. Given our broad definition of culture, it is more likely that an increasing number of individuals belong to several cultures, or at least appreciate a number of cultural perspectives, at the same time. A graphic depiction of this conceptualization is provided in Figure 1.1, showing that within the dominant U.S. culture (which serves as a foundation for our legal and medical system), individuals may be subject to additional cultural influences from their ethnicities, religions, regions in which they were raised, and memberships in other groups. How these cultural perspectives influence one's end-of-life decisions is modified, of course, by one's personal knowledge about and experiences with death, dying, and decision making.

Take, for example, an African American man who was raised Catholic and joins the military. The decisions that he makes about end-of-life may be influenced by all three cultures. If he is married to a woman from Vietnam who was raised Buddhist, then his end-of-life decisions also may be influenced by two additional cultures; at a minimum, he would need to understand and appreciate his wife's traditional end-of-life views and practices. The dictates of these cultures are modified through his personal experience with death and dying. They also are modified by the dominant U.S. culture as it influences the legal and medical structures within which his end-of-life decisions are being made.

Given the growing number of cultures represented in the United States, it is important that helping professionals (a) gain knowledge about the culture or cultures of their clients, (b) increase understanding of their own values and traditions as just one way (rather than the only way) to look at reality, and (c) develop skills at communicating with others that allow for the nonjudgmental exchange of values and traditions in the problem-solving process (Mokuau & Shimizu, 1991).

■ WHY STUDY CULTURE?

The study of other cultures and cultural influence on behavior has many benefits. First, by studying other cultures, one learns about different ways in which to view the world. At the same time, and inseparable from the process, one also learns about one's own culture. This occurs when we are confronted with aspects of other cultures that contrast sharply with our own views. "Sharp contrast events" have been described by Hall (1959, 1976). One of his examples concerns the differences in the conceptualization of time. In the U.S. culture, time is based on the clock (e.g., the meeting starts at 9 a.m.), whereas in another culture, time might be based on events (e.g., the meeting starts when all have finished their morning chores). Another example is the difference between autonomous decision making, a value of the dominant U.S. culture, and

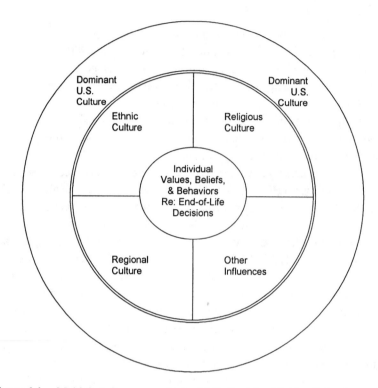

Figure 1.1.   Multiple Influences on End-of-Life Decision-Making Behavior

models of decision making that are more collective (McLaughlin & Braun, 1998). Kluckhorn and Strodtbeck (1961) identified five areas that are useful in examining culture: (a) time orientation (based on the past, present, or future), (b) valued human relations (individual, collateral, or lineal), (c) focus of human activity (on doing, being, or becoming), (d) human nature at birth (basically good, bad, neutral, or mixed), and (e) relationship with the supernatural (one of control, subordination, or harmony).

Second, by studying different cultures, one begins to see the commonalties across them, for example, that all people want the best for their children and that all cultures serve to guide behavior and help their members rationalize confusing, sad, and unknowable aspects of life (DeSpelder & Strickland, 1992). This perspective confirms that, although cultures might differ in how the universe is explained and how people are taught to behave, one culture is not any better or worse than another. Cultures develop, and histories unfold, in response to the environment (Diamond, 1998). This concept also is known as cultural relativism, which means that a client's beliefs and behaviors are considered within his or her own culture's context rather than within the context of the dominant culture or, if different, the provider's culture (Loustaunau & Sobo, 1997). The danger, of course, is that of adopting a rigid view of another culture based on a chapter in a book or a meeting with a single representative of that culture (Brislin, 1993). Generalizations about a specific group must be modified and humanized through interaction with individual members.

Third, the study of different cultures improves our ability to interact with others. Learning and practicing to be nonjudgmental and looking for commonalties with people of different cultures require skills at observation, active listening, and open communication. Improved communication skills will improve human interactions within, as well as across, cultural groups.

■ ORGANIZATION OF THIS BOOK

For this book, we sought the expertise of a diverse group of people interested in and knowledgeable about these fields. The process began as a collaboration among three people in three different fields: geriatric medicine, law, and public health. To this team, we invited professionals from anthropology, bioethics, cardiology, criminology, education, family and community medicine, neurology, nursing, psychiatry, political science, religion, social work, and sociology. Each of these fields has something to contribute to the discussion of end-of-life decision making. In addition, all contributors are both practitioners and scholars, so that their writings are not just theoretical but also enriched by their personal experiences with helping others through the dying process.

Following this introductory chapter, the book is organized into four sections. The first section provides a brief overview of the physical, legal, and ethical aspects of dying. These chapters might seem basic to students of medicine and law, but they provide important contextual information for other readers. The second section presents information from the perspectives of various ethnic groups. All authors in this section start with a caveat against stereotyping, reminding readers that vast differences exist among individuals within a specific ethnic group. Still, general differences in history and worldview can be seen among the ethnic groups, and these are discussed. In the third section, views from a number of religious groups are presented. These authors note that religions are drawing from examples and realities of the distant past, so that no exact recommendations might exist for specific end-of-life decisions faced today. The final section presents perspectives on death and dying from within two institutional cultures (the hospital/nursing home and the U.S. military) and for two specific population groups (people with HIV/AIDS and people with disabilities). The final chapter attempts to help readers to incorporate the information presented throughout the book and put it to practical use in the context of caring for a dying person. Most important, the authors provide suggestions for the types of questions that practitioners should ask patients in an attempt to learn about their values and beliefs related to living and dying and, for dying patients, their perceptions of the situation and their wishes for care.

■ GENERAL THEMES OF THE BOOK

Two general themes emerge from this volume. Given the growing diversity in North American communities, the primary recommendation for practice is to increase cultural competency. As mentioned previously, this requires an increased knowledge about the cultures of our clientele as well as the cultures that shape our own behaviors. Through this, we will increase our ability to anticipate and resolve potential clashes among the clients' cultures, our own cultures, and the cultures of the institutions within which we work. Most critically, however, we should not stereotype clients based on ethnicity, religious preference, sexual orientation, disease status, and so forth. What we know about a culture rarely can be used to accurately predict an individual's behavior. Instead, we should hone our assessment skills, asking clients questions about their values and preferences regarding end-of-life decision making. In some cases, these might be congruent with what we know about clients' cultures. But more likely, individuals are influenced by multiple cultures as well as by personal educational, work, and life experiences and, therefore, are unique.

Our second general observation concerns the unevenness of knowledge and research across the areas of end-of-life decision making presented in this book. As you will surmise when reading the chapters, there are many unanswered questions. This is not surprising given that the societal changes that stimulated us to put together this book—increased longevity, technological advances, growing diversity—are relatively recent phenomena. True, North Americans are paying more attention to end-of-life issues. Still, the field of palliative care is in its infancy. There are many concerns about the effectiveness and workability of our current advance directive laws. Culture is dynamic and changing, and it is subject to regional and socioeconomic variations as well. Traditional religious documents did not address end-of-life issues such as organ donation and mechanical ventilation, leaving today's clergy to discern how to guide their followers. Investigators are only now beginning to document how the cultures that develop in special populations and institutional settings influence decision making at the end of life. Thus, there is plenty of room for further research in this field.

■ REFERENCES

Brislin, R. (1993). *Understanding culture's influence on behavior.* New York: Harcourt Brace.

DeSpelder, L. A., & Strickland, A. L. (1992). *The last dance: Encountering death and dying* (3rd ed.). Mountain View, CA: Mayfield.

Diamond, J. (1998). *Guns, germs, and steel: The fates of human societies.* New York: Norton.

Hall, E. (1959). *The silent language.* Garden City, NY: Doubleday.

Hall, E. (1976). *Beyond culture.* Garden City, NY: Anchor.

Johnson, C. J., & McGee, M.G. (Eds.). (1991). *How different religions view death and afterlife.* Philadelphia: Charles Press.

Kaufman, S. R. (1998). Intensive care, old age, and the problem of death in America. *The Gerontologist, 38,* 715-725.

Kluckhorn, F., & Strodtbeck, F. (1961). *Variations in values orientations.* Evanston: IL: Row, Peterson.

Koenig, B. A. (1997). Cultural diversity in decision making about care at the end of life. In M. J. Field & C. K. Cassel (Eds.), *Approaching death: Improving care at the end of life* (pp. 363-382). Washington, DC: National Academy Press.

Locke, D. C. (1992). *Increasing multicultural understanding: A comprehensive model.* Newbury Park, CA: Sage.

Loustaunau, M. O., & Sobo, E. J. (1997). *The cultural context of health, illness, and medicine.* Westport, CT: Bergin & Garvey.

McLaughlin, L., & Braun, K. L. (1998). Asian and Pacific Islander cultural values: Considerations for health care decision making. *Health and Social Work, 23,* 116-126.

Merriam-Webster. (1998). *Webster's tenth new collegiate dictionary.* Springfield, MA: Author.

Mokuau, N., & Shimizu, D. (1991). Conceptual framework for social services for Asian and Pacific Islander Americans. In N. Mokuau (Ed.), *Handbook for social services for Asian and Pacific Islanders.* Westport, CT: Greenwood.

Williams, R. M. (1970). *American society: A sociological interpretation.* New York: Knopf.

Part 1

The Medical, Legal, and Ethical Context of Death and Dying

This section of the book provides an overview of some of the medical, legal, and ethical concerns relative to end-of-life decision making, such as the following:

- What happens physically when someone dies?
- What symptoms might a dying person experience, and how can they be alleviated?
- What cognitive changes occur with normal aging and with various disease states, and how do these changes affect someone's ability to make decisions?
- What laws are in place to ensure that an individual's end-of-life wishes are followed?
- Who can make decisions for someone who is incapacitated?
- What types of end-of-life conflicts and disagreements occur?

■ How can disputes over end-of-life issues be avoided or resolved before going to court?

The four chapters in this section, written by physicians and lawyers, provide basic information in answering these questions. Readers trained in medicine and law might wish to skip ahead. Readers without experience in these areas, however, will find this information useful in understanding the medical, legal, and ethical context of death and dying within which end-of-life decisions are made.

Chapter 2

Physical Aspects of Dying

JULIE A. PATTERSON FAGO

By the latter half of the 20th century, death had become prominently absent from the day-to-day experience of most Americans. Indeed, death now often is relegated to the hospital or nursing home, where medical science overshadows this natural event for both patients and their families. Currently, between 50% and 80% of people in the United States die in institutions (Wanzer et al., 1989). By contrast, the vast majority of Americans died in their own homes at the start of the 20th century (McCue, 1995).

The process of dying also has changed. Advances in medical science now make it possible to postpone death from days to (in some cases) years. Because of the medicalization of death, the experience of watching a person journey through the various physical stages of dying has changed considerably. Little is written in the medical literature about this process to guide physicians and nurses, who in turn might not be able to adequately prepare patients and their caregivers about what to expect during the final days, weeks, and months of life.

The process of dying is unique to each individual. The symptoms experienced by dying patients reflect their underlying disease processes and organ systems involved, the presence of coexisting conditions, what medical interventions are chosen, and patients' spiritual and emotional states.

13

This chapter is intended to summarize what is known about the physical aspects of dying. The emotional, psychological, and cultural aspects will be covered in other chapters.

■ COMMON SYMPTOMS
FACED BY THE DYING

Pain, difficulty in breathing, nausea, and vomiting are common during the final stages of life (Lynn et al., 1997; Turner et al., 1996). Fatigue, anorexia, restlessness, bowel and bladder dysfunction, and disrupted sleep also are prevalent. In fact, Donnelly, Walsh, and RyBicki (1995) found that dying patients experience an average of 11 troubling symptoms during the months preceding death (range of symptoms = 1-27). The coexistence of symptoms occurs not only because of the effects of the disease process at hand but also because of treatments. For example, opiates used to relieve pain can predispose a patient to nausea, constipation, and anorexia. Failure to adequately treat noxious symptoms has a significant impact on the quality of a dying person's life and contributes to the caregiver's strain. Physicians and caregivers must be mindful of the causes of and solutions to these symptoms, and they must be able to anticipate and prevent their onset (if possible).

Pain

Pain is a common problem in many terminal conditions. Although pain is the most prevalent symptom cited by patients dying of cancer, it also is seen in those dying of other causes. In the Study to Understand Prognoses and Preferences for the Outcomes and Risks of Treatments (SUPPORT), which followed 10,000 critically ill patients, severe pain during the 3 days before death was reported by nearly 35% of those over 80 years of age, 34% of those with chronic obstructive pulmonary disease (COPD), and nearly 45% of those dying of congestive heart failure (Lynn et al., 1997). Pain often is a marker of disease progression, but it also can indicate toxic effects of treatment or an exacerbation of a preexisting condition (Gavrin & Chapman, 1995). Pain interferes with activity, appetite, and sleep. When present, pain can prevent engagement with even simple tasks and enjoyment of life. The psychological effect of severe pain on patients and their caregivers can be devastating. Thus, pain control deserves our highest priority.

There are two major types of pain: nociceptive and neuropathic. Nociceptive pain originates from diseased or damaged tissue and is transmitted by intact healthy nerves. By contrast, neuropathic pain originates from nerve(s) or brain tissue that is itself damaged by disease, trauma, or treatments such as surgery, radiation, and chemotherapy (Agency for Health Care Policy and Research [AHCPR], 1994; Gavrin & Chapman, 1995). The distinction is important because treatment modalities differ. Neuropathic pain is more resistant to standard pain therapy but can be very responsive to alternative approaches.

In patients with cancer, the most common cause of pain is bone metastases. Inflammation of the periosteum and/or increased intraosteal pressure from tumor infiltration lies at the root of the problem. The pain often is described as a diffuse, vague achiness, but the patient also might have intermittent periods of acute, piercing, knifelike pain related to change of position or bearing of weight. Visceral nociceptive pain, caused by tumor infiltration, inflammation, or obstruction, also is a common cause of pain in malignancies. This pain generally is constant, dull, and difficult to pinpoint. If there is obstruction (of the organ or duct), then the pain is colicky with intermittent short but intense bursts of pain. Sympathetic irritation of nearby autonomic nerves can cause nausea, bowel, or bladder dysfunction (Gavrin & Chapman, 1995). Immobilization from bed rest or neuromuscular disease is an overlooked cause of diffuse low-grade pain, particularly in the back.

Neuropathic pain is characterized by dysesthesias (burning, sensation of wetness, and feeling of pins and needles). The pain can be exquisite. The location of the pain corresponds to the area supplied by the affected nerve or central nervous system territory. Skin overlying the area of pain often is hyperesthetic (hypersensitive).

Optimal treatment of pain requires assessing its cause and type, determining the severity, and frequently reviewing the chosen treatment regimen for its efficacy as well as its effect on the patient's mental alertness (Table 2.1). Analgesic medications, prescribed and taken on a fixed round-the-clock schedule, are the mainstay in treating pain in dying patients.

Non-opioid medications, such as nonsteroidal anti-inflammatory drugs (NSAIDs) and acetaminophen, are useful as initial therapy in mild pain and can be used effectively in combination with opioids. NSAIDs, by virtue of their anti-inflammatory properties, are especially effective in treating the pain of bony metastases, although opioids might be needed to control more severe pain. It is important to remember that all non-opioid medications have a ceiling effect; pushing doses higher achieves only increased side effects without any gain in pain control (Gavrin & Chapman, 1995).

TABLE 2.1. Steps for Optimal Pain Relief

1. Define the cause and source of pain.
2. Determine its severity/grade.
3. Institute treatment of regularly scheduled dosages, not as needed.
4. Review treatment for efficacy and side effects.
5. Adjust treatment as needed.
6. Aim for maximum level of alertness possible.

SOURCE: Adapted from Agency for Health Care Policy and Research (1994) and Zerwekl (1984).

Opioid medications are the most important and effective tools for controlling pain and improving quality of life for dying patients. Morphine is the most commonly used opioid for moderate to severe pain in the United States because of its efficacy, tolerability, flexible dosage forms, and relatively low cost. Neuropathic pain often is resistant to treatment with opioids except in high doses but responds well to alternative treatments such as tricyclic antidepressants, anti-epileptic medications, and neuroleptics. The complete discussion of the pharmacological management of pain is beyond the scope of this chapter; however, an excellent resource for treating patients for pain from cancer is available though the AHCPR (1994).

Nonpharmacological approaches are very important adjuncts to overall pain control strategies. Transcutaneous electrical nerve stimulation units and acupuncture activate endogenous pain-modulating pathways by directly stimulating peripheral nerves. Massage and other relaxation techniques, such as visualization, can greatly enhance pain control through alleviation of anxiety and reduction in skeletal muscle tension (AHCPR, 1994). Gentle exercise enhances patient comfort by strengthening weak muscles and mobilizing stiff joints.

Dyspnea

More than half of hospitalized patients with serious illnesses have severe dyspnea (air hunger) during the final 3 days of life (Lynn et al., 1997), and many who die at home or in hospice care suffer from shortness of breath (Turner et al., 1996). The cause depends on the underlying condition and often is complex and multifactorial. Congestive heart failure produces dyspnea through fluid-filled airspaces and hypoxia (oxygen deficiency); in its extreme form, it can impart a sense of drowning. The excess secretions from pneumonia fill alveolar airspaces and bronchial passages, producing partial obstruction and hypoxia. The loss of lung tissue from emphysema or infiltrating cancers also can cause dyspnea from hypoxia and a loss of elasticity. Tenacious secretions or masses from head and neck cancer can produce partial upper airway obstruction. Mediastinal disease (e.g., bulky adenopathy) can compromise both cardiac and pulmonary function. Respiratory muscle insufficiency from neuromuscular diseases or cachexia (malnutrition and wasting) produces dyspnea from hypoventilation and hypercarbia (increased amounts of carbon dioxide in the blood).

Treatment of dyspnea includes correcting the underlying causes (if possible) and alleviating suffering. Opiates play an invaluable role through their effect on reducing air hunger and decreasing cough. They also can improve breathing efficiency and exercise endurance, presumably through opiate receptors in the brain stem (Bruera, Macmillan, Kuehn, Hanson, & MacDonald, 1990; MacDonald, 1995). Oxygen can be helpful even in cases without hypoxemia (insufficient oxygenation of the blood) (Dean, Brown, & Himmelman, 1992), although it can dry the nasal passages and patients might feel claustrophobic when wearing oxygen masks or nose tubes. Bronchodilators are beneficial if there is a component of bronchospasm. Methylxanthines also can be of some (probably minimal) benefit in neuromuscular disease causing respiratory distress (Gavrin & Chapman, 1995). The subjective feelings of dyspnea can be reduced by relaxation techniques, massage (especially with aromatic oils), distraction (music), and increased air movement (open windows, fan) (Regnard, 1990).

During the final hours and days of life, a common change occurs in the neurally mediated respiratory pattern. This is called Cheynes-Stokes respiration and is characterized by periods of rapid respiration alternating with cyclical periods of apnea (temporary cessation of breathing). Generally, when this stage is reached, the person is somnolent (sleepy) due to the disease process. As such, the patient does not suffer. But the appearance of Cheynes-Stokes respiration can be troubling for the caregiver because the periods of rapid respiration make it appear that the person is laboring and the periods of apnea can seem to last for minutes.

As death approaches, the patient often has increasing difficulty in handling respiratory secretions, which can become quite thick and tenacious. This makes conversation difficult. In its extreme form, this manifests as the "death rattle." Chemical agents, such as scopolamine and atropine, will help to dry secretions (Gavrin & Chapman, 1995). Dehydration during the terminal phase reduces pulmonary secretions, thereby improving comfort (Printz, 1992).

Nausea and Vomiting

Nausea and vomiting are common symptoms found in terminally ill patient conditions. The mechanism of nausea and vomiting is complex. Local factors include impaired gastrointestinal (GI) motility (from drugs such as opioids and calcium channel blockers or from autonomic neuropathies), visceral lesions (from inflammation or obstruction), and iatrogenic causes (from drug side effects or irradiation of the GI tract). Central nausea is mediated through the chemoreceptor trigger zone and the nucleus solitarious. Both are located in a highly vascular area of the brain stem and, therefore, are prone to metastases (Donnelly et al., 1995). Vomiting does not always follow nausea but can be hazardous because it promotes dehydration, electrolyte imbalance, and aspiration pneumonia. Anti-emetic drugs work well in most cases.

Fatigue

Fatigue is the most common symptom in dying patients. As death draws near, the person's energy can be drained by even the simplest tasks. In the SUPPORT study, 80% of cognizant patients reported fatigue during the final 3 days of life (Lynn et al., 1997). In addition to enervating effects from the underlying terminal condition, progressive malnutrition from anorexia, endocrine imbalances (e.g., adrenal insufficiency), and/or metabolic derangements (e.g., hypercalcemia) contribute to overall weakness. Pacing oneself is critically important to conserve energy for important emotional, spiritual, and physical tasks.

Anorexia and Cachexia

Loss of the desire to eat is one of the most distressing symptoms to both the family and the patient because of the association of food with nurturing, caring, and compassion. Anorexia is experienced by the vast majority (75%-100%) of patients dying from serious illnesses as death approaches. Associated symptoms include significant weight loss, muscle wasting, changes in autonomic function, and constipation (MacDonald, 1995). The causes vary. In patients with tumors, the anorexia/cachexia syndrome is mediated by a number of cytokines, including tumor necrosis factor, Interleukins 1 and 6, and interferon gamma (Beck, Mulligan, & Tisdale, 1990; MacDonald, 1995). A

commonly overlooked cause of anorexia is mouth pain from dental caries, infection, or poorly fitting dentures (Sheehan & Foreman, 1997). Central nervous system disorders, tumors, delirium, the central effects of metabolic derangements (e.g., hypercalcemia), and drugs can produce anorexia as well. Gastrostasis (decreased stomach activity) from drugs and autonomic dysfunction also are culprits.

Treatment is aimed at ameliorating the underlying cause when possible. Appetite stimulants, such as megestrol, can be helpful in patients with cancer and AIDS. Pro-motility (gastrokinetic) agents (e.g., metoclopramide) can improve gastric emptying associated with diabetic neuropathies and opiate-induced gastrostasis.

Some authors have suggested that specific amino acid supplementation, such as arginine and glutamine, can enhance protein balance, wound healing, and immune function (MacDonald, 1995). As such, "designer" supplements in combination with appetite stimulants can enhance the quality of some patients' lives. However, general dietary supplementation has not been shown to improve biological end points. In fact, particularly as a patient nears death, force feeding (orally, enterally, or parentally) increases suffering. Stated another way, terminal patients who die after cessation of hydration and nutrition die peaceful deaths (Bernat, Gert, & Mogielnicki, 1993). Food deprivation has been shown to increase beta-endorphin levels. An increase in dymorphin, a powerful opioid, is seen in the central nervous system during terminal dehydration (Printz, 1992).

Agitation and Restlessness

Some terminally ill patients experience restlessness and agitation during the final stages. In a small study, 18% of patients dying in hospice care experienced significant agitation during the final 3 days of life (Turner et al., 1996). Restlessness can be due to pain, urinary retention, or constipation. Delirium due to metabolic abnormalities, infection, or drug side effects also might be present. It is important to pay attention to signs that might reveal the cause of the restlessness. Although sedatives, such as benzodiazepines and neuroleptics (in the case of delirium with frightening hallucinations), are very beneficial, ignoring a full bladder is inexcusable. Reassurance, companionship, holding, and massage can enhance overall care and help to alleviate psychic distress.

■ WHEN DOES DYING BEGIN?

Marking the transition from living, even with a life-threatening condition, to the point where one is terminal often is difficult. For some, death is sudden and little preparation is possible. For others, progressive lethal conditions (e.g., end-stage COPD), can lead to death that occurs only after a series of medical crises. Although the process of dying varies with disease, organ systems involved, and treatments undertaken, there are common biological markers that signal the progression toward death (Table 2.2). Not every dying patient will experience all these signs. However, knowledge about what could occur and what is normal greatly helps patients and their caregivers to cope during the patients' final days (Gavrin & Chapman, 1995).

Signs of Approaching Death

During the final days of life, a gradual loss of interest, or "social disengagement," often is seen. There is a physical withdrawal and subtle signs of emotional disorganization (Pattison, 1977). Patients generally become somnolent, although some experience periods of restlessness and agitation. The desire for food wanes. Doyle (1984) noted that the nearer to death, the colder the food preference. During the final days preceding death, most patients will stop eating altogether, and their fluid intake will drop to just sips.

Unless a catastrophic event (e.g., a massive pulmonary embolism) intervenes, circulatory failure gradually progresses during the hours or days before death. If vital signs are taken, one sees a drop in blood pressure and an increased pulse, which often is thready and irregular. The color and temperature of the extremities are one of the most useful signs that death is near. As circulation fails, the hands and feet become cold, blue, and mottled, and this appearance gradually proceeds up the legs. The hands often become colder and increasingly dark as well (Zerwekl, 1984). During the hours before death, the eyes become glazed and the patient often is unrousable. However, because hearing is thought to be the final sense to leave, it is important to speak to a dying person as if every word can be heard (Zerwekl, 1984). Breathing can become more labored, especially if secretions are a problem. The onset of Cheynes-Stokes respiration generally signifies that death is near. Periods of apnea become more prolonged until the final breath is taken.

TABLE 2.2. Signs of Approaching Death

Reduced level of consciousness

Anorexia and decreased thirst

Disorientation with or without visual and auditory hallucinations

Restlessness

Irregular breathing patterns (Cheynes-Stokes respiration)

Excessive pulmonary secretions ("death rattle")

Decreased urine production and incontinence

Progressively cool, purple, mottled extremities

SOURCE: Adapted from Gavrin and Chapman (1995) and Zerwekl (1984).

■ WHEN DOES DEATH OCCUR?

From a biological point of view, death is a gradual process that ends when the entire organism ceases to function (Iserson, 1994). For example, some muscle, skin, and bone cells can live on for days after what one traditionally would consider "death." However, in the absence of life-support technology, a patient is pronounced clinically dead when respiration ceases and the heart no longer beats. For a discussion of "brain death," see Martino's chapter in this volume (Chapter 3). Shortly after death, the eyelids remain slightly open and the pupils become fixed. The muscles initially are flaccid, including the jaw; thus, the mouth often will sag open. *Rigor mortis* (muscle stiffness) generally develops 2 to 6 hours after death. The skin becomes discolored by *livor mortis* (purple-red discoloration over dependent areas of the body) within minutes to hours after death (Iserson, 1984).

■ CONCLUSION

The major symptoms experienced by terminally ill patients described in this chapter are common. Fortunately, there are many tools available to alleviate distress in dying patients. Patients and their caregivers should be told what to expect during the final days, weeks, and months of life. Dying patients need to be freed from both the fear of death and troublesome symptoms so that their dying can become profound and meaningful experiences.

■ REFERENCES

Agency for Health Care Policy and Research. (1994). *Clinical practice guidelines 1994: Management of cancer pain* (Publication No. 94-0592). Rockville, MD: Author.

Beck, S. A., Mulligan, H. D., & Tisdale, M. J. (1990). Lipolytic factors associated with murine and human cancer cachexia. *Journal of the National Cancer Institute, 82,* 1922-1926.

Bernat, J. L., Gert, B., & Mogielnicki, R. P. (1993). Patient refusal of hydration and nutrition: An alternative to physician-assisted suicide or voluntary active euthanasia. *Archives of Internal Medicine, 153,* 2723-2728.

Bruera, E., Macmillan, K., Kuehn, N., Hanson, J., & MacDonald, R. N. (1990). A controlled trial of megestrol acetate on appetite, caloric intake, nutritional status, and other symptoms in patients with advanced cancer. *Cancer, 66,* 1279-1282.

Dean, N. C., Brown, J. K., & Himmelman, R. B. (1992). Oxygen may improve dyspnea and endurance in patients with chronic obstructive pulmonary disease and only mild hypoxemia. *American Review of Respiratory Disease, 146,* 941-945.

Donnelly, S., Walsh, D., & RyBicki, L. (1995). The symptoms of advanced cancer: Identification of clinical and research priorities by assessment of prevalence and severity. *Journal of Palliative Care, 11,* 27-35.

Doyle, D. (1984). Palliative symptom control. In D. Doyle (Ed.), *Palliative care: The management of advanced illness* (pp. 297-329). Philadelphia: Charles Press.

Gavrin, J., & Chapman, C. R. (1995). Clinical management of dying patients. *Western Journal of Medicine, 163,* 268-277.

Iserson, K. V. (1994). I'm dead, now what? In K. V. Iserson (Ed.), *Death to dust: What happens to dead bodies?* (pp. 11-49). Tucson, AZ: Galen Press.

Lynn, J., Teno, J. M., Phillips, R. S., Wu, A. W., Desbiens, N., Harrold, J., Claessens, M. T., Wenger, N., Kreling, B., & Connors, A. F., Jr. (1997). Perceptions by family members of the dying experience of older and seriously ill patients: SUPPORT investigators—Study to Understand Prognoses and Preferences for Outcomes and Risks of Treatments. *Annals of Internal Medicine, 126*(2), 97-106.

MacDonald, N. (1995). Suffering and dying in cancer patients: Research frontiers in controlling confusion, cachexia, and dyspnea. *Western Journal of Medicine, 163,* 278-286.

McCue, J. D. (1995). The naturalness of dying. *Journal of the American Medical Association, 273,* 1039-1043.

Pattison, E. M. (1977). The experience of dying. In E. M. Pattison (Ed.), *The experience of dying* (pp. 43-60). Englewood Cliffs, NJ: Prentice Hall.

Printz, L. A. (1992). Terminal dehydration: A compassionate treatment. *Archives of Internal Medicine, 152,* 697-700.

Regnard, C. (1990). Dyspnea in advanced cancer: A flow diagram. *Palliative Medicine, 4,* 311-315.

Sheehan, D. C., & Foreman, W. B. (1997). Symptomatic management of the older person with cancer. *Clinics in Geriatric Medicine, 13,* 203-219.

Turner, K., Chye, R., Aggarwal, G., Philip, J., Skeels, A., & Lickiss, J. N. (1996). Dignity in dying: A preliminary study of patients in the last three days of life. *Journal of Palliative Care, 12*(2), 7-13.

Wanzer, D. H., Federman, D., Adelstein, S. J., Cassel, C. K., Cassem, E. H., Cranford, E. H., Hook, E. W., Lo, B., Moertel, C. G., & Safar, P. (1989). The physician's responsibility towards hopelessly ill patients: A second look. *New England Journal of Medicine, 320,* 844-849.

Zerwekl, J. V. (1984). The last few days. In J. V. Zerwekl (Ed.), *Hospice and palliative care nursing* (pp. 177-197). Orlando, FL: Grune & Stratton.

Chapter 3

Cognitive Changes That Affect Capacity and End-of-Life Decisions

RONALD A. MARTINO

A great deal of mythology surrounds the process of aging, especially the aging of the brain. Although it is true that the brain undergoes anatomical and functional changes with age, healthy individuals can maintain excellent neurological and psychological functioning well into their 8th, 9th, and even 10th decades. However, a number of disease processes (e.g., Alzheimer's disease, stroke) can affect brain functioning, and many of these illnesses become more prevalent with age. Given that more than 19 million baby boomers will live to be 85 or older by the year 2015 (Hooyman & Kiyak, 1996), it is important to understand the aging process of the brain in terms of what is normal and what is abnormal or disease related. This chapter gives an overview of normal aging processes that affect cognition, followed by a review of some of the conditions that impair memory and personality. The conditions of persistent vegetative state, coma, and brain death also are defined. Other particularly important factors applying to function, including competency and capacity, are discussed along with a common testing measure, the Mini-Mental State Examination (MMSE). This knowledge will permit those who work with the elderly to better assist them and their families in making end-of-life decisions.

■ NORMAL AGING OF THE BRAIN

Anatomical Changes

The brain is composed of neurons (nerve cells) and neuroglia (supporting cells) and is divided into gray and white matter. The gray matter of the brain is made up by nerve cell bodies, whereas the white matter is composed of nerve cell processes that form tracts connecting various parts of the brain with one another (Thomas, 1993).

The number of neurons in the cortex of the brain is maximal at birth (Brody, 1955). But myelination, or the laying down of a protective sheath around parts of neurons, continues well after birth and is related to increases in neurological functioning. Some areas of the brain do not fully myelinate until the second or third decade (Filley, 1996). The ratio of gray matter to white matter is 1:3 at 20 years of age and falls to 1:1 by 50 years of age (Miller, Alston, & Corsellis, 1980).

With aging, there is a steady loss of cerebral cortical cells. Over the course of a lifetime, up to 50% of the large neurons and 35% of the small neurons can be lost from some areas of the cortex (Henderson, Tomlinson, & Gibson, 1980). Neuroanatomical changes in the normally aging brain can be seen with serial neuroimaging studies (Awad, Spetzler, Hodak, Awad, & Cary, 1986; Boone et al., 1992; Fazekas et al., 1993; Filley et al., 1989; Golomb et al., 1993; Hachinski, Potter, & Mersky, 1987; Longstreth et al., 1996), but the clinical significance of these changes is uncertain. Overall, there is a decrease in the weight of the brain and a decrease in total brain volume with advancing age, with the volume declining slightly more in males than in females (Miller et al., 1980). By 100 years of age, the ratio of gray matter to white matter rises to 1:5 as some atrophy occurs (Miller et al., 1980).

General Neurological Changes

The general neurological examination of the healthy elder will reveal only subtle changes, and these changes do not necessarily affect cognitive functioning. For example, pupillary size and reflexes are somewhat diminished, and about 25% of older adults will have a functionally unimportant reduction of upward gaze. Approximately 40% of individuals over 75 years of age have impaired hearing acuity (Morris & McManus, 1991). Motor examination usually shows a mild reduction of grip strength, whereas gait is somewhat shorter and broader based with age, and people 80 and older tend to walk 10% to 20% slower than younger persons (Sudarsky, 1990). Subtle changes in balance occur in the seventh and eighth decades (Camicioli, Panzer, & Kaye, 1997).

Cognitive Changes

When we talk about cognitive functioning, we are referring to one's intelligence, ability to learn and process information, memory, and verbal skills. The good news is that substantial cognitive loss does not necessarily occur with normal aging (Howieson, Holm, Kaye, Oken, & Howieson, 1993). In motivated and well-educated individuals, many verbal skills increase between 20 and 50 years of age (Bayley & Oden, 1955) and are preserved into the seventh decade. Researchers have found an overlap in abilities among some 70-year-old and some 20-year-old individuals, for example, in their abilities to memorize word lists (Carman, 1997; Katzman & Terry, 1983).

It appears that cognitive decrements in visual memory begin to appear by 65 to 70 years of age (Giambra, Arenberg, Zonderman, Costa, & Kawas, 1995). However, no significant correlation has been observed between verbal memory and age (Koss et al., 1991), and little intraindividual covariation between changes in visual memory and verbal memory has been found at any age (Giambra et al., 1995). Although it generally is accepted that secondary verbal memory declines with age (Carman, 1997; Golomb et al., 1993), some investigators have found that it is preserved (Koss et al., 1991) and that it might appear to be impaired only because of decreases in the speed at which older people process information (Salthouse, 1994; Schaie, 1994).

Many older adults complain of being forgetful. However, most studies show little correlation between these subjective memory complaints and objective testing (Flicker, Ferris, & Reisberg, 1993; Jorm et al., 1994). Memory complaints are more likely to be clinically meaningful when they are new for that individual (Schofield, Jacobs, Marder, Sano, & Stern, 1997) and are commonly related to depression and anxiety (Hänninen et al., 1994).

Personality

There is little evidence to support the notion that people become psychologically unstable as they age (Cohen, 1997). In fact, there appears to be great stability in the personality of the elderly and a high level of well-being, even in the presence of chronic physical illness. Older people seem to adapt and are not more likely than younger people to be hypochondriacal (Costa et al., 1987). The greatest stability is observed when self-reported personality surveys are used in studies that collect data on the same individuals over time. In one such longitudinal study (Field & Millsap, 1991), four out of five components of personality remained stable with age; the most stable component was satisfaction. Thus, the elderly not only maintain their lifelong array of coping skills but also seem to find satisfaction through having their basic needs met in their old age (Fisher, 1995).

■ CONDITIONS THAT IMPAIR COGNITIVE FUNCTIONING

There is no clear boundary between changes in memory that occur with normal aging and early changes caused by serious disorders of the brain. The controversial diagnostic category of age-associated memory impairment (AAMI) straddles this boundary. Kral (1962) first introduced the term "benign senescent forgetfulness" during the 1960s to describe mild memory impairment of the elderly. In 1986, the National Institute of Mental Health developed research criteria for AAMI (Crook et al., 1986). Using these criteria, several investigators have found that more than a third of their older subjects do not have AAMI, making it difficult to consider AAMI normal for age (Hänninen et al., 1997; Larrabee & McEntee, 1995). This finding tends to confirm the notion that cognitive impairments are caused by disease states rather than by normal aging.

Dementia

Dementia is defined by impairment of memory and at least one other cognitive function in a previously normal adult. In the fourth edition of the *Diagnostic and Statistical Manual of Mental Disorders* (DSM-IV), a diagnosis of dementia also must be based on the observation of significant impairment in social or occupational roles and the absence of delirium or impaired level of consciousness (American Psychiatric Association, 1994). However, a clinician skilled in the evaluation of dementia often can make a correct diagnosis before there is a noticeable decline in social roles or expectations.

Dementia can be caused by a number of conditions. In some cases, treatment of the condition can reverse the dementia. For example, when dementia is caused by a brain tumor, the dementia might disappear when the brain tumor is surgically removed.

Alzheimer's disease is the most common cause of dementia, however, accounting for well over half of all diagnosed cases of dementia in the United States. Because women have a longer life expectancy than men and Alzheimer's disease is an age-related illness, there is a greater prevalence of the disease in older women. However, when risk is adjusted for differential survival rates, the risk is the same for men and women. A person might have Alzheimer's disease for many years before clinical symptoms are apparent. It is a progressive disease in which there are substantial pathological, cognitive, behavioral, and personality changes. Progressive deficits occur in memory, with memory for recent events more severely impaired than memory for events that occurred years before.

Dementia caused by stroke is called vascular dementia and is the second most common dementia in the United States, Canada, and Europe. In Asia and some developing countries, the incidence of vascular dementia exceeds that of Alzheimer's disease. This variation in prevalence reflects the differences in the population's risks for strokes, injuries, and certain illnesses. For example, there is a higher proportion of people with vascular dementia in populations with higher incidence of stroke related to hypertension, heart disease, smoking, and diabetes mellitus (Lindsay, Hébert, & Rockwood, 1997).

Other causes of dementia include anoxic brain damage, physical trauma to the brain, dementia with Lewy bodies, Parkinson's disease, prolonged vitamin B12 and other serious nutritional deficiencies, and other rarer conditions.

Pseudodementia

Physically healthy elderly individuals can show evidence of decreased memory performance when experiencing clinical or subclinical anxiety or depression (Deptula, Singh, & Pomara, 1993). The term "pseudodementia" was introduced to describe patients who had the appearance of suffering from dementia but who instead suffered from a variety of psychiatric disorders, especially depression (Kiloh, 1961; Wells, 1979). Although pseudodementia can occur at any age, it presents the greatest diagnostic challenge in the elderly, for whom the prevalence of true dementia is greatest (McCullough, 1991). Among people being evaluated for dementia, 10% to 20% of them might have pseudodementia (O'Boyle, Amadeo, & Self, 1990; Sachdev, Smith, Angus-Lepan, & Rodriguez, 1990). Up to 50% of depressed older people will have MMSE

(Folstein, Folstein, & McHugh, 1975) scores lower than 24 (out of 30 points), which strongly suggests the possibility of dementia. However, with pharmacological or electroconvulsive therapy treatment, formerly depressed individuals often regain normal MMSE scores (Fisher, 1995). In evaluating patients, it is helpful to know that the pseudodementia of depression never presents severe cognitive disturbances without depressive symptoms (Fischer, 1996) and that agnosia (loss of comprehension of auditory, visual, or other sensations), agraphia (loss of ability to write), and aphasia (inability to communicate due to brain dysfunction) are very unlikely. Long-term studies show that pseudodementia follows a longitudinal course consistent with mood disorder, not with dementia (Sachdev et al., 1990).

Delirium

Delirium is a state of altered mental status in which a person's ability to pay attention is affected by being either lethargic or hyperexcited. Symptoms can be mild to severe and can include hallucinations and misinterpretations of the environment. Delirium can be of a gradual or acute onset. Common causes include medications, especially narcotic pain medications and sleeping pills, and serious medical illnesses. Depending on the causes, delirium often is reversible, although it can take up to 2 months to fully clear once the causes are eliminated. Therefore, it is important to accurately diagnose this particular condition and prevent confusion with any other illnesses.

■ PERSISTENT VEGETATIVE STATE AND COMA

Persistent Vegetative State

When a person is alert (awake) but not aware, with complete inability to respond to stimuli or to communicate, he or she is said to be in a persistent vegetative state (PVS) (Dougherty, Rawlinson, Levy, & Plum, 1981). One definition of PVS is "a clinical condition of complete unawareness of the self and the environment, accompanied by sleep-wake cycles with either complete or partial preservation of hypothalamic and brain stem autonomic functions" (Multi-Society Task Force on PVS, 1994a, p. 1500).

PVS usually is due to massive damage to the cerebral hemispheres with preservation of brain stem structures (Dougherty et al., 1981). Therefore, the prognosis for the recovery of awareness is poor, and PVS can occur at any age due to a number of causes. When due to traumatic brain injury, the prognosis is better than when caused by a nontraumatic brain injury. When PVS occurs as the final stage of dementia, recovery is not possible (Multi-Society Task Force on PVS, 1994a, 1994b).

The recognition of PVS is critical to making end-of-life decisions. Medical support may be ethically withdrawn from certain patients in PVSs (American Thoracic Society, 1991). Withdrawal of nutrition and hydration from a vegetative patient results in a painless death within 10 to 14 days (Alfonso, Lanting, Duenas, Cullen, & Papazian, 1992).

Coma

Many people confuse PVS with coma and, even worse, use the terms interchangeably. Coma refers to a state of unarousable psychological unresponsiveness in which the eyes remain closed and there is no psychologically understandable response to external stimuli or internal need (Plum & Posner, 1980). In contradistinction to PVS, people in coma lack arousal and give the appearance of being asleep.

■ DEATH OF THE BRAIN

Brain death is a state of deep, irreversible coma with apnea (lack of spontaneous breathing). The definition of brain death requires the permanent loss of activity of the entire brain, including the brain stem (Ad Hoc Committee, 1968). In most Western countries, it is accepted that the death of the brain signals the death of a person. This definition of death was not widely accepted in Japan until 1997 (before that, death was defined as the stopping of the heart) because it is at variance with a number of important cultural beliefs (Ohnuki-Tierney, 1994). Japan's new organ transplantation law was enacted on October 16, 1997, and permits the transplant of hearts, livers, and other vital organs from donors declared legally dead using the "whole brain death" criterion. The donor must be at least 15 years old, and written permission must be obtained from the donor's family. Transplants from living donors, such as kidney transplants, have been widely accepted in Japan for years. Now, there are clear guidelines for other types of organ transplants. More information on this definition of brain death in Japan is provided in Nakasone's chapter in this volume (Chapter 14).

"Brain death" also is a utilitarian social construct that has emerged in response to the development of technology that can ventilate the lungs and circulate the blood within a body in which the brain is dead. The need for organs for transplantation has been a major driving force in this redefinition of death (Taylor, 1997). Donor organs must be removed while they still are being perfused, that is, when the heart still is beating. Hence, a declaration of brain death is required. A non-donor in a hopeless state of deep coma may have medical technical support withdrawn, permitting the heart to stop, without requiring an official determination of brain death (Schneiderman, Necker, & Jonsen, 1990).

Cardiorespiratory arrest, anoxia, head trauma, and stroke are common causes of brain death. These insults frequently increase intracranial pressure and ischemia (diminished blood supply), which destroy the brain in a rostral-to-caudal sequence (Plum & Posner, 1980); that is, the hemispheres stop functioning first, followed by the midbrain, the pons, and the medulla oblongata. The medulla is the part of the brain that regulates basic functions such as blood pressure and respiration. Once the entire brain is dead, cardiac asystole occurs within days or weeks despite all efforts to keep the heart beating (Power & Van Heerden, 1995). There is a useful rationalization for a declaration that a person is legally dead once it has been established that the entire brain has experienced a permanent cessation of function, even if respiration and circulation are maintained artificially. If the whole brain is permanently and completely destroyed, then respiration would cease, circulation would cease within a short period of time, and the traditional standard of death would be met. On a determination of whole brain death, a patient is considered to be legally dead and organ retrieval can be commenced while respiration and circulation are maintained. In addition, if a person is legally dead, then life support can be discontinued. Thus, the use of the whole brain death criterion is useful both to avoid the impression that organs are being withdrawn from a living person and to permit disconnecting life support technology that is maintaining blood and air circulation in an otherwise lifeless person.

There are specific parameters for determining brain death in adults (Quality Standards Subcommittee of the American Academy of Neurology, 1995). There must be a high degree of certainty as to the cause of coma. Reversible causes, such as drug overdose and hypothermia, must be ruled out. There can be no movements other than spinal cord reflexes. All brain stem reflexes, including pupillary light responses, corneal responses, gag reflex, and all eye movement responses, must be absent. There can be no respiratory efforts while

the patient is off the ventilator for 8 minutes (Wijdicks, 1
tion is done at the bedside in the intensive care unit. A rep
hours is recommended, whereas confirmatory tests are o

The family should be kept well informed during th.. p.∪∪∪∪∪ ∪y ∪∪mg
thoroughly educated about brain death. However, the burden and responsibility for declaring the individual dead rests with the physician.

■ COMPETENCY AND CAPACITY

Competency and capacity refer to the ability to manage one's affairs and make sound decisions. Although the terms often are used interchangeably, *competency* generally is used in a legal context, whereas *capacity* frequently appears in a medical context. A person in a vegetative state or a coma clearly is not competent to make decisions. Just as certainly, a healthy older adult usually is competent enough to make decisions. But what about the individual who is diagnosed with a condition that affects cognitive functioning?

First, health care and legal workers must never conceptualize competency as a light switch, that is, either "on" or "off." It is important to recognize that a diagnosis of a neurological or psychological disease does not necessarily mean that a person lacks the capacity for self-determination, that is, to make informed decisions with regard to important life decisions. For example, some individuals with psychiatric disorders might be competent to make decisions when they are maintained on appropriate medications but might not be competent to do so when they go off their medications. Others might have conditions that affect capacity on a temporary basis. For example, underlying conditions that are treatable might cause confusion, disordered speech, and/or hallucinations. These include dehydration, malnutrition, depression, alcohol abuse, overmedication, adverse drug reactions, chemical imbalances, hypoglycemia, brain tumor, and organ damage. Other disorders, such as stroke and hearing loss, can affect a person's ability to engage in conversation but might not affect his or her decision-making capacity. Even individuals with irreversible dementia might be able to make some decisions. For example, although an individual in the early stages of Alzheimer's disease might not be able to balance a checkbook, he or she still might have the capacity to make or revoke a will, complete advance directives, give informed consent for medical treatment, participate as a subject in a research study, refuse treatment, designate a surrogate decision maker, and/or make other end-of-life decisions (Pietsch & Lee, 1998).

TABLE 3.1. Mini-Mental State

Maximum Score	Score	
		Orientation
5	( )	What is the (year/season/date/month)?
5	( )	Where are we (state/county/town/hospital/floor)?
		Registration
3	( )	Name three objects, one second to say each, then ask the patient all three after you have said them. Give 1 point for each correct answer. Then, repeat them until the patient learns all three. Count trials and record.
		Attention and Calculation
5	( )	Serial 7's: Count backward from 100 by 7. Give 1 point for each correct. Stop after five answers. Alternatively, spell "world" backward.
		Recall
3	( )	Ask for the three objects repeated above. Give 1 point for each correct.
		Language
2	( )	Name a pencil and watch (2 points).
1	( )	Repeat the following: "No ifs, ands, or buts."
3	( )	Follow a three-stage command: "Take paper in your right hand, fold it in half, and put it on the floor."
1	( )	Read and obey the following: Close your eyes.
1	( )	Write a sentence.
1	( )	Copy a design.

30 (total)

Assess level of consciousness along a continuum: Alert-Drowsy-Stupor-Coma

SOURCE: Reprinted from Folstein, Folstein, and McHugh (1975) with permission from Elsevier Science.

Professionals assisting individuals with end-of-life decision making often include attorneys and health care providers, and each has the professional responsibility to determine the mental status of the individual to ensure that decisions are informed, voluntary, and not made under the undue influence of another person. This raises difficult questions, however, about which standards to use to judge capacity and whether decisions can be made in advance of any further loss of capacity.

There is no single conclusive test to determine capacity. A common tool used to assess it, however, is the MMSE (Folstein et al., 1975). As shown in Table 3.1, this instrument calls for patients to answer questions about time and place, and it tests their ability to register and recall information, perform calculations, and follow commands. The maximum possible score is 30; a score of less than 24 frequently is indicative of dementia. As mentioned earlier, however, about half of depressed older adults score less then 24 on the MMSE, but these individuals regain a normal mental status after treatment. When there is a question of specific capacity, an opinion should be sought by a clinician skilled in making these assessments (Blanchette & Pietsch, 1999).

■ CONCLUSION

The neurological and psychological functions of the brain show only minor changes well into old age. Specific diseases or a combination of disorders can cause major impairment of the brain and the mind with age. Although dementia becomes more common with age, it is not a normal process of aging. The vegetative state represents the ultimate state of decline. Brain death is an accepted concept in the United States and other Western countries but is not accepted in all countries or cultures. It is important to remember, however, that despite the extremes of normal old age or a diagnosis of disease that can impair cognition in some way, many people retain the capacity to make personal (including end-of-life) decisions or to designate a trusted surrogate to make these decisions for them.

■ REFERENCES

Ad Hoc Committee. (1968). A definition of irreversible coma: Report of the Ad Hoc Committee of the Harvard Medical School to Examine the Definition of Brain Death. *Journal of the American Medical Association, 205,* 337-340.

Alfonso, I., Lanting, W. A., Duenas, D., Cullen, R. F., & Papazian, O. (1992). Discontinuation of artificial hydration and nutrition in hopelessly vegetative children [abstract]. *Annals of Neurology, 32,* 454-455.

American Psychiatric Association. (1994). *Diagnostic and statistical manual of mental disorders* (4th ed.). Washington, DC: Author.

American Thoracic Society. (1991). Withholding and withdrawing life-sustaining therapy. *Annals of Internal Medicine, 115,* 478-485.

Awad, I. A., Spetzler, R. F., Hodak, J. A., Awad, C. A., & Cary, R. (1986). Incidental sub-cortical lesions identified on magnetic resonance imaging in the elderly: Correlation with age and cerebrovascular risk factors. *Stroke, 17,* 1084-1089.

Bayley, N., & Oden, M. H. (1955). The maintenance of intellectual ability in gifted adults. *Journal of Gerontology, 10,* 91-107.

Blanchette, P. L., & Pietsch, J. (1999). Evaluation of competence. In J. J. Gallo, J. Busby-Whitehead, P. V. Rabins, R. Silliman, & J. Murphy (Eds.), *Reichel's care of the elderly: Clinical aspects of aging* (5th ed., pp. 686-691). Baltimore, MD: Lippincott Williams & Wilkins.

Boone, K. B., Miller, B. L., Lesser, I. M., Mehringer, C. M., Hill-Gutierrez, E., Goldberg, M. A., & Berman, N. G. (1992). Neuropsychological correlates of white matter lesions in healthy elderly subjects: A threshold effect. *Archives of Neurology, 49,* 549-554.

Brody, H. (1955). Organization of the cerebral cortex. III: A study of aging in the human cerebral cortex. *Journal of Comparative Neurology, 102,* 511-556.

Camicioli, R., Panzer, V. P., & Kaye, J. (1997). Balance in the healthy elderly. *Archives of Neurology, 54,* 976-981.

Carman, M. D. (1997). The psychology of normal aging. *Psychiatric Clinics of North America, 20*(1), 15-24.

Cohen, G. D. (1997). Sky above clouds: Mental health in later life. *American Journal of Geriatric Psychiatry, 5,* 1-3.

Costa, P. T., Jr., Zonderman, A. B., McCrae, R. R., Cornoni-Huntley, J., Locke, B. Z., & Barbano, H. E. (1987). Longitudinal analyses of psychological well-being in a national sample: Stability of mean levels. *Journal of Gerontology, 42,* 50-55.

Crook, T., Bartus, R. T., Ferris, S. H., Whitehouse, P., Cohen, G. D., & Gershon, S. (1986). Age-associated memory impairment: Proposed diagnostic criteria and measures of clinical change—Report of a National Institute of Mental Health work group. *Developmental Neuropsychology, 2,* 261-276.

Deptula, D., Singh, R., & Pomara, N. (1993). Aging, emotional states, and memory. *American Journal of Psychiatry, 150,* 429-434.

Dougherty, J. H., Rawlinson, D. G., Levy, D. E., & Plum, F. (1981). Hypoxic-ischemic brain injury and the vegetative state: Clinical and neuropathologic correlation. *Neurology, 31,* 991-997.

Fazekas, F., Kleinert, R., Offenbacher, H., Schmidt, R., Kleinert, G., Payer, F., Radner, H., & Lechner, H. (1993). Pathologic correlates of incidental MRI white matter signal hyperintensities. *Neurology, 43,* 1683-1689.

Field, D., & Millsap, R. E. (1991). Personality in advanced old age: Continuity or change? *Journal of Gerontology, 46,* 299-308.

Filley, C. (1996). Neurobehavioral aspects of cerebral white matter disorders. In B. S. Fogel & R. B. Schiffer (Eds.), *Neuropsychiatry* (pp. 913-933). Baltimore, MD: Williams & Wilkens.

Filley, C. M., Davis, K. A., Schmitz, S. P., Stears, J. C., Heaton, R. K., Kelly, J., Culig, K. M., & Scherzinger, A. L. (1989). Neuropsychological performance and magnetic resonance imaging in Alzheimer's disease and normal aging. *Neuropsychiatry, Neuropsychology, and Behavioral Neurology, 2,* 81-91.

Fischer, P. (1996). The spectrum of depressive pseudodementia. *Journal of Neural Transmission, 47*(Suppl.), 193-203.

Fisher, J. B. (1995). Successful aging, life satisfaction, and generativity in later life. *International Journal of Aging and Human Development, 41,* 239-250.

Flicker, C., Ferris, S. H., & Reisberg, B. (1993). A longitudinal study of cognitive function in elderly persons with subjective memory complaints. *Journal of the American Geriatrics Society, 41,* 1029-1032.

Folstein, M. F., Folstein, S. E., & McHugh, P. R. (1975). "Mini-Mental State": A practical method for grading the cognitive state of patients for the clinician. *Journal of Psychiatric Research, 12,* 189-198.

Giambra, L. M., Arenberg, D., Zonderman, A. B., Costa, P. T., Jr., & Kawas, C. (1995). Adult life span changes in immediate visual memory and verbal intelligence. *Psychology and Aging, 10,* 123-139.

Golomb, J., de Leon, M. J., Kluger, A., George, A. E., Tarshish, C., & Ferris, S. H. (1993). Hippocampal atrophy in normal aging: An association with recent memory impairment. *Archives of Neurology, 50,* 967-973.

Hachinski, V. C., Potter, P., & Mersky, H. (1987). Leukoariosis. *Archives of Neurology, 44,* 21-23.

Hänninen, T., Hallikainen, M., Koivisto, K., Partanen, K., Laaskso, M. P., Riekkinen, P. J., Sr., & Soininen, H. (1997). Decline of frontal lobe functions in subjects with age-associated memory impairment. *Neurology, 48,* 148-153.

Hänninen, T., Reinikainen, K. J., Helkala, E., Koivisto, K., Mykkänen, L., Laakso, M., Pyörälä, K., & Riekkinen, P. J. (1994). Subjective memory complaints and personality traits in normal elderly subjects. *Journal of the American Geriatrics Society, 42,* 1-4.

Henderson, G., Tomlinson, B. E., & Gibson, P. H. (1980). Cell counts in human cerebral cortex in normal adults throughout life using an image analyzing computer. *Journal of the Neurological Sciences, 46,* 113-136.

Hooyman, N. R., & Kiyak, H. A. (1996). *Social gerontology: A multidisciplinary perspective* (4th ed.). Needham Heights, MA: Allyn & Bacon.

Howieson, D. B., Holm, L. A., Kaye, J. A., Oken, B. S., & Howieson, J. (1993). Neurologic function in the optimally healthy oldest old: Neuropsychological evaluation. *Neurology, 43,* 1882-1886.

Jorm, A. F., Christensen, H., Henderson, A. S., Korten, A. E., Mackinnon, A. J., & Scott, R. (1994). Complaints of cognitive decline in the elderly: A comparison of reports by subjects and informants in a community survey. *Psychological Medicine, 24,* 365-374.

Katzman, R., & Terry, R. (1983). Normal aging of the nervous system. In R. Katzman & R. D. Terry (Eds.), *The neurology of aging* (Contemporary Neurology Series, pp. 15-50). Philadelphia: F. A. Davis.

Kiloh, L. C. (1961). Pseudodementia. *Acta Psychiatrica Scandinavica, 37,* 336-351.

Koss, E., Haxby, J. V., DeCarli, C., Schapiro, M. B., Friedland, R. P., & Rapoport, S. I. (1991). Patterns of performance preservation and loss in healthy aging. *Developmental Neuropsychology, 7,* 99-113.

Kral, V. A. (1962). Senescent forgetfulness: Benign and malignant. *Canadian Medical Association Journal, 86,* 257-260.

Larrabee, G. J., & McEntee, W. J. (1995). Age-associated memory impairment: Sorting out the controversies. *Neurology, 45,* 611-614.

Lindsay, J., Hébert, R., & Rockwood, K. (1997). The Canadian study of health and aging: Risk factors for vascular dementia. *Stroke, 28,* 526-530.

Longstreth, W. T., Manolio, T. A., Arnold, A., Burke, G. L., Bryan, N., Jungries, C. A., Enright, P. L., O'Leary, D., & Fried, L. (1996). Clinical correlates of white matter findings on cranial magnetic resonance imaging of 3,301 elderly people: The Cardiovascular Health Study. *Stroke, 27,* 1274-1282.

McCullough, P. K. (1991). Geriatric depression: Atypical presentations, hidden meanings. *Geriatrics, 46,* 72-76.

Miller, A. K. H., Alston, R. L., & Corsellis, J. A. N. (1980). Variation with age in the volumes of gray and white matter in the cerebral hemispheres of man: Measurements with an image analyzer. *Neuropathology and Applied Neurobiology, 6,* 119-132.

Morris, J. C., & McManus, D. Q. (1991). The neurology of aging: Normal versus pathologic change. *Geriatrics, 46,* 47-54.

Multi-Society Task Force on PVS. (1994a). Medical aspects of the persistent vegetative state [Part I]. *New England Journal of Medicine, 330,* 1499-1508.

Multi-Society Task Force on PVS. (1994b). Medical aspects of the persistent vegetative state [Part II]. *New England Journal of Medicine, 330,* 1572-1579.

O'Boyle, M., Amadeo, M., & Self, D. (1990). Cognitive complaints in elderly depressed and pseudodemented patients. *Psychology and Aging, 5,* 467-468.

Ohnuki-Tierney, E. (1994). Brain death and organ transplantation: Cultural bases of medical technology. *Current Anthropology, 35,* 233-254.

Pietsch, J. H., & Lee, L. (1998). *The elder law Hawaii handbook.* Honolulu: University of Hawaii Press.

Plum, F., & Posner, J. B. (1980). *The diagnosis of stupor and coma* (3rd ed.). Philadelphia: F. A. Davis.

Power, B. M., & Van Heerden, P. V. (1995). The physiological changes associated with brain death: Current concepts and implications for treatment of the brain dead organ donor. *Anesthesia and Intensive Care, 23*(1), 26-36.

Quality Standards Subcommittee of the American Academy of Neurology. (1995). Practice parameters for determining brain death in adults [summary statement]. *Neurology, 45,* 1012-1014.

Sachdev, P. S., Smith, J. S., Angus-Lepan, H., & Rodriguez, P. (1990). Pseudodementia twelve years on. *Journal of Neurology, Neurosurgery, and Psychiatry, 53,* 254-259.

Salthouse, T. A. (1994). The aging of working memory. *Neuropsychology, 8,* 535-543.

Schaie, K. W. (1994). The course of adult intellectual development. *American Psychologist, 49,* 304-313.

Schneiderman, L. J., Necker, N. S., & Jonsen, A. R. (1990). Medical futility: Its meaning and ethical implications. *Annals of Internal Medicine, 112,* 949-954.

Schofield, P. W., Jacobs, D., Marder, K., Sano, M., & Stern, Y. (1997). The validity of new memory complaints in the elderly. *Archives of Neurology, 54,* 756-759.

Sudarsky, L. (1990). Geriatrics: Gait disorders in the elderly. *New England Journal of Medicine, 322,* 1441-1446.

Taylor, R. M. (1997). Reexamining the definition and criteria of death. *Seminars in Neurology, 17,* 265-270.

Thomas, C. L. (1993). *Taber's cyclopedic medical dictionary.* Philadelphia: F. A. Davis.

Wells, C. E. (1979). Pseudodementia. *American Journal of Psychiatry, 136,* 894-896.

Wijdicks, E. F. M. (1995). Determining brain death in adults. *Neurology, 45,* 1003-1011.

Chapter 4

Autonomy, Advance Directives, and the Patient Self-Determination Act

JAMES H. PIETSCH
KATHRYN L. BRAUN

*T*his chapter addresses issues related to self-determination in medical treatment and the effect that federal and state laws have had on the way in which patients, families, and society make health care decisions. First acknowledged is a fundamental commitment within the constitutional fabric of the United States to patient autonomy and its relationship to informed consent. The chapter then discusses the Patient Self-Determination Act of 1990 (PSDA), an attempt by the U.S. Congress to enhance the effectiveness of state laws governing the rights of individuals to make their own medical treatment decisions. An important component of the PSDA is the advance directive, defined in the law as a written document such as a living will or a durable power of attorney for health care (DPOA-HC) that provides "directions in advance" for medical treatment in case a person becomes incapacitated. The importance of addressing "competency" and "capacity" is stressed. Finally, the chapter highlights some of the difficulties that individuals face in ensuring that their instructions for end-of-life treatment will be followed, and it outlines attempts by some practitioners and community groups to remedy these difficulties.

■ PATIENT AUTONOMY AND INFORMED CONSENT

In the United States, all competent individuals have the fundamental right to control decisions relating to their own medical care, including the decision to have life-prolonging treatments provided, continued, withheld, or withdrawn. The basis for making autonomous decisions centers on the concept of informed consent as well as a person's common law and constitutional right to refuse unwanted medical treatment. This concept was codified in 1973 with the adoption of the Patient's Bill of Rights, which elevated patient self-determination from an ethical concern to a legal obligation for physicians (Edge & Groves, 1994; Foster & Pearman, 1978). Americans regard self-determination as freedom from group expectations, and self-reliance is regarded as a sign of strength. It is not surprising, then, that the United States would ask health care providers to follow moral and legal mandates based on principles of autonomy such as the Patient's Bill of Rights and the PSDA.

Despite a national commitment to patient self-determination, it is important to note that patients and their families have experienced difficulties in having wishes concerning end-of-life medical treatment decisions followed, even when such decisions are documented in writing. This difficulty is due partly to the fact that there is no single national standard on accepting or refusing medical treatment. Instead, each of the 50 states, as well as each of the other U.S. jurisdictions (e.g., American Samoa, District of Columbia, Guam, Puerto Rico, Virgin Islands), establishes its own laws within the country's constitutional framework. Federal actions, such as decisions by the U.S. Supreme Court on key patient autonomy cases and the passage of federal laws such as the PSDA, also influence how states and health care providers approach end-of-life issues.

In every jurisdiction of the United States, a physician has a duty to inform a patient of the consequences and risks of a medical procedure and to obtain the patient's consent prior to performing the procedure. A physician who fails to obtain informed consent can be held liable to the patient for any resulting damages. Consent is expressed ideally in writing, or it may be implied. Consent usually is implied in emergencies, in situations to preserve the life of an unconscious patient, and in cases where a patient actively seeks treatment and manifests a willingness to accept the treatment. Each state can develop its own standards as to how the state ensures that individuals who receive health care in the state are, in fact, informed about their options and consent voluntarily to treatment. Specifically, each state must ensure that mechanisms are in place so that a patient, or a patient's guardian, is reasonably informed of (a) the condition being treated, (b) the nature and character of the proposed treatment or surgical procedure, (c) the anticipated results, (d) the recognized possible alternative forms of treatment, and (e) the recognized serious possible risks, complications, and anticipated benefits involved in the recommended treatment, possible alternative forms of treatment, and nontreatment.

The law also recognizes that competent individuals, once informed of their options, can choose to refuse treatment. But what if a patient does not have the capacity to understand his or her options and make treatment choices, as in the case of Nancy Cruzan?

■ THE *CRUZAN* CASE

The case of Nancy Cruzan served as an important catalyst for the development and passage of the PSDA. Cruzan was a young woman who was rendered incompetent as a result of severe injuries sustained in an automobile accident. She was not brain dead but did not respond to stimuli and could not communicate. After several years in this condition, the family petitioned to have life-sustaining treatments (in this case, tube feeding and intravenous fluids) withdrawn. The patient had no written documentation of her medical treatment wishes, however, and the State of Missouri refused this request.

The case was appealed to the U.S. Supreme Court, which rendered its decision on June 25, 1990 (*Cruzan v. Director, Missouri Department of Health,* 1990). In its decision, the Supreme Court essentially held that a competent person has a liberty interest under the due process clause of the Fourteenth Amendment to the U.S. Constitution in refusing unwanted medical treatment, including the right to refuse lifesaving hydration and nutrition. The court held that this does not mean that an incompetent person should possess the same right given that such a person is unable to make an informed and voluntary choice to exercise that hypothetical right or any other right. The court went on to say that the U.S. Constitution does not prohibit a state from requiring clear and convincing evidence of an incompetent's wishes as to withdrawal of life-sustaining treatment. It further stated that the due process clause does not require a state to accept the "substituted judgment" of close family members in the absence of substantial proof that their views reflect those of the patient (*Cruzan v. Director, Missouri Department of Health,* 1990). Thus, once Cruzan was incapacitated, and absent any clear and convincing evidence of her wishes, no automatic rights of the patient or family, nor any legal recourse, could force the State of Missouri to allow the withdrawal of the tube feeding and intravenous hydration. The issue eventually was resolved in a lower court when the family was able to provide clear and convincing evidence of Cruzan's wishes through testimony by friends and relatives. They testified of having heard, prior to the accident, verbal expressions by Nancy that would have indicated that she would not want to be kept alive under such conditions.

■ THE PSDA AND ADVANCE DIRECTIVES

Building on the concepts of autonomy and informed consent, as well as on the lessons of the *Cruzan* case, the PSDA makes clear that all competent individuals have the fundamental right to control decisions regarding their own medical care. This includes the decision to have provided, continued, withheld, or withdrawn any medical or surgical means calculated to prolong life. It realizes that individuals, through illness or injury, can become incapacitated and lose their ability to make emerging decisions about treatment. An advance directive can be used to document a person's wishes in advance of incapacitation and can be used to provide clear and convincing evidence of how treatment should proceed.

The PSDA became effective on December 1, 1991, and requires all health care facilities and agencies, upon the admission of patients, to provide information to the patients about their medical treatment decision rights. Each facility is to ask whether the patient has completed an advance directive and, if so, to request that the patient or his or her family supply a copy to the facility. If the patient does not have an advance directive, then the facility is to provide information about advance directives.

The PSDA strengthened the effect of codified legal options for individuals wanting to avoid the dilemma confronted by Cruzan and her family. These options are called advance directives. As with standards of informed consent, however, each state establishes its own criteria for making advance medical treatment decisions orally or through documents such as the living will and the DPOA-HC.

This chapter continues with a description of specific advanced directives. It is important to note, however, that state laws regarding advance directives vary and are constantly changing. The current diversity of approaches has led to some difficulties, especially in an increasingly mobile society where advance directives made in one state might need to be implemented in another state. Thus, a Uniform Health Care Decisions Act has been proposed for adoption across states that would provide some consistency in advance directive

TABLE 4.1. Definitions

Term	Definition
Advance directives	Directions given in advance of incapacitation to guide decisions about medical treatment, including "living wills" and DPOA-HC
Comfort-care-only order or out-of-hospital DNR order	Order by a physician that allows a terminally ill person to state in advance that he or she does not want to be resuscitated in an emergency; normally for use outside a hospital or other institution
Do-not-resuscitate order or no-CPR order	Order by a physician for not providing CPR of a patient in the event that he or she suffers cardiac or respiratory arrest; normally for use in a hospital or other institution
Durable power of attorney for health care	Type of advance directive in which a person appoints someone else to make treatment decisions in the event that he or she is incapacitated
Living will	Type of advance directive in which a person gives specific directions about treatment that should be followed in the event of his or her incapacitation; usually addresses life-sustaining medical treatment, including providing food and water by intubation
Patient Self-Determination Act	Federal law that requires health care facilities and agencies to provide information to the patient about his or her medical treatment decision rights
Surrogate decision maker	Person designated, through a DPOA-HC or through state law, to make decisions on another person's behalf
Uniform Health Care Decisions Act	Model act drafted by the National Conference of Commissioners on Uniform State Laws that places provisions about the living will, the DPOA-HC, family consent, and other items into a single statute with a goal of increasing consistency of definitions and approaches to health care decision making in the United States

NOTE: DNR = do-not-resuscitate; CPR = cardiopulmonary resuscitation; DPOA-HC = durable power of attorney for health care.

laws and facilitate cross-state acceptability of advance directives (National Conference of Commissioners on Uniform State Laws, 1994). At the time this chapter was written, the Hawaii state legislature was adopting its own version of the Uniform Health Care Decision Act, and the chapter includes examples from both the new and old (repealed) Hawaii laws pertaining to decision making. Important terms presented in this chapter are presented in Table 4.1.

Living Wills

A "living will" is a written document that directs care on an individual's mental incapacitation. Prior to the *Cruzan* case, most state living will laws did not provide very much help to individuals who wished to make informed and comprehensive decisions about medical treatment if they were to become incompetent. The old laws generally were ambiguous as to what conditions qualified under the law and whether or not it permitted a person to have intravenous hydration and/or tube feeding withheld or withdrawn. After 1990, state legislatures began revising their living will laws. For example, Hawaii updated its statute and expressly recognized the right of an adult person to create a written declaration instructing a physician to provide, continue, withhold, or withdraw life-sustaining procedures. This was so that patients' rights still may be respected after they no longer are able to participate actively in decisions about their care. Also explicitly included were options for directing the insertion, removal, or withholding of tubes to provide food and water (e.g., Medical Treatment Decisions, Hawaii Revised Statutes § 327D-2, repealed).

In general, living will laws place the responsibility on the individual to provide a living will declaration valid under state law to his or her physician and the hospital in which he or she is a patient. Most states require that health care facilities develop systems to visibly identify when a patient's chart contains a living will declaration. These systems also must facilitate the transfer of a patient to another physician if the attending physician refuses or is unable to comply with the terms of the patient's advance directive. Most state laws also outline criminal penalties for coercing or intimidating someone to execute a declaration or for concealing or obliterating a declaration (e.g., Medical Treatment Decisions, Hawaii Revised Statutes § 327D-17, repealed).

Although a written advance directive is desirable, some states do not mandate the patient to write the declaration. For example, in Hawaii, a verbal statement (or statements if they are consistent) made by the patient to either a physician or a friend or relative of the patient may be considered in deciding whether the patient would want life-sustaining procedures to be withdrawn or withheld. Unambiguous verbal statements by the patient, or reliable reports thereof, are to be documented in the patient's medical record. As in many states, Hawaii's law provided that, in the absence of any declaration at all (written or verbal), ordinary standards of current medical practice will be followed (Medical Treatment Decisions, Hawaii Revised Statutes § 327D-21, repealed).

The DPOA-HC

A DPOA-HC is the other advance directive provided for in most states that also is recognized under the PSDA. Very briefly, a power of attorney is a written instrument executed by a person, called the principal, granting another individual, called the agent (or attorney-in-fact), the authority to act on the person's behalf and to perform certain acts. As a general rule, powers of attorney cease to be effective on the death of the principal. In a "nondurable" power of attorney, these powers also are terminated in the event of mental incapacitation of the principal. However, if the document states that the agent's power will not be terminated by the incapacity or disability of the principal, then this creates a durable power of attorney. A "springing" power of attorney is one that takes effect only on some future event or date, for example, in the event of a person's incapacity. A documents that grants the agent power to make decisions regarding medical treatment is called a durable power of attorney for health care (or DPOA-HC).

As in most states, Hawaii law expressly authorized such a document through the Uniform Durable Power of Attorney Act (Title 30, Hawaii Revised Statutes § 551D-2.5, amended), which allowed a designated surrogate to make health care decisions for the principal if he or she is incapacitated, as determined by a licensed physician. The Hawaii law also required, however, that the principal must explicitly state in the document that he or she grants the surrogate the power to withhold or withdraw life-sustaining medical treatment. If this was not specifically stated, then it was presumed that the agent did not have the power to direct the withholding or withdrawing of life-sustaining medical treatment; rather, his or her power was restricted to other medical decisions, that is, those not regarding "life and death."

Hawaii's Uniform Health Care Decisions Act (Modified) was signed into law in July 1999. This act includes rules about the living will, the DPOA-HC, and surrogate decision making, as well as some provisions concerning organ donation, and it replaced previous legislation on these topics (Act 169, Hawaii Legislative Session, 1999).

Advance Directives on the Internet

All 50 states have passed legislation to enforce compliance with a patient's wishes through advance directives. For more information about advance directives in specific states, readers are urged to contact the American Bar Association's Commission on Legal Problems of the Elderly. This group, which regularly publishes updates on all state health decision-making statutes, can be reached through the Internet by accessing the American Bar Association Web site (http://www.abanet.com/elderly/).

■ DO-NOT-RESUSCITATE ORDERS AND COMFORT-CARE-ONLY ORDERS

The enactment of the living will and DPOA-HC legislation demonstrated the intent of states to promote the autonomy and self-determination of individuals concerning their own medical treatment. Depending on particular state laws, however, there are certain circumstances under which these documents might not be followed. For example, a patient who suffers cardiac or respiratory arrest in a hospital will routinely be resuscitated, even if he or she has an advance directive, unless there is a written "do-not-resuscitate" (DNR) order in the medical record. The DNR order is required if the patient wants a health care facility or practitioner to forgo the otherwise automatic initiation of cardiopulmonary resuscitation (CPR).

Under normal circumstances, for the advance directive to be followed, a physician first must certify that the patient is in a certain condition or state of incapacity. For example, Hawaii's living will law required an attending physician, who has been notified of the existence of an advance directive, to first make all reasonable efforts to obtain a notarized copy and then ascertain whether the patient's condition corresponds to the directions on the declaration (Medical Treatment Decisions, Hawaii Revised Statutes § 327D-10, repealed). Hawaii's law relating to DPOA-HC decisions provided that it will be effective only during the period of incapacity of the patient as determined by a licensed physician (Uniform Durable Power of Attorney, Hawaii Revised Statutes § 551D-2.5, amended). These types of determinations are not easily made in the emergency room or when the resuscitation team is speeding to the patient's room. Thus, advance directives might not be very useful in emergency situations. However, to remedy this, some states specifically address resuscitation codes in their advance directive statutes.

In some states, "comfort-care-only" or "out-of-hospital DNR" orders are authorized in specific statutes. For Hawaii, the law allows a terminally ill person to state in advance that he or she does not want to be resuscitated in an emergency (Rapid Identification Documents, Hawaii Revised Statutes § 321-229.5). Such a person must (a) be certified, in a written comfort-care-only document by his or her physician, to be a terminally ill patient of that physician; (b) have certified in the same written comfort-care-only document that he or she directs emergency medical services personnel, first responder personnel, and health care providers *not* to administer chest compression, rescue breathing, electric shocks, or medication to restart the heart if the person's breathing or heart stops and, instead, directs that he or she be given care for comfort only (which may include oxygen, airway suctioning, splinting of fractures, and pain medicine); and (c) be wearing a physician-prescribed comfort-care-only bracelet or necklace.

■ COMPETENCY AND CAPACITY

Intertwined with the concepts of informed consent and advance directives is the concept of competency or mental capacity. Although the terms *competency* and *capacity* often are used interchangeably, competency generally is used in a legal context, whereas capacity frequently appears in a medical context.

Adults age 18 or older initially are presumed to be legally competent to provide informed consent. Parents of minors usually have the authority to make medical treatment decisions for their children. The state, under its *parens patriae* (literally "parents of the country") doctrine, may act to protect the interests of persons under legal disability who are unable to protect themselves. For minors, this doctrine also can be used to give the state the right to override a parent's decision and provide treatment believed to be necessary to safeguard a child's life or health.

Under laws of informed consent, individuals need to have adequate competency/capacity to understand their diagnoses, prognoses, and options. If an adult is incompetent, then advance directives can guide treatment decisions. But an individual needs to possess adequate competency/capacity to complete written advance directives or to have others trust his or her verbal statements about future treatments. Thus, the determination of competency/capacity is a critical issue. Professionals assisting an individual with end-of-life decision making, including attorneys and health care providers, have professional responsibilities to determine the mental status of the individual to ensure that decisions are informed, voluntary, and not made under the undue influence of another person. More information on competence and capacity was provided in the chapter by Martino in this volume (Chapter 3).

■ SURROGATE DECISION MAKING

If a person has not completed a written advance directive, then he or she may verbally provide directions for medical treatment in advance of future incapacitation. The concept of autonomy-enhancing advance directives could even include such things as verbal statements by a patient to a physician when he or she was competent and noncontradicted statements by relatives or friends concerning statements made by the patient at an earlier point in time. Whether or not these verbal statements have much of an effect on decision making really depends on the motivations and integrity of the person hearing or knowing about the patient's earlier requests.

A similar concern exists in considering how decisions are made by legal surrogates such as those empowered to make decisions under a DPOA-HC document or through "default" or "family consent" statutes that have been enacted in many states. These surrogate decision-making statutes typically outline a hierarchy of decision makers. For example, if a patient has no advance directive or guardian, then his or her spouse may be deemed the default surrogate decision maker. If there is no spouse, then decisions might fall to another family member or, if the patient has no family, to a close friend. Different state statutes on surrogate decision making include different limitations. For example, under Hawaii's first surrogate statute, a surrogate could make decisions for the patient only if he or she resided in a nursing facility, and the surrogate could not make decisions to remove tube feeding and/or hydration (Medical Treatment Decisions, Hawaii Revised Statutes § 327D-28-38, repealed). These limitations originally were included to help circumvent possible abuse by a surrogate who might want to end a patient's life for a reason other than "the patient's best interest" (e.g., personal material gain, revenge).

Unlike most states, Hawaii's Uniform Health Care Decisions Act (Modified) does not provide for a common family hierarchy of decision makers for a decisionally incapacitated person. Instead, it provides for decision making by an "interested person," which could be a non-estranged spouse, a reciprocal beneficiary, a parent, an adult sibling, a child, a grandchild, or any adult who has exhibited special care and concern for the patient and who is familiar with the patient's personal values. A surrogate decision maker who was not designated formally prior to the incapacitation, however, faces more restrictions than does a formally designated surrogate.

■ LIMITATIONS OF THE PSDA

Although it should be clear that health care professionals should take advance directives seriously, an accumulation of evidence suggests that the

PSDA has not been effective in increasing the use and usefulness of advance directives.

Who Completes Advance Directives?

Although all 50 states have passed legislation on advance directives and surveys have shown that people are in favor of such legislation, empirical data reveal that the actual use of advance directives is low. In general populations, about 15% to 25% of people say that they have advance directives, reported prevalence among hospitalized patients is 1% to 40%, and research suggests that only 50% of people with terminal cancer or AIDS have advance directives (Miles, Koepp, & Weber, 1996). In addition, people who have executed advance directives tend to be better educated and from higher socioeconomic strata than people who have not, and this limits their usefulness in certain populations. Cultural and religious traditions can play a role in an individual's willingness to complete a written advance directive, as noted in subsequent chapters in this volume.

Who Knows About the Advance Directive?

Even if a patient has executed an advance directive, it might not be entered into hospital record. Research suggests that patients' physicians might not know that their patients have advance directives, patients forget to bring them to the hospital or refer to having them in safe deposit boxes, copies that are in outpatient records might not be duplicated for the hospital record, and so forth (Miles et al., 1996). In other cases, a patient might have completed an advance directive but not shared copies with his or her family members. In other cases, family members might disagree with an advance directive and threaten to make trouble if it is honored. Although the patient's advance directive still must be followed, surprise or disagreement among family members often works to delay decisions to withdraw treatment.

Problems of Portability

If a person has completed a living will in one state, is it valid in another state? Unfortunately, the answer often is no because each state has the right to develop its own statutes relative to advance directives. Thus, just as it is important to check in advance whether an agency, organization, institution, or private party will recognize or accept the power of attorney for financial or legal matters, it might be just as important to make the same assessment concerning advance health care directives. In many cases, state law or practice might require some specific language in the document or require an alternative mechanism such as guardianship. The exception is the Military Advance Medical Directive Law (10 U.S. Code, § 1044c), established under federal law for persons eligible for military legal assistance. Under this statute, an advance medical directive executed in accordance with applicable military regulations will be given the same legal effect as an advance medical directive prepared and executed in accordance with the laws of the state concerned. In other words, such an advance medical directive, no matter where it is executed, must be given the same legal effect as an advance directive prepared and executed in the state where the individual is a patient. For persons who are not eligible for military legal assistance, some states have attempted to address the "portability" of advance directives by expressly recognizing advance directives executed in other states. Widespread adoption of the Uniform Health Care Decisions Act mentioned earlier also would make it easier for advance health care directives made in one state to be implemented in another state.

Are Advance Directives Followed?

Sadly, there is evidence to suggest that advance directives are not very effective in guiding treatment decisions. The best example of this comes from the Study to Understand Prognoses and Preferences for the Outcomes and Risks of Treatments (SUPPORT). In this study involving several hospitals, practice patterns at the end of life were compared prior to and following implementation of the PSDA (SUPPORT Principal Investigators, 1995). In addition, an intervention started after the passage of the PSDA was provided to a random sample of the patients in which trained nurses tried to facilitate communication about end-of-life issues and the use and honoring of advance directives. Researchers found that advance directives did not direct care and that, despite receiving additional information on patient prognoses and preferences, few changes were seen in the frequency of discussions of treatment, use of ventilators, level of pain experienced by dying patients, or cost of care (Hanson, Tulsky, & Danis, 1997; Teno, Licks, et al., 1997; Teno, Lynn, et al., 1997). In other words, "Neither the implementation of the PSDA nor the introduction of the experimental intervention improved end-of-life care" (Fins, 1997, p. 519).

When Should an Advance Directive Be Completed?

The PSDA requires that health care facilities ask patients, on admission, about advance directives. For many, however, admission can be the worst possible time to do so. Psychologically, patients might be traumatized by whatever brought them to the hospital or preoccupied with the experiences they are about to face. Discussions about what should be done in the event of future incapacitation can cause some patients to wonder whether the procedure they are about to undergo might "go wrong." Should not these discussions take place when patients are relatively healthy and fully competent?

Questions also have been raised as to the appropriateness of having hospital admission personnel lead discussions about advance directives. Should not these discussions be initiated by physicians and lawyers who are more likely to have the expertise to provide counsel on these matters? Both the American Medical Association and the American Bar Association opposed the passage of the PSDA (Larson & Eaton, 1997), in part because of doubts that advance directives could work if they were not based on open communication about death and dying among the patient, family, and provider(s). The chapter by Kogan, Blanchette, and Masaki in this volume (Chapter 19) provides more information on talking to patients about end-of-life issues.

■ STRENGTHENING ADVANCE DIRECTIVES

Health care workers, lawyers, and researchers have put forward a number of suggestions to enhance patient autonomy and self-determination through advance directives. For example, on the legal front, state and federal laws can be strengthened, with some advocates calling for statutory sanctions, criminal penalties, and punitive damages against physicians and health care facilities for disregarding advance directives (National Conference of Commissioners on Uniform State Laws, 1994). Some practitioners and researchers, including the SUPPORT Principal Investigators (1995), have proposed incentives to promote dialogue between patients and health care professionals about these issues. If we recommend that discussions about end-of-life preferences begin early while patients are middle-aged and healthy, then perhaps health care providers can be reimbursed for initiating these discussions and getting their patients to execute advance directives. If these discussions result in the appropriate withholding of unwanted (and expensive) lifesaving medical treatment,

then the costs associated with reimbursing upfront counseling would be minimal by comparison (Dunn et al., 1996).

Values History

For practitioners who take the time to broach the topic of death and dying
with their patients, several tools are available. Doukas and McCullough
(1991), in their work with patients, realized that advance directive documents
did not identify patients' underlying values and beliefs regarding end-of-life
issues. They also found that living wills provided general directions for care
but did not, and could not, give specific directions for each eventuality that
might confront the patient and physician. If a patient's values and preferences
could be understood, then physicians and surrogate decision makers would
have more information on which to base decisions in the event that the patient
were incapacitated.

The Doukas and McCullough (1991) tool includes two parts: an explicit
identification of values and the articulation of advance directives based on the
values. For example, in the values section, patients are asked to choose between two statements: (a) "I want to live as long as possible regardless of the
quality of life that I experience" or (b) "I want to preserve a good quality of life
even if this means that I might not live as long." The patient then is asked to review a list of values related to quality of life and to circle (or add) those that are
most important. Examples include the following:

1. I want to maintain my capacity to think clearly.
2. I want to avoid unnecessary pain.
3. I want to be with my loved ones before I die.
4. I want to leave good memories of me to my loved ones.
5. I want to be treated in accord with my religious beliefs and traditions.
6. I want to help others by making a contribution to medical education and research.

In the second section, the patient is to indicate whether he or she would
want to undergo CPR, be placed on a ventilator, have tube feeding, and so forth.
The patients can answer these with a yes or a no but also may specify that he or
she would want this procedure tried for a trial period of a specified length of
time or just to see whether it would be effective (and to be withdrawn if not effective).

Another tool was developed through the National Values History Demonstration Project in New Mexico (McIver-Gibson, 1990). The McIver-Gibson (1990) form is longer than that of Doukas and McCullough (1991) and includes three to eight questions in each of the following categories: one's attitudes toward health, life, illness, dying, and death; perceptions of the role of the doctor and other health caregivers; the importance of independence and control; personal relationships; religious beliefs; living environment; finances; and wishes concerning one's funeral. On the final page, an individual is given the option to write an obituary and brief eulogy about himself or herself.

Physician Orders for Life-Sustaining Treatment Document

Even if a person has completed an advance directive and/or values history, these documents still might not ensure that directions will be followed efficiently. As was mentioned earlier, the advance directive might not provide directions about specific treatments and might not be transferred with the patient to a new facility. Also, each institution may require that its own DNR form be completed (rather than accepting one from another facility).

In response to these problems, a multidisciplinary team at the Center for Ethics in Health Care at Oregon Health Services University worked to develop their Physician Orders for Life-Sustaining Treatment (POLST) document. This team started meeting in 1992 and involved providers from acute and long-term care settings in the creation and testing of, first, a Medical Treatment Coversheet (Dunn et al., 1996) and, later, the POLST form, which is described here.

The POLST form has seven sections to be completed by the attending physician (or another health care provider under the direction of the attending) based on discussions with the patient or surrogate decision maker regarding patient values and preferences. The first four sections allow the documentation of directions for specific treatments or services. Section A asks, in the event that the patient has no pulse and is not breathing, does he or she want to be resuscitated? Section B asks, in the event that the patient has a pulse and/or is breathing, which medical interventions does he or she want? Options include (a) comfort measures only (e.g., hygiene, reasonable efforts to offer food and fluids orally, medications, wound care, pain relief), (b) limited interventions (comfort measures plus use of oxygen, airway suctioning, and manual treatment of airway obstruction), (c) advanced interventions (all of the preceding plus oral/nasal airway, bag-mask/demand valve, monitor cardiac rhythm, medication, and intravenous fluid), (d) full treatment/resuscitation (all of the preceding plus CPR, intubation, and defibrillation), and (e) other instructions (to be specified). Section C asks about the use of antibiotics, that is, none except if needed for comfort, no invasive (intramuscular or intravenous) antibiotics, or full treatment. Section D asks about artificially administered fluids and nutrition with four options: (a) no feeding tube or intravenous fluids, (b) no long-term feeding tube or intravenous fluids, (c) full treatment, or (d) other instructions (to be specified).

Section E requires the attending physician to indicate with whom these orders have been discussed (e.g., patient, health care representative, court-appointed guardian, spouse, specified other). Also to be provided is the basis for these orders. An example is provided in the POLST guidance booklet: "After thorough discussion with the patient and family, and in keeping with the current advance directive, the patient has indicated a desire for no aggressive treatment. The above orders reflect this discussion" (POLST Task Force, 1997, p. 4). The two remaining sections instruct health care workers to attach copies of documentation of patient wishes and to provide guidelines for reviewing and making changes to the POLST as the patient's preferences and/or condition change. A POLST wallet card with a summary of physician orders also is available. In testing the POLST, researchers found that it helped practitioners to make treatment decisions that were more in accord with patient wishes (Dunn et al., 1996).

Unlike the values history documents, the POLST was not developed for distribution to the general public. The authors also acknowledged that the POLST adheres to Oregon's liberal advance directive statutes but might not be legally upheld in other states. However, they encouraged other communities to constitute work groups that can look into the specific problems that their states face in ensuring patient self-determination at the end of life.

■ CONCLUSION

This chapter introduced readers to the concepts of patient autonomy and informed consent and illustrated reasons why, despite the passage of the PSDA, families still can experience difficulties in ensuring that a patient's wishes concerning end-of-life medical treatment decisions are followed. Ways in which to strengthen the effectiveness of the PSDA, through legal action and early patient-provider discussion of these issues, were presented. Widespread adoptions of the Uniform Health Care Decisions Act and the use of tools such as a values history and the POLST can help to facilitate discussion about end-of-life choices and help to ensure that patients' wishes are followed.

■ REFERENCES

Doukas, D. J., & McCullough, L. B. (1991). The values history: The evaluation of the patient's values and advance directives. *Journal of Family Practice, 32,* 145-153.

Dunn, P. M., Schmidt, T. A., Carley, M. M., Donius, M., Weinstein, M. A., & Dull, V. T. (1996). A method to communicate patient preferences about medically indicated life-sustaining treatment in the out-of-hospital setting. *Journal of the American Geriatrics Society, 44,* 785-791.

Edge, R. S., & Groves, J. R. (1994). *The ethics of health care: A guide for clinical practice.* Albany, NY: Delmar.

Fins, J. F. (1997). Advance directives and SUPPORT. *Journal of the American Geriatrics Society, 45,* 519-520.

Foster, M. G., & Pearman, W. A. (1978). Social work, patient rights, and patient representatives. *Social Casework, 59,* 89-100.

Hanson, L. C., Tulsky, J. A., & Danis, M. (1997). Can clinical interventions change care at the end of life? *Annals of Internal Medicine, 126,* 381-388.

Larson, E. J., & Eaton, T. A. (1997). The limits of advance directives: A history and assessment of the Patient Self-Determination Act. *Wake Forest Law Review, 32,* 249-293.

McIver-Gibson, J. (1990). National values history project. *Generations, 14*(Suppl.), 51-64.

Miles, S. H., Koepp, R., & Weber, E. P. (1996). Advance end-of-life treatment planning: A research review. *Archives of Internal Medicine, 156,* 1062-1068.

National Conference of Commissioners on Uniform State Laws. (1994). *Draft Uniform Health Care Decisions Act.* Chicago: Author.

POLST Task Force. (1997). *Physician orders for life-sustaining treatment: Guidance for health care providers.* Portland, OR: Oregon Health Sciences University, Center for Ethics in Health Care.

SUPPORT Principal Investigators. (1995). A controlled trial to improve care for seriously ill hospitalized patients: The Study to Understand Prognoses and Preferences for Outcomes and Risks of Treatments. *Journal of the American Medical Association, 274,* 1951-1958.

Teno, J. M., Licks, S., Lynn, J., Wenger, N., Connors, A. F., Jr., Phillips, R. S., O'Connor, M. A., Murphy, D. P., Fulkerson, W. J., Desbiens, N., & Knaus, W. A. (1997). Do advance directives provide instructions that direct care? *Journal of the American Geriatrics Society, 45,* 508-512.

Teno, J. M., Lynn, J., Connors, J. A. F., Jr., Wenger, N., Phillips, R. S., Alzola, C., Murphy, D. P., Desbiens, N., & Knaus, W. A. (1997). The illusion of end-of-life resource savings with advance directives. *Journal of the American Geriatrics Society, 45,* 513-518.

Cases and Legislation Cited

Cruzan v. Director, Missouri Department of Health, 110 S.Ct. 2841 (1990).

Medical Treatment Decisions, Title 19 Hawaii Rev. Stat. § 327D (repealed June 30, 1999).

Military Advance Medical Directive Law, 10 U.S. Code 1044c.

Patient Self-Determination Act, Omnibus Budget Reconciliation Act of 1990, Public Law No. 101-508 §§ 4206, 4751, codified at 42 U.S. Code §§ 1395cc(a)(1)(Q), 1395cc(f), 1395mm(c)(8), and 42 U.S. Code §§ 1396a(a)(57), 1396a(a)(58), 1396a(w) (1991).

Rapid Identification Documents, Title 19 Hawaii Rev. Stat. § 321-229.5.

Uniform Durable Power of Attorney Act, Title 30 Hawaii Rev. Stat. § 551D (repealed June 30, 1999).

Uniform Health Care Decisions Act (Modified), Act 169, Hawaii Legislative Session, 1999.

Chapter 5

Ethical Considerations and Court Involvement in End-of-Life Decision Making

MARSHALL B. KAPP

rom a humane perspective, the quality of care provided to persons near the ends of their lives in the United States often leaves something to be desired (Institute of Medicine, 1997). The reasons for shortcomings in the care and compassion provided to a significant percentage of dying individuals by the modern health care system are multifold, but clearly, the complexity of relevant ethical issues at the end of life plays a role (Gordon & Singer, 1995). This chapter briefly outlines the most salient of these issues, with particular emphasis on presently identified areas of ethical consensus and dispute. Because anxiety on the part of health care providers about perceived potential legal liabilities can negatively influence their ethical behavior (Kapp, 1998; Perkins, Bauer, Hazuda, & Schoolfield, 1990), the legal parameters within which sequential, multiple, ethical decisions must be made and implemented over time are sketched out (Faber-Langendoen, 1996). Then, strategies for acting ethically while minimizing use of the judicial system for resolving conundrums about the initiation, continuation, withholding, or withdrawal of life-sustaining medical treatments are suggested.

■ DEFINITIONS

Because much confusion emanates from imprecision in the use of terminology, a note on nomenclature is worthwhile at the onset (Brigham & Pfeifer, 1996). The commonly used term *euthanasia,* originally derived from the Greek word meaning "good death," now is used to refer to any action or purposeful inaction by an individual that is intended to encourage the death of another. As such, it becomes an overarching categorical concept that may be defined more specifically through three distinctions.

First, *active* euthanasia is an act of commission in which a person engages in some direct action (e.g., suffocating another person with a plastic bag, administering a lethal injection) to hasten the death of a seriously ill individual. *Passive* euthanasia, by contrast, is an act of omission, ordinarily the withholding or withdrawing of life-sustaining medical interventions (e.g., mechanical ventilation, antibiotics, dialysis, artificial feeding/hydration, cardiopulmonary resuscitation) that results in the predicted and intended death of a seriously ill person.

Second, in a *voluntary* act of euthanasia, the patient clearly has indicated, orally or in writing, an express wish to die, whereas no such desire has been clearly expressed in the case of *nonvoluntary* or *involuntary* euthanasia. Third, euthanasia may be either *physician assisted* or *non-physician assisted.*

■ ETHICAL CONSENSUS

Much attention in contemporary bioethical and medico-legal discussions focuses on disputes and dilemmas. Thus, it is easy to forget that a solid consensus has coalesced during the past two decades around several key concepts pertaining to medical decision making near the end of life ("Measuring Quality of Care," 1997; Moreno, 1995). This chapter concentrates on bioethical consensus achieved in the United States, recognizing that attitudes on many issues vary across diverse cultures (Asai, Fukuhara, & Lo, 1995). Among these are the fundamental concepts of autonomy and beneficence.

Autonomy, the principle of self-rule or self-determination concerning the integrity of one's own body, has been translated into a well-accepted ethical and legal right on the part of mentally capable, critically ill persons to refuse the provision, or to consent to the withholding or withdrawal, of life-sustaining medical treatments (Bajwa, Szabo, & Kjellstrand, 1996). Many individuals have chosen to exercise this option (Fried & Gillick, 1994), concluding that their present or likely future medical situations constitute states worse than death (Pearlman et al., 1993).

However, a large chasm often exists between ethical theory and actual clinical experience (Brink, 1995; SUPPORT Principal Investigators, 1995). Just as in other areas of medical decision making, ethically and legally valid refusal of life-sustaining medical treatment assumes and depends on adequate information about viable alternatives being communicated to and comprehended by the patient. This includes acknowledgment of the current state of medical uncertainty (Ackerman, 1996), the existence of a sufficient degree of cognitive and emotional capacity on the patient's part, and surrounding conditions that can and do support voluntariness of choice. Questions might arise in specific instances concerning the sufficiency of any of these essential elements of an authentic decision to hasten death passively by abating life-sustaining medical treatment (Mezey, Mitty, & Ramsey, 1997; Morrison, Meier, & Cassel, 1996; Patterson, Miller-Perrin, McCormick, & Hudson, 1993; Perrin, 1997; Powell & Lowenstein, 1996).

In circumstances involving patients who are mentally incapacitated at the time when important decisions need to be made, there is consensus that individual autonomy should and may be promoted through respect for the process of substituted judgment. Under this approach, the proxy decision maker takes on the "mental mantle" of the patient, attempting to arrive at those choices that the patient would reach if personally capable of making and expressing autonomous decisions at that time. The wishes of the incapacitated patient are discerned through reference to that person's prior explicit statements or through inference from the aggregation of his or her prior life choices and actions.

There are, it must be noted, a few dissenters who break from the general agreement on substituted judgment, arguing that the vital interests of a person change fundamentally once he or she has become decisionally incapacitated, in essence, that one becomes a "different person" at that point (Dresser, 1994). Hence, according to this distinctly minority view, it is impossible to determine accurately what the patient would have wanted if now competent when that individual is in fact now *not* competent.

Even for supporters of the substituted judgment concept, there are many situations in which substituted judgment is impossible to apply honestly due to the fact that there is no accurate way in which a proxy could discern, with any reasonable degree of confidence, what the now incapacitated person would wish to do under the actual circumstances confronting him or her. In such "clueless" circumstances, the ethical consensus is to make and implement medical choices consistent with the traditional approach to proxy decision making, namely, the best interests standard. Predicated on the ethical principle of beneficence (i.e., doing good for or helping another person), the patient's best interests in any specific situation are judged from the perspective of the proxy decision maker who is acting as the patient's fiduciary or trust agent. This judgment may translate into the forgoing of life-sustaining medical treatment for patients in whom the probable burdens of life-sustaining medical treatments are likely to be disproportionately greater than the anticipated benefits (Payne, Taylor, Stocking, & Sachs, 1996; Society of Critical Care Medicine Ethics Committee, 1992).

But determining which course of medical action is in the best interest of a critically ill, cognitively and/or emotionally incapacitated individual is not always a simple task. For example, the use of mechanical restraints to prevent removal of medical devices such as feeding tubes often contributes to, rather than protects against, patient injuries and also fails to reduce the likelihood of extubation (Morrison et al., 1996). However, there might be rare cases in which no less restrictive alternative is available and restraints provide a benefit.

Among professionals and family members, there exists a strong modern consensus that it almost always is in the best interests, and is consistent with the substituted judgment, of critically ill patients to provide relevant forms of physical comfort or palliative care near the end of life (Hesse, 1995; Lynn, 1997; Lynn et al., 1997). This may include withholding or withdrawing artificial feeding and hydration mechanisms using the same clinical and moral criteria (i.e., disproportionality of burdens and benefits) that apply to abatement of other forms of aggressive medical interventions (Morrison et al., 1996; Printz, 1992; Slomka, 1995). Because payment policies powerfully drive clinical practice, it is significant that the *International Classification of Diseases, 9th Revision, Clinical Modification* recently added a code for patients who receive palliative care related to their primary diagnoses (Cassel & Vladeck, 1996).

Despite general agreement on the principle of comfort care, some disagreements persist among physicians over specific methods for best achieving the comfort objective (Gerber & Scott, 1996; Gilligan & Raffin, 1996; Salon, 1996). These disagreements reflect current shortcomings in technical expertise in this area (Brody, Campbell, Faber-Langendoen, & Ogle, 1997), such as medical uncertainty about the relative benefits and burdens of tube feeding for particular patients (Ackerman, 1996; Sheiman, 1996), rather than deep splits in ethical outlooks.

■ ETHICAL DISPUTES

The developing consensus on several key principles described heretofore is promising. Nonetheless, serious splits in ethical outlooks exist regarding a variety of questions surrounding decisions about the care of patients near the end of life.

There is evidence that surrogate decision makers frequently make decisions about the acceptance or rejection of life-sustaining medical treatment for incapacitated patients that are inconsistent with decisions that the patients themselves would make if able, that is, that violate the principle of substituted judgment (McNabney, Beers, & Siebens, 1994). In light of this discordance, there is no clear ethical consensus on the proper extent of surrogate decision makers' unchecked authority (Veatch, 1993) or on the correct response of health care professionals, family, and friends in the face of specific surrogate choices that comply with neither the substituted judgment nor best interests standards.

Physician-assisted death, referring here to various forms of active euthanasia and facilitated suicide in which a physician is affirmatively involved, is one of the most controversial topics in medical ethics today. Dissension on the issue of physician-assisted death is hardly recent ("A Slander on the Medical Profession," 1896). But the discussion has heated up considerably over the past 5 years with publicity surrounding liberalized laws and practices in a few other countries (Collins & Brennan, 1997; Gevers, 1996) and the U.S. Supreme Court's recent consideration of challenges to state criminal statutes prohibiting physician-assisted death. The court unanimously and unequivocally rejected the existence of any constitutional right for a patient to procure a physician's aid to die by upholding current state laws criminalizing physician-assisted death (*Vacco v. Quill,* 1997; *Washington v. Glucksberg,* 1997). Nevertheless, the Supreme Court left the door open for individual states to decriminalize this area, and this has been done in Oregon (Chin, Hedberg, Higginson, & Flemming, 1999). Vigorous public debate about the moral distinction, if any, between letting a person die, on the one hand, and actively killing that person, on the other (Rachels, 1975), no doubt will continue to be staged in the political arenas of state legislatures and elsewhere. In addition, this debate will increasingly include attention to the nurse's central role in making and carrying out decisions about end-of-life patient care (Asch, 1996).

Another sphere in which ethical consensus has been elusive to this point is that pertaining to the health care provider's obligation, if any, to provide futile or nonbeneficial forms of medical treatment just because they are demanded by the patient or surrogate decision maker. Such demands for aggressive medical interventions still occur, even in the face of dismal survival and quality of life prospects (O'Brien et al., 1997). They can create a clash at the bedside between patient autonomy (exercised personally or through a proxy) and the practitioner's professional conscience (Daar, 1993). In addition, although they are not coextensive, the concepts of futility and economic waste overlap considerably; wasteful treatment, in the minds of many (but not all), offends the ethical ideal of distributive or social justice/fairness (Luce, 1994).

Many have adopted the position that determining whether a particular medical intervention will be futile for a specific patient is a medical matter best left to the physician's scientifically informed judgment. Consequently, according to this ethical perspective, the physician may unilaterally withhold or withdraw particular potential interventions (e.g., resuscitation) without the patient or proxy's permission or even over their express objections (Layson & McConnell, 1996; Society of Critical Care Medicine Ethics Committee, 1997). Conversely, others maintain firmly that because medical choices inevitably are matters of personal values, and because medical benefit can encompass subjective good, no intervention is truly futile (i.e., totally nonbeneficial in every respect) if the patient or proxy wants it. Under this view, the physician has a responsibility to provide, and third parties have a duty to pay for, virtually any medical treatment demanded by the patient or surrogate, with unilateral abatement of a potential treatment by the physician condemned as morally reprehensible (Scofield, 1991).

More unsettled issues relating to the ethics of end-of-life medical treatment revolve around the emergency context. Vexing dilemmas often arise as health care professionals and family members try to interpret and apply express or implied patient preferences in situations not anticipated by the patient when time-consuming discourse and deliberation is not a realistic option (Iserson, 1992, 1996).

■ COURT INVOLVEMENT

Court involvement in end-of-life medical decision making is a relatively rare event. Approximately 2 million people die every year in the United States, about 80% of them in health care institutions. For deaths occurring within institutions, more than 70% involve situations in which patients could have been kept alive longer through the use of aggressive medical intervention. In these cases, a decision is made and carried out to withhold or withdraw some form of life-sustaining medical treatment and to permit the patients to die more naturally.

This means that everyday situations arise in hospitals, nursing homes, hospices, and other health facilities nationwide in which choices to abate some aspects of life-sustaining medical treatment for critically ill patients are made and implemented, with the patients' deaths following shortly thereafter. Yet, since the initial judicial involvement in these matters during the mid-1970s (*In re Quinlan,* 1976), only a few hundred circumstances entailing decisions about the beginning, continuation, withholding, or withdrawal of life-sustaining medical treatment have been presented to the courts. Instead, these decisions most often are made and implemented privately and outside of the judicial system. Informal discussion and negotiation occur among the patient (if still capable of taking part), family, significant friends, physicians, other members of the health care team, and (sometimes) risk managers and attorneys advising the health care provider(s) and/or the patient/family.

Although court involvement is the exception, a body of legal precedent has evolved to set societal parameters within which ethical decisions must be made and implemented (National Center for State Courts, 1992). The most important judicial opinion rendered to date is that of the U.S. Supreme Court in *Cruzan v. Director, Missouri Department of Health* (1990).

In *Cruzan,* the Supreme Court set legal parameters for three categories of patients. First, the court held that adult patients who currently are decisionally capable possess a constitutional right, based on the Fourteenth Amendment's guarantee of personal liberty, to make their own medical decisions, even including decisions to refuse life-sustaining medical treatment. Second, the same constitutional right applies to presently incapacitated patients who previously, while capable, had left clear written or oral instructions regarding future medical care or designated a proxy to make future decisions. Put differently, a person does not forfeit the liberty right to direct his or her medical future just because of subsequent decisional incapacity.

Finally, *Cruzan* held that, for incapacitated patients who had not left advance instructions or proxy designations, each state could set its own evidentiary standard for relying on the decisions of surrogates. Most states permit surrogates to order abatement of life-sustaining medical treatment for an incapacitated, critically ill patient if it is more likely than not (i.e., there is a preponderance of the evidence) that forgoing this treatment is the choice that the patient personally would make under similar circumstances if capable. A few states (e.g., Missouri, New York), however, do not recognize a surrogate's authority unless there is clear and convincing evidence that the surrogate is accurately representing the patient's wishes.

The Supreme Court also resolved a couple of other questions in *Cruzan*. At least from a legal point, it now is established that there is no legitimate distinction between withholding life-sustaining medical treatment in the first place and withdrawing it once it is in place. Similarly, the court ruled that artificial feeding and hydration are forms of medical intervention that should be governed by the same criteria as are other life-sustaining medical treatments. Although these positions now are commonly accepted, some continue to draw ethical distinctions, and many correctly point to psychological distinctions, between withholding and withdrawing (Brody, 1995) and between feeding and providing medical treatments.

■ KEEPING CASES OUT OF COURT

Cases involving dispute over life-sustaining medical treatment that have culminated in litigation usually have taken that course because of the following reasons:

1. Strong, irreconcilable disagreement about appropriate treatment persisted among surrogates or between surrogates and providers.
2. Providers had an overblown but sincere apprehension of their own potential legal liability exposure.
3. Communication among the interested parties was inadequate.

Ineffective communication is especially significant in exacerbating potential misunderstandings (and other barriers to optimal decision making and treatment) that can steer an otherwise benign medical situation toward a courtroom (Hofmann et al., 1997; O'Toole et al., 1994; Pfeifer et al., 1994). Readers are referred to the chapter by Kogan, Blanchette, and Masaki in this volume (Chapter 19) for advice on talking to patients and their families about death and dying.

A strategy for reducing the likelihood that a patient care situation becomes a court case is for health care institutions to develop, adopt, and implement both substantive policies and operational procedures for dealing with questions pertaining to the ethical aspects of treatment for critically ill patients. Such written policies and procedures, as well as their communication to potential patients/surrogates, are mandated in the United States by the federal Patient Self-Determination Act of 1990. Hospitals and nursing homes also are mandated to have such policies and procedures by the Joint Commission on Accreditation of Healthcare Organizations (JCAHO, 1998). Other nations without similar legislation or voluntary accreditation standards lag behind in this respect (Choudhry, Ma, Rasooly, & Singer, 1994).

As an adjunct to their policies and procedures, many institutional and organizational providers have created internal bioethics committees, regularly scheduled educational ethics rounds, or formal ethical consultation arrangements to assist with the analysis and resolution of difficult ethical challenges, including those involving decisions about the use of life-sustaining medical treatment. Another strategy is to promote advance health care planning among patients before illness occurs. This allows patients to maintain a semblance of medical autonomy, especially if they subsequently become incapable of making and expressing autonomous choices, while keeping private decision making out of the judicial arena. Every state has legislation recognizing legal mechanisms through which a presently mentally capable individual may document future preferences. Directions regarding the acceptance or limitation of particular treatments may be documented in a living will. The identification of an agent to act as a surrogate decision maker for the patient in the event of future incapacity may be documented in a durable power of attorney for health care decision (DPOA-HC). Health care professionals should play a significant role in encouraging the advance health care planning process to take place in a timely fashion (Markson et al., 1997). More information on advance directives is provided in the chapter by Pietsch and Braun in this volume (Chapter 4).

The majority of states have enacted legislation generally lumped under the rubric of "family consent statutes." This confers legal authorization on specified categories of people (e.g., spouses, adult children, adult siblings) to make life-sustaining medical treatment decisions on behalf of incapacitated, critically ill patients who have not executed advance health care directives. These statutes, in effect, formally ratify the long-standing but unofficial medical tradition of turning to actual or functional "next of kin" for help with decision making when the patient cannot exercise personal autonomy at the time. Family consent statutes permit life-sustaining medical treatment decisions to be made and implemented without resort to the judicial system.

Even in the absence of specific authorizing legislation, in the majority of cases, the traditional practice of "bumbling through" with unofficial but honest and conscientious next of kin has served the patient's best interests well without causing negative legal repercussions to health care providers (Hesse,

1995). As one realistic author has observed, "Ethicists and lawyers advise designating the surrogate with a formal DPOA-HC. Doing so, however, is rarely needed unless the best surrogate is contentious or the care is to be given in a state where only formal designations are likely to be honored" (Lynn, 1997, p. 1637).

On occasion, a court will appoint an individual to act as the fiduciary or trust agent for an incompetent ward. This person usually is called a guardian or a guardian of the person, but terminology varies among various jurisdictions. In some states, the appointed individual might be called a plenary (total) guardian, a conservator, or a conservator of the person. By whatever title the individual is called, that guardian ordinarily has the legal power to make necessary decisions for that ward concerning life-sustaining medical treatment. In most circumstances, the guardian may make these decisions without additional continual resort to the court for each life-sustaining medical treatment decision.

A growing ethical dilemma for which viable legal solutions have yet to emerge is crafting a proper process of medical decision making for incapacitated older adults who lack both timely executed advance directive instruments and suitable, willing proxy decision makers (American Geriatrics Society Ethics Committee, 1996). Existing approaches, such as poorly funded public and volunteer guardianship programs, appear largely inadequate for protecting the well-being of this group of "unbefriended" persons while respecting their autonomy as much as possible. At the same time, routine resort to the courts to gain explicit approval for discrete medical interventions seems grossly cumbersome administratively and counterproductive to patients' best interests.

■ CONCLUSION

"Every life is different from any that has gone before it, and so is every death. The uniqueness of each of us extends even to the way we die" (Nuland, 1994, p. 3). Nevertheless, there are fundamental ethical principles in American culture at the close of the 20th century that guide us as individuals and as families, friends, and professional caregivers. We strive for a personally acceptable accommodation near the end of life with a voracious, technologically driven health care system that can do much but not everything. This chapter outlined these ethical principles and placed them within the U.S. legal context, acknowledging that society is evolving constantly in its efforts to delineate the respective rights and responsibilities of dying individuals and those affecting their care.

■ REFERENCES

Ackerman, T. F. (1996). The moral implications of medical uncertainty: Tube feeding demented patients. *Journal of the American Geriatrics Society, 44,* 1265-1267.

American Geriatrics Society Ethics Committee. (1996). Making treatment decisions for incapacitated older adults without advance directives. *Journal of the American Geriatrics Society, 44,* 986-987.

Asai, A., Fukuhara, S., & Lo, B. (1995). Attitudes of Japanese and Japanese-American physicians towards life-sustaining treatment. *Lancet, 346,* 356-359.

Asch, D. A. (1996). The role of critical care nurses in euthanasia and assisted suicide. *New England Journal of Medicine, 334,* 1374-1379.

Bajwa, K., Szabo, E., & Kjellstrand, C. M. (1996). A prospective study of risk factors and decision making in discontinuation of dialysis. *Archives of Internal Medicine, 156,* 2571-2577.

Brigham, J. C., & Pfeifer, J. E. (1996). Euthanasia: An introduction. *Journal of Social Issues, 52,* 1-11.

Brink, S. (1995, December 4). The American way of dying. *U.S. News and World Report,* pp. 70-75.

Brody, H. (1995). Withdrawing versus withholding therapy: Still a pernicious distinction. *Journal of the American Geriatrics Society, 43,* 716-717.

Brody, H., Campbell, M. L., Faber-Langendoen, K., & Ogle, K. S. (1997). Withdrawing intensive life-sustaining treatment: Recommendations for compassionate clinical management. *New England Journal of Medicine, 336,* 652-657.

Cassel, C. K., & Vladeck, B. C. (1996). ICD-9 code for palliative or terminal care. *New England Journal of Medicine, 335,* 1232-1234.

Chin, A. E., Hedberg, K., Higginson, G. K., & Flemming, D. W. (1999). Legalized physician-assisted suicide in Oregon: The first year's experience. *New England Journal of Medicine, 340,* 577-583.

Choudhry, N. K., Ma, J., Rasooly, I., & Singer, P. A. (1994). Long-term care facility policies on life-sustaining treatments and advance directives in Canada. *Journal of the American Geriatrics Society, 42,* 1150-1153.

Collins, J. J., & Brennan, F. T. (1997). Euthanasia and the potential adverse effects for Northern Territory aborigines. *Lancet, 349,* 1907-1908.

Daar, J. F. (1993). A clash at the bedside: Patient autonomy vs. a physician's professional conscience. *Hastings Law Journal, 44,* 1241-1289.

Dresser, R. (1994). Missing persons: Legal perceptions of incompetent patients. *Rutgers Law Review, 46,* 609-719.

Faber-Langendoen, K. (1996). A multi-institutional study of care given to patients dying in hospitals. *Archives of Internal Medicine, 156,* 2130-2136.

Fried, T. R., & Gillick, M. R. (1994). Medical decision-making in the last six months of life: Choices about limitation of care. *Journal of the American Geriatrics Society, 42,* 303-307.

Gerber, D. R., & Scott, E. (1996). Withdrawal of life support [letter to the editor]. *Critical Care Medicine, 24,* 1607.

Gevers, S. (1996). Euthanasia: Law and practice in the Netherlands. *British Medical Bulletin, 52,* 326-333.

Gilligan, T., & Raffin, T. A. (1996). Withdrawing life support: Extubation and prolonged terminal means are inappropriate. *Critical Care Medicine, 24,* 352-353.

Gordon, M., & Singer, P. A. (1995). Decisions and care at the end of life. *Lancet, 346,* 163-166.

Hesse, K. A. (1995). Terminal care of the very old: Changes in the way we die. *Archives of Internal Medicine, 155,* 1513-1518.

Hofmann, J. C., Wenger, N. S., Davis, R. B., Teno, J., Connors, A. F., Jr., Desbiens, N., Lynn, J., & Phillips, R. S. (1997). Patient preferences for communication with physicians about end-of-life decisions. *Annals of Internal Medicine, 127,* 1-12.

Institute of Medicine. (1997). *Approaching death: Improving care at the end of life.* Washington, DC: National Academy Press.

Iserson, K. V. (1992). The "no code" tattoo: An ethical dilemma. *Western Journal of Medicine, 156,* 309-312.

Iserson, K. V. (1996). Withholding and withdrawing medical treatment: An emergency medicine perspective. *Annals of Internal Medicine, 28,* 51-54.

Joint Commission on Accreditation of Healthcare Organizations. (1998). *Comprehensive accreditation manual for hospitals.* Chicago: Author.

Kapp, M. B. (1998). *Our hands are tied: Legal tensions and medical ethics.* Westport, CT: Auburn House.

Layson, R. T., & McConnell, T. (1996). Must consent always be obtained for a do-not-resuscitate order? *Archives of Internal Medicine, 156,* 2617-2620.

Luce, J. M. (1994). The changing physician-patient relationship in critical care medicine under health care reform. *American Journal of Respiratory and Critical Care Medicine, 150,* 266-270.

Lynn, J. (1997). An 88-year-old woman facing the end of life. *Journal of the American Medical Association, 277,* 1633-1640.

Lynn, J., Teno, J. M., Phillips, R. S., Wu, A. U., Desbiens, N., Harrold, J., Claessens, M. T., Wenger, N., Kreling, B., & Connors, A. F., Jr. (1997). Perceptions by family members of the dying experience of older and seriously ill patients. *Annals of Internal Medicine, 126,* 97-106.

Markson, L., Clark, J., Glantz, L., Lamberton, V., Kern, D., & Stollerman, G. (1997). The doctor's role in discussing advance preferences for end-of-life care: Perceptions of physicians practicing in the VA. *Journal of the American Geriatrics Society, 45,* 399-406.

McNabney, M. K., Beers, M. H., & Siebens, H. (1994). Surrogate decision-makers' satisfaction with the placement of feeding tubes in elderly patients. *Journal of the American Geriatrics Society, 42,* 161-168.

Measuring quality of care at the end of life: A statement of principles. (1997). *Journal of the American Geriatrics Society, 45,* 526-527.

Mezey, M., Mitty, E., & Ramsey, G. (1997). Assessment of decision-making capacity: Nursing's role. *Journal of Gerontological Nursing, 23,* 28-35.

Moreno, J. D. (1995). *Deciding together: Bioethics and moral consensus.* New York: Oxford University Press.

Morrison, R. S., Meier, D. E., & Cassel, C. K. (1996). When too much is too little. *New England Journal of Medicine, 335,* 1755-1759.

National Center for State Courts. (1992). *Guidelines for state court decision making in life-sustaining medical treatment cases.* Williamsburg, VA: Author.

Nuland, S. B. (1994). *How we die.* New York: Knopf.

O'Brien, L. A., Siegert, E. A., Grisso, J. A., Maislin, G. M., La Pann, K., Evans, L. K., & Krotki, K. P. (1997). Tube feeding preferences among nursing home residents. *Journal of General Internal Medicine, 12,* 364-371.

O'Toole, E. E., Youngner, S. J., Juknialis, B. W., Daly, B., Bartlett, E. T., & Landerfeld, C. S. (1994). Evaluation of a treatment limitation policy with a specific treatment-limiting order page. *Archives of Internal Medicine, 154,* 425-432.

Patterson, D. R., Miller-Perrin, C., McCormick, T. R., & Hudson, L. D. (1993). When life support is questioned early in the care of patients with cervical-level quadriplegia. *New England Journal of Medicine, 328,* 506-509.

Payne, K., Taylor, R. M., Stocking, C., & Sachs, G. A. (1996). Physicians' attitudes about the care of patients in the persistent vegetative state: A national survey. *Annals of Internal Medicine, 125,* 104-110.

Pearlman, R. A., Cain, K. C., Patrick, D. L., Appelbaum-Maizel, M., Starks, H. E., Jecker, N. S., & Uhlmann, R. F. (1993). Insights pertaining to patient assessments of states worse than death. *Journal of Clinical Ethics, 4*(1), 33-41.

Perkins, H. S., Bauer, R. L., Hazuda, H. P., & Schoolfield, J. D. (1990). Impact of legal liability, family wishes, and other "external factors" on physicians' life-support decisions. *American Journal of Medicine, 89,* 185-194.

Perrin, K. O. (1997). Giving voice to the wishes of elders for end-of-life care. *Journal of Gerontological Nursing, 23,* 18-27.

Pfeifer, M. P., Sidorov, J. E., Smith, A. C., Boero, J. F., Evans, A. T., & Settle, M. B. (1994). The discussion of end-of-life medical care by primary care patients and physicians. *Journal of General Internal Medicine, 9,* 82-88.

Powell, T., & Lowenstein, B. (1996). Refusing life-sustaining treatment after catastrophic injury: Ethical implications. *Journal of Law, Medicine, & Ethics, 24,* 54-61.

Printz, L. A. (1992). Terminal hydration: A compassionate treatment. *Archives of Internal Medicine, 152,* 697-700.

Rachels, J. (1975). Active and passive euthanasia. *New England Journal of Medicine, 292,* 78-80.

Salon, J. E. (1996). Withdrawal of life support [letter to the editor]. *Critical Care Medicine, 24,* 1607.

Scofield, G. (1991, November/December). Is consent useful when resuscitation isn't? *Hastings Center Report, 21,* 28-36.

Sheiman, S. L. (1996). Tube feeding the demented nursing home resident. *Journal of the American Geriatrics Society, 44,* 1268-1270.

A slander on the medical profession. (1896). *Journal of the American Medical Association, 27,* 820-821.

Slomka, J. (1995). What do apple pie and motherhood have to do with feeding tubes and caring for the patient? *Archives of Internal Medicine, 155,* 1258-1263.

Society of Critical Care Medicine Ethics Committee. (1992). Attitudes of critical care medicine professionals concerning forgoing life-sustaining treatments. *Critical Care Medicine, 20,* 320-326.

Society of Critical Care Medicine Ethics Committee. (1997). Consensus statement of the Society of Critical Care Medicine's Ethics Committee regarding futile and other possibly inadvisable treatments. *Critical Care Medicine, 25,* 887-891.

SUPPORT Principal Investigators. (1995). A controlled trial to improve care for seriously ill hospitalized patients: The Study to Understand Prognoses and Preferences for Outcomes and Risks of Treatments. *Journal of the American Medical Association, 274,* 1591-1598.

Veatch, R. (1993). Forgoing life-sustaining treatment: Limits to the consensus. *Kennedy Institute of Ethics Journal, 3,* 1-19.

Cases and Legislation Cited
Cruzan v. Director, Missouri Department of Health, 110 S.Ct. 2841 (1990).
In re Quinlan, 355 A.2d 647 (N.J.) (1976).

Patient Self-Determination Act, Omnibus Budget Reconciliation Act of 1990, Public Law No. 101-508 §§ 4206, 4751, codified at 42 U.S.C. §§ 1395cc(a)(1)(Q), 1395cc(f), 1395mm(c)(8) and 42 U.S.C. §§ 1396a(a)(57), 1396a(a)(58), 1396a(w) (1991).
Vacco v. Quill, 521 U.S. 793 (1997).
Washington v. Glucksberg, 521 U.S. 702 (1997).

Part 2

Ethnic Perspectives on End-of-Life Decision Making

This section of the book provides information about the four largest ethnic minority populations in the United States: African Americans, Hispanic Americans, Asian and Pacific Islander Americans, and American Indians and Alaska Natives. For each population, the following questions are addressed:

- How large is this minority group, and what are the major subgroups within this population?
- What has been the group's experience with immigration or colonization?
- Which cultural and religious traditions are important to the group's view of death and the dying process?
- What is known about the group's traditional decision-making practices?
- How do these experiences and traditions affect current-day preferences regarding end-of-life care?

■ What can health care and social service providers do to reduce potential conflict between their institutions and the minority clients they serve?

The four chapters in this section are presented by scholars who represent and/or work closely with the ethnic groups about which they write. They provide information about their populations, but they also warn against the tendency to stereotype people by ethnic membership. Rather, readers are reminded that individual behaviors are affected by education, personal experience, years in the United States, current religion, and other factors in addition to ethnic and religious traditions. Nonetheless, knowledge of each group's history, traditions, and within-group diversity will assist professionals in their efforts to become more sensitive to individual differences and more appropriate in their interactions with clients.

Chapter 6

Cultural and Religious Issues for African Americans

CHARLES P. MOUTON

*D*eath is the poignant end of life for all human beings. As a group, African Americans face this reality on a daily basis. Through the legacy of slavery, segregation, and discrimination, African Americans have developed a perspective on death that is unique to this racial/ethnic group. Views about the end of life are further influenced by the current reality of black-on-black homicide, epidemics of violence in urban areas where many African Americans live, high rates of death from chronic disease, and limited access to health care for segments of this population.

Because the current African American population is a heterogeneous group, one cannot make a definitive characterization of death for every member in this population. Some African Americans are the descendants of slaves and have been part of the United States even before its independence. Some have immigrated from other places in the Western Hemisphere, such as the Caribbean basin, bringing a history of freedom or at least greater success in throwing off the constraints of oppression. Other subpopulations recently have migrated from the African continent and have no history of slavery behind them. Besides the reflection of the African diaspora, the U.S. African American population has variations reflecting geographic locale. With backgrounds from north and south of the Mason-Dixon line and both sides of the Mississippi River, the large intragroup diversity in the African American population does not allow any one study or finding to fit all. Those who work with African Americans always should remember to discuss and make decisions on an *individual* basis, not on group membership.

Caveat aside, this chapter discusses several issues related to end-of-life decision making by African Americans. First, it presents the historical experiences of the majority of African Americans that have shaped cultural attitudes related to death and dying. Then, information on the preferences of African Americans regarding life-extending medical procedures, withdrawal of therapy, and advance directives is presented. Finally, attitudes toward euthanasia and postmortem issues are discussed.

■ HISTORICAL BACKGROUND

Africans have been part of the U.S. landscape since the arrival of Columbus in 1492. They first arrived as indentured servants or as part of ships' crews on voyages with European explorers. In 1619, the first sets of African slaves were transported to U.S. shores (Bennett, 1987; Mintz, 1993). The cross-Atlantic journey for African slaves was a horrible experience. Many slaves died in the process of transport, 10% en route from the interior of the African continent to the African coast and 25% while crossing the Atlantic Ocean. Here is one slave's description of his time aboard a ship during his cross-Atlantic passage: "With the loathsomeness of the stench and the crying together, I became so sick and low that I was unable to eat, nor had I the least desire to taste anything. I now wished for my last friend, Death, to relieve me" (quoted in Mellon, 1988, p. 446).

The slave trade brought Africans to American shores in a subhuman state. Most slaves then endured subhuman conditions during their lifelong servitude. Not surprisingly, death was a common occurrence in the lives of slaves. Half of all slave infants died during their 1st year of life, twice the death rate of Caucasian infants (Mintz, 1993). Life expectancy for slaves was 21 to 22 years, compared to 40 to 43 years for Caucasians. Furthermore, the judicial declaration that slaves were chattel or property allowed their owners to do anything to the slaves. Slave owners resorted to life-threatening practices of torture and mutilation to maintain slaves' productivity. Then, once slaves had outlived their usefulness, they often were killed to reduce the cost of feeding and housing them. In the words of a former slave, "Slavery was the worst days that was ever see'd [sic] in the world" (quoted in Mellon, 1988, p. 18). Because of the hardship that was endured in the daily struggle to survive, death became the ultimate escape from the master.

Life in the post-Reconstruction period was equally harsh. Following slavery, after the Emancipation Proclamation and the Civil War, African Americans were free from the constraints of the legal system of slavery. However, the post-Reconstruction period found many African Americans confronted by a new system of labor control. "African American codes" forced many African Americans to work on plantations in work gangs. Many became trapped in a new system of exploitation called sharecropping. This system was similar to the old form of indentured servitude that was in place before slavery. Although not enforced by whip or hanging post, life during the post-Reconstruction period for African Americans often was as harsh as slavery itself. These former slaves never received the original promise of emancipation or freedom on American soil.

Several programs had been proposed to aid the freed slaves. Educational opportunities, housing opportunities, and land distribution plans were presented in various legislatures. However, some of the more meaningful programs, such as the proposal to give each slave a mule and 40 acres of land to farm, never were executed. Early federal programs that were enacted to assist these newly "freedmen" dried up within two decades after the Civil War (Bennett, 1987). Failure to provide what many newly freed slaves felt was rightfully theirs contributed to a cynicism about institutions and bureaucracy-laden programs. Also, the use of police authority to enforce continued segregation placed the interests of African Americans and local governments at opposite poles.

The shared history of slavery, oppression, and discrimination shaped the African American characterization of death in several ways. Culturally based funeral rituals, such as the New Orleans second line to the postfuneral meal with the family of the deceased in Louisiana, have their roots in the slave experience. In a traditional New Orleans funeral, a procession follows the coffin to the burial site. The first line is made up of the immediate family members who mourn the passing of a loved one. The second line is made up of friends and more distant relatives of the deceased. After the deceased is buried, the second line begins a joyous dancing celebration. The postfuneral meal has its roots in the small break from work that the slave masters gave family members of a deceased slave to mourn after the burial.

Although slavery and segregation have long been abolished and equal opportunity programs have been established, inequities between African Americans and Caucasians in the United States still continue. These differences are reflected in life expectancy and mortality statistics. According to a 1996 report from the Centers for Disease Control and Prevention, the 1993 age-adjusted death rates for the African American population were higher than those for the Caucasian population for all causes of death combined and for 8 of the 10 leading causes of death (Gardner & Hudson, 1996). The report also stated that estimated life expectancy for African American females born in 1993 was 5.8 years less than that for Caucasian females, with differences due to higher death rates among African American females for heart disease, cancer, HIV/AIDS, perinatal conditions, and stroke. Life expectancy for African American males was 8.5 years less than that for Caucasian males; this difference is attributed to higher death rates for homicide, heart disease, cancer, HIV/AIDS, and perinatal conditions for African American males (Gardner & Hudson, 1996).

■ RELIGIOUS BELIEFS ABOUT END OF LIFE

End-of-life decision-making practices also draw on religious characterizations of death. The majority of African Americans adhere to a Christian belief system, with 83% claiming a Protestant affiliation (the majority being Baptist) and 14% claiming a Catholic affiliation (Ellison & Sherkat, 1990). These religious beliefs recognize a transcendent soul that rises to heaven on death. African Americans also have a strong belief in a heaven not of this earth. Furthermore, most African Americans subscribe to an African American theology, a religious doctrine that views God as the fighting God of the Old Testament (Lincoln, 1974; Lincoln & Mamiya, 1991). African American theology embraces both notions of humans' responsibility to work with God and humans' faith that God can handle problems exclusively (Lincoln, 1974, 1984). It also adds features of a Calvinist belief in predetermination and the sovereignty of God.

The historical framework for this core religious belief is a direct relationship between the experience of slavery and the notion of "a divine rescue" (Lincoln & Mamiya, 1991). The hopelessness that slavery, poverty, and social isolation created for African Americans required a power greater than humans to relieve these conditions of suffering. Thus, African Americans have developed a belief in God's power to conquer all and a resilient hope that a miracle will happen.

It is important to note that not all African Americans view death from a religious construct. However, religion does seem to play a greater role for African Americans than for Caucasian Americans. A classic Los Angeles-based study showed that 40% of African Americans felt that religion influenced how they felt about death, compared to only 25% of Caucasians who felt that way (Kalish & Reynolds, 1976). Also, prayer was noted to be the way in which many African Americans coped with stress associated with the dying process (Chatters & Taylor, 1989). Others suggest a more secular view that African Americans demonstrate "magical thinking" when faced with seemingly hopeless situations. They feel that something good will happen, if given a chance, that may or may not be related to notions of divine intervention (Marian Secundy, personal communication, January 1996; Mouton, Johnson, & Cole, 1995).

This belief in God's power, in conjunction with a belief in God's willingness to have the people free, is a major aspect of African American Christianity. These notions might be manifest in patients' attitudes toward continuing medical treatment, suggesting that an aggressive treatment approach needs to be followed as a test of faith and to allow "God's will" to be done (Mouton et al., 1995). Also, patients might feel that enough time needs to elapse for God to "work the miracle."

■ PREFERENCES FOR END-OF-LIFE CARE

An understanding of how history, religion, and personal experience can influence an African American individual's attitude toward the end of life is essential for health care providers who want to render adequate care for older patients. These experiences certainly are reflected in research findings suggesting that African Americans appear less likely than other groups to trust health care providers, communicate treatment preferences, complete advance directives, favor euthanasia, and participate in organ donation. These research findings are reviewed here.

Trust Issues

An unfortunate consequence of the history of racism in this country is African American distrust of the systems established by the dominant Caucasian culture. In addition, some African Americans resent and distrust any person in a position of power over their lives (Levy, 1985). This distrust is not unfounded, as several studies have documented the lack of access of African Americans, women, and other minorities to available health care. These studies specifically suggest that cardiac procedures, bypass operations, and organ transplants all have been performed less frequently on African Americans than on Caucasian Americans (Council on Ethical and Judicial Affairs, 1990; Gonwa et al., 1991; Kjellstand & Logan, 1987; Tielsch et al., 1991; Wennecker & Epstein, 1989). Some authors have suggested that these differences are the result of discriminatory practices and feel that African Americans simply cannot trust Caucasians, their system of truth, or their social institutions (Lincoln, 1974, 1984; Lincoln & Mamiya, 1991). An article by Gamble (1993) pointed to numerous examples of how medicine proceeded with gruesome and unethical experiments on African Americans, justifying these actions by claiming that African Americans were inferior to Caucasians. The 40-year Tuskegee Syphilis Study, in which the U.S. Public Health Service lied to and denied standard treatment to 400 poor African American sharecroppers, is the best-known example of racist practices in biomedical research. Specific to advanced directives, an article by Young and Jex (1992), concerning the implementation of the Patient Self-Determination Act of 1991, pointed out that African Americans often have equated life support with life and that any effort at withholding life-sustaining therapies might be seen as another attempt of genocide by the predominantly Caucasian institution. The combination of these attitudes can lead to a negative view of advance care planning and inhibit African American patients from communicating desires in end-of-life decisions. African Americans also might be concerned about the possibility of neglect and being allowed to die prematurely if they choose or express a palliative treatment preference.

Communication

The normative model of health provider-patient interaction is one of increasing patient autonomy and decreasing provider paternalism. Effective patient autonomy necessitates high levels of patient-doctor communication. However, for some African Americans, this shift away from paternalism has not taken place because African Americans tend to be reluctant to communicate treatment preferences to their health care providers. In a study on communication of treatment preferences among 1,031 AIDS patients, Caucasian patients were twice as likely as African American patients to have discussed their treatment preferences with their physicians, even after adjusting for age, function, education, income, and other covariates. It also was found that African Americans were half as likely as Caucasians to prefer a treatment approach that focused on relieving pain as opposed to extending life (Mouton, Teno, Mor, & Piette, 1997). Another study by Haas et al. (1993) found similar results, where non-Caucasians were half as likely as Caucasians to discuss their preferences for resuscitation with their physicians.

In some instances, the lack of communicating a treatment preference returns the decision-making power to the health care provider; this has been labeled "paternalism by permission" (Cross & Churchill, 1982). In doing this, African American patients passively resist efforts to limit care while inadvertently allowing whatever course the physician chooses. With the great push to have patients make autonomous decisions, paternalism by permission might make physicians uncomfortable and pose difficulty in the patient-provider relationship. But pressuring a patient to express a treatment preference, in the face of an obvious desire not to do so, also might cause damage to the doctor-patient relationship and subsequent communication.

Treatment Preferences

Several studies have found ethnic differences in preferences for life-sustaining care. In a study of 150 dialysis patients, Sehgal et al. (1992) asked whether the patients would want dialysis continued if they developed advanced Alzheimer's disease, and 67% of African Americans said yes, compared to only 34% of Caucasians. Similarly, African American patients with cancer were more likely than Caucasians (67% vs. 41%) to report wanting life-sustaining treatment if they were dying (McKinley, Garrett, Evans, & Danis, 1996). In another study, 2,536 older adults were asked whether they would want lifesaving treatments if they had a terminal illness, and 35% of African Americans expressed a desire for more treatment, compared to only 15% of Caucasians (Garrett, Harris, Norburn, Patrick, & Davis, 1993). Eleazer et al. (1996) found that the African American elders in a case management program were more likely to select full code than were elders of other ethnicities (19% of African Americans vs. 4% of Hispanics, 10% of Asians, and 10% of Caucasians). Finally, Caralis, Davis, Wright, and Marcial (1993) found that African Americans were more likely than the general population to choose life-sustaining treatment, even in the face of futility or low expected quality of life.

Advance Care Planning

Some controversy exists as to whether African Americans are less likely than other ethnic groups to complete written documents to explicitly state end-of-life treatment preferences. A retrospective chart review of 1,193 frail older persons in South Carolina found that African Americans were significantly less likely than Caucasians and Hispanics to have completed advance directives (Eleazer et al., 1996). In a study of an educational intervention to increase advance directive completion, African Americans were significantly less likely than Caucasians (12% vs. 26%) and Asians to complete durable powers of attorney for health care (DPOA-HCs) (Rubin, Strull, Fialkow, Weiss, & Lo, 1994). Even when an advance directive such as a living will or a DPOA-HC was previously executed, another study found that African Americans were less likely than Caucasians (14% vs. 36%) to have advance directives documented on subsequent hospital admissions (Morrison, Olsen, Mertz, & Meier, 1995). Other studies, however, have found no racial difference in rates of completing advance directives (Caralis et al., 1993; Chambers, Diamond, Perkel, & Lasch, 1994). This suggests that African American attitudes toward advance directives might be influenced by African Americans' personal experience or other within-group differences rather than by their shared history.

When one examines the question of advance directive use, access issues emerge as a potential confounding variable. Previous research has shown that African Americans face inequities in terms of access to care for several medical therapies (Council on Ethical and Judicial Affairs, 1990; Gonwa et al., 1991; Kjellstand & Logan, 1987; Tielsch et al., 1991; Wennecker & Epstein, 1989). If an advance directive to withhold life-sustaining therapies is perceived by African Americans as another way of limiting their access to a possible beneficial therapy, then they might be more inclined *not* to complete one. Other articles cite problems with African American patients viewing their physicians as authority figures whose decisions might not be understood but definitely are not to be challenged overtly (Levy, 1985; Satcher, 1973). In this passive-aggressive pattern of interaction, *not* choosing to withdraw or withhold therapy may be viewed as forcing physicians to do their job to provide all possible medical care without demanding it directly.

A corollary to the low use of advance care planning is the low use of hospice services by African Americans compared to that by Caucasians (Gordon, 1995). This disparity is partially explained by lack of access to health services and lack of education about hospice care among African Americans. However, distrust of health care institutions also plays an important role. A trusting relationship must be present because hospice stresses the acceptance of a patient's eminent death and has palliative therapy as the goal of care.

Euthanasia and Physician-Assisted Suicide

As a whole, African Americans are less likely than Caucasians to approve of euthanasia. For example, in a study comparing attitudes toward life-prolonging treatment among 139 patients from a general medicine clinic, only 63% of African Americans approved of stopping life-prolonging treatments, compared to 89% of Caucasians. In addition, 35% of Caucasians approved of physician-assisted suicide, compared to only 16% of African Americans (Caralis et al., 1993).

This finding is corroborated by public opinion polls conducted over the past several decades. Specifically, Singh (1979) found that 40% of African Americans (vs. 65% of Caucasians) felt that a physician should be allowed to help a terminally ill patient die if the patient so requested. In the same survey, only 21% of African Americans (vs. 42% of Caucasians) felt that a person with an incurable illness had a right to end his or her own life. Similar African American-Caucasian differences were found by Ostheimer and Moore (1981); Rao, Staten, and Rao (1988); and Wood (1990). Most recently, a survey of 500 Detroit residents on whether physician-assisted suicide should be legal found support among 76% of the Caucasian respondents but only 56% of the African American respondents (Lichtenstein, Alcser, Corning, Bachman, & Doukas, 1997).

From the health provider standpoint, studies of attitudes toward assisted suicide, euthanasia, and end-of-life decisions do not control for physician race as a variable. In addition, many of these studies were done before the media attention generated by the assisted suicide activities of Dr. Jack Kevorkian. Thus, as the general public's attitude grows in favor of euthanasia and as the number of African American physicians increases, it is unclear whether and how the attitudes of individual African Americans will change.

Organ Donation and Autopsy

African American attitudes to postmortem issues also are drawn from their shared historical, religious, and social experiences. On the whole, African Americans are less likely than Caucasian Americans to agree to organ donation. Most have a strong belief in the resurrection of the body, and this belief inhibits their willingness to donate organs because they will need their bodies to be intact on Judgment Day. Some believe that sick African Americans are allowed to die sooner so that their organs can be removed and used for research; unfortunately, this belief is grounded in historical truth (Savitt, 1982). Through organ donation advocacy groups, religious leaders, and the media, efforts have been made to encourage organ donation by the African American community. It remains to be seen how well this effort will overcome strongly held beliefs against organ donation.

African Americans also are less likely than Caucasians to agree to an autopsy. Whereas overall autopsy rates in the United States generally are low (7.9%), rates for African Americans are even lower (4.0%) (Harrell, Callaway, & Powers, 1993; Shope & Holmes, 1993). Issues similar to organ donation come into play concerning autopsies, for example, concerns about bodily integrity and abuse. The historical abuses of the dead have undermined the trust of African Americans in this procedure.

■ CONCLUSION

The effects of history and religious views, combined with individual life experiences and beliefs, influence African Americans' attitudes about the end of life. Clinicians need to bring to the table a degree of cultural sensitivity to allay some of the mistrust and fear that some African Americans might have when making end-of-life decisions. Failure to explore the underlying perceptions of a patient's illness, hopes and expectations, and concerns about dying without any attempt at life-prolonging treatment does not fulfill the patient autonomy mandate. To get past these barriers, the medical community must develop trustworthy and competent personnel adequately trained in cultural aspects of medical decision making and appropriate communication techniques. Addressing these issues might alleviate some of the apprehension that African Americans feel concerning end-of-life care.

■ REFERENCES

Bennett, L. (1987). *Before the Mayflower: A history of African American America.* New York: Viking Penguin.

Caralis, P. V., Davis, B., Wright, K., & Marcial, E. (1993). The influence of ethnicity and race on attitudes toward advance directives, life-prolonging treatments, and euthanasia. *Journal of Clinical Ethics, 4*(2), 155-165.

Chambers, C. V., Diamond, J. J., Perkel, R. L., & Lasch, L. A. (1994). Relationship of advance directives to hospital charges in a Medicare population. *Archives of Internal Medicine, 154,* 541-547.

Chatters, L. M., & Taylor, R. J. (1989). Age differences in religious participation among African American adults. *Journal of Gerontology: Social Sciences, 44,* S183-S189.

Council on Ethical and Judicial Affairs. (1990). African American-Caucasian disparities in health care. *Journal of the American Medical Association, 263,* 2344-2346.

Cross, A. W., & Churchill, L. R. (1982). Ethical and cultural dimensions of informed consent: A case study and analysis. *Annals of Internal Medicine, 96,* 110-113.

Eleazer, G. P., Hornung, C. A., Egbert, C. B., Egbert, J. R., Eng, C., Hedgepeth, J., McCann, R., Strothers, H., Sapir, M., Wei, M., & Wilson, M. (1996). The relationship between ethnicity and advance directives in a frail older population. *Journal of the American Geriatrics Society, 44,* 938-943.

Ellison, C. G., & Sherkat, S. E. (1990). Patterns of religious mobility among African Americans. *Sociological Quarterly, 4,* 551-566.

Gamble, V. N. (1993). A legacy of distrust: African Americans and medical research. *American Journal of Preventive Medicine, 9*(Suppl. 6), 35-38.

Gardner, P., & Hudson, B. L. (1996). Advance report of final mortality statistics, 1993. *Monthly Vital Statistics Report, 44*(7, Suppl.). (National Center for Health Statistics, Hyattsville, MD)

Garrett, J. M., Harris, R. P., Norburn, J. K., Patrick, D. L., & Danis, M. (1993). Life-sustaining treatments during terminal illness: Who wants what? *Journal of General Internal Medicine, 8,* 361-368.

Gonwa, T. A., Morris, C. A., Mai, M. L., Husberg, B. S., Goldstein, R. M., & Klintmalm, G. B. (1991). Race and liver transplantation. *Archives of Surgery, 126,* 1141-1143.

Gordon, A. K. (1995). Deterrents to access and service for African Americans and Hispanics: The Medicare hospice benefit, healthcare utilization, and cultural barriers. In D. L. Infeld, A. K. Gordon, & B. C. Harper (Eds.), *Hospice care and cultural diversity* (pp. 65-83). Binghampton, NY: Haworth.

Haas, J. S., Weissman, J. S., Cleary, P. D., Goldberg, J., Gatsonis, C., Seage, G. R., III, Fowler, F. J., Jr., Massagli, M. P., Makadon, H. J., & Epstein, A. M. (1993). Discussion of preferences for life-sustaining care by persons with AIDS: Predictors of failure in patient-physician communication. *Archives of Internal Medicine, 153,* 1241-1248.

Harrell, L. E., Callaway, R., & Powers, R. (1993). Autopsy in dementia illness: Who participates? *Alzheimer's Disease and Associated Disorders, 7,* 80-87.

Kalish, R. A., & Reynolds, D. K. (1976). *Death and ethnicity: A psychocultural study.* Los Angeles: University of Southern California Press.

Kjellstand, C. M., & Logan, G. M. (1987). Racial, sexual and age inequalities in chronic dialysis. *Nephron, 45,* 257-263.

Levy, D. R. (1985). Caucasian doctors and African American patients: Influence of race on the doctor-patient relationship. *Pediatrics, 75,* 639-643.

Lichtenstein, R. L., Alcser, K. H., Corning, A. D., Bachman, J. G., & Doukas, D. J. (1997). African American-Caucasian differences in attitudes toward physician-assisted suicide. *Journal of the National Medical Association, 89,* 125-133.

Lincoln, C. E. (1974). *The African American church since Frazier.* New York: Schoken Books.

Lincoln, C. E. (1984). *Race, religion, and the continuing American dilemma.* New York: Hill & Wang.

Lincoln, C. E., & Mamiya, L. H. (1991). *The African American church in the African American experience.* Durham, NC: Duke University Press.

McKinley, E. D., Garrett, J. M., Evans, A. T., & Danis, M. (1996). Differences in end-of-life decision making among African American and Caucasian ambulatory cancer patients. *Journal of General Internal Medicine, 11,* 651-656.

Mellon, J. (1988). *Bullwhip days: The slaves remember—An oral history.* New York: Avon Books.

Mintz, S. (1993). *African American voices: The life cycle of slavery.* St. James, NY: Brandywine Press.

Morrison, R. S., Olsen, E., Mertz, K. R., & Meier, D. E. (1995). The inaccessibility of advance directives on transfer from ambulatory to acute care settings. *Journal of the American Medical Association, 274,* 478-482.

Mouton, C. P., Johnson, M. S., & Cole, D. R. (1995). Ethical considerations in African American elders. *Clinics of Geriatric Medicine, 11*(1), 113-129.

Mouton, C. P., Teno, J., Mor, V., & Piette, J. (1997). Communication of preferences for care among human immunodeficiency virus-infected patients: Barriers to informed decisions? *Archives of Family Medicine, 6,* 342-347.

Ostheimer, J. M., & Moore, C. L., Jr. (1981). The correlates of attitudes toward euthanasia revisited. *Social Biology, 28*(1-2), 145-149.

Rao, P. V. V., Staten, F., & Rao, V. N. (1988). Racial differences in attitudes toward euthanasia. *Euthanasia Review, 2,* 260-277.

Rubin, S. M., Strull, W. M., Fialkow, M. F., Weiss, S. J., & Lo, B. (1994). Increasing the completion of the durable power of attorney for health care: A randomized controlled trial. *Journal of the American Medical Association, 271,* 209-212.

Satcher, D. (1973). Does race interfere with the doctor-patient relationship? *Journal of the American Medical Association, 223,* 1498-1499.

Savitt, T. (1982). The use of African Americans for medical experimentation and demonstration in the Old South. *Journal of Southern History, 89,* 331-348.

Sehgal, A., Galbraith, A., Chesney, M., Shoenfeld, P., Charles, G., & Lo, B. (1992). How strictly do dialysis patients want their advance directives followed? *Journal of the American Medical Association, 267,* 59-63.

Shope, J. T., & Holmes, S. B. (1993). Pathologists' participation in postmortem examination for patients with dementia. *The Gerontologist, 33,* 461-467.

Singh, B. K. (1979). Correlates of attitudes toward euthanasia. *Social Biology, 26,* 247-254.

Tielsch, J. M., Sommer, A., Katz, J., Royall, R. M., Quigley, H. A., & Javitt, J. (1991). Racial variation in the prevalence of primary open-angle glaucoma. *Journal of the American Medical Association, 266,* 369-374.

Wennecker, M. B., & Epstein, A. M. (1989). Racial inequalities in the use of procedures for patients with ischemic heart disease in Massachusetts. *Journal of the American Medical Association, 261,* 253-257.

Wood, F. (1990). *An American profile: Opinions and behavior, 1972-1989.* Detroit, MI: Gale Research.

Young, E. W., & Jex, S. A. (1992). The patient self-determination act: Potential ethical quandaries and benefits. *Cambridge Quarterly of Health Care Ethics, 2,* 107-115.

Chapter 7

Advance Directives and End-of-Life Care: The Hispanic Perspective

MELISSA A. TALAMANTES
CELINA GOMEZ
KATHRYN L. BRAUN

Cultural values, beliefs, religion, and spirituality affect choices that people make about health care treatment and end-of-life decisions. When faced with complex treatment regimes, expensive options for health care, and decisions to withhold treatment, patients and families easily can become overwhelmed, even under the best of circumstances. Additional challenges are presented when a family speaks a different language or has a different educational, economic, social, or cultural background than the provider. This chapter presents an overview of Hispanic elderly in the United States and the roles played by their families, social support systems, religion, and culture in decision making at the end of life. It recommends ways in which health and social service providers can begin to address these very complex issues with Hispanic patients and their families.

■ DIVERSITY OF HISPANIC AMERICANS

In 1990, there were about 22 million Hispanic Americans, representing about 9% of the total U.S. population. By the year 2000, about 31 million of the country's residents were predicted to be Hispanic Americans (U.S. Bureau of the Census, 1993). Looking just at the population of Hispanics age 65 years or over, about 1.1 million were enumerated in 1990, representing about 5.1% of the total Hispanic population. The number of Hispanic elderly was expected to increase by 3.9% each year from 1990 to 2050 (U.S. Bureau of the Census, 1993).

The label of Hispanic American actually encompasses several subgroups, each with important social and cultural differences. Major Hispanic subgroups in the United States include Mexican Americans, Puerto Ricans, Cubans, Central Americans, and South Americans. Based on 1993 data from the National Death Index, about 54% of Hispanic Americans who died that year were of Mexican origin, 13% were Puerto Rican, 10% were Cuban, 8% were Central or South American, and 15% were categorized as "other or unknown" Hispanic (Gardner & Hudson, 1996). These percentages are in line with the 1990 census figures on the national origins of Hispanic elders—49% Mexican, 15% Cuban, 12% Puerto Rican, and 25% other (U.S. Bureau of the Census, 1993).

Differences exist among Hispanic subgroups, and these are related to their countries of origin and their histories of immigration or experience with colonization. The largest of the Hispanic subgroups is the Mexican Americans. The majority of members of this subgroup reside in the region of Texas that was formerly part of Mexico (Gonzalez, 1991). After the Mexican American War of 1846-1848, this territory became part of the United States and its Mexican residents became Americans. Thus, these Hispanic Americans trace their U.S. citizenship back five or six generations. During the Mexican Revolution of 1910-1921, there was a large influx of Mexicans into the United States. Immigration from Mexico has continued over the 20th century, and today the majority of Mexican Americans reside in the southwestern states of Texas, New Mexico, Arizona, and California (Gonzalez, 1991).

Puerto Ricans comprise the second largest Hispanic subgroup in the United States, with significant numbers residing in New York, New Jersey, and Illinois (U.S. Bureau of the Census, 1993). Puerto Rico's link to the United States stems from the Spanish American War; with the U.S. victory in 1898, Puerto Rico became a territory of the United States. Since then, there have been several waves of immigration from Puerto Rico (Sanchez-Ayendez,

1988). Another significant subgroup is Cuban Americans, about 1.1 million of whom have migrated to the United States—mostly to Florida—since the 1959 revolution in Cuba. Members of the older Cuban cohort tend to have higher income and education levels than do elders in other Hispanic subgroups (Bernal & Shapiro, 1996). Immigration from Panama was linked to the U.S. occupation and administration of the Panama Canal. War, political persecution, and economic hardship have resulted in immigration from Spanish-speaking countries in Central America. Cuellar (1990) indicated that regional differences also are important, noting that the practices of Hispanics from the Caribbean basin are influenced by "an amalgamation of Afro-Hispanic mulatto traditions," whereas the practices of Mexicans and Central and South Americans are influenced by "mestizo Indio-Hispanic traditions" (p. 385).

Despite the differences among these subgroups of Hispanics, for the most part, they share a common language, religion, and tradition of family relations as well as several Pan-Hispanic values. For example, although many Hispanics have bilingual capabilities (i.e., Spanish and English), the literature reports that many Hispanic elders prefer to speak Spanish over English, especially in the home (Bastida, 1988; Kravitz, Pelaez, & Rothman, 1990; Sanchez-Ayendez, 1988). In terms of religion, most Hispanics are Catholic, especially elderly Hispanics (Gallego, 1988), although degree of participation in church activities can vary (McCready, 1994). For example, in a study about religion and older Hispanics, 50% of the respondents indicated that they had decreased their frequency of church attendance over the years due to transportation or health problems, and 75% said that they listened to religious programming on television or radio (Gallego, 1988).

Another commonality is the importance of family. Several studies have documented that, in all Hispanic subgroups, strong family ties exist and are characterized by high levels of instrumental, associational, and affective support within and across generations (Bastida, 1988; Cuellar, 1990; Sotomayor & Applewhite, 1988; Sotomayor & Randolph, 1988; Talamantes, 1987). Both foreign-born and U.S.-born Mexican Americans indicate a preference to live with their children if they were to experience declines in health (Angel, Angel, McClellan, & Markides, 1997). In addition to *familismo* (emphasis on the welfare of the family over the individual), Cuellar (1990) described four more cultural themes that influence Pan-Hispanic beliefs and practices: *jerarquismo* (respect for hierarchy), *personalismo* (trust building over time based on the display of mutual respect), *espiritismo* (belief in good and evil spirits that can affect health and well-being), and *presentismo* (emphasis on the present, not the past or future).

As with European American elderly, the three leading causes of death for U.S. Hispanics are heart disease, cancer, and stroke, accounting for about two thirds of deaths for elders in both ethnic categories. Diabetes is the fourth leading cause of death for Hispanic elders, whereas chronic obstructive pulmonary disease is the fourth leading cause for European Americans. The fifth leading cause of death for both ethnic groups is pneumonia/influenza (Gardner & Hudson, 1996). Socioeconomically, census data suggest that 17% of Hispanic elderly live below the poverty level and that Hispanic elders have an average of 5 years of formal education (U.S. Bureau of the Census, 1991).

Regarding race and ethnicity, one should note that when referring to Hispanic Americans, it is important to remember that individuals included under this label can be of any racial group (e.g., indigenous Indian, Negroid, Asian, Caucasian). The label of Hispanic, then, refers to an ethnic or a cultural affiliation rather than to race. This complicates efforts to describe cross-ethnic comparisons. For example, when comparing African Americans and European Americans, the literature refers to them by these labels or might call them blacks and whites. However, the label of white or Caucasian is not applicable to studies with a Hispanic comparison group because some Hispanics are in fact of the Caucasoid race (i.e., persons of European, North African, or Southwest Asian ancestry). Thus, literature that compares Hispanics to other ethnic groups might refer to members of the "white" comparison group as European American, non-Hispanic white, non-Hispanic Caucasian, European American, Anglo, or Euro-Anglo. In this chapter, we use the term European American in reference to a non-Hispanic Caucasian comparison group. When citing studies, we use the terms selected by the cited studies' authors.

■ CULTURE, FAITH, AND RELIGION IN THE DYING AND DEATH EXPERIENCE

Several studies and articles have reported on Hispanic perspectives on dying, death, religion, and spiritual beliefs (Rael & Korte, 1988; Talamantes, Lawler, & Espino, 1995; Villa, 1991; Younoszai, 1993). Younoszai (1993), for example, described a mural by a well-known Mexican artist, Diego Rivera, that depicts death (as a skeleton) walking in the park on the arm of the artist. Interpreting this, the mural suggests an acceptance, and even a celebration, of death in the culture. This also is seen in the observance of a holiday called *Dia de los Muertos* (Day of the Dead), which is a combination of the Pre-Columbian Day of the Dead and the European Catholic All Souls' Day. This holiday, which falls around Halloween, is celebrated throughout Mexico and in Hispanic communities in the southwestern United States. The tradition involves going to cemeteries to place food on the graves of loved ones. It honors the life of the deceased as well as the unity of the family that occurs when there is a death.

In a sociohistorical qualitative study on Hispanic elderly in small rural towns in northern New Mexico, Rael and Korte (1988) found that many traditional practices related to dying and death still are observed. For example, it is common to hold a continued vigil over an older family member with a terminal illness. After death, parishioners offer daily masses or light candles in honor of the deceased. It is believed that dead family members continue to watch over living family members and are prayed to for continued support and strength. Masses held in honor of the anniversary of a family member's death are a common occurrence, as is publishing a semi-poetic paragraph in a local newspaper to remember a loved one's death. These rituals support the view of death as a natural part of the cycle of life and the view of life as only a temporary loan or gift from God (Rael & Korte, 1988).

Villa (1991) explored the concept of *Fe* (spirituality) and found it to be a primary and important coping resource among older Hispanic women. Using a scale to measure Fe, the investigator found that about 60% of Mexican American women said that one could have Fe without being religious and that 86% strongly believed that Fe could help with life's problems such as healing family members and coping with caregiving responsibilities. Older Puerto Rican, Cuban, and Mexican American women caring for terminally ill family members rely on their faith in God for strength to cope with the suffering and ultimate deaths of their loved ones. Their use of *dichos* (sayings) such as *Dios es Grande* (God is great) and *Yo ruego a Dios que lo alivie de su sufrimiento y que se alivia* (I pray to God to heal his suffering and to heal him), is a testament to the importance of their faith when faced with illness and death (Talamantes et al., 1995).

■ KNOWLEDGE AND PREFERENCES ABOUT END-OF-LIFE DECISION MAKING

Studies that have examined Hispanic beliefs and practices regarding end-of-life decision making are limited but are reviewed here. First noted are studies about patient autonomy, followed by studies about advance directives, life-prolonging treatment, hospice, euthanasia, and autopsy/organ donation.

Patient Autonomy

A study in Los Angeles by Blackhall, Murphy, Frank, Michel, and Azen (1995) compared Mexican Americans, Korean Americans, African Americans, and European Americans on several issues related to patient autonomy. They found that Mexican and Korean Americans were less likely than the other two groups to believe that a patient should be told about a metastatic cancer diagnosis. Mexican and Korean Americans also were less likely to believe that a patient should be told about a terminal diagnosis or make decisions about using life support. Instead, Blackhall and colleagues found that Mexican and Korean American elders were more likely than African and European American elders to want family members to make these decisions. In stepwise multiple regression, ethnicity was the strongest predictor of these patient autonomy issues, although years of schooling and personal experience with illness also were significant predictors for all groups. For Mexican Americans, the investigators also found differences by income, acculturation, and age; younger respondents, more acculturated respondents, and those with annual incomes over $10,000 were more likely to favor truth telling about the diagnosis (Blackhall et al., 1995).

Talamantes and Gomez (1996) explored these issues among Mexican American elders residing in the San Antonio area in Texas. Focus groups were employed to help refine a survey instrument later administered to a random convenience sample of 50 Hispanic elders. When asked about general medical treatment decisions, 46% responded that they would want their doctors to make these decisions, 24% would prefer to make their own decisions, and 18% would discuss the decision with their families. At the same time, nearly 90% said that their physicians did not know what the elders wanted if they were to become so ill that they could not make their own decisions. When asked why, many patients responded with *"Nunca me han hablado de eso"* (They never have discussed that) or *"No he estado enfermo"* (I have not been sick).

In response to the question of whether it bothered them to talk to their families about these issues, 84% said that it did not. Common responses included *"Quiero que sepan lo que pienso yo"* (I want them to know how I feel) and *"Mis hijos saben"* (My children know). When asked which people could make decisions regarding life-support measures if they were unable to decide themselves, 28% selected daughters, 14% selected spouses, and 12% selected doctors (Talamantes & Gomez, 1996). This finding is in contrast to the findings of other investigators who have reported that older Hispanics might be reluctant to discuss terminal illness and death with family members (Koenig, 1997).

Advance Directives

The Los Angeles study on patient autonomy mentioned earlier also compared the Mexican American, Korean American, African American, and European American groups on knowledge and completion of advance directives. They found that Mexican and European Americans were significantly more knowledgeable than the Korean and African American groups about advance directives. However, of those who had knowledge of advance directives, only 22% of the Mexican Americans actually possessed advance directives, compared to 40% of the European Americans. The authors also found that Mexican Americans who had advance directives scored higher on the acculturation scale than did those who did not have them (Murphy et al., 1996).

Caralis, Davis, Wright, and Marcial (1993) conducted a multicultural study at the University of Miami in Florida, looking at the influence of ethnicity on attitudes toward advance directives, life-prolonging treatments, and euthanasia. In terms of advance directives, the investigators found that Hispanic patients in the study, the majority being Cuban Americans, were less knowledgeable about living wills than were the African American and non-Hispanic white participants.

Similar evidence comes from a random sample survey in New Mexico ($N = 883$), which asked about advance directives and use of life support. In terms of advance directives, the authors found that Hispanic elderly were less likely than non-Hispanics to know about and have advance directives, even after controlling for socioeconomic variables (Romero, Lindeman, Koehler & Allen, 1997).

Eleazer and colleagues (1996) looked at advance directive use among 1,193 participants in PACE (Program for All-inclusive Care of the Elderly), a comprehensive managed care demonstration serving frail older adults at 10 sites across the country. The investigators found that only 40% of the 146 Hispanic participants had their health care wishes recorded in their medical records, compared to 80% or more of the 385 non-Hispanic white, 364 African American, and 288 Asian participants. The authors also found that more Hispanics than non-Hispanics refused to give any form of advance directives and that the Hispanic group was least likely to select a "no code" status.

An effort to increase advance directive completion rates among patients age 65 years or over in a health maintenance organization in San Francisco was reported by Rubin, Strull, Fialkow, Weiss, and Lo (1994). The authors randomly assigned 1,101 older patients into two groups; one served as a control, and the other received educational materials on durable power of attorney for health care (DPOA-HC). On follow-up, 18% of the intervention group completed DPOA-HC documents, compared to less than 1% of the control group. Analysis by ethnicity, however, suggested that only 4% of Hispanics in the intervention group completed DPOA-HC documents, compared to 12% of the African Americans, 22% of the Asians, and 26% of the non-Hispanic whites in the intervention group.

In interviews among older Mexican Americans in San Antonio ($N = 50$), Talamantes and Gomez (1996) found that 36% were knowledgeable about the Patient Self-Determination Act of 1991, 26% knew about various advance directive options, and only 10% had completed advance directives. In contrast to findings reported by other investigators, respondents had a positive attitude toward completing advance directives and expected that their physicians would explore this topic with them. A measure of acculturation also was used in this study and was not a significant factor in advance directive knowledge or completion rates; this finding differs from findings by the Los Angeles team that found that Hispanics with advance directives were more acculturated than those without advance directives (Blackhall et al., 1995; Murphy et al., 1996).

Life-Prolonging Treatments

Some of the studies reviewed in the previous section also examined attitudes toward use of life-prolonging treatment at the end of life. For example, in the study by Caralis et al. (1993) that compared three ethnic groups in Miami, Hispanic and African American respondents were more likely than non-Hispanic whites to report wanting their doctors to keep them alive regardless of how ill they were (42% and 37% vs. 14%, respectively). In line with this finding, only 59% of Hispanics and 63% of African Americans agreed to stop life-prolonging treatment, compared to 89% of the non-Hispanic white participants. In cases where there was no living will and the family and physicians disagreed over life-prolonging treatment, Hispanics were more likely to defer to a doctor's judgment than were African Americans and non-Hispanic whites (49% vs. 38% and 35%, respectively).

In their New Mexico study, Romero et al. (1997) asked participants to respond to a scenario about someone with a terminal illness. The investigators found that Hispanics were more likely than non-Hispanics to approve of the use of cardiopulmonary resuscitation, hospitalization, use of antibiotics, intubation, feeding tube placement, and intravenous nutrition in this situation.

Hospice

A few studies have suggested that Hispanics are low users of hospice services. In New York City, for example, a study found that only 14% of the patients and 2% of the hospice users affiliated with St. Luke's/Roosevelt Palliative Care Service were Hispanic (Pawling-Kapling & O'Connor, 1989). Wallace and Lew-Ting (1992) suggested that low hospice use is related to physician referral patterns; for example, physicians might not refer Hispanic patients to hospice because they observe families providing the care themselves and believe that hospice might be unnecessary or culturally inappropriate. Other potential reasons for low use are lack of awareness about hospice, lack of health insurance, language barriers, and unpleasant experiences with or distrust of the health care system (Sotomayor & Randolph, 1988; Treviño, 1988; Wells, Golding, Hough, Burnam, & Karno, 1988).

Euthanasia

The Florida-based study by Caralis et al. (1993) included questions about physician-assisted death. Of the three groups surveyed, the Hispanic group's responses were intermediate to those of the African American and non-Hispanic white groups. Specifically, 53% of Hispanics agreed that there were circumstances under which doctors should assist patients to die, compared to only 36% of African Americans and 61% of non-Hispanic whites. If faced with a terminal illness or permanent unconsciousness, 26% to 29% of Hispanics said that they would want a doctor's assistance to die, compared to 14% to 16% of African Americans and 38% of non-Hispanic whites. In the face of dementia, however, Hispanic responses were more similar to African American responses; only 10% of Hispanic respondents would want a doctor's assistance to die, compared to 8% of African Americans and 25% of non-Hispanic whites.

Autopsy and Organ Donation

A two-part study comparing autopsy rates between Mexican Americans and European Americans in San Antonio was reported by Perkins, Supik, and Hazuda (1993). In the first part of the study, autopsy rates were calculated for both groups. For autopsies required by law, the rates were 9% for Mexican Americans and 16% for European Americans. The authors believed that this was due to the fact that more European Americans than Mexican Americans were admitted to this hospital as trauma cases. Of autopsies granted voluntarily by families, the overall age-adjusted rates were 29% for Mexican Americans and 34% for European Americans. The rates were most different for two age groups: stillborn and adults over 40 years of age.

In the second part of the study, Perkins et al. (1993) interviewed 19 Mexican American and 12 European American key informants, using a case presentation followed by questions about whether a "typical" family from the culture would grant an autopsy. Analysis of the interview transcripts suggested cultural differences in several areas. Specifically, Mexican Americans were more likely than European Americans to see the information gathered at autopsy as useless and of no benefit. This was especially true if the autopsy was not seen as beneficial to the immediate family; European Americans, by contrast, hoped that autopsies would benefit people beyond their own families. Mexican Americans were more likely to perceive an autopsy request before death occurs as something harmful that can hasten death; by comparison, more European Americans felt that this pre-death request would be beneficial and supportive of the planning process. Mexican Americans were more concerned about God wanting a "whole body back" at death, whereas this was less of an issue for European Americans. Finally, Mexican Americans were concerned that the soul, which they believed remained in or near the body for up to 9 days after death, would be upset or perhaps feel the incision; by contrast, European Americans thought that the soul left the dead body immediately, and they did not think an autopsy would hurt a dead person.

Few articles were found that referred to organ donation among Hispanics. One (McQuay, 1995) noted that fear of mutilation and continued suffering among Hispanics presented barriers to organ donation. Findings from the Perkins et al. (1993) autopsy study reinforce McQuay's (1995) observations. Specifically, the last two areas—God wanting a whole body back and concern that the soul would feel any incisions—would likely limit acceptance of organ donation in the same way as they limit acceptance of autopsy.

■ DISCUSSION

From this review of the literature, it appears that Hispanic Americans are less likely than European Americans to appreciate autonomous decision making, complete advance directives, endorse the withholding or withdrawal of life-prolonging treatment under seemingly futile conditions, support physician-assisted death, use hospice services, or embrace organ donation and autopsy. In this section, we speculate as to why this might be and then discuss implications of these findings for patient care, community outreach, and professional education.

Why?

A number of investigators have speculated as to why Hispanic Americans differ from European Americans on matters of end-of-life decision making. Several authors have pointed to cultural values as a reason. For example, Cuellar (1990) pointed out that collectivist rather than individualist decision making is supported by the Pan-Hispanic value of familismo and that deference to the physician is in line with the value of jerarquismo. Advance care planning might appear antithetical to the value of presentismo. Perkins et al. (1993) described how traditional beliefs about the soul can hinder organ donation and autopsy. The commandment "Thou shalt not kill" presents a barrier to discussions of withdrawing or withholding treatment in this predominantly Catholic group. A summary of Pan-Hispanic themes that can influence end-of-life decisions is provided in Table 7.1.

Other authors have suggested educational reasons for differences in end-of-life preferences; that is, Hispanic Americans are less knowledgeable than other ethnic groups about advance directives and end-of-life options (Caralis et al., 1993; Romero et al., 1997). Others have presented social reasons such as low literacy, lack of health insurance, and linguistic isolation (Sotomayor & Randolph, 1988; Treviño, 1988; Wells et al., 1988). We suspect that many of these factors work together to discourage end-of-life discussions among Hispanics. An area of disagreement in the literature seems to be that of the role of acculturation; some authors have found that advance directive completion is related to level of acculturation (Blackhall et al., 1995), whereas others have not (Talamantes & Gomez, 1996). This issue needs further exploration.

Patient Care

We believe that patient care at the end of life can be improved for Hispanic Americans in a number of ways. First, it is important for health care profes-

TABLE 7.1. Hispanic Cultural Themes That Can Influence Beliefs and Practices Concerning End-of-Life Decisions

Theme	Meaning	Implications for Practitioners
Familismo	Emphasis on the well-being of the family over the individual	• Include family members in health care and end-of-life discussions
Personalismo	Trust building over time based on the display of mutual respect	• Learn about patients and their culture • Family physicians should start end-of-life discussions when clients are middle-aged
Jerarquismo	Respect for hierarchy	• Check whether patients are not just saying yes out of deference to physician • Families might expect physicians, hospitals, or God to be able to perform miracles, even under seemingly futile conditions, and might delay use of hospice services
Presentismo	Emphasis on the present, not on the past or the future	• Can hinder acceptance of advance care planning
Espiritismo	Belief in spirits, that is, good and evil spirits that can affect well-being and the spirit of the dead person that can stay near the body for 9 days after death	• Individuals might believe that requesting an autopsy prior to death will hasten death • Family members might delay organ donation if they believe that the deceased person would feel the incision

SOURCE: Adapted from Cuellar (1990) and Perkins, Supik, and Hazuda (1993).

sionals to expand their knowledge about Hispanic Americans. They should become familiar with the history of immigration/colonization for the various Hispanic subgroups and some of the family, social, and religious values associated with Hispanic culture. Learning some Spanish would be useful. Even showing an interest in the culture and learning about it from the patients' perspective would display respect and help build confidence and trust in congruence with the value of personalismo. It also is important for health care professionals to keep in mind the broad diversity among Hispanics and not to stereotype patients.

Second, we recommend that physicians include family members in discussions about patients' wishes about end-of-life care. There might be some cases in which Hispanic clients are "not content in their extended family contexts," but in most cases the families will want to be involved (Cuellar, 1990, p. 397).

Third, we recommend that conversations with Hispanic Americans about end-of-life care query their values about life and their expectations of Western medicine as well as their desires for care. This will take time, so these discussions should begin when clients are middle-aged and decisionally capacitated, not when they are elderly and/or in crisis.

The use of a values history form has proven useful to practitioners who want to stimulate discussion of end-of-life issues. One such form was developed by the Medical Treatment Guardian Program of the University of New Mexico's Institute of Public Law (McIver-Gibson, 1990). This form originated in response to a need for this program's clients to begin to process and document their preferences, values, and choices regarding medical care. A more streamlined values history form is offered by Doukas and McCullough (1991). Providing clients with a values history form to complete at home will signal that the issue is important and will give patients a chance to think about and discuss the form with their families. Reviewing the completed form is critical because it furthers the patient-physician relationship and offers a chance to ask questions of each other. In this way, the underlying values of patients become known, and it is these values that guide treatment decisions in the case of incapacity. Relying solely on advance directives is inadequate because they often are vague and/or do not give instructions for every situation. Knowing patients well and establishing trust always should precede discussions about advance directives. A Spanish-language version of the New Mexico values history form has been piloted in San Antonio.

In all cross-cultural care, we are partial to a model proposed by Good and Good (1980) that employs a meaning-centered approach to clinical practice. This "hermeneutic" or interpretive model takes a different approach to treatment than does the biomedical model. It guides the practitioner to gain an understanding of the patient's illness through his or her eyes, to find out what the illness and suffering mean to the patient and family, and to examine the language and symbols used by the patient and family to describe their experience. The final therapeutic goal is to treat the patient experiences, which often are found to be linked to important values of the patient. At the same time, using this model promotes open communication, cultural accommodation, and a mutual understanding among the physician, patient, and family.

Community Education and Outreach

Community education and outreach must be provided consistently over time, not just once or twice. Consistent with the value of personalismo, outreach should be provided by health professionals and other people who have the respect of the target audience and who show a high degree of caring for the audience. Second, community education should be aimed at a broad audience that includes entire families rather than just the elderly, consistent with the cultural value of familismo.

Third, education approaches need to go beyond brochures. These do not work well because the technical language used in many brochures is complex and above a 12th-grade reading level (Doak, Doak, & Root, 1996). The lack of sensitivity to reading level was evident in a survey of patient education materials at 19 acute, rehabilitation, and psychiatric hospitals in the San Antonio area. All materials in English were above a 12th-grade reading level; the Spanish brochures were at an 11th-grade reading level or higher and were literal Spanish translations (Talamantes, 1993).

Instead, educators are urged to take a grassroots approach to providing information about advance directives and end-of-life issues. Successful grassroots workers can identify community members interested in this topic to serve as discussion leaders. They also can identify community members who had family members in end-of-life situations and might be willing to share these experiences for purposes of education. In addition to short lectures and panel discussions, the use of song, dance, drama, and comedy (in skits or theater) has been found to be effective in grassroots education (Safer & Harding, 1993; Valente, Poppe, Alva, Vera de Briceno, & Cases, 1995). Participants in community outreach efforts should be offered ways to get further information or ask personal questions. Recruiting hospice volunteers from the Hispanic community will serve both to increase awareness of end-of-life issues among volunteers and to make sure that Spanish-speaking volunteers are available for Spanish-speaking hospice patients (Talamantes et al., 1995).

Professional Education

Research suggests that outpatients, regardless of ethnicity, want their doctors to initiate discussions about advance planning and that these discussions should occur after their physician-patient relationship is established but while the patient still is well (Miles, Koepp, & Weber, 1996; Talamantes & Gomez,

1996). The absence of any communication can lead to misunderstandings, which can cause dissatisfaction in the physician-patient relationship. Thus, current and future physicians need to learn ways to talk about end-of-life issues with their patients. More information about communicating with patients about death and dying is provided in the chapter by Kogan, Blanchette, and Masaki in this volume (Chapter 19).

All health care provider training programs, but especially medical school and residency programs, should require courses on death and dying, advance directives, palliative treatment, and bioethics. The curriculum should allow trainees to become familiar with advance directive documents. These courses should allow presentation and discussion of cases, including those in which the patient/family needs to be told about a terminal diagnosis, needs to be told that further treatment is futile, or is dealing with the late stages of the dying process. If possible, students and residents should have opportunities to discuss patients in a forum where a medical ethicist is present and can help with the process. Of primary importance, faculty must feel comfortable talking about these issues with their own patients before they can serve as role models to their students. It also would be important for faculty to have talked to their own families about their end-of-life wishes and to have completed their own advance directives. Some training programs videotape physicians-in-training as they engage in family/patient education; analysis of these tapes can be helpful in increasing awareness of mannerisms that can be misinterpreted. Other programs require medical students to spend a 6-week rotation as hospice volunteers.

■ CONCLUSION

A number of variables influence beliefs and practices at the end of life, and these are complicated by the specific circumstances of each patient such as his or her type and duration of illness, prognosis, level of pain and suffering, and familial support as well as the patient's personal values and beliefs in relation to choices that need to be made. This chapter presented an overview of Hispanic American decision making and practice at life's end within the context of Hispanic American history and culture. Although our goal is to help raise awareness about this population, practitioners are reminded to approach all patients with openness and curiosity as they assess the patients' knowledge about and preferences for care at the end of life.

■ REFERENCES

Angel, J. L., Angel, R. J., McClellan, M. A., & Markides, K. S. (1997). Nativity, declining health, and preferences in living arrangements among elderly Mexican Americans: Implications for long-term care. *The Gerontologist, 36,* 464-473.

Bastida, E. (1988). Reexamining assumptions about extended familism: Older Puerto Ricans in a comparative perspective. In M. Sotomayor & H. Curiel (Eds.), *Hispanic elderly: A cultural signature* (pp. 163-181). Edinburg, TX: Pan American University Press.

Bernal, G., & Shapiro, E. (1996). Cuban families. In M. McGoldrick, J. Giordano, & J. K. Pearce (Eds.), *Ethnicity and family therapy* (pp. 155-168). New York: Guilford.

Blackhall, L. J., Murphy, S. T., Frank, G., Michel, V., & Azen, S. (1995). Ethnicity and attitudes toward patient autonomy. *Journal of the American Medical Association, 10,* 820-825.

Caralis, P. V., Davis, B., Wright, K., & Marcial, E. (1993). The influence of ethnicity and race on attitudes toward advance directives, life-prolonging treatments, and euthanasia. *Journal of Clinical Ethics, 4*(2), 155-165.

Cuellar, J. B. (1990). Hispanic American aging: Geriatric education curriculum development for selected health professionals. In M. S. Harper (Ed.), *Minority aging: Essential curricula content for selected health and allied health professions* (DHHS Publication No. [HRS] P-DV-90-4, pp. 365-413). Washington, DC: Government Printing Office.

Doak, C. C., Doak, L. G., & Root, J. H. (1996). *Teaching patients with low literacy skills.* Philadelphia: J. B. Lippincott.

Doukas, D. J., & McCullough, L. B. (1991). The values history: The evaluation of the patient's values and advance directives. *Journal of Family Practice, 32,* 145-153.

Eleazer, G. P., Hornung, C. A., Egbert, C. B., Egbert, J. R., Eng, C., Hedgepeth, J., McCann, R., Strothers, H., Sapir, M., Wei, M., & Wilson, M. (1996). The relationship between ethnicity and advance health directives in a frail older population. *Journal of the American Geriatrics Society, 44,* 938-943.

Gardner, P., & Hudson, B. L. (1996). Advance report of final mortality statistics, 1993. *Monthly Vital Statistics Report, 44*(7, Suppl.). (National Center for Health Statistics, Hyattsville, MD)

Gallego, D. (1988). Religiosity as a coping mechanism among Hispanic elderly. In M. Sotomayor & H. Curiel (Eds.), *Hispanic elderly: A cultural signature* (pp. 117-135). Edinburg, TX: Pan American University Press

Gonzalez, G. (1991). Hispanics in the past two decades, Latinos in the next two: Hindsight and foresight. In M. Sotomayor (Ed.), *Empowering Hispanic families: A critical issue for the '90s* (pp. 1-19). Milwaukee, WI: Family Service America.

Good, B. J., & Good, M. J. (1980). The meaning of symptoms: A cultural hermeneutic model for clinical practice. In L. Eisenberg & A. Kleinman (Eds.), *The relevance of social science for medicine* (pp. 165-196). Boston: D. Reidel.

Koenig, B. A. (1997). Cultural diversity in decision making about care at the end of life. In M. J. Field & C. K. Cassel (Eds.), *Approaching death: Improving care at the end of life* (pp. 363-382). Washington, DC: National Academy Press.

Kravitz, S. L., Pelaez, M. B., & Rothman, M. B. (1990). Delivering services to elders: Responsiveness to populations in need. In S. A. Bass, E. A. Kutza, & F. M. Torres-Gil (Eds.), *Diversity in aging: Challenges facing planners and policymakers in the 1990's* (pp. 47-71). Glenview, IL: Scott, Foresman.

McCready, W. C. (1994). Culture and religion. In P. S. J. Cafferty & W. C. McCready (Eds.), *Hispanics in the United States: A new social agenda* (pp. 49-61). New Brunswick, NJ: Transaction Publishers.

McIver-Gibson, J. (1990). National values history project. *Generations, 14*(Suppl.), 51-64.

McQuay, J. E. (1995). Cross-cultural customs and beliefs related to health crises, death, and organ donation/transplantation: A guide to assist health care professionals understand different responses and provide cross-cultural assistance. *Critical Care Nursing Clinics of North America, 7,* 581-594.

Miles, S. H., Koepp, R., & Weber, E. P. (1996). Advance end-of-life treatment planning: A research review. *Archives of Internal Medicine, 156,* 1062-1068.

Murphy, S. T., Palmer, J. M., Azen, S., Frank, G., Michel, V., & Blackhall, L. J. (1996). Ethnicity and advance care directives. *Journal of Law, Medicine, & Ethics, 24,* 108-117.

Pawling-Kaplan, M., & O'Connor, P. (1989). Hospice care for minorities: An analysis of a hospital-based inner-city palliative care services. *American Journal of Hospice Care, 6*(4), 13-21.

Perkins, H. S., Supik, J. D., & Hazuda, H. P. (1993). Autopsy decisions: The possibility of conflicting cultural attitudes. *Journal of Clinical Ethics, 4*(2), 145-154.

Rael, R., & Korte A. O. (1988). *El ciclo de la vida y muerte:* An analysis of death and dying in a selected Hispanic enclave. In S. R. Applewhite (Ed.), *Hispanic elderly in transition: Theory, research, policy, and practice* (pp. 189-202). Westport, CT: Greenwood.

Romero, L. J., Lindeman, R. D., Koehler, K. M., & Allen, A. (1997). Influence of ethnicity on advance directives and end-of-life decisions. *Journal of the American Medical Association, 277,* 298-299.

Rubin, S. M., Strull, W. M., Fialkow, M. F., Weiss, S. J., & Lo, B. (1994). Increasing the completion of the durable power of attorney for health care: A randomized controlled trial. *Journal of the American Medical Association, 271,* 209-212.

Safer, L. A., & Harding, C. G. (1993). Under Pressure Program: Using live theater to investigate adolescents' attitudes and behavior related to drug and alcohol abuse education and prevention. *Health Education Research, Theory, and Practice, 4,* 213-223.

Sanchez-Ayendez, M. (1988). Elderly Puerto Ricans in the United States. In S. R. Applewhite (Ed.), *Hispanic elderly in transition: Theory, research, policy, and practice* (pp. 17-31). Westport, CT: Greenwood.

Sotomayor, M., & Applewhite, S. R. (1988). The Hispanic elderly and the extended multigenerational elderly. In S. R. Applewhite (Ed.), *Hispanic elderly in transition: Theory, research, policy, and practice* (pp. 121-134). Westport, CT: Greenwood.

Sotomayor M., & Randolph, S. (1988). A preliminary review of caregiving issues and the Hispanic family. In M. Sotomayor & H. Curiel (Eds.), *Hispanic elderly: A cultural signature* (pp. 137-160). Edinburg, TX: Pan American University Press.

Talamantes, M. A. (1987). *An exploratory study of the nature of sibling relationships among older Mexican American adults.* Master's thesis, Baylor University.

Talamantes, M. A. (1993, March). *Community education on advance health care directives.* Paper presented at the annual meeting of the American Society on Aging, Chicago, IL.

Talamantes, M. A., & Gomez, C. (1996, November). *Knowledge and use of advance health directives by Mexican American elderly.* Paper presented at the annual meeting of the Gerontological Society of America. Washington, DC.

Talamantes, M. A., Lawler, W. R., & Espino, D. V. (1995). Hispanic American elders: Caregiving norms surrounding dying and the use of hospice services. *Hospice Journal, 10*(4), 35-49.

Treviño, M. C. (1988). A comparative analysis of need, access, and utilization of health and human services. In S. R. Applewhite (Ed.), *Hispanic elderly in transition: Theory, research, policy, and practice* (pp. 61-72). Westport, CT: Greenwood.

U.S. Bureau of the Census. (1991). *The Hispanic population in the United States: March 1986 and 1987.* Washington, DC: Government Printing Office.

U.S. Bureau of the Census. (1993). *Racial and ethnic diversity of America's elderly.* Washington, DC: Government Printing Office.

Valente, T. W., Poppe, P. R., Alva, M. E., Vera de Briceno, R., & Cases, D. (1995). Street theatre as a tool to reduce family planning misinformation. *International Quarterly of Community Health Education, 15,* 279-290.

Villa, R. F. (1991). *La fe de la mujer.* In M. Sotomayor (Ed.), *Empowering Hispanic families: A critical issue for the '90s* (pp. 43-58). Milwaukee, WI: Family Service America.

Wallace, S. P., & Lew-Ting, C. (1992). Getting by at home: Community-based long-term care of Latino elders. *Western Journal of Medicine, 157,* 337-344.

Wells, K. B., Golding, J. M., Hough, R. L., Burnam, M. A., & Karno, M. (1988). Factors affecting the probability of use of general and medical health and social/community services for Mexican Americans and non-Hispanic whites. *Medical Care, 26,* 441-451.

Younoszai, B. (1993). Mexican American perspectives related to death. In D. P. Irish, K. F. Lundquist, & V. Jenkins Nelsen (Eds.), *Ethnic variations in dying, death, and grief: Diversity in universality* (pp. 67-78). Washington, DC: Taylor & Francis.

Chapter 8

*Cultural Issues in
End-of-Life Decision
Making Among Asians
and Pacific Islanders in
the United States*

GWEN YEO
NANCY HIKOYEDA

Some of the oldest cultures in the world are from Asia, and as in all cultures, strong beliefs and traditions established over time have helped individuals to deal with death. When individuals migrate from Asia to the United States, not only the health care but also the "death care" might seem inappropriate and strange. The same is true for individuals from the diverse populations in the Pacific Islands, whether they migrated or, as in the case of Native Hawaiians, had a foreign culture imposed on them.

The starting point in understanding the potential cultural disparity that individuals face is to recognize the vast range of cultural differences found among the populations classified in

AUTHORS' NOTE: This work was partially supported by a grant from the Bureau of Health Professions for Geriatric Education Centers.

the United States as "Asian/Pacific Islander." Although the category provides a convenient label for official census classification of the many relatively small populations, it is almost meaningless when cultural understandings are the goal. More than 30 countries of origin are lumped together to categorize Asian/Pacific Islander American (APIA) individuals. They span over half the globe and contain literally hundreds of language and ethnic subgroups, many vastly different from one another in cultural ideology and traditions about death. For most subgroups, there is very little literature about those traditions, especially as they are practiced by APIA individuals residing in the United States. To add to this complexity, vast differences in rural/urban background, education, and other characteristics are seen within each ethnic subgroup. These factors also influence the degree to which ethnic subgroup beliefs differ from those of Americans of European ancestry. This chapter reviews end-of-life issues identified for the largest groups within the rapidly growing APIA population where there is some literature, although the depth of the research differs enormously from one ethnic population to another.

Cautionary Notes

Before attempting to describe the cultural traditions that might be relevant and helpful for providers to increase their understanding of issues involved in end-of-life decision making, a caveat is in order. Koenig (1997) warned against the overly simplistic call for culturally competent care that ignores the dynamic nature of culture or considers culture a predictor of decision making at the end of life. One cannot assume that patients and their families from certain geographic areas or religious backgrounds will approach decisions about death in a particular culturally related way.

An important example relates to the interpretation of Buddhist traditions among the many Asian populations who practice Buddhism. It is important to recognize the differences among the sects of Buddhism that have developed in the respective countries of origin. Although the basic doctrines are similar, there are very clear differences in rituals and practices, especially those teachings relating to reincarnation and the role of ancestral spirits. For example, it is common for Chinese and Southeast Asian Buddhists to believe in the important influence of ancestral spirits, whereas Japanese American Buddhists tend to honor their ancestors but not attribute supernatural powers to them.

■ ISSUES ON WHICH SOME APIA POPULATIONS MIGHT CONFLICT WITH AMERICAN MEDICAL PRACTICES

The following areas have been found to present dilemmas in some cases for both Western-trained health care providers and APIA patients when the beliefs and expectations influencing end-of-life decisions differ. The awareness that there might be potential cultural conflicts is an important first step for providers to become more culturally competent.

Family Versus Individual Decision Making

Traditions of filial piety and family responsibility in Asian countries influenced by Confucian ideals can produce conflicting expectations with the current ethical and legal model of decision making in the United States that emphasizes individual autonomy. Even if an older patient clearly is competent to make decisions, for example, one or more family members might feel that it is their duty to protect their elder by assuming the decision-making role.

Disclosure of Terminal Illness

It is very common in many Asian countries to have both providers and family members feel that patients should not be told that they have a terminal illness such as advanced-stage cancer. Because informed consent is required in U.S. medicine and this information is essential for a patient to make informed autonomous decisions about treatments (e.g., life support), there is a clear potential for misunderstanding and conflict between providers and family members.

Advanced Directives

It is not uncommon to find disinterest among some APIA elders in controlling the decision making about their own health. In addition, some individuals believe that talking about death, even in a theoretical or hypothetical way, is taboo. Therefore, executing advanced directives can become problematic.

Life Support

Varying beliefs and attitudes can influence decisions about life support by APIA individuals and family members. Cultural values might emphasize longevity over quality of life, especially for one's parent. Some families do not want to make decisions that would preclude the possibility of a miracle from either God or the American medical system, of which they might have unrealistically high expectations. For example, in a large geriatric practice in nursing homes and home care, Fowkes (1995) found that patients from Asian backgrounds were five times as likely as Anglo patients to die with feeding tubes. Klessig (1992) compared 230 patients from eight different ethnic backgrounds in Los Angeles on their attitudes toward beginning and ending life support based on their responses to scenarios of terminally ill or hopeless situations. Respondents from the three Asian populations were much more likely to favor beginning life support and less likely to end it compared to the reference group of non-Jewish Caucasian respondents.

Autopsy or Organ Donation

A belief that the body belongs to one's ancestors can make it difficult to consider any procedure that would make the body less than whole. A similar constraint might be found among some Asian Catholic patients who feel that it is important to return one's nonmutilated body to God.

Traditions at the Time of Death

Strongly held beliefs frequently specify certain rituals about placement or treatment of the dying person or the body, and these can differ dramatically from one APIA culture or subculture to another. If death occurs in the hospital, then the cultural practice of not disturbing the body for a given period of time or of needing to attend it in special ways might conflict with the usual hospital practice of removing the body quickly, often within an hour of death (Hallenbeck, Goldstein, & Mebane, 1996). In some cases, more acculturated individuals from Asian backgrounds have indicated that they have voluntarily given up practicing rituals that would be common in their countries of origin to avoid the difficulties that would be involved in trying to practice them in the United States. It should be noted that the U.S. funeral industry has made adaptations to many cultural practices.

Families of terminally ill APIA elders who want to "go home to die" to Asian countries of origin face a particularly poignant situation. This is not an uncommon request of older immigrants, especially if they came to the United States as "followers of children." A family might experience economic hardship if there is a strong wish by the elder to be buried in his or her country of origin.

Hospice Care

For all the reasons mentioned heretofore, the European model of hospice care might not meet the expectations of APIA patients and their families. Although flexibility is one of hospice's strengths, the lack of intervention except to relieve pain and discomfort can make it less acceptable to APIA families who want more aggressive care.

■ BELIEFS ABOUT DEATH AND DYING IN SEVEN APIA GROUPS

To begin to understand culturally based behavior and perspectives of individual patients and families in the trajectory of dying in clinical care, it is extremely important to go beyond seeing them as "Asian." This chapter provides more detail about the seven largest APIA groups residing in the United States—Chinese Americans, Filipino Americans, Japanese Americans, Asian Indian Americans, Korean Americans, Vietnamese Americans, and Native Hawaiians—and about smaller APIA populations residing in the country. Table 8.1 summarizes the religious traditions and history of immigration/colonization for each of the seven largest groups. The following subsections summarize the available literature regarding death and dying. The varying amounts of information available for the different populations are obvious and dramatic.

Chinese Americans

Chinese Americans not only comprise the largest APIA subgroup but also are the most diverse. Because they were the first Asian population to immigrate in large numbers, with continued immigration from various parts of mainland China, Taiwan, Hong Kong, and (in some cases) Vietnam, Chinese individuals and families are at varying stages of acculturation to the American health care

TABLE 8.1. Background Information on the Seven Largest Asian/Pacific Islander American Populations

Ethnic Group	Population in 1990[a]	Predominant Religious Traditions[b]	Immigration Periods[b]	
Total persons, United States	248,709,873	—		
Total Asians	6,908,638	—		
Chinese	1,645,472	Confucianism, Taoism, and Chinese Buddhism	1850-1860:	First wave (male sojourners)
			1900-1920:	Laborers and families; immigration of "paper" sons and daughters after San Francisco earthquake and fire destroyed official records
			1924:	Immigration Act excludes all Asians; Chinatowns emerge
			1940-1960:	Repeal of Exclusion Act; second wave (wives, scientists, professionals)
			1965-present:	Third wave (families, those with special skills); increased immigration from Hong Kong and Taiwan
Filipinos	1,406,770	Catholicism	1903-1910:	First wave (students or *Pensionados*)
			1900-1920:	Male students and Hawaii plantation laborers
			1924:	Immigration Act
			1920-1940:	Second wave (male laborers or *Pinoys*)
			1940-1960:	Family members and veterans
			1960-present:	Third wave (professionals and families)
Japanese	847,562	Japanese Buddhism and Christianity	1868-1882:	Male contract laborers
			1900-1920:	Primary immigration period (agricultural laborers, picture brides)
			1940-1960:	World War II internment and 45,000 Japanese war brides
			1980-present:	Skilled workers, students, relatives, businessmen, and families

Group	Population	Religion		
Asian Indians	815,447	Hindu, Muslim, and Sikh	1900-1920:	Male laborers to U.S. West Coast
			1920-1940:	Emigration from United States due to Thind Decision (i.e., Indians no longer "white persons" for immigration)
			1940-1960:	Small number of professionals and family reunification
			1965-present:	Large influx of educated middle-class immigrants
Koreans	798,849	Christianity, Confucianism, and Korean Buddhism	1900-1920:	Small group of male laborers to Hawaii and U.S. West Coast and picture brides
			1924:	Immigration Act
			1940-1960:	Students, picture brides, and war orphans
			Post-1965:	Highly educated men and women
			1970-present	Followers of children
Vietnamese	614,547	Vietnamese Buddhism and Catholicism	1975:	First wave (elite from former South Vietnam after fall of Saigon)
			1980-present:	Second wave (diverse cross section of population from unified Vietnam)
Total Pacific Islanders	365,029[c]	—		
Hawaiians	211,014	Christianity and Native Hawaiian traditions	—	

a. SOURCE: U.S. Bureau of the Census (1993a).
b. SOURCE: Yeo et al. (1998).
c. SOURCE: U.S. Bureau of the Census (1993b).

and value systems. There also are vast differences in financial and educational background and language spoken.

The literature about Chinese American attitudes toward death and dying is more abundant than for other APIA populations. One of the most pervasive comments is the cultural barrier against talking about death, with authors and respondents in studies reporting that it brings bad luck and/or is rude and disrespectful (Braun, 1998; Braun & Nichols, 1996; Crain, 1997; Koenig, 1997; Matocha, 1998; Muller & Desmond, 1992; Orona, Koenig, & Davis, 1994; Yeo, 1995). Some believe that the word *death* or its synonyms are especially to be avoided during holidays. In some instances, words that have sounds similar to the word death also are considered to bring bad luck and should not be used, for example, the word for the number *four* and the word for *clock*. The color white also is associated with death in some Chinese traditions, so one wonders how patients with this orientation might feel in the hospital surrounded by individuals in white. With these constraints, it is easy to imagine the difficult misunderstandings that can occur in cross-cultural clinical interactions. Physicians and nurses, and sometimes even hospital admission clerks, trying to fulfill their obligations to obtain information on patient preference for life support or resuscitation in the current climate emphasizing autonomy and advanced directives can unwittingly violate closely held cultural taboos of Chinese patients who hold traditional beliefs. Of course, many patients of Chinese ancestry might *not* be offended and might concur with the value of autonomous decision making, but at this point, clinicians have little direction in knowing how to make the distinction.

On Lok Senior Health Services in San Francisco serves a large population of frail elders of Chinese ancestry. Doreen Der-McLeod, On Lok's director of social services, reported success in obtaining preferences for most of its Chinese American participants' life-support wishes in the context of an established trusting relationship between the multidisciplinary team members and the Adult Day Health Center clients (Der-McLeod, 1995). Careful, culturally appropriate requests of their preferences were made within a discussion of information that the staff needed in case of emergencies. Even in this context, some participants declined to discuss the issues, deferring to the wishes of one or more of their children.

In Hawaii, when Chinese Americans at senior centers and churches were approached to participate in a survey on attitudes toward end-of-life options, three fourths of them declined, and the Chinese interviewer said that a common reason for not participating was that it would be "bad luck" to do so (Braun, 1998). Among those 48 who did respond, however, only 6% agreed that it was bad luck to talk about or plan for death. But they were more likely than Caucasian and other APIA groups to agree with statements indicating that there was no need to plan for death. This is evident in the high level of agreement with the statements "If it is your time to die, you will" (60%) and "It is in God's hands" (42%). The majority thought that a person should prepare by completing advance directives, and three out of four respondents thought that they should discuss death and dying with their families and physicians (Braun, 1998).

Crain (1997), however, reported only a 5% refusal rate among Chinese American elders (who were born in China) in a survey to explore their views on advance directives, smaller than the refusal rate of those of European ancestry. In this research, the 60 primarily monolingual non-English-speaking older homebound respondents in New York's Chinatown viewed independence as less important and expressed less preference for their own participation in their health care decision making and more preference for participation of physicians, compared to their counterparts from European backgrounds. The respondents born in China were less familiar than European Americans with the various types of life-support technologies, were less likely to say that they would refuse life-prolonging treatments, and were more likely to be undecided about it.

Life support also was relatively more important to the Chinese American respondents in the Los Angeles study reported by Klessig (1992). In response to scenarios, 53% preferred to start life support, compared to 17% of the white reference group, but nearly as many in the Chinese sample (65%) as the reference group (71%) agreed to end life support. Historical Chinese traditions honoring longevity support the preference for life support, but traditions also value avoiding undue suffering.

The importance of nutrition in dying patients can influence decisions about life support. A "good death" in some Chinese traditions includes not only dying peacefully in old age surrounded by family members but also dying with a full stomach (Der-McLeod, 1995). In an international study of nurses' attitudes toward feeding and hydration in terminally ill and severely demented patients who refuse to eat, nurses in the People's Republic of China were more uniformly in favor of feeding than were nurses in six Western countries (Norberg et al., 1994).

Decisions regarding life support also can be influenced by perceptions of what might be medically possible. Jump (1994) conducted pilot interviews with older Chinese Americans, who did not speak English, about their health care preferences in case of incapacity. It was found that many have a great belief in the potential for miracles in the American health care system, which made them less likely to accept the hopelessness of health conditions and more likely to want to prolong life with life support.

The importance of family members in health care decision making with Chinese American adults has been emphasized by many authors (Der-McLeod, 1995; Muller & Desmond, 1992; Orona et al., 1994; Yeo, 1995). In interviews with Chinese relatives of cancer patients in San Francisco, Orona and colleagues (1994) found that family members tended to define their duty as protecting the patients and making their remaining time comfortable and free of distress. The need to keep information about the disease and prognosis from the patient was important to avoid suffering and sadness. It is interesting to note, however, that in the Hawaii surveys, 100% of the 48 Chinese American respondents (who probably were among the more acculturated in the population given that three fourths of those approached declined to participate in the study) said that they would want to be told if they were fatally ill, and 84% said that they would want to make their own decisions (Braun, 1998). In some cases, the expectation or insistence of family members from Chinese backgrounds that the patient be protected from knowing of a terminal illness for fear that he or she will give up hope has come into serious conflict with members of the health care team intent on applying the principles of individual autonomy (Muller & Desmond, 1992). Gould-Martin and Ngin (1981) called the tradition of family members from Chinese backgrounds not telling a terminally ill patient of his or her prognosis a "conspiracy of silence" (p. 166). They suggested that the physician explain the terminal prognosis to family members and ask their permission to tell the patient or, if the physician feels that it is very important to tell the patient without permission, to do so in private so that the patient can pretend ignorance with the family. In Hawaii, key informants and focus group members of Chinese ancestry emphasized the importance of taking care of older parents and treating them with respect (filial piety) so that they may avoid the punishment of a premature death. They also indicated that resistance to organ donation stems from the desire to die intact and from the Confucian belief that one's organs are gifts from one's parents and that it would be disrespectful to destroy them or give them away (Braun & Nichols, 1996). Other writers also have described the traditional Chinese belief that one's body belongs to one's ancestors rather than to the individual, so that the family should make decisions regarding organ donation and life support.

As might be expected from the preceding discussion, advanced directives do not seem to be highly valued among Chinese Americans, although there is little direct research on the subject. Respondents in the Hawaii study indicated that there has been little traditional emphasis on advance decision making but that longtime U.S. residents and younger generations in Asia and the United States are more open to living wills, especially if they have witnessed Western medicine's ability to prolong life (Braun & Nichols, 1996).

The American health care literature has little to say about Chinese traditions around death, although it is not uncommon to hear descriptions of cases in which family members request that the bed be turned in a certain direction, that certain items such as mirrors or adornments be put under or on the bed, or that ritual bathing of the body be performed by the eldest son after death.

In summary, given the massive heterogeneity within the Chinese American population in religion, region of origin, education, rural/urban background, length of time in the United States, and acculturation level, one should expect enormous diversity in traditions around dying. Simply asking whether there are any cultural traditions that health care workers should keep in mind during the patient's stay or in the event of death should help elicit information to guide practice.

Filipino Americans

Compared to the literature on Chinese American views of death and dying, information on the second-largest APIA group, Filipino Americans, is much more limited. Only three studies of decision-making issues in terminal illness were found. This sparse information should be viewed in the context of the vast heterogeneity among Filipino Americans who immigrated to the United States in different waves for different reasons from a country with more than 1,000 inhabited islands and more than 70 languages and dialects. They represent vast ranges of education, income, rural/urban background, and occupation. Because of the long Spanish domination of the Philippines, most Filipinos in the United States are Catholic; however, churches such as *Iglesia ni Christo* and *Aglipay* are growing in influence. The ancestral religion (*Bathala*) and Islam also are found among the beliefs of some Filipinos (Miranda, McBride, & Spangler, 1998). The 1990 census found that 95% of Filipino Americans over 65 years of age were born outside the United States (Young & Gu, 1995) and that many elders continue to immigrate to join their adult children in the United States. However, many younger Filipino Americans were born in the United States and have strongly "Americanized" values and attitudes.

Miranda et al. (1998) indicated that deeply religious Filipinos tend to believe that illness happens for reasons that they often attribute to God or a higher power. The predominant belief in the causes of disease or other situations is the "will of God," even though individuals also believe in personal responsibility. Other Filipinos believe in the power of good and evil spirits to prevent, eliminate, or induce illness. Other important issues that might affect the interactions between providers and Filipino patients and their families in the context of terminal illness include a strong respect for elders taught in the culture, a strong reliance on family as decision makers in case of illness, strong expectations of care by the family, and a culturally based practice of indirect communication to avoid stressful interpersonal conflicts and confrontations (Kim, 1983; Miranda et al., 1998).

Klessig (1992) included a sample of 28 Filipino Americans in her study of attitudes toward starting and stopping life support. In response to the scenarios, 80% of the Filipino participants agreed to start life support and 14% agreed to stop it, which represented the most pro-life support position of any of the eight ethnic groups in Klessig's study.

There were two studies of end-of-life attitudes in Hawaii, including Filipino American participants. In the focus group and key informant interviews, Filipino respondents said that Catholic beliefs were an important influence on their culture's views of death (Braun & Nichols, 1996). Those who were the most recent immigrants and least educated expressed the view that Filipinos do not like to talk about death or funerals but might have picked cemetery plots. Those who were better educated, on the other hand, had thought about or executed living wills and funeral plans. Organ donation did not seem to be antithetical to their beliefs, but none had become donors (Braun & Nichols, 1996). In the survey consisting of five ethnic populations, 82% of the Filipino respondents agreed that people should prepare for death by writing living wills, but only one third thought that they should think about donating organs. Their definitions of a dignified death commonly meant a peaceful death free from pain and not being burdensome to others. Filipinos were the least likely to feel that there were conditions under which physician-assisted suicide should be considered (Braun, 1998).

Japanese Americans

Japanese Americans, as a whole, are the most acculturated and assimilated of the APIA subpopulations. However, they are a heterogeneous subgroup with significant generational, geographic, and historical differences that can influence their behaviors, attitudes, and beliefs about death and dying (Kitano, 1993).

Attitudes toward the end of life have been found to differ by the five distinct generations of Japanese Americans presently residing in the United States (Braun & Nichols, 1996; Kalish & Reynolds, 1976). The *Issei* are the early pioneers who immigrated to the United States at the turn of the 20th century. Although most of the Issei now are deceased, they maintained the traditional Japanese culture and language. The *Nisei* are the American-born descendants of the Issei. They attended American schools and English was their primary language, but they also went to Japanese-language schools and churches. Both the Issei and Nisei endured significant anti-Japanese discrimination, although those in Hawaii experienced much less than did their mainland counterparts. More than 110,000 Americans of Japanese descent were forcibly removed from their homes on the West Coast during World War II and detained in 10 concentration camps (Kitano, 1969). The *Sansei* are the children of the Nisei, and the *Yonsei* are their offspring. The *Kibei* are Nisei educated in Japan who later returned to the United States. Other Japanese Americans include those who immigrated after 1965; the *Shin-Issei* are primarily businessmen and their families, and the *Newcomers* include the war brides of U.S. servicemen (Kitano, 1993). *Nikkei* is a relatively recent term used to refer to Japanese Americans as a whole.

Nikkei families have maintained a high degree of traditional Japanese culture and values drawn from Confucian, Buddhist, Shinto, and Samurai traditions that differ from mainstream American mores. There are explicit cultural prescriptions for how Nikkei should behave both individually and as a group that undoubtedly influence their beliefs and behaviors at the end of life. These cultural mandates emphasize collectivity over individuality, obligation and duty over free will, and hierarchical structure and interdependence over self-reliance and independence within families (Kitano & Daniels, 1988). Common Japanese terms reflect the values and norms maintained by Nikkei families; they emphasize filial piety; strict self-discipline and self-restraint or stoicism (e.g., not complaining of pain so as not to upset others); obligation toward the family and Japanese community that share a family member's shame, guilt, or humiliation; quiet forbearance and endurance due to a sense of fatalism; and deferential behavior, modesty, or reticence, particularly in the presence of those in positions of authority (e.g., physicians). Some Nikkei have an extreme concern of "social sensitivity" toward evaluation by, and feelings of, others that has resulted in restricted interpersonal communication and limited emotional expression (Kalish & Reynolds, 1976).

Most Japanese Americans belong to either a Japanese Buddhist sect or a Christian denomination. Because attitudes toward death seem more philosophical and ritualistic than religiously based, it is difficult to assess the influence of religion on Nikkei. Most Japanese Buddhists in Hawaii believe that death is part of the life cycle and that the faithful are reborn into the Pure Land (Nirvana), which is a better place than life on earth (Braun & Nichols, 1996). Both Buddhist and Christian Nikkei tend to maintain a controlled accepta. of death (Kalish & Reynolds, 1976), which has been described as "death-accepting" compared to the American "death-denying" culture (Hirayama, 1990). Readers are referred to the chapter by Nakasone in this volume (Chapter 14) for more information on Japanese Buddhist beliefs.

Relatively little has been documented regarding Japanese Americans and end-of-life issues. However, four studies have begun to examine attitudes toward death and dying maintained by specific Nikkei subgroups. Kalish and Reynolds (1976) interviewed a Los Angeles population, including many Issei, Nishimura and Yeo (1992) interviewed older Nikkei in the San Francisco Bay Area, and Braun and Nichols (1996) conducted focus groups in Hawaii. Braun (1998) also surveyed the attitudes toward end-of-life issues of older and younger members of five ethnic groups in Hawaii, including Japanese Americans, 90% of whom were born in Hawaii. These results are not necessarily representative of all Japanese Americans, but they provide baseline information for establishing culturally sensitive and appropriate services for Nikkei.

In Japan, it is believed that a patient should not be informed of a terminal illness because he or she would lose the strength and hope needed to cope with the illness. However, half of the Los Angeles respondents thought that a dying person should be told of a terminal condition, but they were not sure who should do the telling. Most said that they would want to be told and would accept death peacefully rather than fight it. Others responded that they would not want the family to know if they were about to die because the family would worry too much. They would feel guilty placing such a burden on their families (Kalish & Reynolds, 1976). In fact, Nikkei traditionally endure pain, suffering, and hardship with little or no complaints so that family members will not worry (Hirayama, 1990). The younger generations in the Los Angeles study, however, wanted more control over their life situations and found the attitude of acceptance difficult to understand (Kalish & Reynolds, 1976). In the Hawaii survey, all but one of the 49 Japanese American respondents said that they would want to be told if they had a fatal illness, and 91% said that they would want to make their own decisions (Braun, 1998). The majority agreed that people should discuss death and dying with their family (90%), physicians (73%), and ministers (71%). Fear of dependence and fear of burdening their families were given by 90% of the interviewees as influences on their decisions about treatment if they were fatally ill (Braun, 1998).

Nikkei Buddhist focus group participants in Hawaii felt that planning for death is a good idea and that advance directives are both practical and useful (Braun & Nichols, 1996). All of those who were interviewed in the later survey expressed similar attitudes, saying that a person should prepare for death by completing a living will. In addition, 98% said that a surrogate decision maker should be chosen (Braun, 1998). Nishimura and Yeo (1992) found that the most common reason for use of advance directives in the California sample of older Japanese Americans was to avoid becoming a burden to their children. Most of the older Nikkei expected important medical decisions to be made by physicians and/or family members if they were incapacitated. However, only a few respondents had discussed their preferences with their physicians, and many believed that their doctors would know what should be done. Furthermore, few had discussed these issues with family members, and three fourths of those who preferred that family members make decisions did *not* think that their families knew of their preferences but expected that decisions would be made by their families in the best interests of the families.

Nishimura and Yeo (1992) also found that the durable power of attorney for health care was confusing and complex; few individuals had a reasonable understanding of the meaning of life-sustaining technologies. Overall, an advance directive was viewed not as an expression of individual rights but rather as an escape from life-prolonging treatment.

Nikkei in the Hawaii focus groups believed that Buddhism would support a family's decision regarding withholding or withdrawing life supports. They maintained that a natural death is preferred over the use of life-sustaining technologies. Regarding organ donation, resistance to the idea was supported by two traditions. First, the body is believed to be a gift from ancestors, and it would be disrespectful to have it mutilated in any way. Second, those believing in reincarnation would not want to be reborn without body parts. Other respondents, however, interpreted Buddhist doctrine as supportive of organ donation, saying that only the soul is reborn (not the body) and that Buddhism would approve of the intent to help others (Braun & Nichols, 1996).

Despite the cultural norms and expectations briefly described here, it appears from the limited research that Nikkei families attempt to reconcile their cultural heritage with those of contemporary American life when making end-of-life decisions. In fact, gaps have been noted between expressed cultural norms and actual behaviors. Nikkei often have two sets of interpretations for these cultural norms: a traditional Japanese meaning and an American adaptation (Osako, 1979). The Japanese cultural mandates toward death and dying have been reinforced for two generations in the United States, but there is evidence of their dilution with younger generations (Osako, 1979). Even though Nikkei as a whole are becoming more assimilated, health professionals and other service providers cannot assume that individuals have abandoned their centuries-old traditional Japanese customs and attitudes toward the end of life.

Asian Indian Americans

Although a great deal has been written about Asian Indian history and immigration patterns, minimal information is available on attitudes and cultural practices regarding death and dying among Asian Indian immigrants. Also known as Indo-Americans, East Indians, or South Asians, this group is extremely diverse in the United States as well as in India, where there are 16 recognized languages plus numerous tribal ones. About 83% of the Indian population are Hindus, but there also are Muslims (11%), Christians (2%), Sikhs (2%), and others (e.g., Buddhists, Jains). In the United States, Asian Indian Americans represent wide variations in geographic region of origin, beliefs and customs, language, education, income, and acculturation. The two major waves of immigration were (a) large groups of Sikh farmers from Punjab who came at the turn of the 20th century escaping British imperialism and (b) well-educated urban, English-speaking professionals who immigrated after World War II (Franks, 1993; Melendy, 1977; Ramakrishna & Weiss, 1992).

The Asian Indian view of health and illness is founded on traditional *Ayurvedic* medicine, which sees illness as a disruption of homeostasis in the five universal elements (water, fire, earth, wind, and ether), especially as they are expressed in their analogous elements in the body—bile, phlegm, and wind. Ramakrishna and Weiss's (1992) article provides the only information that could be found on end-of-life beliefs and practices among Asian Indians. Family involvement is the norm when someone is ill in India. The family attends to all but the medical needs of the patient and also provides psychological support. Families are protective of those who are ill and prefer not to disclose information about a terminal illness or to talk about impending death because such talk might make it happen or cause the patient to give up hope and die. It is not clear whether specific Asian Indian subgroups or Asian Indians as a whole commonly hold these beliefs. It is clear that the gaps in the bioethics research regarding Asian Indians are very wide.

Korean Americans

Although some immigration to the United States from Korea has been occurring during much of the 20th century, in recent decades their numbers have been increasingly dramatic. In 1990, 92% of older U.S. residents of Korean ancestry were not born in the United States, 80% did not speak English well, and 53% were linguistically isolated (Young & Gu, 1995). Korean families have been characterized as having a high regard for filial piety, clearly defined family roles, and family collectivity and interdependence overriding individualism and independence (Chin, 1993; Kitano & Daniels, 1988). Many Korean Americans are Christian, and churches serve as social and educational centers.

A major study of decision-making issues among Korean Americans was one in Los Angeles where responses toward advance directives and patient autonomy were compared in four ethnic populations: European Americans, Mexican Americans, African Americans, and Korean Americans (Blackhall, Murphy, Frank, Michel, & Azen, 1995; Murphy et al., 1996). The study consisted of 100 females and 100 males age 65 years or over from each group. Attitudes toward patient autonomy were examined by asking whether a diagnosis should be disclosed to patients and who should make decisions regarding life-supporting technology. Less than half of the Korean American sample believed that a patient should be told about a diagnosis of metastatic cancer (47%) or terminal illness (35%), the lowest of the four ethnic samples on both questions. Korean Americans also were the least likely to believe that the patient should make decisions about life support, with 28% in favor. Instead, the majority felt that the family should make the decision. Acculturation was measured as a potential covariate, but the analysis could not be performed for the Korean sample because 100% had scores below 3, reflecting low acculturation. (All Korean participants chose to be interviewed in Korean rather than in English.) Koreans who were less likely to favor truth telling were older (vs. younger), Buddhist (vs. Christian), and more educated (vs. less educated).

Another analysis from the same study examined the participants' attitudes toward advance directives. The Korean American and African American elders had the least knowledge about advance directives, with only 13% and 12%, respectively, indicating such knowledge. The Korean sample had the most negative attitude toward advanced directives of the four groups, slightly higher than the Mexican American sample. None of the Korean Americans possessed an advance directive, compared to 28% of the European Americans, 10% of the Mexican Americans, and 2% of the African Americans. The Klessig (1992) study, also based in Los Angeles, included 23 Korean Americans' responses to scenarios of terminal illness. They were much more likely to agree to begin life support (74%) and less likely to agree to stop it (30%) than were those in the reference group of non-Jewish Caucasian Americans (17% and 71%, respectively).

Vietnamese Americans

Because the vast majority of Vietnamese Americans and others from Southeast Asia immigrated after the U.S. war in Vietnam, they are among the most recent arrivals in large numbers and contain the largest percentage of first-generation Americans. Despite recent immigration, four distinct waves have been identified, with each containing different populations in terms of education, occupation, rural/urban origin, gender, and age. Although the relevance of cultural issues in decision making with dying Vietnamese patients and their families is high, there are relatively few sources in the literature to guide providers in an appropriate approach.

Despite the fact that many of the Vietnamese in the United States are Catholic, there is strong historical importance of Confucianism (from some 1,000 years of Chinese domination), Taoism, and especially Buddhist beliefs in cyclic continuity and reincarnation as well as concern with ancestral spirits in this life that can influence decision making around death (Nowak, 1998; Ta & Chung, 1990). For example, there might be a cultural aversion to hospitals, especially as a place to die, because of the belief held by some that those who die outside the home become wandering souls with no place to rest. In another example, agreeing to terminate life supports for a parent might be viewed as contributing to the death of an ancestor, who then might influence the fate of the living (Muecke, 1983). The Hawaii study also emphasized the importance of the Buddhist concepts of karma and karmic debts, especially in the belief that "terrible" deaths might be punishments for bad deeds in this life or former lives by the person who dies or by someone else in the family (Braun & Nichols, 1996).

Nowak (1998) quoted studies reported by Calhoun (1985, 1986) in which 60% of Vietnamese women indicated that if someone in their family were dying, they would not want that person told. Preparing for death, however, is common among Vietnamese elders, and it is not unusual for people to put aside money to pay for burials, choose burial sites with favorable orientations, buy coffins (sometimes stored under household altars), or buy burial clothes long before they are actually needed (Nowak, 1998; Ta & Chung, 1990). In the Hawaii study, Vietnamese participants said that preparation for death included praying a lot and/or preparing wills for distribution of property, but very few were familiar with living wills or other advance directives (Braun & Nichols, 1996).

Few of the Vietnamese in the Hawaii study were in favor of organ donation because they did not want to be born into the next life missing organs. A Vietnamese Buddhist priest who was interviewed in Hawaii indicated that theoretically, organ donation would be a good idea because the body means nothing; only the soul is reborn, and it would help others. But in reality, he thought that few in his congregation would consider it (Braun & Nichols, 1996).

In Vietnam, there were traditional rituals that should be performed after the death of a family member, lasting until the second anniversary of the death, but it is not clear how many of those rituals have survived in the Vietnamese American communities. Ta and Chung (1990) advised social workers with Vietnamese clients to understand that sadness is considered a normal part of life, so that coping with the death of a family member might not involve expressing grief and mourning in the Western style of bereavement counseling but instead might be centered on providing the appropriate rituals. Because commemoration of ancestors is an extremely important part of traditional Vietnamese culture, the most important piece of furniture in one's home frequently is the ancestral altar, where offerings of food and drink often are made and prayers are said to the spirits of the dead. Rituals are believed to assist the deceased in passing to the other world and "wander[ing] freely in the peaceful land" (p. 201).

Native Hawaiians

As might be expected, little data are available on decision making about death in the Native Hawaiian culture, especially outside the state of Hawaii. Indigenous Hawaiians are likely to have both non-Hawaiian and Hawaiian ancestors because less than 1% of the population in the state are "full-blooded" Hawaiians (Braun, 1998). They are very aware of their history of being defeated and oppressed and of having their culture decimated by the dominant culture. Following contacts with the West, many thousands of the original inhabitants of the islands died of infectious diseases. The survivors, who became a minority in Hawaii, were forced to give up their language, religion, and traditional way of life.

Information from interviews with key informants and from focus group participants reported by Braun and Nichols (1996) indicated that current Native Hawaiian beliefs are influenced both by Native Hawaiian traditions and Christianity. Participants agreed that wills or living wills were not talked about by many Native Hawaiians. Some elders believed that talking about death will bring on death, but many Native Hawaiians do make their wishes about death and funerals known to their loved ones.

For the follow-up survey interviews on attitudes toward end-of-life issues with five ethnic populations, three fourths of the Native Hawaiians who were approached declined to participate in the study. Those 50 who did participate were primarily Christian but respected the traditional Hawaiian values of *ohana* (family) and *kokua* (mutual cooperation and support), which tend to support a collaborative decision-making model rather than the autonomy model of health care decisions in the dominant culture (Braun, 1998). They rated their own health as the lowest among the five groups studied and had the most experience with caregiving, illness, hospice, and suicide. They thought that it was very important to have control over medical decisions that affected them and expressed low trust in physicians and moderate trust in family members to make the right decisions for them. Although 78% of the interviewees thought that a person should prepare for death by completing a living will, only 44% had living wills. In addition, 86% favored the thought that a person should choose a surrogate decision maker, but only 22% had surrogate decision makers. The influences of a painful death and burdening the family were significantly lower influences on decisions about treatment in case of fatal illness among the Native Hawaiian participants than among the participants in any of the other four groups (Braun, 1998).

Attitudes toward organ donation among Native Hawaiians in the two studies were mixed. In the focus groups, they ranged from a participant who already had designated herself as an organ donor on her driver's license to one who said that neither she nor any member of her family would donate organs because each wanted to return his or her body to God, its maker, as it is. Others were unsure about organ donation (Braun & Nichols, 1996). In the survey, only 36% felt that people should prepare for death by thinking about donating their organs, the lowest proportion among the five ethnic groups (Braun, 1998).

Smaller Populations in the United States

Although very limited, some information is available on certain aspects of death and dying in a few other APIA populations residing in the United States.

Samoan Americans

The majority of the relatively small populations of Samoan Americans live primarily in Hawaii and on the West Coast of the mainland. During the 1950s, however, several hundred individuals were brought from American Samoa to Hawaii to serve in the U.S. military, so those military families have been stationed in bases throughout the country.

Health care among Samoan Americans has been characterized as family centered. If a member of a family has a health crisis and needs care, then members of the extended family frequently cooperate to designate and support one member to be the caregiver, even if it means providing transportation to another part of the country. High use of emergency rooms and lack of follow-up for chronic illness have been reported (King, 1990), although no statistical data seem to be available to confirm these trends.

In traditional Samoan culture, illness, pain, and death are accepted stoically, and death is reported to be regarded as a natural event, with an acceptance of what is considered to be "God's will" (Ablon, 1971). If the bones are not treated respectfully, then the spirit might return to cause trouble such as accidents, pain, disease, and/or death, especially if the deceased had been a prominent person such as a *Matai* (chief) (Goodman, 1971).

In the Samoan communities on the West Coast, funerals are reported to be Christian ceremonies, usually attended by large numbers of family and friends, most often on the weekends and sometimes lasting several days. If a Matai is not available locally, then one might travel from Samoa to attend. Money commonly is donated to the immediate family of the deceased, and the funeral is paid in full in cash at the end of the service (Ablon, 1971; King, 1990). The body is prepared by Samoan women, who also provide the choir that sings traditional songs and hymns. The giving of traditional fine mats, which are increasingly rare in the United States, was reported during the 1970s as ritualized along with money donations, but because these mats were so difficult to obtain, the surviving family members often returned them to the donors after the services (King, 1990).

Cambodian Americans

The population of Cambodian Americans consists largely of refugees from the terror of Pol Pot and his Khmer Rouge regime in Cambodia, during which about one third of the population died. After their escapes, Cambodians frequently spent many years in refugee camps in Thailand or other countries before being allowed to enter the United States during the late 1970s and 1980s. Many were farmers from rural areas in Cambodia, and the level of education of the older Cambodians is very low. A study of 76 Cambodians age 50 years or over living in San Jose, California, in 1993 found a mean of 1.3 years of schooling (Handelman & Yeo, 1996).

A largely Buddhist religious orientation influences Cambodian Americans' attitudes toward illness, death, and dying. This sometimes includes a somewhat fatalistic belief in karma, which holds that the quality of one's current life is heavily dependent on the number of merits that one achieved in a past life. Some believe that pain and suffering are relieved by a life hereafter, especially if the person has "carried his burden with courage, grace, patience, and dignity" (Lang, 1990, p. 206). Buddhism sees birth as a rebirth immediately or 49 days after a death. Spirit possession also sometimes is used to explain illness (Lang, 1990). By contrast, respondents in the San Jose study overwhelmingly described a condition called *pruit chiit/kiit chraen* as the cause of their most common chronic illness, severe headaches accompanied by dizziness (Handelman & Yeo, 1996). Pruit chiit/kiit chraen is roughly translated as sadness from thinking too much, usually about the loss of family members or traumatic events under the Khmer Rouge.

Terminal illness has been described as difficult to explain to Cambodian Americans, especially those who are not old, because death tends to be seen as a natural result of old age. Another common experience is the decision by family members not to inform a seriously or terminally ill patient about his or her diagnosis. This is described by one social worker as the cause of a great deal of "psychic pain and unfinished emotional business for all the family members" and is illustrated by the case of a terminally ill patient who continued a vain search for a better doctor and another patient who blamed her increasing weakness on the drawing of blood by the nurses (Lang, 1990, pp. 207-209).

For patients who are in severe pain or dying, friends and family traditionally gather around the bedside to pray together, sing rituals, and/or tell stories about Buddha. Sometimes, a Buddhist monk is called in to recite prayers from the *Pali,* the Buddhist rituals, and the patient is encouraged to repeat the monk's words so that the words from the rituals will be on his or her lips at the time of death (Lang, 1990).

After death, family members traditionally offer food, money, and other gifts to the monks and the poor to assist the spirit of the deceased to be received into the afterlife. Funerals are important and sometimes costly events that can last several days with multiple rituals, but mourners frequently display little emotion. Home altars with pictures of the deceased are centers for offerings of food, incense burning, and prayers. Communication with the spirit of the deceased directly or through dreams is not unusual (Lang, 1990).

■ CONCLUSION

The most significant result of reviewing the current state of knowledge about APIA populations and their preferences regarding end-of-life issues is that there are some ethnic populations that are very disadvantaged by the lack of data available. This is especially true for the Asian Indian population. Although there are recurrent themes among the different APIA populations in terms of values of family-based decision making and protection of terminally ill patients from knowledge of their prognoses, the variations in their histories in the United States and specific cultural norms make it obligatory that clinicians make every effort to recognize the uniqueness of the individuals and ethnic populations for whom they give care.

■ REFERENCES

Ablon, J. (1971). Bereavement in a Samoan community. *British Journal of Medical Psychology, 44,* 329-337.

Blackhall, L. J., Murphy, S. T., Frank, G., Michel, V., & Azen, S. (1995). Ethnicity and attitudes toward patient autonomy. *Journal of the American Medical Association, 274,* 820-825.

Braun, K. L. (1998). *Surveying community attitudes on end-of-life options.* Honolulu: University of Hawaii, Center on Aging.

Braun, K. L., & Nichols, R. (1996). Cultural issues in death and dying. *Hawaii Medical Journal, 55,* 260-264.

Calhoun, M. A. (1985). The Vietnamese woman: Health/illness attitudes and behaviors. *Health Care for Women International, 6*(1-3), 61-72.

Calhoun, M. A. (1986). Providing health care to Vietnamese in America: What practitioners need to know. *Home Healthcare Nurse, 4*(5), 14-22.

Chin, S-Y. (1993). Korean migration. In S. Yamamato, S-Y. Chin, W. L. Ng, & J. Franks (Eds.), *Asian Americans in the United States* (Vol. 2, pp. 83-87). Dubuque, IA: Kendall/Hunt.

Crain, M. (1997). *Medical decision-making among Chinese-born and European-American elderly: A comparative study of values.* New York: Garland.

Der-McLeod, D. (1995, November). *Ethical issues in working with Chinese American elders on end-of-life issues.* Paper presented at the annual meeting of the Gerontological Society of America, Los Angeles.

Fowkes, W. (1995, May). *Ethnicity and choice at the end of life.* Paper presented at the annual meeting of the Society of Teachers of Family Medicine, San Diego.

Franks, J. (1993). Asian Indian and Pakistani immigration. In S. Yamamoto, S-Y. Chin, W. L. Ng, & J. Franks (Eds.), *Asian Americans in the United States* (Vol. 2, pp. 95-100). Dubuque, IA: Kendall/Hunt.

Goodman, R. A. (1971). Some Aitu beliefs of modern Samoans. *The Polynesian Society Journal, 80,* 463-479.

Gould-Martin, K., & Ngin, C. (1981). Chinese Americans. In A. Harwood (Ed.), *Ethnicity and medical care* (pp. 130-171). Cambridge, MA: Harvard University Press.

Hallenbeck, J., Goldstein, M. K., & Mebane, E. (1996). Cultural considerations of death and dying in the United States. *Clinics in Geriatric Medicine, 12,* 393-406.

Handelman, L., & Yeo, G. (1996). Using explanatory models to understand chronic symptoms of Cambodian refugees. *Family Medicine, 28,* 271-276.

Hirayama, K. K. (1990). Death and dying in Japanese culture. In J. K. Parry (Ed.), *Social work practice with the terminally ill: A transcultural perspective* (pp. 159-174). Springfield, IL: Charles C Thomas.

Jump, B. (1994, May). *Preferences for life-sustaining treatment among Chinese American elders.* Poster presented at the annual meeting of the American Geriatrics Society, Washington, DC.

Kalish, R. A., & Reynolds, D. K. (1976). *Death and ethnicity: A psychocultural study.* Los Angeles: University of Southern California Press.

Kim, S. S. (1983). Ethnic elders and American health care: A physician's perspective. *Western Journal of Medicine, 139,* 885-891.

King, A. (1990). A Samoan perspective. In J. K. Parry (Ed.), *Social work practice with the terminally ill: A transcultural perspective* (pp. 175-189). Springfield, IL: Charles C Thomas.

Kitano, H. H. L. (1969). *Japanese Americans: The evolution of a subculture.* Englewood Cliffs, NJ: Prentice Hall.

Kitano, H. H. L. (1993). *Generations and identity: The Japanese American.* Needham Heights, MA: Ginn Press.

Kitano, H. H. L., & Daniels, R. (1988). *Asian Americans: Emerging minorities.* Englewood Cliffs, NJ: Prentice Hall.

Klessig, J. (1992). The effects of values and culture on life-support decisions. *Western Journal of Medicine, 157,* 316-322.

Koenig, B. (1997). Cultural diversity in decision-making about care at the end of life. In Institute of Medicine (Ed.), *Approaching death: Improving care at the end of life* (pp. 363-382). Washington, DC: National Academy Press.

Lang, L. T. (1990). Aspects of the Cambodian death and dying process. In J. K. Parry (Ed.), *Social work practice with the terminally ill: A transcultural perspective* (pp. 205-211). Springfield, IL: Charles C Thomas.

Matocha, L. (1998). Chinese-Americans. In B. J. Paulanka & L. D. Purnell (Eds.), *Transcultural health care: A culturally competent approach* (pp. 163-188). Philadelphia: F. A. Davis.

Melendy, H. B. (1977). *Asians in America: Filipinos, Koreans, and East Indians.* Boston: Twayne.

Miranda, B. F., McBride, M. R., & Spangler, Z. (1998). Filipino Americans. In L. D. Purnell & B. J. Paulanka (Eds.), *Transcultural health care: A culturally competent approach* (pp. 245-272). Philadelphia: F. A. Davis.

Muecke, M. A. (1983). Caring for Southeast Asian refugee patients in the USA. *American Journal of Public Health, 73,* 431-438.

Muller, J., & Desmond, B. (1992). Ethical dilemmas in a cross-cultural context: A Chinese example. *Western Journal of Medicine, 157,* 323-327.

Murphy, S. T., Palmer, J. M., Azen, S., Frank, G., Michel, V., & Blackhall, L. J. (1996). Ethnicity and advance care directives. *Journal of Law, Medicine, & Ethics, 24,* 108-117.

Nishimura, M., & Yeo, G. (1992, November). *Ethnicity, medical decisions, and the care of the Japanese American elders.* Paper presented at the annual meeting of the American Geriatrics Society. Washington, DC.

Norberg, A., Hirschfeld, M., Davidson, B., Davis, A., Lauri, S., Lin, J. Y., Phillips, L., Pittman, E., Vander Laan, R., & Ziv, L. (1994). Ethical reasoning concerning the feeding of severely demented patients: An international perspective. *Nursing Ethics, 1*(1), 3-13.

Nowak, T. T. (1998). Vietnamese Americans. In L. D. Purnell & B. J. Paulanka (Eds.), *Transcultural health care: A culturally competent approach* (pp. 449-477). Philadelphia: F. A. Davis.

Orona, C., Koenig, B., & Davis, A. (1994). Cultural aspects of nondisclosure. *Cambridge Quarterly of Healthcare Ethics, 3,* 338-346.

Osako, M. (1979). Aging and family among Japanese Americans: The role of ethnic tradition in the adjustment to old age. *The Gerontologist, 19,* 448-452.

Ramakrishna, J., & Weiss, M. G. (1992). Health, illness, and immigration: East Indians in the United States. *Western Journal of Medicine, 157,* 265-270.

Ta, M., & Chung, C. (1990). Death and dying: A Vietnamese cultural perspective. In J. K. Parry (Ed.), *Social work practice with the terminally ill: A transcultural perspective* (pp. 191-204). Springfield, IL: Charles C Thomas.

U.S. Bureau of the Census. (1993a). *We the . . . American Asians.* Washington, DC: Government Printing Office.

U.S. Bureau of the Census. (1993b). *We the . . . American Pacific Islanders.* Washington, DC: Government Printing Office.

Yeo, G. (1995). Ethical considerations in Asian and Pacific Island elders. *Clinics in Geriatric Medicine, 11,* 139-151.

Yeo, G., Hikoyeda, N., McBride, M., Chin, S-Y., Edmonds, M., & Hendrix, L. (1998). *Cohort analysis as a tool in ethnogeriatrics: Historical profiles of elders from eight ethnic populations in the U.S.* Palo Alto, CA: Stanford Geriatric Education Center.

Young, J. J., & Gu, N. (1995). *Demographic and socio-economic characteristics of elderly Asian and Pacific Island Americans.* Seattle, WA: National Asian Pacific Center on Aging.

Chapter 9

End-of-Life Decision Making in American Indian and Alaska Native Cultures

NANCY WESTLAKE VAN WINKLE

*D*iscussing end-of-life issues such as living wills, health care proxies, autopsies, and organ donations can be difficult for patients and health care professionals (Edinger & Smucker, 1992; U.S. General Accounting Office, 1995). When a largely non-Indian health care workforce is caring for an American Indian and Alaska Native population, differences in values, beliefs, and health care practices can make these discussions even more problematic (Hepburn & Reed, 1995). Even hospital policies for advance care planning that are mandated by the Patient Self-Determination Act of 1991 (PSDA) can raise ethical questions for some American Indian groups (Carrese & Rhodes, 1995).

Although some literature exists that discusses American Indian and Alaska Native views of death and death rituals (Brokenleg & Middleton, 1993; Grossman, Putsch, & Inui, 1993; Lewis, 1990; Turner-Weeden, 1995), studies specifically addressing end-of-life issues such as advance directives, autopsies, and organ donations are rare (Carrese & Rhodes, 1995; Ventres, Nichter, Reed, & Frankel, 1993). The purpose of this chapter is to review the literature relevant to end-of-life decision making among American Indians and Alaska Natives in the context of their history. A discussion of demographics of the American Indian and Alaska Native populations; historical background; health care delivery and health status; views on death and dying; end-of-life decision making; and suggestions for practice, policy, and research are included.

■ BACKGROUND ON AMERICAN INDIANS AND ALASKA NATIVES

Demographics

American Indians and Alaska Natives comprise a small but growing part of the U.S. population. The 1990 U.S. census reported 1,959,000 American Indians and Alaska Natives, which was less than 1% of the general U.S. population. Nearly one half of the population lived west of the Mississippi River, with Oklahoma, California, Arizona, New Mexico, and Alaska having the largest populations (U.S. Bureau of the Census, 1993).

In addition to being small, this group is extremely heterogeneous. There are more than 300 federally recognized tribes, 100 state historical tribes, several dozen tribes with no formal recognition, and about 200 Alaska Native villages. More than 150 languages are spoken by these widely diverse groups (Manson & Trimble, 1982). Tribes vary in how they determine membership. Some tribes base membership on a certain proportion of Indian ancestry (e.g., one fourth), whereas other tribes (e.g., Cherokee) base membership on whether individuals can trace their ancestry back to the Dawes rolls (discussed later in this chapter).

According to the 1990 census (U.S. Bureau of the Census, 1993), the American Indian and Alaska Native population is young, with a median age of 26 years, compared to 33 years for the general U.S. population. About 8% of those in this group are age 60 years or over, substantially less than the 13% in the total population. In addition, 66% of American Indians and Alaska Natives age 25 years or over graduated from high school, compared to 75% for the total population.

The financial situation of many American Indians and Alaska Natives is poor. Median income is low ($21,750) when compared to that of the general population ($35,225). In 1989, about 31% of all American Indians and Alaska

Natives, and about 51% of Indians living on reservations and trust lands, had incomes below the poverty level. Although many people think that most Indians live on reservations, in fact only 22% live on reservations and trust lands. Another 15% live in some type of tribal or Alaska Native village statistical area (U.S. Bureau of the Census, 1993), whereas about 50% live in urban areas (John, 1994; Starr, 1996).

In terms of religion, American Indians and Alaska Natives may subscribe to traditional beliefs, Christianity, and/or the Native American Church. The latter incorporates traditional Indian beliefs and elements of Christianity. For example, the pantheon includes Indian and Christian spiritual beings. Rituals make use of some Christian elements but also use eagle bone whistles, water drums, and gourd rattles. Peyote, a nonaddictive drug made from drying the tip of the mescal cactus, is used to induce contact with the supernatural during ceremonies. The Native American Church, which began on the Southern Plains of the United States during the late 1800s, was officially organized in 1918. It has an estimated 250,000 members today (Josephy, 1991).

Historical Background

American Indians and Alaska Natives were the original inhabitants of North America. Although there is no consensus on how many people inhabited the coterminous present-day United States at the time of European contact, 5 million is the approximate figure reported by Josephy (1991). Because of warfare and disease, this number plummeted to 220,000 by 1910.

As Europeans began populating North America, treaties were made and often broken, and conflict arose between Indians and whites as settlers pushed westward. During the 1800s, many tribes were decimated by European illnesses, had suffered military defeats, and were placed on reservations. The Indian Removal Act of 1830 forced the Indians in the southeastern United States to move west to Indian Territory, which later became Oklahoma. On reservations, their ability to govern themselves and to pursue a traditional subsistence lifestyle was taken away, and they became wards of the government. The Department of the Interior, through bureau agents and missionaries acting as agents, "governed" the Indians and made all decisions for them in a paternalistic pattern of interaction that lasted for many years.

Assimilation became the thrust of federal policy toward the tribes. Indian children were sent away to boarding schools where they were forbidden to speak their native language or practice native customs. The Dawes General Allotment Act of 1887 provided for the division of some tribal reservations into land allotments for individual tribal members, thereby turning communal landholdings into privately owned property. Indian people were encouraged to farm their allotments. It was hoped that this would accelerate assimilation into European American society, but it only succeeded in reducing the Indian land base.

The Indian Reorganization Act of 1934 ended the allotment policy and, among other things, allowed the development of tribal self-government and tribal management of some of their affairs. However, the Department of the Interior still maintained control of many things, including financial matters, legal matters, and the tribes' natural resources. Even as late as the 1950s, the federal government instituted a program to physically relocate Indian people from reservations to urban areas for economic progress and assimilation (Harjo, 1993; Josephy, 1991). Termination policy, also initiated during the 1950s, was an attempt by the federal government to promote assimilation and terminate the government-to-government relationship that tribes, as sovereign nations, had with the federal government. This termination policy would have absolved the federal government of providing treaty-guaranteed services such as health care (Harjo, 1993; Rhoades & Deer Smith, 1996).

During the 1960s, after a stormy period of Indian relations culminating in the Indian occupation of Wounded Knee, South Dakota, there was a reemphasis in federal policy on self-determination with legislation such as the Indian Self-Determination and Education Assistance Act of 1975 and the Indian Health Care Improvement Act of 1976. Also during this period, more funding became available for social and economic development, and the sovereign power of the tribes was strengthened. This trend continued with legislation such as the Native American Graves Protection and Repatriation Act of 1990 and the Tribal Self-Governance Program of 1992 (Josephy, 1991; Rhoades & Deer Smith, 1996). Many tribes now contract with the federal government for funding to administer education, health care, law enforcement programs, and other services for their people (Harjo, 1993). More Indians are getting advanced education and training and are successfully developing and administering culturally relevant programs for their tribes (Josephy, 1991).

This historical background has provided insight into why some American Indians and Alaska Natives might react negatively to people and policies (including those related to end-of-life decision making) of a government-sponsored health care system.

Health Care Delivery and Health Status

As a result of the cession of most of the Indians' land, the U.S. government incurred obligations toward the Indians, including the provision of health care. As Rhoades and Deer Smith (1996) explained,

> Health services provided by the federal government for Indian people are not a gift. They are the result of business arrangements between two parties that resulted in a prepaid health plan. The health plan was prepaid by cession of the entire lands (except for small parcels "reserved" for Indians to live on and for other federal purposes) of the United States. (p. 166)

Prior to 1954, minimal health services were provided to the Indian people through the Bureau of Indian Affairs (Starr, 1996). In 1955, the Indian Health Service (IHS), an agency of the U.S. Public Health Service, began providing health care to American Indians. This service delivery program currently provides preventive, curative, rehabilitative, and environmental services through IHS-operated facilities, contracts with providers in the private sector, tribally operated programs, and 34 urban Indian health programs. IHS services are provided in 35 states. Approximately 60% of all American Indians and Alaska Natives living in the United States are eligible for IHS services, although not all of them use these services (IHS, 1996a, 1996b). To be eligible for care from the IHS, persons must be of Indian descent (i.e., they must be members of a federally recognized tribe or have a certificate provided by the Bureau of Indian Affairs) and have close ties to a federally recognized tribe (Rhoades & Deer Smith, 1996).

Although Congress never has appropriated sufficient funds to adequately cover the health care needs of Indian people (Rhoades & Deer Smith, 1996), health outcomes for American Indians and Alaska Natives have improved since the IHS began providing health care. According to IHS service area statistics, from 1972–1974 to 1991–1993, maternal mortality dropped from 27.7 to 6.9 per 100,000 live births, infant mortality dropped from 22.2 to 8.8 per 1,000 live births, and life expectancy at birth increased from 63.5 to 73.2 years (IHS, 1996b).

Like other groups, the American Indian and Alaskan Native population has experienced a shift from dying from acute and infectious diseases to dying from chronic and degenerative diseases (Kramer, 1997). Thus, the 10 leading causes of death among American Indians and Alaska Natives today are similar to the causes of death in the overall U.S. population: diseases of the heart, malignant neoplasms, accidents, diabetes mellitus, chronic liver disease and cirrhosis, cerebrovascular diseases, pneumonia and influenza, suicide, homicide, and chronic obstructive pulmonary diseases. However, age-adjusted mortality rates for chronic liver disease and cirrhosis, tuberculosis, accidents, diabetes mellitus, pneumonia and influenza, suicide, and homicide are higher in American Indian populations than in the general U.S. population (IHS, 1996b). Alcoholism and alcohol abuse are factors in many of these deaths (May, 1995). Age-adjusted rates for disease of the heart, malignant neoplasms, chronic obstructive pulmonary disease, and HIV infection are lower than those for the general U.S. population (IHS, 1996b). For more details, John (1997) provided an insightful discussion of mortality data for the American Indian population and the problems with and limitations of these data.

Mortality rates can vary by region (IHS, 1996a), urban/rural designation (Grossman, Krieger, Sugarman, & Forquera, 1994), and tribe. For example, research on suicide conducted in New Mexico showed a high variation in rates by cultural group, by tribe, and over time (Van Winkle & May, 1986, 1993). Variation by cultural group was seen in age-adjusted suicide rates for 1980-1987, with the Apache rate at 48.8 per 100,000 population, the Pueblo rate at 32.0 per 100,000, and the Navajo rate at 18.2 per 100,000. Suicide rates for the various Pueblo tribes in the study varied from 0.0 to 76.5 per 100,000 between 1957 and 1987. Variation over time also was observed, with rates peaking every 5 to 6 years among the Apache and every 7 to 8 years among the Pueblo. Van Winkle and May (1986, 1993) speculated that these peaks might be associated with social and economic trends and with the phenomenon of clustering, in which one suicide sets off a series of imitative suicides. May (1990) identified three commonalties of suicide experience across tribes: Suicides can occur in clusters among youth, often are alcohol related, and result from using methods that have a high success rate (e.g., firearms, hanging). The literature also shows that, among American Indians, suicide rates usually are highest for males in their late teen or early adult years. For the general population, by contrast, they are highest for older white males (Duclos & Manson, 1994).

Prevalence data for diseases among the American Indian and Alaska Native population is limited. Results of the Survey of American Indians and Alaska Natives component of the 1987 National Medical Expenditure Survey (Johnson & Taylor, 1991) show that diabetes and gallbladder disease have a higher prevalence in the Indian and Alaska Native population than in the general population. Prevalence of some other chronic diseases, such as cardiovascular disease, emphysema, hypertension, rheumatism, and arthritis, are about the same as in the general population, and prevalence of cancer is lower. Although prevalence of cancer is lower, American Indians have the lowest cancer survival rate of all groups in the United States (Burhansstipanov & Dresser, 1993). Alcoholism and alcohol abuse are problems in many tribes (May, 1995). Thus, although the health of American Indians and Alaska Natives has improved since the IHS became the main provider of health care, there still is much room for improvement to raise the health status to that of the general population (Starr, 1996).

■ VIEWS ON DEATH AND DYING

Keeping in mind that there is variation in beliefs and customs among and within tribes, some authors have suggested that a few beliefs regarding death and dying are held in common across tribes. For example, many American Indians and Alaska Natives view death as a natural and accepted part of life. Death and dying might not be discussed openly in all tribes, but it is not hidden either. Through stories and tribal ceremonies, even children learn about the naturalness of death and are taught to accept it as part of life.

Life and death are viewed in a circular pattern rather than in a linear pattern that is more typical of a Western worldview. Within this circular view, life and death are seen as a unitary concept (Lewis, 1990). Lombardi and Lombardi (1982) suggested, "Native Americans thus comprehend the harmony of the endless circle of creation and re-creation: Their interred bodies return nourishment to the earth; the earth makes the plants grow; the plants feed the animals; the animals feed humanity" (p. 36).

According to Turner-Weeden, a hospice nurse of American Indian ancestry, many Indian people believe in some type of existence after death. Her description is of a spirit world inhabited by their ancestors. Regarding the time leading up to death, Turner-Weeden (1995) wrote, "This should be a time of peace and understanding, a time to communicate, . . . to settle differences, to make peace with ourselves and others. Then we are prepared to take the next step through the 'Big Open Door' into the spirit world, to greet our Creator and all of our ancestors" (p. 13).

Despite these more common themes regarding death and dying, there is heterogeneity among tribes and within tribes regarding beliefs and behaviors surrounding death and dying. The values and mores of the traditional culture, the influence of Christianity, and the level of acculturation are some factors that can influence beliefs and behaviors of both communities and individuals (McCabe, 1994). Discussions of some traditional beliefs, values, and rituals surrounding death and dying in specific U.S. tribes can be found in historical ethnographies, for example, on the Cheyenne of Montana and Oklahoma (Hoebel, 1960), on the Wyandot (Huron) of Oklahoma and Kansas (Trigger, 1969), and on the Comanche of Oklahoma (Wallace & Hoebel, 1952). More contemporary pieces have been written about the Lakota Sioux of South Dakota (Brokenleg & Middleton, 1993) and the Tanacross Athabaskans of Alaska (Simeone, 1991). There also are some interesting accounts of death beliefs and behaviors of Canadian Indians (Kaufert & O'Neil, 1991; Preston & Preston, 1991).

Because several of the articles on end-of-life issues that are discussed in what follows concern Navajo people of Arizona, New Mexico, and Utah, a brief discussion of traditional Navajo beliefs and behaviors is provided. The Navajo, a very traditional people, often have been characterized as being fearful of death and the dead (Kluckhohn & Leighton, 1946/1962; Lewis, 1990; Webb & Willard, 1975). When a Navajo person dies, other Navajo are not supposed to touch the body. If they do, then the spirit of the deceased might contaminate them and they will require a cleansing ceremony (French & Schwartz, 1976). Some Navajo believe that ghosts of the dead might return to their homes and harass the living to avenge wrongs committed. If a person is dying at home in the traditional hogan, then the family might build a temporary hogan close to the original structure and move the ill person into it so that he or she dies there. On death, the temporary structure will be burned (French & Schwartz, 1976). Some terminally ill Navajo are sent to hospitals when they are dying (Lewis, 1990). The dead are quickly buried away from the village and living areas.

Navajo tend to avoid discussions of death and dying, and the name of the dead person is not spoken. Some authors suggest that the Navajo believe in an afterlife, but it is "only a shadowy and uninviting thing" (Kluckhohn & Leighton, 1946/1962, p. 184). It is not tied to rewards for good behavior in one's earthly life. Some Navajo believe that the spirit of a person who commits suicide or is a witch would be segregated in this afterlife. The spirit of a suicide victim is destined to carry the implement used for his or her death in the afterworld (Kluckhohn & Leighton, 1946/1962; Morgan, 1936). As mentioned earlier, however, beliefs held by an individual Navajo will vary, depending on his or her personal experiences; level of acculturation; and belief in traditional religion, Christianity, and/or the Native American Church.

■ END-OF-LIFE DECISION MAKING

Very little has been written about end-of-life decision making among American Indians and Alaska Natives today. Few research studies have been conducted, and most of these used qualitative approaches. They are summarized here.

First, however, it is important to note that two ethical principles, autonomy and self-determination, are the focus of much of this literature. The principle of autonomy states that a person has complete control over his or her body and mind and has the right to decide what is best for himself or herself (McCabe, 1994). The principle of self-determination is embodied in the PSDA. This federal legislation set certain expectations of all health facilities that are funded by Medicare and Medicaid. These expectations include requiring health facilities to provide (a) written information on state laws and hospital policies about the patient's rights to accept or refuse treatment, including the right to complete an advance directive and (b) education for staff and the community on advance directives. The goal of this legislation was to increase patient participation in end-of-life decision making. Despite the passage of this act in 1991, studies have shown that only 10% to 25% of Americans have completed advance directives (U.S. General Accounting Office, 1995), and these percentages generally are lower among minority groups (Murphy et al., 1996). Studies also have indicated that advance directives might not always be implemented in the way that the patients intended (U.S. General Accounting Office, 1995).

The principles of autonomy and self-determination imply that providers must discuss all aspects of care with patients, including negative information. These principles were the focus of an ethnography on end-of-life issues in a Navajo community. Carrese and Rhodes (1995) interviewed 34 Navajo informants, including some biomedical health care providers and traditional healers. Traditional Navajo believe that thought and language shape reality and influence events. Positive language helps to maintain or restore health, and negative language can be harmful. Carrese and Rhodes learned that discussion of negative information, such as disclosure of risk in informed consent, bad-news telling, and advance care planning for future illness, was a violation of these traditional Navajo values and could actually be harmful to the patient. The authors also noted that two IHS policies come into conflict in this situation: the policy requiring advance directives to be discussed under the PSDA and the policy to respect tribal views.

Ventres et al. (1993) conducted an ethnographic study to evaluate the use of the Limitation of Medical Care form (a document developed by an Arizona teaching hospital to address, in part, resuscitation issues) in actual hospital practice. The authors illustrated their findings through two case reports, one of a 35-year-old urban Indian male who was given a terminal diagnosis of hepatorenal syndrome while hospitalized. The intern felt that, because the patient was not competent to make all of the necessary decisions, his family should participate in the decision making. Two family conferences were held, and the patient's mother emerged as the lead decision maker. The intern's interactions with the family led to the completion of the Limitation of Medical Care form, an institutional objective. However, Ventres et al. suggested that the process of getting the form completed actually limited the intern's understanding of the social, emotional, and family context in which decisions were made. They also suggested that it caused the family members to believe that their concerns were not heard. For example, the intern went into great detail about the resuscitative procedures, even after the family members said that they did not want any to be used. One family member felt that this meant the physician did not trust the family's judgment. The intern never understood how the family members' past experience with resuscitative decisions of friends and the patient's past history of pain influenced their decision.

Hepburn and Reed (1995) reviewed the literature on end-of-life decision making and Indian elders. Because they found only one study dealing with Indian elders, they gathered some data themselves through telephone interviews with 12 health care workers, including physicians, nurses, social workers, and administrators, who had worked with a variety of Indian groups. Respondents were asked open-ended questions about the concepts of autonomy, advance directives, competence, and surrogate decision making. Especially important was how they approached these issues, how easy it was to approach Indian elders and their families about these issues, and suggestions for how to have discussions regarding these concepts with elders and their families. Respondents felt that individual autonomy was upheld in Indian communities and that the community would support an individual's decisions. Respondents also found that discussing advance directives with Indian elders before life-threatening events was problematic. Although patient and family wishes usually could be ascertained through discussion, formal documents might not be signed. Including family in discussions of competence and in most other discussions was viewed as important. Surrogate decisions could be made, but it might take some time and be an indirect process.

Ethical issues of medical futility and the role of the community in decision making were raised in the case of a 3-year-old American Indian girl born with numerous anomalies (Carter & Sandling, 1992). To survive, the child needed lifelong intravenous (IV) nutrition. The child's mother did not want the child to have IV nutrition initiated. However, the tribal elders wanted the girl to receive IV nutrition and return home. The mother deferred to the tribe, and the child was placed on IV nutrition and transferred to a local community hospital, where she received medical care but little support from family or tribe. Her mother became pregnant again and delivered another child with the same problems. This time, the mother did not consent to the initiation of IV feeding. This child died. This case demonstrates a challenge to the concept of medical futility and describes how tribal leaders can be involved in end-of-life decision making.

Historically, death songs were sung by members of many of the tribes that inhabited the Great Plains. The songs prepared the person psychologically and spiritually for death. Gordon (1990), an IHS physician, related a poignant story of a Hochungra elder approaching 100 years of age as she sang her death song. This elder had been brought to the IHS hospital by her family, and her prognosis was poor. Gordon gave her "ordinary medical care," that is, IV fluids and antibiotics. Her family did not want her sent 25 miles away to a better equipped hospital; instead, family members wanted the woman to stay at the IHS hospital so that she could "die close to home and family" (p. 1889). She survived and eventually was transferred to a nursing home 30 miles away. Although her family visited her often, she did not appear happy. Gordon mused, "I pondered her death and began to wonder if I had done either the patient or her community a service by snatching her from sure death. She had been ready to die, [and] her family and her community had been ready for her death. My therapy had shattered the integrity of her final life event" (p. 1889).

French and Schwartz (1976) contrasted two case studies of terminally ill patients from different cultures who were living at home. One of the patients was a 59-year-old Navajo woman diagnosed with cervical and osteoblastic cancer. The authors chronicled her compassionate care at home and the rituals prior to and after death. The authors discussed (a) the mutually respectful attitudes of home care staff and a Navajo medicine man, (b) the building of a temporary hogan for the patient (which was burned upon her death), (c) the request for the nurse to prepare the body so that the ghost of the patient would not contaminate the family, and (d) the sacrifice of burying the family's wealth with her (e.g., blankets, satin comforter, jewelry, money).

In her book of case studies of cultural conflicts in American hospitals, Galanti (1991) related two cases that are relevant. One concerned an 83-year-old Cherokee woman who entered the hospital with a bowel obstruction. She refused to sign the consent form for surgery and wanted to see a medicine man.

Because the medicine man was brought to the hospital and allowed to conduct a healing ceremony in the patient's room, the patient was willing to sign the consent form for the surgery. Surgery was successful, and the patient recovered.

The other case concerned a 15-month-old American Indian girl who was brought to the hospital by her grandmother with dehydration and fever. When the child's head was shaved for the IV, her grandmother was sure that the girl would die because of the tribal taboo of cutting a child's hair. When the child was not permitted to keep a medicine bundle next to her to counter the effect of breaking the taboo, her grandmother took the child home. The next day, the child's mother brought the child back to the hospital. This time, hospital personnel agreed to let the medicine bundle stay with the child after the mother explained the traditional beliefs about it, and the child's condition improved.

McCabe (1994) presented a Navajo perspective on the PSDA. She suggested that certain Western biomedical ethical principles have analogies in the Navajo culture. The principle of autonomy is part of the Navajo belief system, but it is accompanied by the principle of cooperation or consensus. This means that end-of-life decisions usually are not made by the patient without consulting the family. The principle of beneficence (i.e., doing what is good for another) has the Navajo corollary of giving help or aid for the good of the culture without expecting anything in return. The principle of confidentiality is viewed differently by the Navajo, again reflecting the principle of cooperation and consensus. As McCabe described it, "There is no hierarchical or vertical line of decision making; instead, there is a horizontal line—all concerned individuals are involved in some form or another in a major decision" (p. 420). McCabe also discussed the principle of truth telling as honesty. The principle of social justice fits in well with the Navajo belief that no one should strive for wealth for himself or herself but rather should share it and support one's culture. McCabe stressed the need for health care professionals to understand and respect these views when discussing death and dying with traditional Navajo patients.

■ RECOMMENDATIONS

Very little literature about American Indian and Alaska Native end-of-life decision making could be found. There was virtually nothing in the literature on organ donation or physician-assisted suicide. Brokenleg and Middleton (1993) made the only reference to autopsies, reporting that Lakota avoid them because they view the body as being sacred and housing the essence of the deceased. Most of the end-of-life literature reviewed in this chapter deals with advance directives and issues of patient autonomy and self-determination.

By considering the few research studies and case studies identified, historical and cultural information about these groups, and some literature on cross-cultural counseling, the following suggestions are offered for health care and social service providers' consideration, for policy considerations, and for research directions when working with American Indian and Alaska Native populations.

For health care or social service providers to discuss end-of-life issues in a culturally appropriate way with their patients, they must understand the range of values, beliefs, and health care practices that exist in their service population. It is important that providers recognize the existence of great diversity both among and within tribal and cultural groups. No two tribes have exactly the same values, beliefs, and proscribed behaviors regarding death, dying, and end-of-life decision making. There also is a wide range of values, beliefs, and behaviors within tribes due to factors such as acculturation and religious affiliation. It is helpful, therefore, for health professionals to learn as much as possible about the groups with which they work. In the actual encounters, it is important to keep this information in mind, but remember that the patient is an individual who might subscribe to some, none, or all of the traditional beliefs and behaviors.

It seems that many American Indians and Alaska Natives subscribe to the principles of patient autonomy coupled with consensus and cooperation as described by McCabe (1994). Individuals are involved in decision making but often include extended family members and even elders of the community in the process. Lewis (1990) suggested that the extended family as well as the patient be involved in decision making with regard to the outcome of a life-threatening illness. Members of the extended family should be defined by the patient or family, and the decision makers should emerge from within the family. In his commentary on the case study of the 3-year-old girl being sustained by IV feedings, Truog (1992) supported the involvement of tribal communities to help in crisis situation decision making. Although the tribal community was not helpful in this case, he felt that it is appropriate to incorporate community and cultural values into end-of-life decision making. Blackhall, Murphy, Frank, Michel, and Azen (1995) suggested "that physicians ask patients if they wish to be informed about their illness and be involved in making decisions about their care or if they prefer that their family handles such matters. In either case, the patients' wishes should be respected" (p. 825).

Many American Indians and Alaska Natives believe that it will help a sick or dying person to recover if many family members stay with him or her to provide support (Lewis, 1990). Also, many tribes believe that a person should not be alone at the time of death (Brokenleg & Middleton, 1993). Hospital administrators should consider modifications in hospital policy when possible to provide culturally relevant, compassionate care. Perhaps intensive care visiting hours could be extended, more than just two people could be allowed in the room, and family members could be allowed to stay round-the-clock.

Although about half of American Indians and Alaska Natives live in urban areas, many come long distances from reservations or rural areas to receive medical care. They might have to spend many days in the city while their relatives are receiving care at a tertiary care hospital. Perhaps more options such as Ronald McDonald Houses could benefit the dying patient and family and could contribute to holistic health care.

A number of communication issues should be considered when working with American Indian and Alaska Native patients on end-of-life issues. Can the patients and other decision makers speak English, and if not, then are interpreters available? Trained medical interpreters who know the culture usually are ideal. They have been taught how to explain medical terms that do not exist in the native language, and they usually can be objective in translating the meanings (Haffner, 1992). They also can help health care professionals to understand patients' behaviors and beliefs by acting as cultural brokers (Kaufert & O'Neil, 1991). In reality, trained medical interpreters often are not available, and family members and friends are used. Be aware that some medical terms might be problematic and that translations might not always be accurate if the interpreters want to please the health professionals or protect the patients (Buchwald et al., 1993).

Be aware that communication styles of the patient and health professional might differ (Paniagua, 1994). For some American Indians, sustained eye contact is rude and disrespectful. Silence is valued, and some Indians will be silent for much longer than Western health professionals are comfortable with while they consider what has been said and formulate what they want to say. Sometimes, communication is indirect. Hepburn and Reed (1995) gave an example of an American Indian elder who indirectly discussed her preferences for end-of-life care by referring to the death of a friend and how that was a good death.

When discussing advance directives, American Indians and Alaska Natives might not be willing to sign a form to indicate their wishes and might only be willing to discuss their wishes verbally. A history of inadequate health care and broken treaties and promises might contribute to some being suspicious of Western health providers and not wanting to sign a form. Hepburn and Reed

(1995) suggested that the goal should be the understanding of a patient's wishes without allowing formal procedures to hinder the process, as occurred in the case reported by Ventres et al. (1993). Because formal documentation might not be obtained, Hepburn and Reed suggested that this could necessitate some review of and change in clinical policy.

Some of the case studies reviewed for this chapter (French & Schwartz, 1976; Galanti, 1991) illustrate how holistic medical care can be given to patients when Western health professionals and traditional healers work together. Some IHS hospitals have rooms set aside for traditional healing ceremonies (Starr, 1996). Other hospitals should work with patients and traditional healers to allow healers to perform their ceremonies in the hospital rooms if at all possible.

There is an open arena for future research on end-of-life decision making among American Indians and Alaska Natives, given that so little work has been done to date. Qualitative and quantitative studies need to be conducted with a variety of tribes to identify the commonalties and variability in values, beliefs, and behaviors regarding end-of-life issues among and within these cultural groups. Studies of advance directives, autopsies, organ donations, physician-assisted suicides, and appropriate places to die all are needed. Studies of how health care personnel interact with American Indian patients regarding these issues also are important. Studies to understand the attitudes of American Indians and Alaska Natives toward ethical principles such as autonomy and self-determination are needed as well.

Researchers should work closely with tribes throughout the whole research process, from the development of the research design to interpreting results. Some tribes might not want such studies to be conducted if they believe that discussing end-of-life issues is unethical or could cause their people harm. Of course, findings should be made accessible to the tribes for their own use in the development of policy and community education programs. Among other things, results of this research can be used to inform a variety of policymakers and to develop culturally sensitive instructional material for health care providers and students who work with American Indian and Alaska Native populations.

■ REFERENCES

Blackhall, L. J., Murphy, S. T., Frank, G., Michel, V., & Azen, S. (1995). Ethnicity and attitudes toward patient autonomy. *Journal of the American Medical Association, 274,* 820-825.

Brokenleg, M., & Middleton, D. (1993). Native Americans: Adapting, yet remaining. In D. P. Irish, K. F. Lundquist, & V. J. Nelsen (Eds.), *Ethnic variations in dying, death, and grief* (pp. 101-112). Washington, DC: Taylor & Francis.

Buchwald, D., Panagiota, V. C., Francesca, G., Hardt, E. J., Marjorie, A. M., & Putsch, R. W., III. (1993). The medical interview across cultures. *Patient Care, 27*(7), 141-166.

Burhansstipanov, L., & Dresser, C. M. (Eds.). (1993). *Native American Monograph No. 1: Documentation of the cancer research needs of American Indians and Alaskan Natives* (National Cancer Institute, NIH Publication No. 93-3603). Washington, DC: Government Printing Office.

Carrese, J. A., & Rhodes, L. A. (1995). Western bioethics on the Navajo reservation: Benefit or harm? *Journal of the American Medical Association, 274,* 826-829.

Carter, B. S., & Sandling, J. (1992). Decision making in the NICU: The question of medical futility. *Journal of Clinical Ethics, 3*(2), 142-145.

Duclos, C. W., & Manson, S. M. (1994). Calling from the rim: Suicidal behavior among American Indian and Alaska Native adolescents. In *American Indian and Alaska Native Mental Health Research: The Journal of the National Center Monograph Series* (Vol. 4). Denver, CO: National Center for American Indian and Alaska Native Mental Health Research.

Edinger, W., & Smucker, D. R. (1992). Outpatients' attitudes regarding advance directives. *Journal of Family Practice, 35,* 650-653.

French, J., & Schwartz, D. R. (1976). Terminal care at home in two cultures. In P. J. Brink (Ed.), *Transcultural nursing: A book of readings* (pp. 247-255). Englewood Cliffs, NJ: Prentice Hall.

Galanti, G. A. (1991). *Caring for patients from different cultures: Case studies from American hospitals.* Philadelphia: University of Pennsylvania Press.

Gordon, S. F. (1990). The last death song. *Journal of the American Medical Association, 264,* 1889.

Grossman, D. C., Krieger, J. W., Sugarman, J. R., & Forquera, R. A. (1994). Health status of urban American Indians and Alaska Natives. *Journal of the American Medical Association, 271,* 845-850.

Grossman, D. C., Putsch, R. W., & Inui, T. S. (1993). The meaning of death to adolescents in an American Indian community. *Family Medicine, 25,* 593-597.

Haffner, L. (1992). Translation is not enough: Interpreting in a medical setting. *Western Journal of Medicine, 157,* 255-259.

Harjo, S. (1993). The American Indian experience. In H. P. McAdoo (Ed.), *Family ethnicity: Strength in diversity* (pp. 199-207). Newbury Park, CA: Sage.

Hepburn, K., & Reed, R. (1995). Ethical and clinical issues with Native American elders: End-of-life decision making. *Clinics in Geriatric Medicine, 11*(1), 97-111.

Hoebel, E. A. (1960). *The Cheyennes: Indians of the Great Plains.* New York: Holt, Rinehart & Winston.

Indian Health Service. (1996a). *Regional differences in Indian health: 1996.* Rockville, MD: Author.

Indian Health Service. (1996b). *Trends in Indian health: 1996.* Rockville, MD: Author.

John, R. (1994). American Indian elders' health, income security, and formal and informal support systems: The need for praxis. *Bold, 4*(4), 7-13. (International Institute on Aging, United Nations, Malta)

John, R. (1997). Aging and mortality among American Indians: Concerns about the reliability of a crucial indicator of health status. In K. S. Markides & M. R. Miranda (Eds.), *Minorities, aging, and health* (pp. 79-104). Thousand Oaks, CA: Sage.

Johnson, A., & Taylor, A. (1991, July). *Prevalence of chronic diseases: A summary of data from the Survey of American Indians and Alaska Natives* (AHCPR Publication No. 91-0031). Rockville, MD: Public Health Service.

Josephy, A. M., Jr. (1991). *The Indian heritage of America.* Boston: Houghton Mifflin.

Kaufert, J. M., & O'Neil, J. D. (1991). Cultural mediation of dying and grieving among Native Canadian patients in urban hospitals. In D. R. Counts & D. A. Counts (Eds.), *Coping with the final tragedy: Cultural variations in dying and grieving* (pp. 231-251). Amityville, NY: Baywood Publishing.

Kluckhohn, C., & Leighton, D. (1962). *The Navaho* (rev. ed.). Garden City, NY: Doubleday. (Original work published 1946)

Kramer, B. J. (1997). Chronic disease in American Indian populations. In K. S. Markides & M. R. Miranda (Eds.), *Minorities, aging, and health* (pp. 181-202). Thousand Oaks, CA: Sage.

Lewis, R. (1990). Death and dying among the American Indians. In J. K. Parry (Ed.), *Social work practice with the terminally ill: A transcultural perspective* (pp. 23-31). Springfield, IL: Charles C Thomas.

Lombardi, F., & Lombardi, G. S. (1982). *Life and death: The circle is timeless.* Happy Camp, CA: Naturegraph Publishing.

Manson, S. M., & Trimble, J. E. (1982). American Indian and Alaska Native communities. In L. R. Snowden (Ed.), *Reaching the underserved: Mental health needs of neglected populations* (pp. 143-163). Beverly Hills, CA: Sage.

May, P. A. (1990). Suicide and suicide attempts among American Indians and Alaska Natives: A bibliography. *Omega, 2*(3), 199-214.

May, P. A. (1995). The epidemiology of alcohol abuse among American Indians: The mythical and real properties. *IHS Primary Care Provider, 20*(3), 41-50.

McCabe, M. (1994). Patient Self-Determination Act: A Native American (Navajo) perspective. *Cambridge Quarterly of Healthcare Ethics, 3,* 419-421.

Morgan, W. (1936). *Human wolves among the Navajo* (Yale University Publications in Anthropology, No. 11). New Haven, CT: Yale University Press.

Murphy, S. T., Palmer, J. M., Azen, S., Frank, G., Michel, M., & Blackhall, L. J. (1996). Ethnicity and advance care directives. *Journal of Law, Medicine, & Ethics, 24,* 108-117.

Paniagua, F. A. (1994). *Guidelines for the assessment and treatment of American Indians in assessing and treating culturally diverse clients: A practical guide.* Thousand Oaks, CA: Sage.

Preston, R. J., & Preston, S. C. (1991). Death and grieving among northern forest hunters: An East Cree example. In D. R. Counts & D. A. Counts (Eds.), *Coping with the final tragedy: Cultural variation in dying and grieving* (pp. 135-155). Amityville, NY: Baywood Publishing.

Rhoades, E. R., & Deer Smith, M. H. (1996). Health care of Oklahoma Indians. *Journal of the Oklahoma State Medical Association, 89*(5), 165-172.

Simeone, W. E. (1991). The northern Athabaskan potlatch: The objectification of grief. In D. R. Counts & D. A. Counts (Eds.), *Coping with the final tragedy: Cultural variation in dying and grieving* (pp. 157-167). Amityville, NY: Baywood Publishing.

Starr, E. R. (1996). Health care systems in Indian country. In A. G. Sharon (Ed.), *Health of native people of North America* (pp. 7-44). Lanham, MD: Scarecrow Press.

Trigger, B. G. (1969). *The Huron farmers of the North.* New York: Holt, Rinehart & Winston.

Truog, R. D. (1992). Beyond futility. *Journal of Clinical Ethics, 3*(2), 143-145.

Turner-Weeden, P. (1995). Death and dying from a Native American perspective. *Hospice Journal, 10*(2), 11-13.

U.S. Bureau of the Census. (1993). *We the . . . First Americans.* Washington, DC: Government Printing Office.

U.S. General Accounting Office. (1995). *Patient Self-Determination Act: Providers offer information on advanced directives but effectiveness uncertain* (GAO/HEHS-95-135). Washington, DC: Author.

Van Winkle, N. W., & May, P. A. (1986). Native American suicide in New Mexico, 1957-1979: A comparative study. *Human Organization, 45,* 296-309.

Van Winkle, N. W., & May, P. A. (1993). An update on American Indian suicide in New Mexico, 1980-1987. *Human Organization, 52,* 304-315.

Ventres, W., Nichter, M., Reed, R., & Frankel, R. (1993). Limitation of medical care: An ethnographic analysis. *Journal of Clinical Ethics, 3*(2), 134-145.

Wallace, E., & Hoebel, E. A. (1952). *The Comanches: Lords of the South Plains.* Norman: University of Oklahoma Press.

Webb, J. P., & Willard, W. (1975). Six American Indian patterns of suicide. In N. L. Farberow (Ed.), *Suicide in different cultures* (pp. 17-33). Baltimore, MD: University Park Press.

Part 3

ℛeligious 𝒫erspectives on ℰnd-of-𝔏ife 𝒟ecision ℳaking

𝒯his section of the book provides information about the major religious traditions practiced by North Americans—Christianity (and Catholicism, one of Christianity's denominations), Judaism, Islam, and Buddhism. Each chapter addresses questions such as the following:

- How many people are affiliated with this religion, and what are the major subgroups within the faith?
- What are some of the beliefs of the faith, and how are they relevant to end-of-life decision making?
- How are religious tenets being applied to questions of assisted suicide, organ donation, and advance planning?

Readers will find that all faiths affirm the value of life and oppose suicide and killing. Yet, in the face of life-extending technology, the issues rarely are black and white; rather, they pose difficult questions for which answers are not clearly discerned in historical religious doctrine.

The five chapters in this section are presented by individuals who are, at the same time, both religious scholars and practitioners; two also are physicians, two also are pastoral counselors, and one also is a nurse-bioethicist. Their chapters provide information about religious-based views of death and dying. More important perhaps, they demonstrate how these views are evolving through ongoing debate among scholars and practitioners within these religious groups.

An editorial note is in order here. In noting historical dates, these authors use the abbreviation B.C.E. (for Before the Common Era) to signify dates prior to the birth of Jesus Christ and the abbreviation C.E. (for Common Era) to signify dates after the death of Christ.

Chapter 10

Christian Perspectives on End-of-Life Decision Making: Faith in a Community

MARY ROWELL

*W*ithin the Christian community, considerable diversity exists in the ways in which faith is interpreted and expressed. Much of this has been shaped by historical, cultural, and social factors. For a balanced and fair presentation of Christian responses to end-of-life decision making, it is necessary to reflect a range of perspectives found within the faith community. There is no single expression of the framing of issues or responses that can be said to be *the* Christian one. Nevertheless, there is a significant level of agreement across denominations on fundamental beliefs and approaches that influence the debate. This chapter focuses on what is shared across denominations and provides a grounding for discussion of differing interpretations and a basis for a practical response.

■ THE CHRISTIAN COMMUNITY

An estimated 28% of the world's population is Christian. Of these Christians, 56% are Roman Catholic; the other main denominations are Eastern Orthodox and Protestant. The Anglican communion, which commonly is included in surveys as Protestant and experienced to be so by some of its members, defines itself more strictly as Catholic, stressing the continuity of Catholicism beyond the Reformation while not identifying specifically with Roman Catholicism. In terms of development, Christianity has grown the fastest in Africa and Asia over the past 30 years. During that period, Pentecostal and charismatic groups have represented the fastest growth globally, with their numbers increasing from approximately 12 million to an estimated 154 million (Brierley, 1997).

In North America, immigration patterns have influenced the composition of the Christian community. In Canada, the dominant religious group is Roman Catholic, accounting for 45% (9.3 million) of adult Canadians in 1990. Members of Protestant denominations accounted for 30% of the adult population. Women tend to be more actively engaged in the church than do men, and older people are more likely to attend church than are younger adults. By contrast, the United States is predominantly Protestant. A 1988 Gallup survey, reported by Baril and Mori (1991), identified 59% of the U.S. population as Protestant and 27% as Roman Catholic. The makeup of the Protestant denominations in the two countries varies as well. In Canada, the United and Anglican churches have the largest affiliations, followed by the Presbyterian, Lutheran, and Baptist churches. In the United States, more people are members of the Baptist Church, followed by the Methodist and Lutheran churches. Baril and Mori also noted a significant decline in church attendance and an increase in both countries of people reporting "no religion."

The wide denominational variations are illustrative of the diversity of interpretation within the Christian community. Differences in faith expression and practice, together with reported trends in religious activity, might help underscore the continuing ambiguity and debate within the Christian Church around issues relating to end-of-life decision making. The situation is compounded in the context of a rapidly changing and increasingly secular society in which Christianity is not uncommonly marginalized. The emphasis on the primacy of individualism in North America has shifted the focus of society. An explosion in science and technology as it is applied in complex ways to medical care leaves many confused about how their faith is to be interpreted. Even in those churches where specific teachings are strong, it can be difficult for members to be clear about the application of such teachings in the context of new technology and personal situations.

■ BACKGROUND CONSIDERATIONS

Debates around end-of-life decision making, and in particular those concerning physician-assisted suicide and euthanasia, have become commonplace in contemporary industrialized societies that have technologically advanced medical systems. Such debates have gained increased momentum in the light of high-profile legal cases and the activities of Dr. Jack Kevorkian.

Within such societies, patterns of dying and death have changed. In the past, people commonly would be cared for in their homes, within the family, and with support from the surrounding community. In that setting, there was a certain ethos of acceptance, informed significantly by Christian traditions, within which death was seen as a part of life or a stage on a spiritual journey. In today's industrialized societies, however, dying and death are more likely to be associated with greater fear and embarrassment and to be viewed with a sense of defeat. The process is highly medicalized as well. There appear to be cultural dimensions and variations at work, and these differ significantly across the industrialized, predominantly Christian societies. It is, for example, initially strange to many Europeans who move to North America that Americans speak of people "passing away" or "passing on" but rarely of people "dying." It might be suggested that North American terminology better reflects a Christian perspective on afterlife. But it is more likely premised on fear, embarrassment, and avoidance than on any conscious theological foundation. Such factors tend to smooth the way for an acceptance of inappropriate technological interventions and demands for treatments that are nonbeneficial. These subsequently can lead to conflict with respect to withholding or withdrawal of aggressive therapies. Thus, although advances in medicine have saved lives and, in many cases, have alleviated suffering, it also is the case that such interventions can prolong dying and increase the suffering of patients. These complex issues are, at least in part, at the root of calls for the legalization of physician-assisted suicide and euthanasia. It is against such a backdrop, and necessarily through its theological foundations and pastoral ministry, that the Christian Church inevitably is drawn into the debate.

■ SCRIPTURAL ROOTS

To understand some of the roots of Christian thought that are applied to end-of-life discussions, several key concepts from Christian scripture are reviewed here.

Thou Shalt Not Kill

The Christian tradition historically has affirmed the value of life entrusted to us by God. It is a gift seen as something greater than the individual's ownership of it and, therefore, is not ours to be discarded. The intentional taking of one's own life or the deliberate killing of another is considered wrong, although exceptions to this have been applied in situations of self-defense, war, and (in some cases) capital punishment. Exceptions aside, the Church consistently has condemned assisted suicide and prohibited euthanasia. The basis for this condemnation is found in the story of Cain and Abel in Chapter 4 of the Biblical book of Genesis and in the prohibition of killing in the Ten Commandments (Exodus 20:13). It is to this scriptural foundation that Pope John Paul II referred in his encyclicals *Veritatis Splendor* (John Paul II, 1993) and *Evangelium Vitae* (John Paul II, 1995), both of which affirmed the dignity and sanctity of human life and the sovereignty of God over human life. In line with this thinking, rejection of assisted suicide and euthanasia continue to be widely upheld across the Christian denominations today.

But it is clear that individual attitudes and understandings vary, and the traditional stance is somewhat nuanced by changing theological reflections on the nature of suffering within the context of a highly technological and strongly individualistic age. Significantly, within the tradition, life has not been seen in terms of an absolute good that must be extended at all costs.

Created in the Image of God

Based in Scripture, Christians assert the fundamental dignity of the human person, created in the image and likeness of God (Genesis 1:26), saved by Jesus Christ (Ephesians 1:10), and destined for eternal life with God (1 Corinthians 15:42-57). This foundational belief, focusing on the person, is developed in detail in this volume by Alexander in his chapter on Catholic perspectives on euthanasia and assisted suicide (Chapter 11). In his writing, Alexander presents the roots of Christian belief underpinning respect for life and a recognition of the principle of the sanctity of life, a foundation held in common by Christians generally. Furthermore, a belief in the dignity of the human person, created in the image of God, has been extended to encompass a theology of relationship. Anderson (1993), a United Church theologian, expressed it in the following way: "To be created in the image of God, therefore, is to be created . . . for relationship in love, as the very being and character of God displays. Authentic humanity means being in relationship with God, with one another, and with other-than-human creation" (p. 163).

Such thinking has its source in the commands of the Christian gospel to love one another and, therefore, to build community in our lives: "I give you a new commandment: Love one another, as I have loved you, so you are to love one another. If there is love among you, all will know that you are my disciples" (John 13:34-35). A relational understanding of this type provides a basis for the Christian commitment to care for others and to attend to the needs of those who suffer.

There is, however, a seeming paradox here, for although the tradition historically has been life affirming and committed to the care of those who suffer as evidenced in the great foundations for care initiated by the Church, at the same time there has been a traditional theology of suffering set in contradistinction to this.

Suffering in the Christian Context

Accounts of suffering in both the Hebrew Scriptures and the New Testament have been used by Christians to shape various views about suffering. One account has held that suffering is in some sense deserved. It is a view set in a theology of retributive justice in which God is seen to be kind to those who are good and to inflict evil on those who do wrong or on their descendants or community (Deuteronomy 28:1-2, 28:15; Isaiah 3:11; Jeremiah 17:10; Psalm 1). A second view has been that suffering is educative and a means of spiritual development through which humans may learn to rely on God and come closer to God (Deuteronomy 8:5; Judith 8:27; Sirach 18:13). Talbert (1991), in his book on the educative value of suffering in the New Testament and its milieu, pointed out that this also was the dominant focus in the Greco-Roman world, which has had an enduring philosophical influence on Christian thinking. Scriptural references to suffering also have portrayed it in terms of meaninglessness and hopelessness (Psalm 8). In the book of Job, detailed but conflicting views of suffering are portrayed. The predominant account of suffering in the New Testament is one in which suffering is seen to be for the benefit of others, the pivotal account here being that of the suffering and crucifixion of Jesus Christ. In the text, Christ describes his suffering as necessary for human salvation (Mark 8:21; Matthew 16:21; Luke 9:21-22; Luke 24:26). Those who follow Christ are asked to take up their cross and suffer for the sake of the gospel (Matthew 16:24-27).

Thus, in Christian thinking, it has been held that the followers of Jesus Christ can expect to suffer so as to witness to their faith (Williams, 1998). Traditionally, suffering has been valorized in the Church. From this arises the suggestion that suffering in faithfulness to, and as a witness of, the Christian life is not to be avoided; rather, it is to be embraced and celebrated. However, as a report on assisted suicide developed within the Episcopal Diocese of Newark (1996) pointed out, such endorsements of suffering are to be understood only in the context of suffering *for the sake of the gospel*. These accounts should not be taken to refer to suffering more generally. Within recent times, approaches toward suffering have expressed it as a mystery with which every faith community wrestles in its encounters with human tragedy. This is well articulated in a discussion paper titled *Caring for the Dying* (Canada Executive, 1994), prepared for the Congregations of the United Church of Canada, that reflects a contemporary view that is shared across Christian denominations:

> We do not believe that suffering is God's punishment for sin or that suffering is ever intended by God. Our calling is to ease and relieve suffering in every way possible short of intentionally causing the person to die. Some suffering can be transformative; however, we reject any theological perspective that claims suffering is intended by God for redemptive purposes. We believe that the loving God revealed in Jesus Christ wills healing, wholeness, and relief of pain throughout the whole of creation. (p. 26)

Although more traditional understandings of suffering continue to exert some influence within the Christian community, the preceding expression of belief is well accepted generally and is foundational to approaches to end-of-life decision making. It underscores a Christian commitment to care for those who suffer, entails a recognition that life does not have to be preserved at all costs, and supports the generally held view that intentionally ending a person's life or one's own life is wrong. Continuing reflection on the nature of suffering within the Christian context, however, has contributed to varying attitudes and to some support to the view that, in certain circumstances of extreme suffering, assisted suicide or euthanasia might be morally acceptable and compatible with the exercise of a Christian faith.

■ CHRISTIAN DEBATE ON END-OF-LIFE ISSUES

Withholding and Withdrawal of Treatment

There is a long tradition in the Christian Church that allows for the withholding or withdrawal of therapies that are deemed to be useless and disproportionately burdensome. This is based on the premise that such therapies serve to prolong the dying process rather than to save life. Gula (1994) pointed out that such omissions and acts are not considered to be killing and that, from a moral point of view, withholding treatment is to be evaluated in the same way as withdrawing treatment. This position assumes a moral distinction between killing and allowing to die. In the Roman Catholic tradition, this is clearly set out in the encyclical of Pope Pius XII (1953), *Divine Aflante Spiritu.* In this encyclical, Pius XII made the well-known distinction between ordinary and extraordinary treatment, a distinction he repeated in his address to the Italian Anaesthesiological Society in 1957 and one that was reiterated in the 1981 Vatican Declaration on Euthanasia (Lane, 1985). Practical application of this teaching was demonstrated in the intervention of the Roman Catholic Church in the case of Karen Ann Quinlan in which Bishop Joseph Casey gave support to the request for removal of artificial ventilation on the grounds that it constituted extraordinary treatment that was both ineffective and unduly burdensome.

The acceptance of a distinction between killing and letting one die is apparent in a range of reports and discussion documents of a variety of denominations. The Anglican report titled *On Dying Well,* for example, expressed the concept in the following way:

Euthanasia implies killing, and it is misleading to extend it to cover decisions
not to preserve life by artificial means when it would be better for the patient
to be allowed to die. Such decisions, coupled with determination to give the
patient as good a death as possible, may be quite legitimate. (Church Information Office, 1975, p. 61)

Across the denominations, there has been consistent support for, and practical participation in, the development of effective palliative care and pain control, even where such pain relief might accelerate a patient's death. What is
seen to be critical here is the nature of intention. In neither case, it is argued, is
the intention to kill the patient. Rather, it is to provide comfort for the patient
during his or her dying while allowing the natural disease process to run its
course. To oppose this natural process is to deny respect for the person. Resist-
ing death and dying, it is argued, is not respectful of the gift of life; it diminishes a respect for the sanctity of life and falsely asserts human control over
life. What the Christian Church is called to do is not to preserve life at all costs.
Instead, it is to provide a suffering person with a community of faith, comfort,
love, and support.

Within recent years, however, there has been significant criticism of this
distinction between killing and letting one die (Gula, 1994). Some argue that
there is no moral difference at all. Such a position is supported by the Hemlock
Society and by philosophers such as Jonathan Glover, Peter Singer, and James
Rachels. For example, Rachels (1986) contended that the distinction is quite
simply a difference in the way in which actions to terminate life are described;
whether others actively participate in bringing about the death of the person or
passively allow him or her to die makes no moral difference. Thus, according
to Rachels, our acceptance of allowing someone to die ought to include active
killing when such killing is more merciful, and some would argue that this
position is compatible with Christian obligations to love. Others, while maintaining the distinction, argue that in extreme circumstances it might not be held
to apply. Ramsey (1970, 1978), for example, did not in principle accept euthanasia on the grounds that it breached a covenantal fidelity that is owed to others. But Ramsey, a Protestant, did support the view that some patients, such as
those in irreversible comas and those suffering intractable pain, might have
moved beyond a point at which they are able to receive care and comfort, and
at that point the distinction between killing and letting one die simply dis-
solves.

Although such discussion has carried some weight, generally the Christian churches have maintained that intention is important and is central to a

necessary distinction. In the case of withdrawal of ineffective treatment, a doctor does not kill a patient but simply removes artificial barriers to the natural process of dying. A distinction is to be made "between what we intend and the foreseeable consequences of our actions" (Anglican Church of Canada, 1998, p. 21). Even so, as Kirk (1927) pointed out, simply because a distinction is made, it does not follow that we have no moral responsibility for the foreseen consequences of our actions. What might be argued here is that a serious commitment to a Christian ethos requires that our actions and their foreseeable consequences be examined in the light of a faith response of caring.

Suicide and Christianity

The Christian condemnation of killing generally has been held to apply to the taking of one's own life. Although it is clear that there is nothing in the Scriptures analogous to contemporary understanding of physician-assisted suicide or euthanasia, some Christians have argued that the accounts of suicide in Scripture may provide a basis for its justification. There are, in fact, few accounts of suicide in the Bible, and none of these includes explicit discussion of the moral status of the act (Lockman Foundation, 1977). They are, rather, biographical accounts of those who have committed suicide to avoid shame and dishonor.

Traditionally, however, the condemnation of suicide has been strong. The 1997 Report of the Episcopal Diocese of Washington pointed out, "The silence of Scripture on the moral status of suicide cannot be counted as approval of or indifference to the practice" (Cohen, 1996, p. 371). In his *City of God,* Saint Augustine (1963) condemned suicide as a cowardly act in the face of pain and suffering. In the *Summa Theologica,* Saint Thomas Aquinas (1947-1948), adopting the view of the Jewish scholar Maimonides, made the claim that suicide violates a natural self-love, offends the community, and offends God who gives the gift of life, which must not be disrespectfully abandoned under any circumstances. In the Protestant tradition, neither Luther nor Calvin approved of suicide or taking the life of another in the face of suffering (despite their own experiences of extreme ill health).

The document by the Episcopal Diocese of Washington (1997) noted several examples of Christians who wrote positively of suicide and euthanasia. In his *Utopia* (1949), Thomas More (a Roman Catholic) appears to depict Utopia as a place in which suicide and euthanasia were to be encouraged for those suffering terminal illness and great pain. This work, nevertheless, is considered to have been satirical in form, a claim that is supported by the fact that More, while awaiting his own execution, wrote *A Dialogue of Comfort: Against Tribulation*, in which he argued against such acts. The Christian poet and Anglican divine, John Donne, wrote a defense of suicide in his *Biathanatos*, (1982) but it does not appear that he defended the act for purposes of self-interest. During the 20th century, some Anglican writers have suggested that euthanasia and assisted suicide may be morally permissible to end extreme suffering at the end of life (Fletcher, 1954; Inge, 1930; Rashdell, 1907). Fletcher (1954), for example, argued that the overriding moral commitment for Christians is one of love and that, in practice, this will mean a necessary response to the particular situations of those who are suffering. He suggested that euthanasia, in some circumstances, might be the appropriate Christian response in affirming the dignity of the person and in preventing the dehumanizing realities of terminal illness, which can deprive an individual of the meaning and worth he or she has experienced in life.

Küng (1995), a Catholic theologian, recently added his voice, albeit tentatively, to this debate. It must be noted that Küng is at variance with traditional and formally accepted Roman Catholic teaching, but on this topic he posed an interesting argument. He maintained that suicide in response to situations of despair, such as the breakup of a relationship, a career collapse, or a generalized tiredness in life, are irresponsible and morally illegitimate for Christians. He argued, however, that it might be acceptable within a Christian context to accept the possibility of providing active help in dying for those who are at the end of their lives, who are going irreversibly toward death, and whose suffering is unbearable.

Küng (1995) based his claim on a modification of the traditional arguments, grounded in beliefs about the gift of life and God's sovereignty over life. He asserted that an understanding of life as a gift from God encompasses an understanding of a gift of freedom and responsibility for life. He stated, "With freedom, God has also given human beings the right to utter self-determination" (p. 30). Thus, he held that "no one should be compelled or even urged to die a day or even an hour earlier than he or she wants. But conversely, no one should be forced to go on living at all costs" (p. 31). From these claims, Küng argued that as part of God's gift, a person ought to be enabled to choose to end a life of unbearable suffering in a responsible manner that takes others into account but allows a dignified death. He saw the traditional commitment to a belief that people must endure their "ordained end" as founded on a misguided view of God taken from one-dimensional and literal interpretations of Biblical texts. Küng wrote,

So, for the terminally ill, our theological task is not a spiritualizing and mysti-fication of suffering or even a pedagogical use of suffering but—in the foot-steps of Jesus, who healed the sick—one of reducing and removing suffering as far as possible.... There are said to be theologians who fear a "society free of suffering"—and one asks what kind of world they live in. Indeed, there are theologians who in this connection call for a "share in Christ's suffering"—as though Jesus would have argued for the intolerable suffering of a terminally ill patient kept alive on drugs. (pp. 26-27)

With these reflections, Küng made a plea, even within the context of Catholic moral theology, for a shift from "rigoristic standpoints" to an emphasis on "hu-man values to which biologic life is subordinate" (p. 37).

Exceptions such as these within the Christian tradition are, however, rare and especially so in a Catholic faith context. Generally, the prohibitions of euthanasia and suicide persist. Nevertheless, these comments refer to formal writings, and it is not known in any conclusive way what views exist at an infor-mal level. This is complicated further by the fact that even where polls have been taken of the "ordinary person in the pew," it remains unclear just what the definitional understanding of those surveyed might be. What does seem to be clear is that, as the social and theological debate continues, more intensive dis-cussion will and must arise within the Church and across its denominations.

■ VALUES INFLUENCING ARGUMENTS FOR AND AGAINST ASSISTED SUICIDE AND EUTHANASIA

Arguments in the Christian tradition for and against assisted suicide and euthanasia rest largely, then, on values and beliefs with respect to life as a gift, sanctity of life, the sovereignty of God, and stewardship.

Life as the Gift of God

According to Christian belief, life is God's gift to us and is our responsibil-ity. It is a belief derived from the creation narratives found in the book of Gene-sis (1:2-4). As God's gift, life is not our own and may not be discarded at will. Life is given to us in sacred trust, and our role is one of responsible steward-ship. But that stewardship is limited by the sovereignty of God (Genesis 2:7), and our oversight does not extend to a right to take life. This foundation under-pins the traditional Christian rejection of assisted suicide and euthanasia.

Some, however, have pointed to the inconsistencies in Christian teaching given the exceptions to the rule against taking life, noted previously, in the context of war and in defense of capital punishment. Because such exceptions to the commandment against killing have been accepted, some have argued that similar exceptions might be extended to allow the taking of a life to alleviate pain and suffering near death.

It also might be argued that, as a gift, life is for the service of God and others. Where this ceases to be possible because of extreme illness and unremitting suffering, the experience of life no longer is one of a gift but rather is one of a burden. In the face of such meaninglessness, might it not be acceptable to end that life, confident of a loving God's mercy? Nevertheless, a belief in life as a gift of God suggests that Christians should be wary of the rhetoric of individual autonomy in its abstract formulations that seem to imply that life is one's own to dispose of at will. Such a position clearly runs counter to a very fundamental Christian belief in the sovereignty of God.

Sanctity of Life

The Christian belief in God as the creator and sustainer of life underpins and entails an attitude of respect and reverence for life. Acknowledgment of the sanctity of life is a deeply held Christian principle in recognition that the person is made in the image of God. Although it does not encompass the belief that life is an absolute good to be preserved at all costs, it does provide the foundation for the Christian Church's generally held prohibition of assisted suicide and euthanasia. But some commentators have suggested that because life is not held as an absolute good, a distinction might be drawn between simply biological life and a quality of life that makes possible the living out of a life of faith in relationship to God and others. When this no longer is a possibility, might it be the case that life can be terminated at its end and in the face of intense suffering, and might this be a more appropriate expression of respect for the sanctity of life? This is supported by the notion that, for a Christian, faith is marked by a promise of redemption and resurrection. Once again, however, the views that support such arguments seemingly are in the minority within the Church.

Autonomy

Respect for a principle of autonomy has taken primacy in secular expressions of bioethics in North America. It also is at the center of arguments that support the individual's right to choose to terminate his or her life. Christians have compelling reasons to give respect to the principle because a central element of the image of God that we bear is our capacity to make free choices. Some have, therefore, held that we have a right to choose to end our lives when we no longer are able to render service to God or others. This position was made clear in the report prepared by the Episcopal Diocese of Newark (1996) in which it was stated that assisted death would be acceptable if the decision to hasten death was a free and informed one. In this way, autonomy and control of the process of dying are in the hands of the dying person. In the argument proffered by Küng (1995), this line of thinking also is apparent. What remains unclear, however, is whether the concept of autonomy that is enshrined in the pervading liberal individualism of North American society is so clearly compatible with Christian faith. Opponents of assisted suicide and euthanasia in the Christian Church appeal to principles of divine sovereignty and common good.

As we have seen, a Christian belief in life as a gift encompasses an attitude of reverence for life that is not properly exercised by placing others at the disposal of one's intentions or to serve some utilitarian end. This view entails an assertion that God has absolute dominion over creation, in which we share but in a limited way (Gula, 1994). The responsibilities that we have are those of stewardship, not ownership. Haring (1973) stated that we exercise our freedom by accepting ourselves as belonging to God and in facing our powerlessness over death. Human freedom does not extend to a right to bring about our death at a time or in a manner specified by us.

Even those writing within the secular context have begun to question the ways in which abstract ethical principles, of which autonomy is the preeminent one, are to be applied. In the current applications, a sense of the context within which such principles are exercised has been lost. Of this, O'Neill (1993) stated that abstract principles may serve as guides but do not provide an algorithm for judgment. Such principles somehow refer to abstract individuals, and "a world of abstract individuals assumes away relations of dependence and independence" (p. 303). This might especially be the case within the context of serious illness, dying, and death. O'Neill's view also is one that seems to fit with ease the Christian understandings of encompassing community and mutuality.

Moreover, the view in turn dovetails into issues concerning common good. For a Christian, living is or ought to be about living with and for others. Strong arguments have been put forward that a Christian understanding of autonomy necessarily entails individual limits for the well-being of others more generally. The argument is that there is a "good" for society as a whole that is a good beyond that of the individual person. In this framework, individual interests are respected and served, but ultimately the collective good is the greater. Indeed, individuals flourish within such societies (Dougherty, 1993; Gula, 1994). From this standpoint, the issues of assisted suicide and euthanasia are essentially social community issues and do not belong primarily to the realm of individual choices. Following this line of thinking, Callahan (1992) progressed to address so-called "slippery slope" arguments in which he claimed that the practice of euthanasia would threaten to weaken the general prohibition against killing in society and that we would end up valuing life less. Such thinking clearly also is encapsulated in the papal encyclical *Evangelium Vitae* in which John Paul II (1995) referred to the contemporary "culture of death" and the need for Christians to affirm life. This view has been echoed in the reports of numerous Christian denominations, albeit with somewhat varying interpretations of what it is to be life affirming. Generally, it is such views around autonomy that hold sway in the Christian community despite the dissenting voices in the Church.

Compassion

One of the more initially attractive arguments made in favor of assisted suicide and euthanasia by some Christians is based on an appeal to Christian compassion. As we have seen, this is the approach used by Fletcher (1954, 1966). Advocates of this view claim that, in some extreme circumstances, the ending of a life of insurmountable suffering not only is consistent with Christian teachings on compassion but also might be the desired Christian response to such suffering, one that best maintains the dignity of the person made in the image and likeness of God. But others would argue that in most circumstances, suffering represents frank evidence of failure on the part of the Christian community and the community at large. At a practical level, there is considerable evidence that in our contemporary society, in which costs of care are being downloaded onto patients and their families, technological interventions prevail inappropriately. Time is consumed by an absorption in models of material productivity, and there is little real commitment to community for those who suffer. Moreover, there is strong evidence of the underuse or inappropriate application of pain relief. The majority of Christian commentators have seen this as a challenge to those who espouse Christian values of life and care rather than as an argument for assisted suicide and euthanasia. In her recent book, *Stewards of Life,* Wheeler (1996) stated this eloquently:

> Unlike the prevailing culture, which must deny death at all costs since it shares no account of a good more fundamental than survival, Christian communities live in the belief that life is directed toward and fulfilled in the knowledge and love of God, goods which cannot be thwarted by death. These convictions can enable a kind of courage and even cheerfulness in the face of death that does not depend on the pretense of personal invulnerability. Thus, Christians need not flee from the intimations of our own mortality which are inevitably borne by the sick and the dying. We will look, therefore, for a greater readiness to be with, and to be truthful with, the sick and those facing death. (p. 24)

■ COMMON CONCERNS AND SHARED PERCEPTIONS

A discussion document, *Care in Dying* (Anglican Church of Canada, 1998), places emphasis on the importance of concerns and perceptions that unite even those who disagree deeply on certain approaches to end-of-life decision making. In a report prepared by the Committee on Medical Ethics of the Episcopal Diocese of Washington (1997), such shared foundations are outlined clearly:

> [Both] Christians who accept and those who reject assisted suicide and euthanasia share certain convictions. Both have a sense of the sovereignty of God; both want to protect human dignity and individual freedom to choose how to confront human finitude and death; both view life as a good in relationship to the broader purposes of life; both recognize that human life, especially in situations of death and dying, can confront us with conflict between physical life and other purposes or goods of life; [and] both feel compassion toward those who suffer at the end of life. Moreover, both recognize that Christian principles of social justice call us to remedy a public policy that provides inadequate social support to the poor and very sick as well as to those who are better off financially yet lack medical and social resources during illness. (p. vii)

Thus, there is within the Christian community a broad level of agreement on central theological foundations. Such agreement makes possible continuing dialogue, but it does little to resolve the conflict about the application of those foundations on a practical level.

■ CONCLUSION

From all that has been said in this chapter, it is clear that there is no single Christian response to problematic questions around issues relating to end-of-life decision making. There is, however, a generally prevailing ethos that is consistent with that described by Alexander in this volume about the Roman Catholic perspectives (Chapter 11). Nevertheless, such a view does not go un-challenged across all the denominations. Although this creates difficulty for the articulation of one Christian stance, it should be kept in mind that there is more that is shared in common than is disagreed on. This paves the way for continuing and sensitive dialogue in the community and might provide an ef-fective basis for the involvement of the Church across denominations and with others in the very practical concerns of those who suffer.

In the end, this is not so much a theological debate for the community as it is a challenge to pastoral care, and there is a great deal to be done to address these issues in the community. A task for the Church at present is to continue to wrestle with such questions and problems by appealing to our common heri-tage in faith. It will be a task that demands of the Church a critical, analytical, and caring role consistent with the teachings of Jesus Christ.

■ REFERENCES

Anderson, T. (1993). *Walking the way: Christian ethics as a guide.* Toronto: United Church Pub-lishing House.

Anglican Church of Canada. (1998, June). *Care in dying: A consideration of the practices of euthanasia and physician-assisted suicide.* Paper prepared for discussion at the Synod meeting by the Task Group of the Faith, Worship, and Ministry Committee of the Anglican Church of Canada, Montreal.

Augustine, Saint. (1963). *City of God* (J. W. C. Ward, Trans.). London: Oxford University Press.

Baril, A., & Mori, G. (1991). Leaving the Fold: Declining church attendance. In *Canadian Social Trends* (p. 1). Ottawa: Statistics Canada.

Brierly, P. (Ed.). (1997). *World churches handbook.* London: Christian Research Association.

Callahan, D. (1992). When self-determination runs amok. *Hastings Center Report, 22,* 52-55.

Canada Executive. (1994, June). *Caring for the dying: Choices and decisions.* Paper approved for discussion in the congregations of the United Church of Canada by the Division of Mission in Canada Executive, Toronto.

Church Information Office. (1975). *On dying well: An Anglican contribution to the debate on euthanasia* (General Synod Board for Social Responsibility). London: Author.

Cohen, C. B. (1996). Christian perspectives on assisted suicide and euthanasia: The Anglican tra-dition. *Journal of Law, Medicine, and Ethics, 24,* 369-379.

Donne, J. (1982). *Biathanatos* (M. Rudick & M. P. Battin, Eds.). New York: Garland.

Dougherty, C. (1993). The common good: Terminal illness and euthanasia. *Issues in Law and Medicine, 9,* 151-166.

Episcopal Diocese of Newark. (1996). *Report on the Task Force on Assisted Suicide.* Paper presented at the annual convention of the Episcopal Diocese of Newark, Newark, NJ.

Episcopal Diocese of Washington. (1997). *Are assisted suicide and euthanasia morally acceptable for Christians? Perspectives to consider* (Report of the Committee on Medical Ethics). Washington, DC: Author.

Fletcher, J. (1954). *Morals and medicine.* Princeton, NJ: Princeton University Press.

Fletcher, J. (1966). *Situation ethics.* Philadelphia: Westminster Press.

Gula, R. M. (1994). *Euthanasia: Moral and pastoral perspectives.* New York: Paulist Press.

Haring, B. (1973). *Medical ethics.* Notre Dame, IN: Fides Publishers.

Inge, W. R. (1930). *Christian ethics and moral problems.* New York: Putnam.

John Paul II. (1993). *Veritatis splendor: Encyclical letter.* London: Catholic Truth Society.

John Paul II. (1995). *Evangelium vitae: The gospel of life.* Boston: Pauline Books and Media.

Kirk, K. (1927). *Conscience and its problems: An introduction to casuistry.* London: Longmans, Green.

Küng, H. (1995). A dignified dying. In H. Küng & W. Jens (Eds.), *A dignified dying: A plea for personal responsibility* (pp. 1-40). London: SCM Press.

Lane, G. A. (1985). *Euthanasia: A survey of world religions on the right to die.* Los Angeles: Hemlock Publishing.

Lockman Foundation. (1977). *New American standard Bible.* La Habra, CA: Author.

More, T. (1949). *Utopia* (H. V. S. Ogden, Trans.). New York: Appleton-Century Crofts.

O'Neill, O. (1993). Justice, gender, and international boundaries. In M. C. Nussbaum & A. Sen (Eds.), *The quality of life* (pp. 303-323). Oxford, UK: Clarendon.

Pius XII. (1953). *Divine aflante spiritu: Encyclical letter.* Rome: Roman Catholic Church.

Rachels, J. (1986). *The end of life: Euthanasia and morality.* New York: Oxford University Press.

Ramsey, P. (1970). *The patient as person.* New Haven, CT: Yale University Press.

Ramsey, P. (1978). *Ethics at the edges of life.* New Haven, CT: Yale University Press.

Rashdell, H. (1907). *The theory of good and evil: A treatise on moral philosophy.* Oxford, UK: Clarendon.

Saint Thomas of Aquinas. (1947-1948). *Summa theologica.* New York: Benziger Brothers.

Talbert, C. H. (1991). *Learning through suffering: The educative value of suffering in the New Testament and its milieu.* Collegeville, MN: Liturgical Press.

Wheeler, S. E. (1996). *Stewards of life: Bioethics and pastoral care.* Nashville, TN: Abingdon Press.

Williams, A. (1998, May). *When life is at stake: Theological reflections on end-of-life decision making.* Paper presented at the annual Palliative Care Conference, Toronto.

Chapter 11

Catholic Perspectives on Euthanasia and Assisted Suicide: The Human Person and the Quest for Meaning

MARC R. ALEXANDER

The Catholic community is as diverse as it is large, with communities throughout the world. Available statistics from the *Catholic Almanac* indicate that, worldwide, nearly 976 million people, or 17% of the total population, are Catholic (Our Sunday Visitor Press, 1997). There are two branches of the Catholic Church—the Roman Catholic or Latin Church and the Eastern Catholic Rites or Churches—each with its own rituals and legal system. Both the Latin and Eastern Churches fall under the pastoral care and teaching of the pope in Rome. In the United States, Catholics comprise 23% of the population, with membership in excess of 61 million (P. J. Kenedy & Sons, 1997).

AUTHOR'S NOTE: For more information on the Catholic perspective, I recommend contacting the secretariat for pro-life activities, National Conference of Catholic Bishops, 3211 Fourth Street, N.E., Washington, DC 20017-1194; phone: (202) 541-3070; fax: (202) 541-3054. I acknowledge the assistance of Richard Doerflinger of that office and Rev. Kevin O'Rourke, director of the Center for Health Care Ethics, Saint Louis University, for bibliographical and content assistance. I also acknowledge Pat Gates, application support specialist, University of Hawaii at Manoa, for assistance in obtaining literature. I, however, am responsible for any errors.

The attitudes of Catholics, and even of the population in general, concerning end-of-life issues are difficult to ascertain. In general, one can safely say that Catholics oppose assisted suicide, support compassionate help for the dying (e.g., pain management, hospice), and base their position on religious convictions. Several surveys specific to physician-assisted death have been reported. For example, a survey conducted by the Tarrance Group (1994) for the National Conference of Catholic Bishops found that 73% of Catholics who attend mass weekly opposed physician-assisted suicide because of religious beliefs. In a survey of physicians, Shapiro, Derse, and Gottlieb (1994) found that 79% of Catholic physicians would be unwilling to perform euthanasia and suggested that their religious beliefs might influence this stance. Similar findings were reported by Baume and Bauman (1995) and Waddell, Clarnette, and Kellehear (1996) in Australia, by Verhoef and Kinsella (1996) in Alberta, and by Siaw and Tan (1996) in Hawaii. The reasons for this stance are discussed in this chapter.

■ AN OVERVIEW OF CATHOLIC AUTHORITY

The Catholic Church is a community of faith committed to continuing the mission and work of Jesus Christ. The primary reference for information about the nature of the Catholic Church, its mission, and its structure is found in a document called *Lumen Gentium* (Dogmatic Constitution on the Church) (Vatican II, 1964). The Church bases its teachings in faith and morals (Fransen, 1978-1979) on Scripture (both canonical books of the Old Testament and New Testament) and on Tradition (the collective wisdom of the Church as it reflects on the meaning of Scripture for our lives). Another document, *Dei Verbum* (Dogmatic Constitution on Divine Revelation), discusses how divine revelation is transmitted in Scripture and passed on through Tradition (Vatican II, 1965a). The entire process is empowered by the Holy Spirit through the ministry of the official teaching office of the Church, the magisterium, composed of bishops in union with the pope.

Worldwide, there are 3,267 bishops, some 2,500 of whom are responsible for specific geographical territories called *dioceses* (Our Sunday Visitor Press, 1997; Vatican, 1996). Each bishop has "ordinary" authority in his diocese, although each reports to the pope every 5 years. Contrary to popular belief, the pope does not interfere in the normal operation of a diocese. It is the teaching of the magisterium—not of theologians, philosophers, and scientists—that demmands the particular attention of believers when dealing with matters of faith and morals.

Lumen Gentium distinguishes between teachings that require "adherence of faith" and those that require "a religious respect." Whereas these distinctions were incorporated into the Codes of Canon Law for both the Roman (Vatican, 1983) and Eastern Churches (Vatican, 1990), Pope John Paul II in 1998 issued *Ad Tuendam Fidem,* which added a third category, integrating it into both codes of canon law. This new category fell in between the previously defined two and required that teachings on "faith and morals" that have been "definitively" set forth by the magisterium must be "firmly accepted and held." For the first time, the official commentary included with this document offered examples of teachings for each of the three categories. The prohibition against euthanasia is a "definitive" teaching. Other writings recognize the right of members to make their opinions known, with "due regard for the integrity of faith and morals" (Vatican II, 1964, § 37). Different church documents enjoy different levels of authority, but the exact determination of such authority is not always simple (Sullivan, 1996). In a somewhat simplified form, one may say that a teaching has increasing authority as it finds increased testimony and support from the magisterium, especially the pope, over time. Thus, in this chapter, I concentrate on magisterial documents, using other resources to the extent that they clarify and amplify official teaching.

Although the Catholic Church does not decide doctrine in a democratic manner, it would be incorrect to conclude that the faithful have no role to play. *Lumen Gentium* affirms the classic concept of the *sensus fidei,* or the sense of the faith, which inspires members of the Church to give witness to the truth of a teaching in the practice of their lives (Beinert, 1995; Vatican II, 1964, § 12, 37). Thus, the witness of active Catholics is an important preparation and affirmation of the Church's teaching.

The subsequent sections examine central topics critical to a Catholic understanding and approach to end-of-life issues, especially in regard to the question of assisted suicide and euthanasia. This chapter is limited to the Catholic perspective, although most of what is written would be compatible with general Christian teaching. Furthermore, because literature addressing specific topics from a Catholic perspective is abundant, this chapter focuses on critical principles that too frequently are overlooked but that underpin Catholic teaching on specific issues. O'Rourke and Boyle (1993) provide a convenient resource that contains excerpts from many Catholic documents on issues of medical ethics. In general, the Catholic approach to moral issues is characterized by its appeal to natural law (Gula, 1989), that is, that right and wrong can be determined on the basis of reason and our common human nature. In this chapter, however, I approach the subject from the perspective of religious belief that, according to Catholic teaching, is compatible with natural law.

■ THE CATHOLIC UNDERSTANDING OF THE HUMAN PERSON

The understanding of the human person remains the backdrop for every discussion involving human action (Ashley & O'Rourke, 1997). Vatican II's (1965b) *Gaudium et Spes* (Pastoral Constitution on the Church in the Modern World) placed the human person at the very center of attention. It also asked the question, but what is the human person? In answering this question and addressing special issues of contemporary concern, the document and its official commentary (Vatican II, 1965c) made clear that the morality of human actions must be "determined by objective standards" that are "based on the nature of the human person and his [or her] acts" (Vatican II, 1965b, § 51). The commentary noted, in particular, that the human person must be "integrally and adequately considered" (Vatican II, 1965c, § 37-38).

Janssens (1980) provided one of the best analyses of the *Gaudium et Spes* in terms of the description of the human person in all of his or her dimensions. He identified eight fundamental and constant dimensions of the person that must be respected to guarantee the dignity of the human person. In effect, Janssens demonstrated that the magisterium offers, through *Gaudium et Spes,* a fundamental description of the human person adequately considered that must be used in assessing the morality of any human action (Vatican II, 1965b). This will form the basis for the Church's more specific teaching in regard to end-of-life issues in general and to assisted suicide and euthanasia in particular.

The Human Person Is a Subject

The person may not be treated as an object or as a means to an end (Vatican II, 1965b, § 27). As a subject, the person is able to act responsibly (§ 31, 55), in freedom (§ 17), and in accord with his or her conscience (§ 16). The fundamental dignity of the human person flows from our creation in the image of God (Genesis 1:26; Vatican II, 1965b, § 12, 24), saved by Jesus Christ (Ephesians 1:10; I Timothy 2:4-6; Vatican II, 1965b, § 13, 22), and destined to eternal life with God (I Corinthians 15:42-57; Vatican II, 1965b, § 18, 39). Expressed another way, we believe that God has created everything and everyone and that God alone is the author of life. Human beings, therefore, are stewards of creation, including our own lives.

The Human Person Has a Body

The body is part of who and what we are and, together with the spiritual, forms one being (Vatican II, 1965b, § 14). Consequently, anything that affects the body also affects the person. Thus, we are obligated to respect and maintain our own health and balance of life as well as that of others (§ 27).

The Human Person Is Part of the Material World

The things of the world are seen as fundamentally good with the potential to be further developed. Through our labor, the goods of the world are used for the benefit of the human community (Vatican II, 1965b, § 33-39) and for the development of culture (§ 53-62). Using our gifts, we are called to "unfold the Creator's work" (§ 34).

The Human Person Is in Relationship to Other Human Persons

We need to be in relationship with others (e.g., parents, siblings, friends, spouses) to develop fully as human persons (Vatican II, 1965b, § 12). It is in this context that the man-woman relationship in marriage has special importance (Genesis 1:27; Vatican II, 1965b, § 48-49).

To Be a Human Person Is to Be Part of a Community

We do not just relate to others as individuals, we participate in society (Vatican II, 1965b, § 23-32). We require structures and institutions to prosper (§ 25, 29, 73-76). This social dimension means that we cannot be concerned only about the individual (§ 30); we also must care for the common good (§ 26, 74). Consequently, individual actions must be considered in light of the impact that they might have on the welfare of the community and vice versa.

The Human Person Is in Relationship to God

Having been created in God's image, the human person is fundamentally directed to God and finds his or her happiness in doing God's will. As such, we maximize our potential as humans when we come to know, worship, and glorify our God (Vatican II, 1965b, § 12, 34-39, 48). God's sovereignty is acknowledged through this dimension.

The Human Person Is a Being With a Story/History

To be a human being is to have a past, present, and future. Furthermore, our personal history is deeply intertwined with social history—the past, present, and future of the society of which we are a part (Vatican II, 1965b, § 4-9, 36, 54-59). We affect history and are affected by history (§ 55). To recognize our historicity is to acknowledge that the past has something to teach us, just as the present has something to offer. It is to see that we have a responsibility to the future because we contribute to it today.

The Fundamental Equality and Originality of All Human Persons

Janssens (1980) held that one of *Gaudium et Spes*'s major insights is that "all human persons are fundamentally equal, but at the same time each is an originality" (p. 12). The fundamental equality of every human being is absolutely affirmed (Vatican II, 1965b, § 29). This is why certain moral demands are truly universal; we all share a common nature and dignity, regardless of our sex, age, race, status, and so on. But every human person also is unique, endowed with his or her own gifts and liabilities, personality, and drives. In a highly technological, pragmatic, and globalized world, it is easy for the balance between equality and originality to be upset. When that happens, the human person is compromised.

These eight continuing dimensions define the human person adequately and totally. It is the entire human person, so defined, that must be considered in the evaluation of any human action. When one or another dimension is ignored or demeaned, human dignity is violated. It is within this understanding of the human person that we are now prepared to explore the Church's specific teaching on end-of-life issues.

■ OFFICIAL TEACHING ON END-OF-LIFE ISSUES

When discussing end-of-life issues such as assisted suicide and euthanasia, we should put these subjects within a broader view of the role of religion in health care (Pellegrino & Thomasma, 1997) and, more specifically, the Catholic understanding of illness and death (Catholic Health Association, 1993). As noted in *Gaudium et Spes,* "It is in the face of death that the riddle of human existence becomes most acute" (Vatican II, 1965b, § 18). When facing the prospect of death, the human person experiences not only suffering and questions about life's meaning but also a desire to go on living. The Church teaches that Jesus Christ has come as redeemer to save us from all sin, including a death that comes with the passing of the body (I Corinthians 15:55-57). We believe that the end of our earthly life is not the end of life itself, for God calls us to eternal life (Osborne, 1997; Phan, 1997). Furthermore, as discussed later in the chapter, we believe that suffering, although not something pleasurable, can be redemptive and meaningful.

To be a disciple of Jesus does not mean, however, that we simply wait for eternal life. Just as Jesus Christ responded with love and justice to human suffering and death (Matthew 4:23-25; Mark 1:34; Luke 7:22; John 11:1-57), so must we, as individuals and as a community, who profess to continue his work (Matthew 10:8; Mark 16:15-18; Act 3:6; James 5:13-16). Jesus entered into people's human condition and, by his powerful presence, gave healing and hope to the poor and suffering. What he did, we now continue. In other words, we embrace a Christocentric ethic, even in respect to illness and death (Pellegrino & Thomasma, 1997; Vatican, 1992; Vorgrimler, 1992). The Catholic Church sees illness as one of those special occasions during which one should pray for spiritual and physical healing. This is celebrated in the sacrament of the Anointing of the Sick (Vatican II, 1964, § 11), which draws the faithful closer to God by submitting one's illness into divine care.

Within the framework of the Catholic understanding of the human person, belief in the saving work of Jesus Christ, and commitment to model our lives after Jesus Christ, we now can look at the Church's specific teaching on euthanasia, assisted suicide, and care of the dying.

Definitions

From the beginning, terms must be carefully defined so as not to create confusion. Whereas the root meaning of *euthanasia* comes from Greek meaning "good death," its common meaning more closely approximates an action or an omission of an action with the intention of relieving suffering by causing the death of a person, even though there is a moral requirement to preserve life (Gula, 1994). The principal components of this definition focus on the intention involved and whether or not there is a moral obligation to preserve life (John Paul II, 1995; National Conference of Catholic Bishops, 1994; Vatican, 1980).

Three additional distinctions frequently are recognized: voluntary euthanasia (the person wants to be euthanized), involuntary euthanasia (the person does not want to be euthanized), and nonvoluntary euthanasia (the wish of the person is unknown). In euthanasia per se, an agent other than the dying person carries out the requisite action or inaction, whereas in the case of assisted suicide, the agent only provides the means for death and the dying person carries out the actual action. Because the direct agent of death and the assisting agent have morally equivalent roles, the ethical analysis of euthanasia and assisted suicide is the same. Thus, from now on in this chapter, the use of the term *euthanasia* includes assisted suicide.

Perhaps the most important distinction to be drawn in this debate is between euthanasia and *allowing the patient to die* (Ashley & O'Rourke, 1997). In the case of euthanasia, death is caused by human intervention or nonintervention. In the case of allowing the patient to die, the fatal pathology causes the death. In the first case, one intends to eliminate suffering by causing death, even though one is morally obliged in that situation to support life. In the second case, after having examined all necessary information, the patient or proxy has determined that therapeutic options are not effective and/or carry too great a burden for the person and/or community. In this case, the intention is not to cause death so as to eliminate suffering; rather, one seeks to avoid futile treatment and disproportionate burden, allowing the patient to die with human dignity intact. This is the proper context within which the discussion of withholding or withdrawing nutrition and hydration should take place, and it is why the subject is not addressed separately in church documents. It should be noted that, to date, there has been no definitive teaching concerning the use of artificial nutrition and hydration for those who are in persistent vegetative states or irreversible comas (National Conference of Catholic Bishops, 1992). Thus, the same principles of burden, benefit, and futility must be applied on an individual case-by-case basis. As explained previously, euthanasia is not permissible, whereas allowing the patient to die is permissible and at times might even be morally obligated (John Paul II, 1995; National Conference of Catholic Bishops, 1994; Vatican, 1980).

Two final expressions can be defined briefly. *Futile treatment* is a therapeutic intervention that is deemed likely to fail in curing, benefiting, or aiding
the patient. *Disproportionate burden* refers to a treatment that entails excessive
hardship on the patient and/or community. The assessment of burden and benefit must include physical, social, psychological, and spiritual factors and circumstances. For example, it might be appropriate in a particular case to prolong life to give a person an opportunity to better prepare for death. On the
other hand, to forgo a treatment that is burdensome is not euthanasia. Too often, people continue to equate refusal to undergo a burdensome treatment with
passive euthanasia. Although it is preferable not to use the expression *passive
euthanasia,* it more properly refers to withheld or denied treatment that is morally obligated with the intention to end life. Although the basic definitions of
these expressions are straightforward, their identification and application in
specific cases are more nebulous and subjective, requiring prudential judgment on the part of the patient. Such a judgment more closely resembles art
than science. Having defined some basic terms and distinctions, we now high-
light four principles that are the pillars of the Church's teaching against euthanasia, drawing from official church documents by John Paul II (1995) and the
Vatican (1980) as well as from professional (O'Rourke, 1996) and popular literature (Gregory, 1997; McGann, 1997).

Sanctity of Human Life

First, human life is sacred. It is basic, fundamental, and the condition for
all other rights. Life is a precious gift of love from God that is to be cherished
and nurtured. Euthanasia, as an act against life, is just as wrong as murder. As
O'Rourke (1996) summarized,

> According to Catholic teaching, human life is a gift of God's love which we
> are called upon to preserve and make fruitful; intentionally causing one's own
> death (through suicide or euthanasia) is equally wrong as murder. Through
> suicide, one fails to fulfill one's responsibility to God, violates one's own
> natural desire to exist, betrays self-love, and injures one's own community.
> The human person is created individually by God; thus, the human person is
> dependent upon God, even though the person freely cooperates with God in
> achieving his/her destiny. (pp. 442-443)

Thus, euthanasia, from the perspective of the sanctity of life alone, violates at
least five dimensions of the human person adequately considered. This is

why *Gaudium et Spes* specifically called euthanasia an infamy (Vatican II, 1965b, § 27).

The Dominion and Sovereignty of God Over Life

Second, God has absolute dominion and sovereignty over life. This builds on the sanctity of life. This principle must be carefully nuanced. On the one hand, it must not be interpreted in a way that removes all freedom and responsibility from the human person. God has made us stewards of creation, including life, and in exercising our stewardship we use reason and freedom. Believing that life is not reduced to biological life, we do not cling to material life as if it is all that there is. Thus, for example, we are able to make decisions concerning medical treatment based on the totality of the human person, not merely on his or her biological dimension.

On the other hand, to acknowledge God's sovereignty is to reject the claim of absolute autonomy of the human person. We are held accountable for our actions by God, and we cannot view our actions in an individualist way, in isolation from God and others. In *Veritatis Splendor* (The Splendor of the Truth), John Paul II (1993) stated, "Man's genuine moral autonomy in no way means the rejection but rather the acceptance of the moral law, of God's command.... Human freedom and God's law meet and are called to intersect" (§ 41). Accordingly, genuine freedom is expressed when we choose to act in a way that respects human dignity, that is, is consonant with the nature of the human person (Vatican II, 1965b, § 51; John Paul II, 1993, § 40).

Love and True Mercy

Third, we are called to embrace a path exhibiting love and true mercy. Again and again in the documents of the Church, there is the plea for genuine compassion for the ill and those near death. The example of the Good Samaritan (Luke 10:29-37) serves as a model of compassionate action, which means that one does not kill but rather shares in the pain and suffering of another. True compassion assists those who are ill to find meaning and worth and to experience hope in the victory of Jesus Christ and the promise of resurrection. Finally, true compassion seeks ways in which to alleviate pain and suffering, even if life is unintentionally shortened. Hospice programs are a good example of compassionate care. Pellegrino and Thomasma (1997) were insightful when they wrote, "The ancient grounding of medicine in care and compassion is seriously challenged by a biomedical model that defines medicine simply as applied biology" (p. 27). To speak of compassionate care means a commitment to the care of the total person, including the spiritual dimension.

Helping the Poor

Finally, we are committed to a preferential option for the poor. So often, people think only of economic poverty when speaking of the poor. For Christians, the poor refers to anyone who is ostracized, sick, suffering, without the basic necessities of life, or deprived of human dignity (John Paul II, 1995). Thus, following the example of Jesus Christ, we must give special attention to those most in need, most vulnerable, and most isolated. In the church document *Evangelium Vitae* (The Gospel of Life), we read, "It is above all the poor to whom Jesus speaks in his preaching and actions. The crowds of the sick and the outcasts who follow him and seek him out find his words and actions a revelation of the great value of their lives and of how their hope of salvation is well founded" (John Paul II, 1995, § 32).

In the context of end-of-life issues, the poor would include the very sick, elderly, terminally ill, and disabled (Gigliotti, 1997). It is these individuals who are most vulnerable to euthanasia as a means of cost cutting and whose lives might not be deemed as requiring as much protection as others (John Paul II, 1995, § 15). In a lecture at Catholic University of America, Pellegrino (1997) argued that euthanasia would have a deleterious impact on society because it likely would lead to the "devaluation" of certain groups of people, including the disabled and retarded. He also expressed his belief that there would be "economic, social, and political appeal" to shorten some lives.

The Church's concern for the vulnerable is justified by empirical studies. Koenig, Wildman-Hanlon, and Schmader (1996), for example, concluded that whereas frail elderly patients opposed physician-assisted suicide, nearly 60% of their relatives supported it. Furthermore, they found that thoughts of suicide were rare and almost always were linked to clinical depression. The New York State Task Force on Life and the Law (1994) warned that, if legalized, euthanasia and assisted suicide would

> be practiced through the prism of social inequality and prejudice that characterizes the delivery of services in all segments of society, including health care. Those who will be most vulnerable to abuse, error, or indifference are the poor, minorities, and those who are least educated and least empowered. This risk does not reflect a judgment that physicians are more prejudiced or

influenced by race and class than the rest of society, only that they are not exempt from the prejudices manifest in other areas of our collective lives. (p. 125)

From the perspective of Catholic teaching, euthanasia opens the door to another attack on those who are most vulnerable. In our utilitarian and economically minded culture, it is but a short step from a "right to die" to a "duty to die."

The Meaning of Suffering

Nothing moves human beings to tears, even hopelessness, more quickly than the witnessing of suffering and death (John Paul II, 1995). And few experiences still remain as elusive for explanation. This is the focus of *Salvifici Doloris* (On the Christian Meaning of Human Suffering) by John Paul II (1984). To be sure, human suffering cannot be reduced to just a physical component, for to do so would be to deny the wholeness of the human person with his or her physical, psychological, social, and spiritual dimensions. A careful analysis of suffering indicates that a person's spiritual vision has more of an impact on one's experience of suffering than does one's physical condition. The questions that a suffering person asks (e.g., Why am I suffering? Why must I die? How can I bear my pain?) cannot be answered by technology and biology. It is both arrogant and counterfactual to assert that only physical answers and actions are an acceptable response to such questions. In such a situation, euthanasia represents not only the ultimate physical response to the experience of suffering but also the final denial of anything as real except the physical (Catholic Health Association, 1993; John Paul II, 1984).

To the integral experience of suffering, the Catholic tradition brings both a strong commitment to its elimination and a belief that suffering and death can be transformed. At the outset, it must be said that suffering is not linked to sin as it has been, and continues to be, in certain strands of religious thought (John Paul II, 1984, § 10-11; Pellegrino & Thomasma, 1997). Also, no one can escape the experience of suffering, broadly defined. It is part of being human. The question of suffering must then focus on how to deal with it, not on how to avoid it (Hauerwas, 1986). The Catholic Church teaches that suffering finds meaning when compared to the death of Jesus Christ on the cross. We believe that although Christ suffered death, ultimately his free acceptance of his suffering and death was transformed into resurrected life. This not only brought us redemption but also redeems human suffering itself (John Paul II, 1984,

§ 19). Consequently, we are able to discern meaning in suffering, even if we pursue its elimination and acknowledge its mystery. Thus, in *Evangelium Vitae,* we read,

> Living to the Lord also means recognizing that suffering, while still an evil and a trial in itself, can always become a source of good. It becomes such if it is experienced for love and with love through sharing, by God's gracious gift and one's own personal and free choice, in the suffering of Christ crucified. In this way, the person who lives his suffering in the Lord grows more fully conformed to him and more closely associated with his redemptive work on behalf of the Church and humanity. (John Paul II, 1995, § 67)

The experience of illness, suffering, and death also can be an event of love in another way. In the experience of suffering, one may experience love from the human relationships that nurture and define human dignity. Illness and suffering are real occasions for compassion and mercy to be expressed and received. The *ars moriendi* (the art of dying) is practiced when a person is loved and cared for within the community of which he or she is a part. In vulnerability, one can experience selfless love from one's brothers and sisters as well as love in return as one who has only love to give (John Paul II, 1984, § 4). "Even pain and suffering have meaning and value when they are experienced in close connection with love received and given" (John Paul II, 1995, § 97).

Catholics believe that, in caring for the whole person, we must indeed seek to eliminate pain. But suffering can be addressed only by bringing meaning, which is a human phenomenon, to the total event. To avoid this dimension of meaning would be to ignore part of what it means to be a human person, reducing the human person to merely an animal. This point of view diminishes the following argument: We put animals out of their misery, so we should do the same for humans. This represents a denial of the difference between the human person and an animal. Animals have no capacity for meaning, whereas human persons do (Pellegrino & Thomasma, 1997).

■ CONCLUSION

The official teaching of the Catholic Church is founded on a holistic understanding of the human person. It offers a principled approach that steers a middle ground between extremes. On the one side are those who would do anything to "save" the physical self. On the other side are those who stand ready to end life once its "quality" falls below some standard. Although the official teaching of the Church is not always what its members embrace, it does carry a certain undeniable weight. Health care professionals will be able to understand and assist their Catholic patients and families more effectively if they are familiar with the foundation and framework of this belief system.

■ REFERENCES

Ashley, B., & O'Rourke, K. (1997). *Healthcare ethics: A theological analysis* (4th ed.). St. Louis, MO: Catholic Health Association.

Baume, P., & Bauman, A. (1995). Professed religious affiliation and the practice of euthanasia. *Journal of Medical Ethics, 21*(1), 49-54.

Beinert, W. (1995). *Sensus Fidelium.* In W. Beinert & F. S. Fiorenza (Eds.), *Handbook of Catholic theology* (pp. 655-657). New York: Crossroad.

Catholic Health Association. (1993). *Care of the dying: A Catholic perspective.* St. Louis, MO: Author.

Fransen, P. (1978-1979). A short history of the meaning of the formula (*Fides et Mores*). *Louvain Studies, 7,* 270-301.

Gigliotti, L. K. (1997). *Hear my voice: A cry for a truly compassionate society.* Washington, DC: U.S. Catholic Conference.

Gregory, W. D. (1997). *Why the church opposes assisted suicide* (Catholic Update Series). Cincinnati, OH: St. Anthony Messenger Press.

Gula, R. M. (1989). *Reason informed by faith: Foundations of Catholic morality.* Mahwah, NJ: Paulist Press.

Gula, R. M. (1994). *Euthanasia: Moral and pastoral perspectives.* Mahwah, NJ: Paulist Press.

Hauerwas, S. (1986). *Suffering presence: Theological reflections on medicine, the mentally handicapped, and the church.* Notre Dame, IN: University of Notre Dame Press.

Janssens, L. (1980). Artificial insemination: Ethical considerations. *Louvain Studies, 8,* 3-29.

John Paul II. (1984). *Salvifici Doloris* (On the Christian meaning of human suffering). Rome: Vatican Press.

John Paul II. (1993). *Veritatis Splendor* (The splendor of the truth). Rome: Vatican Press.

John Paul II. (1995). *Evangelium Vitae* (The gospel of life). Rome: Vatican Press.

John Paul II. (1998). *Ad Tuendam Fidem* (To protect the faith). Rome: Vatican Press.

Koenig, H. G., Wildman-Hanlon, D., & Schmader, K. (1996). Attitudes of elderly patients and their families toward physician-assisted suicide. *Archives of Internal Medicine, 156,* 2240-2248.

McGann, J. R. (1997). To care for the dying. *Origins, 26,* 640-648.

National Conference of Catholic Bishops. (1992). *Nutrition and hydration: Moral and pastoral reflections.* Washington, DC: Author.

National Conference of Catholic Bishops. (1994). *Ethical and religious directives for Catholic health care services.* Washington, DC: Author.

New York State Task Force on Life and the Law. (1994). *When death is sought: Assisted suicide and euthanasia in the medical context.* New York: Author.

O'Rourke, K. (1996). Physician-assisted suicide: A religious perspective. *St. Louis University Public Law Review, 15,* 433-446.

O'Rourke, K., & Boyle, P. (1993). *Medical ethics: Sources of Catholic teachings* (2nd ed.). Washington, DC: Georgetown University Press.

Osborne, K. B. (1997). *The resurrection of Jesus: New considerations for its theological interpretation.* Mahwah, NJ: Paulist Press.

Our Sunday Visitor Press. (1997). *Catholic almanac.* Huntington, IN: Author.

P. J. Kenedy & Sons. (1997). *The official Catholic directory.* Providence, NJ: Author.

Pellegrino, E. D. (1997, March). *Assisted suicide in medical ethics: In the patient's best interest?* Lecture at Catholic University of America, Washington, DC.

Pellegrino, E. D., & Thomasma, D. C. (1997). *Helping and healing: Religious commitment in health care.* Washington, DC: Georgetown University Press.

Phan, P. C. (1997). *Responses to 101 questions on death and eternal life.* Mahwah, NJ: Paulist Press.

Shapiro, R. S., Derse, A. R., & Gottlieb, M. (1994). Willingness to perform euthanasia: A survey of physician attitudes. *Archives of Internal Medicine, 154,* 575-584.

Siaw, L. K., & Tan, S. Y. (1996). How Hawai'i's doctors feel about physician-assisted suicide and euthanasia: An overview. *Hawai'i Medical Journal, 55,* 296-298.

Sullivan, F. A. (1996). *Creative fidelity: Weighing and interpreting documents of the magisterium.* Mahwah, NJ: Paulist Press.

Tarrance Group. (1994). *A survey of voter attitudes in the United States in the period of September 25-28, 1994.* Houston, TX: Author.

Vatican. (1980). *Declaration on euthanasia.* Rome: Vatican Press.

Vatican. (1983). *Code of canon law, 1983.* Rome: Vatican Press.

Vatican. (1990). *Code of canons of the Eastern churches, 1990.* Rome: Vatican Press.

Vatican. (1992). *Catechism of the Catholic Church.* Rome: Vatican Press.

Vatican. (1996). *Annuario Pontificio.* Rome: Vatican Press.

Vatican II. (1964). *Lumen Gentium* (Dogmatic constitution on the Church). Rome: Vatican Press.

Vatican II. (1965a). *Dei Verbum* (Dogmatic constitution on divine revelation). Rome: Vatican Press.

Vatican II. (1965b). *Gaudium et Spes* (Pastoral constitution on the Church in the modern world). Rome: Vatican Press.

Vatican II. (1965c). *Schema constitutionis pastoralis de Ecclesia in mundo huius temporis: Expensio modorum partis secundae* (Schema for the pastoral constitution on the Church in the modern world). Rome: Vatican Press.

Verhoef, M. J., & Kinsella, D. T. (1996). Alberta euthanasia survey: 3-year follow-up. *Canadian Medical Association Journal, 155,* 885-890.

Vorgrimler, H. (1992). *Sacramental theology* (3rd ed.). Collegeville, MN: Liturgical Press.

Waddell, C., Clarnette, R. M., & Kellehear, A. (1996). Treatment decision-making at the end of life: A survey of Australian doctors' attitudes towards patients' wishes and euthanasia. *Medical Journal of Australia, 165,* 540-544.

Chapter 12

Jewish Perspectives on End-of-Life Decision Making

WILLIAM KAVESH

*M*odern Judaism has its origins in a religious and intellectual tradition dating back about 3,500 years. This tradition includes a wellspring of legal and ethical literature that has been created over that period and that continues to be written to this day as new issues arise. The sources for this chapter are drawn primarily from the writings of contemporary thinkers who represent the major viewpoints of American Jewish religious thought. Although many Jews make important contributions to the general literature of medical ethics, the current review is confined to those who consciously include Jewish sources as part of their intellectual frame of reference. My personal perspective is that of a geriatric physician who has been thinking, teaching, and writing about Jewish medical ethics for more than 20 years.

Demographic data regarding the American Jewish community are presented first, followed by a description of the major religious movements within American Jewry and some perspectives on how Jewish thinking has evolved regarding issues that arise at the end of life. Then, Jewish views regarding autonomy, assisted suicide, pain and suffering, passive euthanasia, and advance directives are discussed. Finally, Jewish healing circles and the national Jewish hospice movement are described.

History of the American Jewish Community

In view of the prominent and, at times, passionate role played by Jews in the sphere of contemporary medical ethics, it often is surprising to many that the worldwide Jewish community numbers only 13 million. The largest concentration of Jews is in the United States, estimated at 5.5 million in 1990 (Goldstein, 1992; Singer & Seldin, 1992).

The Jewish community in America began more than 300 years ago with the arrival of Dutch and then English immigrants. However, the major waves of immigration occurred considerably later. The first, arising primarily from German lands, resulted in an increase in the U.S. Jewish population from 15,000 in 1840 to 280,000 by 1880. The most significant increase occurred during the subsequent 40 years, when nearly 2.5 million Jews arrived in the United States from Eastern Europe. These immigrants scattered all over the country in search of a livelihood; however, the majority ended up in large metropolitan areas, especially New York City, Chicago, and Philadelphia. Although there has been movement to other centers throughout the country, New York City still boasts the largest concentration; in 1990, its five boroughs were home to 1.05 million Jews (Singer & Seldin, 1992).

Most American Jews who identify themselves with a religious movement belong to one of the four major streams of American Jewish religious thought: Orthodox, Conservative, Reform, or Reconstructionist. According to the National Jewish Population Survey conducted in 1990, U.S. Jews indicated their preferences as follows: Reform, 38%; Conservative, 35%; Orthodox, 6%; Reconstructionist, 1%; nondenominational, 10%; miscellaneous, 9% (Goldstein, 1992). Because these affiliations have implications for the ethical perspectives that arise from their adherents, a review of the origins of these different streams might be helpful.

The Talmud and Legal Codifications

The Bible contains the most coherent description of early Jewish life. Its first five books, known as the Torah and considered to be of divine origin, contain historical information as well as a large body of rules describing appropriate religious behavior in a variety of life situations. This system of rules gradually expanded over many generations and became known as the *halakhah* (the way), a comprehensive system of legal ordinances affecting every aspect of a traditionally observant Jew's life. This system is all encompassing. It tells the traditional Jew the ritually correct way in which to slaughter animals and the types of pots in which food should be cooked. It tells how to give charity sensitively and, germane to our discussion, how to behave ethically (Kavesh, 1976).

The halakhah harks back to legal traditions imbedded in the Bible but received early full exposition in the Talmud, an enormous multivolume work compiled in late antiquity. The Talmud probably is most often thought of as a compendium of legal debates and decisions by rabbis, but it also is filled with anecdotes, folk tales, and other materials, including health rules and remedies. After the time of the Talmud, the legal tradition was transmitted through the rabbis, who compiled answers (known as *responsa*) to questions that arose in their own time. Periodically, outstanding rabbinic scholars compiled encyclopedic codes that summarized the thinking up to their own periods, and later commentators fleshed out the codes even further with additional perspectives. Until the 17th century, there were two major post-Talmudic traditions: the Ashkenazic (originating in Central Europe) and the Sephardic (originating in Spain and spreading over Europe, the Mediterranean basin, and the Middle East after the expulsion from Spain in 1492). The last code to receive general approbation, the *Shulhan Arukh,* was written during the 16th century by Joseph Caro, an Israeli Sephardic rabbi, with additional authoritative comments by Moses Isserles, a contemporaneous Polish Ashkenazic rabbi. It probably is a reflection of the fragmentation of the Jewish community brought on by the Enlightenment that no subsequent code has received such widespread acceptance.

Pre-Enlightenment Jewish Communal Structure

Prior to the Enlightenment, Jewish communities in Europe, Asia, and Africa were semiautonomous entities governed by a lay and religious leadership to which wide powers were ceded by the general authorities. The reasons for these arrangements involved a mixture of anti-Semitism and pragmatism. Because of the anti-Semitism, Jews often were restricted to living in contiguous areas of a town or country. The authorities taxed the Jewish community as a whole, leaving it up to the leadership of the community to decide how to raise the money. At the same time, so long as it provided the money, the Jewish community had a good deal of authority to run its own affairs, including its legal and religious affairs. The religious affairs were run according to the halakhah, as interpreted by the community rabbi. Difficult questions often were referred to regional rabbinic scholars whose authority stemmed from the respect of their peers. This system did not always prevent uncertainties or disagreements, but on its own terms, it had a certain logical coherence (Kavesh, 1976; Soloveitchik, 1983).

Reform and Conservative Movements

Beginning during the 18th century but accelerating after the French Revolution, this relatively coherent system began to break down. During the 19th century, two streams—the Reform and Conservative movements—grew up outside the traditional autonomous context. Initially developing in Germany, both movements thrived when transplanted to the open society of the United States. The Reform movement has classically rejected the halakhic model outright, denying eternal validity to any given formulation of Jewish belief or codification of Jewish law. In its place, Reform developed the notion of prophetic Judaism, based on what were felt to be the universal values of the Jewish prophetic writings that could be shared among all people (Macmillan, 1971; Samuelson, 1975). Various thinkers in the movement have written on medical ethical issues. The rabbinical arm has had a Responsa Committee for many years, and its congregational arm has established a Committee on Bioethics that has issued program guides on some of the topics related to end-of-life decision making. However, there is no such thing as a binding halakhic model in Reform Judaism. Interestingly, there have been recent suggestions by some within its rabbinical arm that thought be given to such an approach, and the phrase "the mood of Judaism" also has appeared in at least one position paper (Address, 1993, p. 10; R. F. Address, personal communication, November 26, 1997).

The Conservative movement, which developed a few decades after the Reform movement (and which some regarded as an explicit reaction to Reform), takes what might be viewed as a middle ground, arguing that the halakhic system under rabbinical leadership still has validity but that modern times require novel approaches to the interpretation of specific issues (Jewish Theological Seminary of America, 1988). The movement has a Committee on Jewish Law and Standards to develop Conservative halakhic positions on various issues and has addressed most of the concerns related to end-of-life decision making during the past decade.

Reconstructionism

A small but growing number of American Jews associate themselves with the Reconstructionist movement, a 20th-century American phenomenon grounded in the rejection of a supernatural God and the consequent rejection of a legal system based on such a belief. During the past 5 years, Reconstructionism has established a Center for Jewish Ethics that has convened an advisory committee to look into a variety of issues, including biomedical ethics.

Orthodoxy

The remaining 6% of American Jews who identify with a religious movement classify themselves as Orthodox. Although a close look reveals much more variety in outlook than one might expect, these Jews are the most religiously observant of all the movements. Most see themselves as heirs to the religious tradition that existed before the Enlightenment, bound by a halakhic Judaism (Bleich, 1973). Orthodox rabbis and thinkers have written extensively on most of the topics considered in this chapter. Interestingly, even though one would think that only one normative Orthodox view would emerge on each issue, in fact this is not the case. The key to Orthodox practice in such situations often depends on the scholarly reputation of the person addressing the question at hand.

This brief survey of the Jewish religious scene indicates how complex it could be to discern a single Jewish view about any of the issues related to end-of-life decision making. And this does not take into account others in the Jewish community (including various non-rabbinic academic thinkers, physicians, and secular organizations) who have put out opinions in professional journals, position papers, and legislative testimony. Nonetheless, there are some areas of consensus and, in those areas of disagreement, important and thoughtful nuances that offer insights. This chapter refers primarily to the approaches developed by the Orthodox, Conservative, and Reform movements and brings in other perspectives as appropriate.

■ END-OF-LIFE ISSUES

The Value of Saving Life

Underlying most Jewish thinking about issues of life and death is the notion of *pikuah nefesh* (saving life). Pikuah nefesh is a cardinal virtue in Judaism. It is so important that it takes precedence over nearly all other religious requirements imposed on Jews (Rosner, 1995). For traditionally observant Jews, this translates into permission to violate usually forbidden activities such as

using electricity and driving on the Sabbath. But even for those who do not subscribe to a traditional approach, this notion of valuing the preservation of life is
pervasive.

There are many suggestions in Biblical sources that ethical behavior, such
as honoring one's parents, treating animals with compassion, and spurning ill-
gotten gains, will be rewarded with long life (Sonsino & Syme, 1994). Old age
often was regarded as a blessing, for example, in the case of Abraham, who
lived 175 years (Genesis 25:7-8). However, positive views were balanced with
the sense that long life is a mixed experience: "So, appreciate your vigor in the
days of your youth, before those days of sorrow come and those years arrive of
which you will say, 'I have no pleasure in them,' before sun and light and moon
and stars grow dark, and the clouds come back again after the rain" (Ecclesia-
stes 12:1-2).

Death at an early age, especially with suffering, was regarded in some
Jewish sources as punishment for sin. But the rabbis were aware that many apparently blameless people died, and they devoted a good deal of attention to
speculating about the reasons. One explanation frequently offered was that
suffering in this world was rewarded in the "world to come" (Babylonian Talmud, Pirket Avot 4:22).

In this century, Judaism has been portrayed as a "this-worldly" religion,
and examples from the Bible can be adduced to support this perspective, for example, "The dead cannot praise the Lord, nor any who go down into silence"
(Psalm 115:17). However, Jewish belief in the resurrection of the dead goes
back to the Biblical books of Daniel (12:1-2) and Ezekial (37:1-10), and this
view was considered part of mainstream Jewish rabbinical doctrine until the
20th century. By the Middle Ages, elaborate mythical writings arose, depict-
ing the journeys of the soul in the afterlife. The belief in reincarnation of souls
also developed in mystical Jewish circles during the medieval period and became widespread after the renaissance of Jewish mysticism in Israel during the
16th century (Raphael, 1994).

In these circles, which continue to function up to the present time, solace
for the death of the young was found in the belief that a person who died at a
young age was inhabited by a soul who needed to return to earth to finish an un-
completed task or to atone for sins committed in the earlier life. Because many
20th-century Jews saw this belief as an embarrassing intrusion of a supersti-
tious past, it receded from view until the past few decades, during which a re-
vival of interest in nontraditional religious beliefs has occurred.

Jewish Views of Autonomy and Assisted Suicide

The principle of autonomy underlies most contemporary American attitudes toward end-of-life decision making. This notion, that the individual or
someone appointed by that individual should have the ultimate right to decide
the timing and extent of health care treatments, has been enshrined in contemporary ethical and legal parlance for more than a decade (Kavesh, 1994). Taken
to its logical conclusion, such a view would seem to be consistent with the idea
of suicide and assisted suicide. Reines (1993), a philosopher at the Hebrew Union College (the Reform rabbinical seminary), expressed this position by declaring, "Reform asserts that every person is the ultimate owner of
her[self]/himself with . . . the moral right to commit suicide . . . [and who] can
transfer [this moral right] to another person . . . to assist her/him to commit suicide" (pp. 14-16). Judging from the responses collected in a bioethics program
guide on *Voluntary Active Euthanasia–Assisted Suicide* (Address & James,
1993), however, Reines stands in relative isolation within the Reform movement. Many of the writers have acknowledged their previous embrace of a Reform tradition heavily weighted toward the principle of autonomy, but they either acknowledged a personal change as the "certainties of youth give way to
the ambiguities of maturity" (Gordon, 1993, p. 7) or realized that "many of us
lost our old, ultimate faith in Western civilization and acknowledge how wise
Judaism remained" (Borowitz, 1993, p. 24). In place of the language of autonomy, several of the Reform thinkers have spoken in terms of "all life [as] a gift
from God and ultimately God's decision as to its end" (Address, 1993, p. 3);
"God's ownership of life" (Bookman, 1993, p. 6); the "historic Jewish tradition
which affirms life" (Zlotowicz & Seltzer, 1993, p. 17); and the traditional Jewish notion that we are created "*b'tzelem elohim*—in the image of God" (Kahn,
1993, p. 25). Finally, A. James Rudin, a Reform rabbi who is the national inter-
religious affairs director for the American Jewish Committee (a secular organization that frequently comments on issues of public or political import), gave
testimony to a congressional committee in March 1997 opposing assisted suicide from a Jewish perspective. In his testimony, he asserted that "life is a divine gift, and it is God alone who determines how and when death will come"
(Rudin, 1997).

This remarkable Reform about-face on autonomy brings the Reform position quite close to both Conservative and Orthodox positions on assisted suicide. Representatives of these movements are unanimous in their condemna-

tion of active euthanasia, whether or not accompanied by suicide (Bleich, 1996; Dorff, 1991; Jakobovits, 1975; Klein, 1979). This view receives its primary impetus from passages in the Talmud that (a) regard all persons—even those who are near death—as living entities and (b) regard any form of active euthanasia as a capital crime. Three decades ago, the head of the Jerusalem Religious Court perhaps anticipated the current debate when he wrote, "[The patient's] consent can grant no permission to extinguish God's candle that is within him [or her]" (Waldenberg, quoted in Zohar, 1997, p. 39). Thus, at least on these matters, one can conclude that there seems to be a relative unanimity in the Jewish community on views of assisted suicide.

Pain and Suffering

At the same time as Judaism condemns active euthanasia and assisted suicide, there is a rather rich and divergent tradition regarding approaches to the patient who is suffering great pain. From Talmudic times, there was general agreement that the relief of pain is meritorious: "Whoever is in pain, let him go to the physician" (Babylonian Talmud, Bava Kama:46b). This perspective is endorsed by Reform, Conservative, and Orthodox thinkers (Jacob, 1992; Jakobovits, 1975; Reisner, 1991).

On the other hand, there is considerable disagreement as to what to do when the patient is at risk of dying from a high dose of the pain medication when this is the only dose that will relieve pain. Leading Reform thinkers tend to look favorably on such an approach:

> We must be equally concerned with the pain of the terminally ill. There is a fine line of distinction between alleviating pain and prescribing a drug which may hasten death. When the pain is great, the physician should alleviate the pain and not be overly concerned about the latter consequence, as death is certain in any case. (Jacob, 1992, p. 239; see also Freehof, 1975)

There is less unanimity in Conservative and Orthodox circles. The Committee on Jewish Law and Standards of the Conservative movement actually has validated two different positions as having legitimacy in these matters. One position asserts that intent to treat is the crucial factor; administration of a high dose of morphine and other pain medications might be required to relieve pain, although this could suppress the respiratory system and simultaneously hasten death (Dorff, 1991). The other position disagrees, stating that the ultimate consequence of death, regardless of intent, overrides the benefits (Reisner, 1991).

In the same vein as Reisner (1991), Bleich (1981) felt that Judaism certainly supports the preservation of life over the relief of pain. But rather than stop at this point, he proposed an alternative approach that certainly is novel (although it raises a host of other questions about the role of invasive procedures), writing, "There is, however, no *halakhic* objection to providing such medication in the case of terminal patients and maintaining such patients on a respirator" (Bleich, 1981, p. 139, italics in original). Other Orthodox scholars do not require the respirator solution but rather take a point of departure similar to that of Dorff (1991). Thus, Immanuel Jakobovits, a recognized leader in the field of modern Jewish medical ethics, wrote,

> Quite different is the problem of indirect euthanasia, when the patient's death is merely the unpremeditated result of some medication given only to relieve pain or consequent on the withdrawal of treatment. Analgesics may be administered, even at the risk of possibly shortening the patient's life, so long as they are given solely for the purpose of rendering him [or her] insensitive to acute pain. (Jakobovits, 1975, p. 276)

An Orthodox physician provided additional perspective by bringing a religious approach to a professional dilemma:

> The decision is easily formulated but difficult to understand. In Jewish law, shortening of life is defined as murder. Euthanasia is also forbidden. Why, then, is a physician permitted to shorten the life of a patient when his [or her] intent is to alleviate pain? In the framework of *halakhic* discussions of these principles, some rabbis stress the physician's *intent.* Unlike euthanasia, where the intent is to kill, administering high doses of narcotic medication for pain is intended to *help* the patient. The shortening of life is merely an undesired side effect. . . . Despite the difficulty in understanding the *halakhah,* it is definitive and is applied in actual cases everywhere. (Halperin, 1993, p. 273, italics in original)

Thus, there seems to be a general, but not unanimous, sanction in Jewish tradition for the notion that adequate sedation should be given to patients in great pain even if there is a risk of suppressing respiratory drive and shortening life.

Passive Euthanasia

Our detailed discussion of Jewish attitudes toward preservation of life, active euthanasia, assisted suicide, and treatment of pain provides valuable background for addressing one of the core issues in end-of-life decision making: passive euthanasia. The tension between Judaism's bias for life and compassion for a patient in severe pain, for most thinkers, seems to resolve itself in the direction of compassion, at least when it comes to the administration of pain-relieving medications. But how should we look at the situation of a terminally ill person who requires active interventions simply to keep him or her alive, whether in pain or not? Should antibiotics be given for pneumonia, even though it will simply prolong the inevitable end? Should a feeding tube be placed for the person who no longer can eat? Under what circumstances, if any, should interventions that already have been started be discontinued?

Reform, Conservative, and prominent Orthodox thinkers point to examples in the Talmud and subsequent Jewish writings indicating that death is the preferred alternative to intractable pain. In the words of one Orthodox source, the "removal of an impediment to death or the withholding of a life-prolonging measure to allow death to occur naturally is not only sanctioned but praised" (Tendler & Rosner, 1993; see also Dorff, 1991; Freehof, 1960; Reisner, 1991). Traditional precedence dates to the era prior to effective pain control when prayer was an oft-used and important intervention. A commonly cited Talmudic precedent involves the maid-servant of one of the great compilers of Jewish law, Judah haNasi:

> We are told that the rabbis gathered in ceaseless prayer to keep him alive, but his servant-maid (who, by the way, was honored as a learned woman in the Talmud), seeing how hopeless was his case and how much he suffered, prayed that he be given the privilege of death. When the rabbis insisted on praying that he be kept alive a little longer, she threw down from the roof a huge earthen jar in order to . . . stop their prayers so that Rabbi Judah might peacefully die. The Talmud quotes this action of this learned woman with evident approval. (Freehof, 1960, p. 119)

The third source often cited in discussions about passive euthanasia is a statement by Isserles in the *Shulhan Arukh* (Yoreh De'ah 339:1):

> It is forbidden to do anything to hasten the death of one who is in a dying condition (*goses*). . . . If, however, there is something that causes a delay in the

exit of the soul, as, for example, if near to this house there is a sound of pounding as one who is chopping wood, or there is salt on his [or her] tongue, and these delay the soul's leaving the body, it is permitted to remove these because there is no direct act involved here, only the removal of an obstacle. (Kavesh, 1976, p. 132, italics in original)

Many draw from these sources the notion that the removal of impediments is reasonable. But two significant questions remain. First, who is in *goses* (a "dying condition"), and second, what does it mean to remove impediments? In regard to goses, most Orthodox scholars cite sources indicating that this condition applies only to the final 72 hours of life (Bleich, 1996; Jakobovits, 1975). Others, however, are inclined to interpret the category of goses more liberally (Newman, 1995). In regard to impediment, Jakobovits (1975), a respected Orthodox scholar, seemed to define this as any factor "extraneous to the patient himself [or herself], or not which may artificially delay his [or her] demise in the final phase" (p. 124).

But Moshe Feinstein offered a more nuanced opinion based, apparently, on the idea that Isserles must have been talking about regarding someone who is dying in pain. On the one hand, the rabbi indicated that "no medical intervention is permitted for a *goses* since physicians have already concluded that no intervention can benefit him [or her]. Routine hospital procedures, such as drawing blood or even taking temperature, have no place in the final hours of a patient's life" (quoted in Tendler, 1991, p. 48, italics in original). But when the question was put to Feinstein again at a later time, he replied, "It seems obvious to me that if the patient is not suffering any pain—in other words, if there is no burden in [the patient] maintaining his [or her] present state—there is no reason why [the patient] should not be given all medical care to prolong his [or her] life as much as possible" (p. 55).

On the other hand, Feinstein offered an opinion regarding a patient with a terminal illness who develops a second illness, such as pneumonia, for which there is a cure:

If the patient's illness is causing him [or her] great pain, and [the patient] would prefer to die rather than live under these conditions, it may well be proper not to treat him [or her] in any manner that would prolong the dying process. This means that it might be best to withhold treatment for the second illness since if the pneumonia is cured, it would impose upon the patient the burden of his first disease, for which relief is not available. . . . When the patient is incompetent, his [or her] family must be consulted. (quoted in Tendler, 1991, pp. 56-57)

This does not seem to be talking about a goses, and many of the difficult problems facing physicians today seem to fall into this category. However, Bleich (1996) quoted a recent pronouncement of a group of Israeli rabbinic decisors: "Heaven [forbid] that the demise of a terminal patient be hastened by withholding nutrients or medical treatments in order to lessen his [or her] suffering" (p. 58). It probably is reasonable to conclude that there still is ferment in the Orthodox community on this issue.

Conservative, Reform, and academic scholars have no more unanimity about what to do in these situations. Analogies to legal categories involving fatal injuries have been drawn by some in an effort to find a position that would justify minimizing or withdrawing therapy for those who are slowly dying or irreversibly comatose but who have not reached the 72-hour limit (Dorff, 1991; Weisbard, 1979). There are two positions accepted by the Conservative movement as legitimate options regarding care of the terminally ill. One permits the withdrawal of the terminally ill from respirators as well as antibiotics, artificial nutrition, and hydration (Dorff, 1991). The second permits the withdrawal of machinery but not nutrition and hydration (Reisner, 1991).

So, what is "the Jewish view" here? I am inclined to turn back to my own perceptions of the issue 20 years ago because the basic issues have not changed much so far as I can tell:

> The problem today is that modern technology has extended the state of *goses* far beyond what naturally would have occurred. Patients with massive strokes, cancer refractory to medication, and other terminal conditions often spend their last days or months vegetating, essentially unresponsive to any stimulus except overwhelming pain from bedsores, irritating intravenous or stomach feeding tubes, and the pain of the illness itself. In these cases, the removal of feeding tubes and other impediments to dying would seem perfectly consistent with Jewish tradition as expressed by Rabbi Isserles [in the 16th-century writings in the *Shulhan Arukh*]. (Kavesh, 1976, p. 132)

Advance Directives

Who should be empowered to make the critical life-and-death decisions for a person who is ill? We have seen in the preceding that most thinkers of the three major Jewish religious movements seem to agree on limiting autonomy when it comes to assisted suicide. However, as a general rule in other settings, the three movements diverge on the issue of autonomy.

Orthodox thinkers advocate restrictions on autonomy in most situations (Bleich, 1996), but as we have seen, when a terminally ill person is in pain, the choice of whether to initiate new therapies might be left up to the individual. Similarly, patient autonomy might be expanded in a situation where a new but very risky treatment is being considered (Tendler, 1991). But generally, the Orthodox perspective reflects a view that important questions about life and death are a matter of divine rather than individual choice and that a rabbi must be consulted to determine what is consistent with the divine will (Tendler, 1991).

This perspective is expressed in an advance directive created by the largest body of American Orthodox rabbis. It begins with appointment of a health care agent and an instruction to health personnel that food and liquids be given in all cases. It has a place for the listing of an Orthodox rabbi whose decision will govern the agent and doctors in situations not covered by the directions within the document. At the same time, it provides a lengthy list of checkoffs to be decided by the person filling out the form for various health care situations. In some of these situations, such as irreversible brain damage "that makes me unable to recognize people or communicate in any fashion," the options include the rejection of mechanical ventilation or major surgery. The form indicates that "pain medication, even if it dulls consciousness and indirectly shortens my life, should be provided" (Rabbinical Council of America, n.d.). This form, in many ways, embodies the mainstream Orthodox philosophy that has evolved from the discussions documented earlier. It provides autonomy to the individual, but in the context of a format approved by the rabbis. It reflects the notion that there are limits to which physicians should go to preserve life in a dying person. Finally, it provides a rabbinic presence that, in its most positive light, provides support to family and other surrogates who often, in my experience, find the decision-making process agonizing and a source of guilty feelings.

The Reform movement has prepared a detailed guide for individuals and families to express their wishes for extraordinary medical treatment and financial arrangements. It includes guidance for preparing an ethical will (a traditional Jewish document offering reflections and instructions for one's children) and a suggested ritual for saying good-bye. Interestingly, the advance directive form included as part of this guide is not a specially created Reform document but rather the medical directive that was published in 1989 in the *Journal of the American Medical Association* (Address, 1994).

The Conservative movement's Committee on Jewish Law and Standards has prepared an advance directive document that includes only those options allowed within the parameters of Conservative halakhah. In this sense, the philosophy underlying the document is more like that of the Orthodox than the

Reform movement. On the other hand, reflecting the ambivalence that prompted the committee to approve two different positions on end-of-life decision making as noted previously, the advance directive document has two options: one that requires nutrition, hydration, and medication (the Reisner option [in italics]) and one that allows the rejection of all interventions, including these three (the Dorff option [in standard type]). The document has a poetic and poignant introduction reflecting its Jewish character and offers choices for a number of likely end-of-life scenarios. It offers the option for rabbinic consultation. Its major weakness, like the medical directive offered by the Reform movement, is that it offers only a set of scenarios rather than a set of value guidelines. Situations can occur that were unanticipated under the scenarios, and in such cases, no options are available to guide the decisions; for example, there is an option to refuse amputation in the setting of an infection even if other means are less likely to prolong life, but there is no option discussed about amputation if the alternative is intractable pain (Kavesh, 1994). Both the Reform and Conservative documents, like the Orthodox one, include forms for the appointment of surrogate agents in the event the person loses decision-making capacity.

The Reconstructionist movement also offers an advance directive document created by a Jewish lawyer/ethicist that includes similar options. However, it is more value focused than the Reform and Conservative versions (Weisbard, 1995).

Organ Transplants

Judaism views the body, both alive and after death, with great reverence. Although there were concerns on the part of some Orthodox scholars during the early days of transplantation, the predominant view in all sections of the Jewish community today is that transplantation of organs from both cadaver and living donors is consistent with the value of pikuah nefesh and that this is overriding (Rosner & Tendler, 1997). The Orthodox advance directive just described includes a section permitting donation of five named organs but requiring the "concurrence of an Orthodox rabbi" before organs are taken.

Jewish Healing Circles and Hospice

The emotional turmoil that accompanies many of the difficult decisions that must be made at the end of life has stimulated increasing numbers of Jews to seek support and solace in community. One manifestation of the Jewish spiritual renaissance noted earlier is Jewish healing circles, which have become widespread during the past decade. Built around meditation, music, sharing, and prayer, these groups have attracted a significant following among sophisticated baby boomers who are entering middle age and are struggling with the illnesses and deaths of parents and, more frequently, of peers. They have received impetus from work in the secular realm apparently validating the powerful effects of prayer on healing (Dossey, 1993). Older mystical ideas, modern poetry, and new rituals are used freely in these circles.

Hospice is a concept that also fits easily into the framework of Jewish healing. The national Jewish hospice movement developed more than a decade ago and incorporates general hospice ideals of volunteerism and the primacy of controlling physical and psychological pain. Communal groups have organized home visits, provided pre-cooked meals, and supplied transportation as well as other necessary assistance. Spiritual nourishment draws on the same resources as do Jewish healing circles. The concept of *bikur holim* (visitation of the sick) is an honored custom in traditional Jewish circles. The Jewish hospice movement has brought this idea to a much wider audience.

■ CONCLUSION

In the struggle to elicit meaning in dealing with difficult life-and-death issues, Judaism offers two faces to the world. On the one hand, the long tradition of halakhic decision making provides a framework for approaching specific ethical questions. Even Reform thinkers, who reject halakhic authority, invariably rely heavily on this framework. Although other thinkers have suggested that reliance on a halakhic framework be rethought (Newman, 1995; Zohar, 1997), in my opinion, no one has come up with a coherent and consistent alternative. Even for those who do not accept the authority of the rabbis or the notion of precedent as a source of ethical understanding, the rabbinical immersion in these issues provides a Jewish starting point. As one Talmudic rabbi advises: "Do not look at the flask but at what it contains; a new flask may be filled with old wine, and an old flask may be empty even of new wine" (Babylonian Talmud, Avot 5:25). Judaism comes with the baggage of history, which we invariably must confront.

The other face of Judaism is the spiritual communal face, the face of Jewish healing circles and Jewish hospice. This face teaches us that we do not live by philosophy alone. We must have a framework for life, but when life gets hard, there is no substitute for friends and family.

■ REFERENCES

Address, R. F. (1993). Redefining the dialogue on voluntary euthanasia. In R. F. Address & D. F. James (Eds.), *Voluntary active euthanasia–assisted suicide.* Philadelphia: Union of American Hebrew Congregations.

Address, R. F. (1994). *A time to prepare.* New York: Union of American Hebrew Congregations Press.

Address, R. F., & James, D. F. (1993). *Voluntary active euthanasia–assisted suicide.* Philadelphia: Union of American Hebrew Congregations.

Babylonian Talmud. (1949). *Siddur HaShalem: The daily prayer book* (P. Birnbaum, Trans.). New York: Hebrew Publishing.

Bleich, J. D. (1973). Establishing criteria of death. *Tradition, 14,* 94-112.

Bleich, J. D. (1981). *Judaism and healing: Halakhic perspectives.* New York: Ktav.

Bleich, J. D. (1996). Treatment of the terminally ill. *Tradition, 30*(3), 51-87.

Bookman, T. A. (1993). Assisted suicide. In R. F. Address & D. F. James (Eds.), *Voluntary active euthanasia–assisted suicide* (pp. 5-6). Philadelphia: Union of American Hebrew Congregations.

Borowitz, E. (1993). The crux of liberal Jewish thought: Personal autonomy. In R. F. Address & D. F. James (Eds.), *Voluntary active euthanasia–assisted suicide* (p. 24). Philadelphia: Union of American Hebrew Congregations.

Dorff, E. (1991). A Jewish approach to end-stage medical care. *Conservative Judaism, 43*(3), 3-51.

Dossey, L. (1993). *Healing words: The power of prayer and the practice of medicine.* San Francisco: Harper.

Freehof, S. (1960). *Reform responsa.* Cincinnati, OH: Union of American Hebrew Congregations.

Freehof, S. (1975). *American Reform responsa, No. 36.* New York: Central Conference of American Rabbis.

Goldstein, S. (1992). Profile of American Jewry: Insights from the 1990 national Jewish population survey. In D. Singer & R. Seldin (Eds.), *American Jewish yearbook* (pp. 77-173). New York: American Jewish Committee.

Gordon, H. L. (1993). Reflections on assisted suicide. In R. F. Address & D. F. James (Eds.), *Voluntary active euthanasia–assisted suicide* (pp. 7-9). Philadelphia: Union of American Hebrew Congregations.

Halperin, M. (1993). *Proceedings of an international colloquium on medicine, ethics, and Jewish law.* Jerusalem: Schlesinger Institute.

Jacob, W. (1992). *Questions and Reform Jewish answers: New American Reform responsa.* New York: Central Conference of American Rabbis.

Jakobovits, I. (1975). *Jewish medical ethics.* New York: Bloch.

Jewish Theological Seminary of America. (1988). *Emet Ve-Emunah: Statement of principles of Conservative Judaism.* New York: Author.

Kahn, Y. H. (1993). Excerpt from "On Choosing the Hour of Our Death." In R. F. Address & D. F. James (Eds.), *Voluntary active euthanasia–assisted suicide* (p. 25). Philadelphia: Union of American Hebrew Congregations.

Kavesh, W. N. (1976). Jewish medical ethics. In R. Siegel, S. Strassfeld, & M. Strassfeld (Eds.), *The Jewish catalog* (pp. 123-150). Philadelphia: Jewish Publication Society.

Kavesh, W. N. (1994). Self-determination and long-term care. In M. B. Kapp (Ed.), *Patient self-determination in long-term care* (pp. 11-42). New York: Springer.

Klein, I. (1979). *A guide to Jewish religious practice.* New York: Jewish Publication Society.

Macmillan. (1971). *Encyclopedia Judaica.* Jerusalem: Author.

Newman, L. E. (1995). Woodchoppers and respirators: The problem of interpretation in contemporary Jewish ethics. In E. N. Dorff & L. E. Newman (Eds.), *Contemporary Jewish ethics and morality* (pp. 140-160). New York: Oxford University Press.

Rabbinical Council of America. (n.d.). *Health care declaration.* New York: Author.

Raphael, S. P. (1994). *Jewish views of the afterlife.* Northvale, NJ: Jason Aronson.

Reines, A. J. (1993). Reform Judaism, bioethics, and abortion. In R. F. Address & D. F. James (Eds.), *Voluntary active euthanasia–assisted suicide* (pp. 14-16). Philadelphia: Union of American Hebrew Congregations.

Reisner, A. I. (1991). A halakhic ethic of care for the terminally ill. *Conservative Judaism, 43*(3), 52-89.

Rosner, F. (1995). Jewish medical ethics. *Journal of Clinical Ethics, 6,* 202-217.

Rosner, F., & Tendler, M. D. (1997). *Practical medical halachah.* Northvale, NJ: Jason Aronson.

Rudin, A. J. (1997, March 6). *Statement of Rabbi A. James Rudin on assisted suicides.* Testimony presented before the House Committee on Commerce Subcommittee on Health and Environment.

Samuelson, N. (1975). *Introduction to modern Jewish philosophy.* Albany: State University of New York Press.

Singer, D., & Seldin, R. (1992). *American Jewish yearbook.* New York: American Jewish Committee.

Soloveitchik, J. B. (1983). *Halakhic man.* Philadelphia: Jewish Publication Society.

Sonsino, R., & Syme, D. (1994). *What happens after I die?* Northvale, NJ: Jason Aronson.

Tendler, M. D. (1991). *Responsa of Rav Moshe Feinstein: Care of the critically ill* (Vol. 1). Hoboken, NJ: KTAV.

Tendler, M. D., & Rosner, F. (1993). Quality and the sanctity of life in the Talmud and the Mishnah. *Tradition, 28*(1), 22-27.

Weisbard, A. J. (1979). On the bioethics of Jewish law: The case of Karen Quinlan. *Israel Law Review, 14,* 337-368.

Weisbard, A. J. (1995). A model integrated advance directive for health care: Unto the third generation. *American Bar Association Bioethics Bulletin, 4*(2), 2-13.

Zlotowicz, B., & Seltzer, S. (1993). Suicide as a moral decision: A response to Dr. Alvin J. Reines. In R. F. Address & D. F. James (Eds.), *Voluntary active euthanasia–assisted suicide* (pp. 17-19). Philadelphia: Union of American Hebrew Congregations.

Zohar, N. (1997). *Alternatives in Jewish bioethics.* Albany: State University of New York Press.

Chapter 13

Muslim Perspectives Regarding Death, Dying, and End-of-Life Decision Making

HAMID ABDUL HAI
ASAD HUSAIN

*A*ny provider of health or social services to the people of the United States must bear in mind the multicultural makeup of today's American population. One of the new groups emerging as a significant religious minority in the United States is the Islamic community, estimated to comprise 2.2% of the American population. In issues relating to death, dying, and end-of-life decision making, religious affiliation always has played an important role. For this group, it is no exception.

■ THE CONTEMPORARY ISLAMIC COMMUNITY IN NORTH AMERICA

The Islamic community in North America has grown progressively during the past several decades. An estimated 6 million Muslims lived in the United States in 1990, and this number was expected to reach 8 to 10 million by the turn of the century (Husain & Husain,

1996; Stone, 1991). This rapid increase is accounted for both by immigration and by conversion to Islam. Muslims have somewhat distinctive religious and cultural practices; therefore, it is advisable for health care, social, and legal workers in this country to be aware of their needs and concerns.

Immigration often occurs in waves. Social and political situations in one part of the world cause people to migrate to distant and promising lands with the intent of finding new opportunities for employment and freedom from oppression. Once a few immigrants arrive and settle down successfully, their families, relatives, and acquaintances follow, usually settling in the same areas. Muslim immigration to North America has followed this pattern.

The earliest Muslim arrivals to the United States probably were slaves from West Africa during the 18th and early 19th centuries. The first well-known American to convert to Islam was Alexander Russell Webb. As American consul to the Philippines, he came in contact with Indian Muslims and embraced Islam in 1887, later returning to the United States and preaching his new faith (Saeger, 1993).

The first large wave of Muslim immigrants, however, came to the United States just before World War I. These were people departing from the collapsing Ottoman Empire in Turkey and the Middle East. The second wave also came from the Middle East during the 1920s and 1930s. These were largely blue-collar workers who settled mostly in the Midwest; Dearborn, Michigan, came to have the largest population of Arabs outside the Middle East (Husain & Husain, 1996).

The third wave of Muslim immigrants arrived after the end of World War II. With the division of the Middle East into smaller countries and the establishment of Israel, significant numbers left Palestine, Egypt, Jordan, Syria, and Lebanon and settled in different parts of the United States and Canada. This group consisted of more educated people who were largely absorbed into white-collar jobs.

The fourth wave of Muslim immigrants came to the United States and Canada starting from the late 1960s and continuing into the 1990s. The largest numbers of these came from the Indian subcontinent (India, Pakistan, and Bangladesh). Many immigrated with professional degrees (e.g., medicine, engineering), whereas others came as university students and stayed on as professionals. This last wave consists of by far the largest and most influential of the Muslim immigrants (Husain & Husain, 1996).

Meanwhile, a number of movements arose in the African American community that caused large numbers of African Americans to convert to Islam.

The Black Muslims, based in Chicago under the leadership of Elijah Muhammad, form the most important of these groups. A son of Muhammad, Warith Deen Muhammad, is the leader of a community that follows mainstream Islam. Several other important African American groups in New York City, Atlanta, and elsewhere have joined the Islamic faith. These movements have resulted in the conversion of approximately 8% to 10% of the African American community to Islam, and their numbers continue to rise. In addition, there have been some conversions in the local white and Hispanic communities.

More than one quarter of Muslim Americans live in just three metropolitan areas: New York (12%), Los Angeles (10%), and Chicago (6%). By national origin, African Americans form the largest group, consisting of 42% of the American Muslim population; immigrants from India, Pakistan, and Bangladesh constitute 24.4%; Arabs comprise 12.4%; Africans, Iranians, Turks, and Southeast Asians together constitute another 14.2%; American whites comprise 1.6%; and others (e.g., Bosnians, Albanians, other Eastern Europeans) make up about 5.6%. Thus, the national, linguistic, and racial backgrounds of American Muslims are quite varied, and this needs to be kept in mind while ministering to them (Nu'man, 1985).

In addition, there are denominational differences among American Muslims. The majority (about 85%) belong to Sunni denominations. Although there are five schools among which Sunni Muslims are divided, their differences are minor and relatively insignificant. There are, however, certain minority groups that deserve mention. The largest minority group is Shia' (or Shiite) Muslims, comprising about 10% of the Muslims in America. Shia' Muslims are subdivided into the Athna Ashri (or Twelvers), the Ismailis (or Agha Khanis), and the Bohras. All three groups have their separate communities in major cities such as Chicago and New York. The Ismailis differ more than the others from mainstream Muslims in their religious practices.

The Nation of Islam, led by Louis Farrakhan, has significant differences in beliefs and practices from mainstream Muslims. Most Muslims do not consider Nation of Islam followers to be Muslim. The hateful remarks attributed to their leader against Jews, and against white people in general, are totally un-Islamic. Furthermore, the belief in Fard Muhammad as God-incarnate and the late Elijah Muhammad as a prophet of God are considered blasphemous. Another such group is the Ahmadis (or Quadianis). These are the followers of Mirza Ghulam Ahmad, who claimed to be a prophet of God in India about 100 years ago. Although they might represent themselves as Muslims at times, they do not participate in or relate to mainstream Islamic centers. The whole world of Islam unanimously considers them to be non-Muslims.

■ INTRODUCTION TO ISLAMIC BELIEF SYSTEM AND PRACTICES

Misinformation and misconceptions about Islam, on which most Westerners have been raised, at times form barriers to the delivery of social services to these clients. Therefore, we attempt here to give a brief outline of the Islamic faith and religious practices.

Certain terms need to be clearly understood. The religion is called Islam, a word that means "submission" (to the will of God). The follower of this religion is called a Muslim, with the "Mus" pronounced as in "full," not as in "dull." The Arabic word for God is Allah. Muslims, Christians, and Jews who are Arabic speaking all refer to God as Allah. When doing so, they are not referring to a different entity from the God most of us worship. The Holy Book of the Muslims is the *Qur'aan,* which is believed to be the revealed word of God to the Prophet Muhammad.

The founder of the religion of Islam was Muhammad, who was born in Makkah, a city in Arabia, in the year 570. The Prophet preached that he was not establishing a new religion but rather that he was the last of a long chain of prophets starting from Adam and continuing through Noah, Abraham, Ishmael, Isaac, Moses, and Jesus Christ. Muhammad and his followers were severely persecuted for the 13 years during which he preached in Makkah. At that time, he migrated to Madina, where he founded a new society based on the ethical principles that he preached. His Makkan persecutors repeatedly waged war on the infant Islamic society, but the Prophet ultimately triumphed over them. When he reentered Makkah as the victor, he magnanimously forgave his persecutors, and all of them joined his community. Soon, Islam spread to all of Arabia. During the years that followed the death of the Prophet, the new religion was challenged by the neighboring powers. But it repeatedly won on the battlefield and also won the hearts of the people so that, within a few years, the whole region known as the Middle East became Muslim (Lewis, 1976). Through mystics and merchants, Islam spread to Southeast Asia, where the largest populations of Muslims are found today. Worldwide, about 1 billion people profess to belong to the Islamic faith today and share the following beliefs.

Oneness of God and Oneness of Humanity

Muslims believe that God is one. God is unique, omnipresent, and omnipotent. God is the creator and master of the world, and nothing happens without God's assent, including death and illness. God sends trials to all creatures to test their faith and steadfastness. God created Adam and Eve, and all of humanity is their family. All human beings are equal in the sight of God and have equal rights and duties. The lordship of humans over humans is unjust, with the only true Lord being God. Men and women are different but equal.

The Concept of the Day of Judgment

Islam teaches that a day will come when the dead will rise and face their maker regarding all the deeds they did—good or evil—in the present life. No one will be spared this judgment, and no deed—however small—will be omitted. Furthermore, the present life is only a period of testing and trial for the eternal life. Death is the transition from this life to the next. Although the general concept of this belief is shared by Christians and Orthodox Jews as well, the Islamic emphasis on *deeds* as the primary basis of salvation (as opposed to intercession or simply belief) is very strong (*Qur'aan* 2:254).

Prophethood

Muslims believe that God has sent numerous prophets to humanity, among them Abraham, Moses, and Jesus Christ. All of them brought the same religion of submission (Islam) to the will of God. All prophets, therefore, are to be honored. Muhammad, however, was the last and greatest of them. Muslims customarily say "Peace be upon him" after mentioning the name of any of the prophets.

These beliefs manifest through "five pillars" of religious practice with which a believer upholds his or her faith. The first is *Shahadah* (the declaration of beliefs). A Muslim should declare openly that he or she believes in the oneness of God and in God's prophets, especially the final prophet, Muhammad. At the moment of death, the Shahadah should be on the believer's lips if he or she is conscious. Second, it is obligatory for the Muslim to pray five times a day in the prescribed manner and at the prescribed times. In the context of illness, a religious Muslim will pray even when ill, in any position he or she is lying if too ill to get up. Ablution (*wudu*), the ritual washing of face, forearms, and feet, is required before prayers unless it is harmful due to illness. If so, then a dry ritual ablution is done. During prayer, the Muslim faces Makkah, standing, bowing, and prostrating before God.

The third pillar is fasting, which means avoiding all eating, drinking, smoking, and sex from dawn to sunset. Even swallowing a drop of water or medication breaks the fast. Fasting is done daily during the lunar month of *Ra-madam*, lasting 29 or 30 days. If a believer is too ill, too old, or otherwise unable to fast, then that person may put off fasting until he or she is able to do it.

The fourth pillar of Islamic religious practice is *Zakat* (the purification of wealth), requiring believers to give $\frac{1}{40}$ (2.5%) of what they own (except for things of personal use) to the poor every year. The fifth pillar is the *Hajj* (pilgrimage to Makkah). This is required once in life for anyone physically and financially able to perform it. Hajj is conducted in the month of *Dhu al-Hijjah*, and Muslims from all over the world aspire to go to Makkah on those particular days. Makkah is the place where the holiest mosque, the House of God, is located.

Some of the customs that Muslims follow can affect health behavior. In terms of dress, many Muslim women will insist on covering their whole bodies except for their faces, hands, and feet, keeping them out of view to men outside their close families. The head cover is called the *Hijab*. Women will dislike being touched by unrelated men except when absolutely necessary, and they might refuse to remove clothes in front of male physicians. It is customary for men to avoid touching unrelated women, and some will avoid even shaking hands with women. Some men will avoid looking directly at unrelated women when they talk, an act that might be interpreted as unfriendliness or lack of cooperation. Rather, in Islamic custom, there is an emphasis on separation of sexes. Whenever possible, a same-sex health professional is appreciated.

Pork and pork products are prohibited, as are intoxicants. Many Muslims will not eat meat unless it is *Halal* (Islamic kosher). Halal meat is available in many U.S. cities today but not always in hospitals. Whenever possible, ritual cleanliness is maintained even in illness; for example, Muslim patients would want to avoid even tiny amounts of urine, feces, or blood on clothes, bedsheets, and the like.

■ END-OF-LIFE PRACTICES AND CONSIDERATIONS

Every soul shall taste of death. In the end, to us will
ye be brought back.

—*Qur'aan* 29:57

With reference to the Islamic system of beliefs described earlier, death represents not the end of life but rather the transition from one stage of life to another. The time spent alive is full of trials. At death, the period of trial ends, and the reward of the faithful begins.

Muslims believe that at death, there is migration of the soul outside the body. On the Day of Judgment, the soul will reenter the body, which will be re-formed, and present itself to the judgment seat of God. The body is a temporary gift from God, entrusted to the believer for his or her use while alive. At death, it is entrusted to his or her family for proper and respectful disposition.

These concepts lead logically to certain conclusions relating to decision making at the end of life. Whereas classical Islamic law (*Shariah*) has ad-dressed many of the age-old issues that relate to end-of-life decision making, legal understanding and reasoning (*Fiqh*) allow for application of these basic principles to new circumstances. Accordingly, Islamic organizations, such as the Islamic Medical Association of North America through its Committee on Medical Ethics, have addressed the contemporary issues relating to this area in light of recent developments in the medical sciences.

Usual Procedures Relating to Death of a Muslim Client

At the time of death, if the patient is conscious, then it is customary for by-standers to recite and encourage him or her to recite the Shahadah. Also, it is customary to recite a certain chapter of the *Qur'aan,* Surah Ya-sin, at the time of death.

After death, the eyes and mouth are gently closed. The body is washed in its entirety and shrouded in simple white cloth. One piece is wrapped around the lower half of the body. The deceased's left hand is placed on his or her chest first, and the right hand is placed over it. Then, the second piece of cloth is wrapped around the body except for the head. A third piece of cloth that is longer than the others is wrapped around the whole body from above the head to below the feet. Four rolled strips of the same cloth are tied, one above the head, one below the feet, and two in between. In the case of female bodies, two extra pieces of cloth are used: one around the waist (like underwear) and one around the chest. The latter piece may be a large one, which has a hole in it for the head and falls to the feet both in front and back like a sleeveless shirt. Per-fume or perfumed water is applied to the face, neck, hands, knees, and feet. It is not customary to use a coffin, although it often is done in the African American community; this group also might uncover the face of the deceased for view-ing. Holding a wake, making up the face, or dressing the deceased in street clothes is not done.

At the service, members of the community stand in line facing Makkah. The shrouded body is placed with its head to the right side. An *Imam* (Muslim religious leader) leads the prayer. If women are present, then they stand in a line behind the men. The prayer is brief, invoking God's forgiveness for the deceased and for the community. Burial is done promptly, usually within 24 hours of death (cremation is unacceptable). Most Muslim communities in North America either have their own burial grounds or have an arrangement to use a portion of a Christian or Jewish cemetery. The Muslim grave is a simple, deep, long trench in the ground, dug perpendicular to the direction of Makkah. Either the body is placed on its right side to face Makkah or, if the deceased is lying flat, the face is turned toward Makkah. A variety of prayers and readings from the *Qur'aan* are performed during and after the burial. It is not customary to place flowers or candles on the grave. A child or a miscarried fetus of 4 months of age or over is washed, prayed over, and buried in a similar manner. A miscarried fetus of less than 4 months of age is not considered to be a person yet. Therefore, it is just wrapped and buried or otherwise disposed of; washing and ritual prayer are not required for it (Siala, 1996).

Within the next few days after burial, people gather at the house of the deceased or in the mosque to recite the Holy Book and make prayers for the deceased (*Fatiha*). In some families, this event will be repeated on one or more occasions until the 40th day after the burial and then yearly. Death is, of course, a sad occasion due to the loss of a loved one, especially if it is a premature or unexpected loss. Therefore, it is natural for people to be weeping and for others to be extending their condolences. However, it is considered undesirable to moan and cry aloud, and there is no public show of sadness by wearing black clothes, arm bands, and the like. Acceptance of God's will in taking the deceased and an expression of satisfaction that the deceased has reached his or her reward are customary.

Prolonging of Life by Artificial Means

The line dividing hopefulness and hopelessness in the continuing of long-term life sometimes is hard to define in our state of knowledge. Various types of coma and other illnesses occurring in the setting of serious organ damage (e.g., stroke) in an elderly person, who also might have cardiovascular, respiratory, renal, and/or metabolic disease, make it less and less likely with the passage of time that the patient will recover to have a meaningful life. Contemporary trends in American intensive care treatment, unfortunately, clearly have erred in favor of prolonging life in cases where all reasonable and likely chances of recovery have been exhausted. In a review of all deaths occurring in a medical institution over a period of several months, the first author found that considerable artificial prolongation of life was being practiced, with its attendant pain and inconvenience to the patients and families. Such artificial prolongation of life is not desirable by ethics or common sense. The application of the principles of Fiqh would appear to oppose it. The Medical Ethics Committee of the Islamic Medical Association (IMA) of North America has indicated that "maintaining a terminal patient on artificial life support for a prolonged period in a vegetative state is not encouraged" (Athar, 1996). Living wills and other advance directives are allowed, including the appointment of a case manager by limited power of attorney.

Refusing Life-Prolonging Treatment

In Islam, any form of treatment is considered to be inherently voluntary. Thus, refusal of any or all treatment is a valid choice. However, in the case of a curable illness, it is strongly recommended that one seek treatment. A well-known saying of Muhammad, as quoted by *Bukhari* (the most respected collection of sayings of the Prophet), goes, "God has sent no disease for which He has not sent the treatment." Furthermore, the Prophet repeatedly advised his companions to seek medical treatment when they were ill. In the case of incurable or terminal illness, however, it is acceptable for a person to refuse life-prolonging treatment. One also is allowed to secure a do-not-resuscitate (DNR) order when treatment appears futile and prolongation of life is not necessarily desirable. Hospices provide comfort to people who have terminal illnesses. This is not only justified, it is highly recommended. The classical way of treating a terminally ill person in the Islamic tradition is to provide comfort and pain relief in a quiet setting where family and friends can be present. This, indeed, is what is done in hospice.

Suicide and Physician-Assisted Death

Because life is a sacred trust given by God, who alone is the creator and disposer of life, it is not acceptable to try to end life in any way by one's own devices. The *Qur'aan* says "Do not kill yourselves" (4:29) and "Do not cast yourselves into destruction" (2:195). Thus, suicide is absolutely forbidden. Because God is the one who sends suffering, a person is expected as a good believer to accept it, and there is a reward for those who patiently persevere despite suffering (*Qur'aan* 2:177, 39:53). Whereas it is desirable to get medical help to cure illness or relieve symptoms such as pain, one is not allowed to end one's own life or to request help to end it. This prohibition is reflected in a 1997 policy statement by the Medical Ethics Committee (1997a) of the IMA of North America: "The IMA endorses the stand that there is no place for euthanasia in medical management, under whatever name or form (e.g., mercy killing, suicide, assisted suicide, the right to die, the duty to die). Nor does it believe in a willful and free consent in this area" (p. 100).

Organ Donation

There has been much discussion among Muslim physicians during recent years regarding organ donation. There seems to be unanimity that one is allowed to donate organs for the purpose of saving someone's life or improving his or her health (Athar, 1996; Mishal, 1997; Rahman, 1987). Concern has been raised about defining death (Khan, 1986; Yasmeen, 1991), but Islamic jurists are unanimous in proclaiming organ donation to be acceptable and, in fact, an act of piety (Medical Ethics Committee, 1997b). This is analogous to blood donation, which for many years has been called an act of piety by contemporary Islamic scholars.

Autopsy

In classical Islamic Shariah law, autopsy was forbidden because no benefit was felt to accrue from its practice. Present understanding (Fiqh) of the value of autopsies as a means of understanding the mechanisms of illness and also of investigating crimes must be balanced against unnecessary dissection of the dead. Where required by law, Muslim jurists and ethicists agree that it is allowed (Athar, 1996). Voluntary permission for autopsy either during life or after death by relatives generally is scoffed at because it delays the usually prescribed methods of disposition of the body. However, because there is no clear-cut injunction against autopsy in the *Qur'aan* or *Hadith* (a collection of sayings and actions of the prophet), there is room for discussion. If the benefits to society can be clearly documented, then voluntary autopsy, in the opinion of the present authors, may be considered.

■ THE ORGANIZATION OF THE MUSLIM SOCIETY IN THE AMERICAN CONTEXT: SOCIAL SUPPORT SYSTEMS

The Muslim society in North America is primarily organized around its Islamic centers. These act as mosques (places of worship), but they also act as community centers for social and religious events and often as schools for children and adults, sites for political and social gatherings, and places for bereavement-related activities. The Imam or other members of the community often will provide social services such as individual counseling, marriage counseling, mediation, and support for poor families by donation of food and clothing. In addition, nonprofit organizations providing educational and social services to Muslims have been developed in communities where large numbers of Muslims are living. For example, Islamic Health and Human Services (phone: 313-961-0678) in Detroit, Michigan, and Total Islamic Hospital Care in Detroit Riverview Hospital (phone: 313-499-4000) provide comprehensive Islamic assistance to hospitalized Muslim patients. Oasis Communications (phone: 800-569-3399) is run by American-born Muslim registered nurses and provides education, public relations, and advice on matters relating to Muslim and/or Arab patients. Finally, national organizations such as the Islamic Society of North America, the Islamic Circle of North America, and the Islamic Medical Association have been established.

With reference to death-related services, the following are available in many areas via local Islamic centers: pre-death counseling of patient and family, counseling regarding end-of-life decision making, *Janazah* services (preparation of the body for burial, the prayer for the dead, and the actual burial services), postburial support and counseling, and other social needs (e.g., emergency support, supervision) as a result of an unexpected death in a family.

For assistance in locating an Islamic center, a useful reference is the *Directory of* Masajid [mosques] *and Muslim Organizations in North America,* which can be obtained from the Council on Islamic Education, P.O. Box 20186, Fountain Valley, CA 92728-0186, phone: (714) 839-2929; fax: (714) 839-2714; e-mail: cie@apc.net.

■ RECOMMENDATIONS

In our experience, misconceptions and misinformation about Islam, its prophet, its history, and its Holy Book are common among otherwise well-informed American professionals. Therefore, we have attempted to give an outline of Islamic religious beliefs in this chapter. In addition, Muslims are sensitive about their "differentness" in contemporary American society, especially in personal and religious matters such as death, dying, and end-of-life decision making. Therefore, it is necessary to treat them with gentleness and with respect for their religion. A few positive remarks regarding their religion often will put Muslim clients at ease and elicit their cooperation, giving one the opportunity to provide the best client care.

If a Muslim client appears to be insisting on doing something (or refusing to do something), then he or she often will have a religious reason for doing (or not doing) it. It is worthwhile to simply ask "Why?" (or "Why not?") and to try to understand the reason. Religious matters are not necessarily based on simple logical reasoning. If something is forbidden in the perception of the client, then it is forbidden. It does not work to argue over it. One may, however, explain the pros and cons of that action and ask whether, in these unusual circumstances of serious illness, it might be allowed so as to save a client's health or life. Failing this, one would work around the difficulty and offer alternatives. Referral to an Imam or other learned person from an Islamic background, including a Muslim physician on one's staff, might help a great deal.

Many Muslims are immigrants and might have difficulty in comprehending complicated explanations given in the English language. Furthermore, as in many Eastern cultures, it is typical to show deference to an authority figure by saying "yes" without necessarily agreeing with what is being said. It is worthwhile to take the extra time to explain tests, procedures, and treatment and to make sure that one's explanations really are understood.

For a hospitalized Muslim, it would be helpful to allow the patient's Imam to visit and to allow the patient to pray and read his or her Holy Book, when possible, without disturbing others. Modesty and privacy are very important, and some elements of a physical examination can be done over a gown. A same-sex physician or nurse is appreciated (if possible). If not, then a male physician should examine a female patient in the presence of another female. Pork, lard, and other pork products (e.g., bacon, sausages), as well as alcoholic beverages, all are forbidden and are to be avoided. Many, but not all, Muslims will refuse to eat meat unless it is Halal. It might be appropriate to allow families to bring in food for the patients.

■ CONCLUSION

To summarize practices regarding end of life, blood transfusion and organ transplants are allowed with the usual screening precautions. Living wills and advanced directives are allowed, including the appointment of a case manager by limited power of attorney. When not required by law, Muslim clients generally will not desire autopsies. However, where required by law, autopsies are allowed. Receiving adequate pain control and refusing treatment, especially if it is futile, are acceptable practices. Assisted suicide and euthanasia, however, are forbidden.

■ REFERENCES

Athar, S. (1996). *Information for health care providers when dealing with a Muslim patient.* Downer's Grove, IL: Islamic Medical Association of North America.

Husain, A., & Husain, I. (1996). A brief history and demographics of Muslims in the United States. In A. Husain, J. E. Woods, & J. Akhter (Eds.), *Muslims in America: Opportunities and challenges* (pp. 27-31). Oak Brook, IL: International Strategy and Policy Institute.

Khan, F. A. (1986). The definition of death in Islam: Can brain death be used as a criterion of death in Islam? *Journal of the Islamic Medical Association, 18,* 18-21.

Lewis, B. (1976). *The world of Islam.* London: Thames and Hudson.

Medical Ethics Committee. (1997a). Care at the end of life and euthanasia. *Journal of the Islamic Medical Association, 29,* 100-101.

Medical Ethics Committee. (1997b). Death: Islamic Medical Association Ethics Committee statement. *Journal of the Islamic Medical Association, 29,* 99.

Mishal, A. A. (1997). Islamic perspective on transplantation. *Journal of Islamic Medical Association, 29,* 116.

Muslim World League. (1997). *Qur'aan* (M. Pickthall, Trans.). New York: Author.

Nu'man, F. H. (1985). The Muslim population in the U.S. In Y. Y. Haddad & J. Smith (Eds.), *Muslim communities in North America* (pp. 231-259). Albany: State University of New York Press.

Rahman, F. (1987). *Health and medicine in the Islamic tradition.* New York: Crossroads.

Saeger, R. H. (Ed.). (1993). *The dawn of religious pluralism.* La Salle, IL: Open Court.

Siala, M. E. (1996). *Janazah guide.* Ann Arbor, MI: Islamic Assembly of North America.

Stone, C. L. (1991). Estimates of Muslims living in America. In Y. Y. Haddad (Ed.), *The Muslims of America* (pp. 25-36). New York: Oxford University Press.

Yasmeen, M. N. (1991). The end of human life in light of the opinion of Muslim scholars and medical science. *Journal of the Islamic Medical Association, 23,* 74-81.

Chapter 14

Buddhist Issues in End-of-Life Decision Making

RONALD Y. NAKASONE

A discussion of issues in end-of-life decision making for a Buddhist devotee requires an understanding of the spiritual goals that govern the Buddhist life, its doctrines, the practical demonstration of its ideals, and its assimilation of other religious beliefs and cultural practices. To this end, this chapter begins with a brief description of the origins and development of Buddhism. Next, it turns to its major doctrines and practices. Finally, it focuses on individual and community attitudes and dynamics involved in organ transplant and end-of-life decision making.

Buddhist cultures are many and complex. This chapter concerns itself primarily with the beliefs and practices of an East Asian Buddhist community, the Japanese Pure Land Buddhist devotees in Hawaii and the continental United States. This group is the largest and oldest organized Buddhist community in the United States. This chapter's reflections on brain death, organ transplants, and important end-of-life decision-making issues, however, also require a review of Chinese Confucianism and the Buddhist encounter with Chinese views of filiality, birth, death, and the afterlife as well as an understanding of funeral and memorial observances. Thus, although the chapter focuses on the Japanese Buddhist community, much of what follows concerning life, death, and ancestral veneration can be applicable to Chinese and other East Asian cultures that have come under the influence of Confucianism and other Chinese religions.

However, it is important to clarify that scholars have difficulty applying the word *religion* to Japanese and Chinese spiritual beliefs. Much of the predicament lies in the definition of the divine. Whereas the English word *religion* signifies a bond between the human and the divine, the Japanese and Chinese make no clear distinction between the profane and the sacred, and East Asian Buddhists maintain that illusion is reality and the mundane is sacred (Ching, 1993).

Buddhism in the United States

The 1990 U.S. census recorded 849,809 Japanese, but it is not certain how many claimed to be Buddhists. The 1996 *Annual Reports* of the 85th Legislative Assembly of the Honpa Hongwanji Mission of Hawaii reported a total of 9,414 members, 31 ministers, and 36 temples (Honpa Hongwanji Mission of Hawaii, 1997). The 1996 *Annual Report* of the Buddhist Churches of America listed 61 temples and 16,902 dues-paying members (Buddhist Churches of America, 1997). Both of these are *Jōdoshin* (Pure Land) Buddhist organizations, the largest Buddhist group in the United States; although other Japanese Buddhist sects are active, their numbers are quite small. Traditionally, a Buddhist temple serves the entire community; those who are not dues-paying members also attend major services, support the temple in a variety of ways, and turn to the temple for funeral and memorial services.

■ ORIGIN AND SPREAD OF BUDDHISM

Buddhists trace the genesis of their faith to the spiritual insight of Siddhārtha Gautama (563-483 B.C.E.), a prince of the *Sākya* clan. Gautama shared his insight and established a faith community in northeast India and present-day Nepal. The community remained a single unit until about 100 years after the death of its founder. A schism centering over the status of the arhat (noble one), the essence of the historical Buddha, and the *Vinaya* (the monastic rules of conduct) split the early community into two groups: the Theravāda (tradition of the elders) and the Mahasmaghika (great assembly).

The Theravādins argued for the perfectibility of human nature in the guise of the *arhat,* the humanity of the historical Buddha, and strict observance of the *Vinaya* outlined by its founder. Present-day Theravāda claim to observe the faith established by its founder. The Mahāsmaghika, on the other hand, believed that becoming an *arhat* did not free one from all impurities. They understood the historical Gautama to be a manifestation of a transcendental Buddha who is free from impurities, infinite, and eternal. The Mahāsmaghika stressed the spirit of the Vinaya, not its letter. These initial disagreements led to further splintering. Buddhist documents mention as many as 34 monastic sects between the second and fourth centuries after the Buddha's passing.

Mahāyāna Buddhism (Great Vehicle) emerged during the two centuries between 100 B.C.E. and 100 C.E. Its origins are obscure. Many scholars believe that Mahāyāna Buddhism emerged from the Mahāsmaghika and related sects as reaction against the aloofness of the monastic sects (Conze, 1962; Robinson & Johnson, 1982). Other scholars, notably Hirakawa (1974/1990), argued that Mahāyāna began as a lay movement that appeared almost immediately after the death of the historical Buddha. The movement evolved from devotees who worshipped and maintained the monuments that housed the relics of the Buddha (Hirakawa, 1974/1990). In time, they developed their own liturgies, doctrines, and institutions. Early Mahāyānists emulated the Buddha and referred to themselves as bodhisattvas (beings who aspire to wisdom). The bodhisattva, an outgrowth of the idealization of the historical Buddha, chooses to minister to the spiritually dispossessed and vows to save all beings before he or she achieves full enlightenment. Mahāyāna followers believe that all beings are ferried across the sea of *samsara* (illusion and desire) to nirvana, whereas they feel that Theravāda Buddhism restricts passage to only the most devoted of followers. Mahāyāna's spiritual vision appealed to the East Asians, and its more liberal attitudes enabled its advocates to accommodate all manners of foreign cultures and beliefs.

Buddhism was one of many spiritual movements until the Gupta king, oka Asoka (ca. 274-236 B.C.E.), embraced the faith. A s oka sent Buddhist missions throughout India, Sri Lanka, North Africa, Macedonia, and Central and South Asia. In Southeast Asia, Asoka's efforts initiated a gradual spread of Buddhism and Indian culture to Thailand and Vietnam and across Indonesia. Meanwhile, the now extinct Central Asian kingdoms of Khotan, Kucha, and Turfan had a well-established Buddhist presence by the second century B.C.E. Straddling the caravan routes, these flourishing trade centers exchanged goods and ideas and served as a natural transition for Buddhism's entry into China. There, after a period of adaptation, Buddhism became an integral part of the national life. During its most prosperous and creative period (500-800), distinctive Chinese forms of Buddhism—*T'ien-t'ai* (Tendai), *Hua-yen* (Kegon), *Ch'ing-tu* (*Jōdoshin* or Pure Land), and *Ch'an* (Zen)—emerged. The northeastward advance of Buddhism transmitted these sects to Manchuria, Korea, and Japan. Buddhism officially entered Japan from Korea in 552. After 600 years, the Japanese evolved forms of Buddhism that suited and reflected their temperament. In contrast to early forms of Buddhism that required regular and long practice, these new movements distilled Buddhist practice to the single practice of reciting the *nembutsu* (*namu amida butsu* [praise the Amida Buddha]) or the *daimoku* (*namu hō renge kyō* (praise the Sutra of the Dharma Blossom). The founder of Japanese *Sōtō Zen, Dōgen* (1200-1253), introduced meditation as an independent single practice. The simplicity of the practice appealed to the common people, and for the first time, Buddhism embraced the majority of the populace. It was these forms of Buddhism that the majority of Japanese immigrant laborers brought to Hawaii and the United States at the end of the 19th century and the beginning of the 20th century.

■ BUDDHIST BELIEFS AND DOCTRINE

Pratītyasamutpāda

Gautama, the founder of the Buddhist faith, began his spiritual journey with the question of human suffering that accompanies old age, sickness, and death. The future Buddha sought his answer through 6 years of spiritual exercises. On that morning of the enlightenment, Gautama realized the Dharma, the truth of *pratītyasamutpāda* (interdependence) and became the Enlightened or Awakened One. He awakened to the truth that all existences are mutually related and mutually dependent. Simply, no single cause or event determines how a thing or being is created or destroyed or how an event is established or transpires. Furthermore, because the multiplicity and sequence of causes and conditions are continually changing, and because all things and beings are concomitantly established, the Buddha understood that there are no eternal or self-sustaining entities and selves.

As a doctrine, *pratītyasamutpāda,* a theme that is common to all Buddhist thought and practice, represents the ideological content of the Buddha's enlightenment. It establishes the Buddhist view of reality and its vision of the universe. We live in a complex, ever-changing web of interrelationships. Conze (1962) stated, "Interdependence is a law of the multiplicity of causes and conditions. No event has one single cause, but invariably a multitude of conditions are involved" (p. 148). Those who are ignorant of this reality suffer because they cling to beliefs such as "life continues forever" and they possess an abiding self that exists without any relationships with others. On a more practical level, *pratītyasamutpāda* explains how events come about and how they can influence and change the courses of people's lives. This doctrine explains how human predicaments arise and how we should comprehend them.

As an idea, *pratītyasamutpāda* can be understood as an extension of the law of karma. The idea of karma (literally "action") appeared approximately two or three centuries before the birth of Gautama. The ancients associated karma with the idea of samsara and personal responsibility. They believed, although not universally, that the deeds committed in the present life affected one's passage into the next life. An individual's present station in life, exalted or lowly, had been determined by the moral quality of action, or karma, that one had generated in his or her previous life. The ideas of karma and samsara quickly obtained universal acceptance. These ideas, no doubt, explained many inequalities that existed at the time. They rarely have been challenged. Although Buddhists accept the idea of individual moral responsibility, they recognize that a strictly personal interpretation of karma is not adequate to explain the complexity of the human experience and the impact that an individual could have on his or her life and the world.

A second and more fundamental aspect of the doctrine of *pratītyasamutpāda* describes the cooperative and mutually supportive relationships among all existences. Cause and effect are not sequential but rather simultaneous. We can illustrate the simultaneous presence of cause and result by a piece of fabric. The individual threads of the warp and woof are the cause of the cloth. The cloth is the product or result of the individual threads from which it is made. Without the individual threads that constitute the fabric, there would be no fabric. Individual threads establish the whole fabric; the fabric, in turn, defines each thread in relation to all other threads. The metaphor illustrates the mutual dependency of cause and result and, by extension, the mutuality of all things. In a mutually dependent universe, not only do we exist in the world, but by being involved in the world we help to create the world through the manner in which we live and act.

Four Noble Truths

According to Buddhist lore, the Buddha preached the Four Noble Truths at his first sermon. The Four Noble Truths, the Buddha's method to spiritual health, assumed karma as a law of cause and effect. The Four Noble Truths profile the condition of our lives, explain the cause of suffering, and explain the means by which we, residing in a samsaric world, can extract ourselves and realize an abiding spiritual reality. The Four Noble Truths are (a) the Noble Truth of suffering; (b) the Noble Truth that the cause of suffering is illusion and desire; (c) the Noble Truth of nirvana, a realm free from suffering; and (d) the Noble Truth of the Noble Eightfold Path, the way to enlightenment or nirvana. The Noble Eightfold Path consists of Right View, Right Thought, Right Speech, Right Action, Right Livelihood, Right Effort, Right Mindfulness, and Right Meditation.

The Four Noble Truths parallel the steps that summarize the medical treatment of a disease—diagnosis, etiology, recovery, and therapeutics (Buddhaghosa, 1956). In the First Noble Truth, the Buddha acknowledges that spiritual suffering, although the most serious, was just one of many ills. The cause or etiology of this suffering, the Second Noble Truth, stems from illusion and desire. Illusion is the belief in a substantial self and an unchanging world; desire refers to wishing for unattainable things. The Fourth Noble Truth is the Eightfold Noble Path that releases the individual from ignorance and delusion. The Eightfold Noble Path is the medicine or spiritual therapy that leads to the Third Noble Truth—wisdom or nirvana. The Four Noble Truths are a method to transcend, not escape, suffering through understanding. As a means for spiritual transformation, the Four Noble Truths do not take into account karmic forces that might deter or prevent an individual from realizing Buddhahood. Illness or an early death, for example, might cut short a devotee's spiritual path.

Transference of Merit

Responding to the reality that not everyone has the personal and economic resources to undertake the task of spiritual release, devotees appealed to the wisdom and compassion of the celestial Buddhas and Bodhisattvas. Amida Buddha, perhaps the most popular of the celestial Buddhas in East Asia, is an idealization of the virtues associated with the historical Buddha and an expression of humanity's deep yearning to be free from suffering. Amida saves all beings by transferring the vast store of merits he has accumulated to the most needy so that they too can enter the Pure Land. *Parinama* (transference of merit) is a soteriological idea based on the belief that an individual's life is irrevocably linked with all beings and things. The transference of merit does not mean that Buddhas and Bodhisattvas literally withdraw merits from their merit repositories and deposit them in others just like one would transfer money from one account to another. Merits of these heroes are "transferred" because we benefit from their spiritual exercises. In an interdependent world, we rise and fall as one body. On an existential level, parināma softens the harsh and uncompromising individualism of karma.

Pure Land devotees take refuge in Amida Buddha for spiritual release. Shinran, the 13th-century Japanese cleric and founder of *Jōdoshinshu* or the True Pure Land Sect, reflecting on the moral frailty of humanity, repeatedly wrote on the unconditional compassion of Amida. Birth in the Pure Land (i.e., attainment of enlightenment or spiritual release) is possible to those who entrust themselves wholeheartedly to the compassionate embrace of Amida. Even those with blind passion (all conscious and unconscious forces from the infinite past and those of the present that tie us to samsara, the world of illusion and desire) are embraced by boundless compassion. Amida's compassion flows most abundantly to the least worthy and most needy. Thus, Shinran (1962) wrote in the third chapter of the *Tanni shō*, "Even a good person is born in the Pure Land, how much more so is an evil person" (p. 23).

■ BUDDHISM'S ENCOUNTER WITH CONFUCIANISM

The Indian practice of a celibate monastic life and beliefs in karma, transmigration, and rebirth into another life form came into immediate conflict with the Confucian society that venerated ancestors, valued family, and desired descendants. The ancient cult of ancestral veneration is linked with *hsiao* (filiality), a fundamental social and religious concept of the Chinese. The ideograph 孝 consists of the graph for "child" 子 directly supporting the graph for "old" 耂. We may interpret the image to mean that the child supports the older person or simply represents affection. In either instance, the combination of the two graphs crystallizes what the ancients believed the relationship between parent and child should be. The sentiments of gratitude and reverence toward parents and ancestors formed the original rationale for ancestral veneration as an extension of filial piety. A filial child serves the parents in life, provides a proper burial, and continues to honor the parents by observing rites dedicated to their memory. Proper ritual sacrifices ensured that the ancestors would look after the well-being of their decedents. In addition, the Chinese believed that the cultivation of the relationship between parent and child, the most intimate of human relationships, is the basis for an individual's capacity to relate to others, the community, and the state. Confucius (552 or 551-479 B.C.E.) and his

followers helped to codify the ancestral cult, which had its origins during the
Shang period (1523-1028 B.C.E.). The importance of rites and associated ancestral veneration remain central to Chinese life and accounts for the significance of the family crypt, memorial tablets, and family lineage.

Confucian ideas have been a constant and prevailing influence on Japanese culture and civilization. Visitors from Korea introduced Confucianism in
404 C.E. Two centuries later in 604, Shōtoku Taishi (574-622) promulgated
the Seventeen Article Constitution, a document with Confucian overtones.
The main thrust of the Constitution was the duty of the people toward their sovereign and the need for harmony between inferiors and superiors. During subsequent centuries, Confucian values defused into Japanese culture. The Confucian heritage is defined in values such as a secular and this-worldly
orientation, personal discipline, diligence, ordered family life, respect for hierarchy and authority, social harmony, and an emphasis on education. An example of this theme of duty and loyalty toward the sovereign, ordered relationships, and filial piety in the Bushidō code is enacted in *Chūshingura* (Treasury
of Loyal Retainers). In this very popular Japanese tale, 47 loyal retainers plot
for 17 years before carrying out a vendetta to avenge the wrongful death of
their lord. Confucian values also found their way into the popular and urban
culture. Chikamatsu Monzaemon (1653-1725), author of Kabuki and Jōrui
plays, incorporated Confucian ideas into his puppet and Kabuki theaters,
where he dramatized the conflict between duty (*giri*) and human feelings
(*ninjō*). During the Meiji period (1868-1912), Japanese nationalists merged
Confucian moral principles with nationhood. In the Meiji Constitution, the
emperor was presented as a benevolent sovereign, the father of his people and
moral preceptor of the nation. Loyalty and filial piety were designated as cardinal virtues, and nationalist leaders prescribed Confucian moral principles as
the basis for education. The 1890 Imperial Rescript on Education is essentially
a Confucian document.

Probably very few Japanese would consider themselves Confucian or attribute their economic success to Confucianism. Most would disavow any significant role of Confucianism in modern Japan. Yet, stability and order in family relationships, harmony and hierarchy in the workplace, loyalty to
employers and supervisors, education, and self-cultivation are qualities that
Confucians prize. Granted, we cannot definitively attribute these widely held
values to be Confucian ideals or assert that they were derived from some Confucian ideas. Nevertheless, these values have endured and shaped not only
Japanese attitudes and values (Reischauer, 1977) but also Japanese American
values.

■ BUDDHIST-CONFUCIAN SYNTHESIS SEEN IN JAPANESE AMERICAN DEATH RITUALS

Memorial Services

Before the introduction of Buddhism, the Chinese did not believe in the continual existence of an individual through successive rebirths. At death, one passed from this world to the world of the ancestors in heaven above or purgatory below. By contrast, Buddhism introduced the idea of successive births. The *Sarvāstivāda*, an important school that exerted great influence on East Asian Buddhism, proposed an intermediate state (in Sanskrit, *antarābhava;* in Japanese, *chūin* or *chū'u*) that commences with death and continues until one takes on another life form. By positing a 49-day intermediate stage, Buddhists could assert that no physical or temporal discontinuity exists between one life and the next life.

In keeping with the Buddhist idea of karma and transmigration, the Chinese came to believe that the deceased passed through seven hells and met with 7 judges who weighed the merits and demerits of a person and meted out the appropriate punishment. The family displayed filial piety by diligently observing services every 7th day for 7 weeks over this 49-day period. The scriptural basis for these observances is the *Shí wáng jīng* (Sutra of the Ten Kings). In the Sutra, the Buddha preaches filial piety, the need for children to sponsor services for their deceased parents, and the advantages of making offerings to the Ten Kings. Besides the original 7 judges noted previously, the Sutra lists 3 additional judges to whom the 100th-day, 1st-year, and 3rd-year services correspond. After leaving the 10th judge, the individual is released from purgatory and is reborn into a realm determined by his or her moral ledger. Chinese funeral and postfuneral rituals are concerned with aiding the deceased's passage through the 10 purgatory courts and providing a comfortable material life until the "soul" would be reincarnated. In return, the ancestral spirits will watch over and protect their descendants. The Chinese understood these services as a way of transferring merit and aid to the deceased as he or she met with the judges.

The Japanese added to this cycle the 7th-, 13th-, 25th-, 33rd-, and 50th-year memorial services. The Japanese American Buddhist community, however, has abbreviated the traditional memorial cycle. Unlike in the past, families today often live great distances apart, and the modern work schedules make it difficult to observe the traditional memorial sequence. However, most families observe the 49th-day and the 1st-, 3rd-, and 7th-year services. The memorial services reinforce family solidarity and the memory of the deceased.

Children too young to know or born after the death of a grandparent connect
with their roots. The Japanese believe that until the 13th-year memorial service, the memory of the deceased remains strong. As the years pass, memory of
the deceased dims. The 33rd-year, or more recently the 50th-year, memorial
service is the final service dedicated specifically to the memory of an individual unless the person is especially noted. By then, the living memory of the deceased is lost and is honored as an ancestor; he or she belongs to the ages. Buddhists honor all ancestors, family, and nameless individuals at the annual
Etaikyō (perpetual memorial service). Temples normally observe this service
in November.

Obon

The Chinese believed that during the seventh lunar month, usually July,
the gates of purgatory stand open and the spirits of those without descendants
are free to wander about. Special care is taken during the month to placate these
wandering spirits. This belief has its origins in remote antiquity and has been
incorporated by Japanese Buddhist *Obon* observance. After its introduction in
the year 657, Obon changed greatly and became not only a service of gratitude
to departed ancestors but also an occasion for joy. The Japanese commonly accept the account that during Obon their ancestors return to their earthly homes.
At that time, offerings are made at the *butsudan* (family Buddhist altar) to welcome them. Lanterns are lit to guide the spirits. It is a time of great festivity.
Families place special foods on the altars to welcome their ancestors. Temples
sponsor bazaars and *Obon odori* (festive community dancing) to welcome the
ancestors and to honor the memory of the deceased. In some locales, families
float lanterns in the river to guide the ancestral spirits back to the other world
during the *Tōrōnagashi* ritual.

Obon and other memorial rituals reveal a reciprocal and unbroken relationship between the living and the dead. The living or a person facing death is
assured that he or she will continue to remain an active member of the family.
The belief that they will be able to communicate with the deceased comforts
the survivors. These rituals tie past, present, and future generations. Sugimoto
(1966) affectionately wrote in *A Daughter of the Samurai* of her childhood
memories of Obon:

> It was the most dearly loved of our festivals, for we believed that our ances-
> tors never lost their loving interest in us, and this yearly visit kept fresh in all
> our hearts a cheerful and affectionate nearness to the dear ones gone. (p. 74)

... Like all children, I had always looked forward with pleasure to visit the ancestors, but after Father's death, I felt a deep personal interest, and my heart was beating with excitement, as the family met at the shrine. (p. 77)
    ... The anxious look that Mother's face had lost during the last few days did not come back, and I felt that Father had really been with us bringing comfort and help to all of us; and now he is gone, leaving behind him not loneliness but peace. (p. 81)

Finally, the traditional cultures of China and Japan believe that malevolent spirits and disgruntled ancestral spirits cause suffering for the living. Malevolent spirits have no decedents to honor them. The Chinese and, to a lesser extent, the Japanese believe that disgruntled ancestral spirits return to remind their descendants through omens that they have forgotten to offer sacrifices (Thompson, 1996). My mother was extremely sensitive to unusual signs. Once when a pet hen crowed, she and my father immediately consulted a shaman, who informed my mother that the family had neglected to make an offering to a distant relative. She sponsored a simple service. The hen stopped crowing, and my mother's anxieties were relieved. Offerings appease and placate malevolent spirits and ensure that they will not harm the living. In many traditional cultures, diseases were not limited to the physical body. A physician might be competent to treat physical ailments, but a shaman or some other religious figure would be consulted when angry ancestors and malevolent spirits intruded into the world of the living.

■ END-OF-LIFE ISSUES

These religious and cultural traditions affect end-of-life decision making among Japanese American Buddhists in several ways, some of which influence Buddhists of other denominations and others of which are specific to Japanese Pure Land devotees. This chapter provides a limited discussion of views on organ donation and decision making. Readers are referred to Yeo and Hikoyeda's chapter on Asian and Pacific Islander Americans in this volume (Chapter 8) for additional information on these issues.

Brain Death and Organ Transplants

As noted by other authors, organ donation is not widely practiced in Japan or by Japanese Americans. The question of brain death and the appropriateness of organ transplants has generated great concern and a range of opinions in the

Buddhist community. The controversy lies, in part, in conflicting definitions of life and death. The United States and other countries in which transplants are routine define death as the absence of brain activity, which often occurs before the heart stops beating. This definition is critical for the success of organ transplants because once the heart stops beating, organs quickly deteriorate and become unsuitable for transplant. However, some Buddhists object to the brain death criterion of death, instead defining death as the stopping of the heart because Buddhists traditionally have associated life with sentience, which in its broadest sense includes animals and plants. Sentience also implies feeling, helping to explain the reluctance of many Buddhists to endorse organ (and especially heart) transplants. Some believe that cutting the corpse or taking away organs pains the individual even after death. In addition, traditional Buddhists understand that death is the dissolution of mind and body, and they believe that death of the mind is not death of the person. Curiously, even today we observe this distinction. We begin funeral preparations when the heart has been removed or has stopped beating, not when the brain is dead.

Another pervasive attitude against organ transplants is the assumption that life is impermanent. Because life is transient and death is inevitable, there is no meaning to artificially extending life. Most Buddhists also believe that a person has his or her own karmic destiny. The extension of life by organ transplant disrupts the natural karmic life span. Moreover, organ transplants are possible only at the expense of another's life, a violation of the precept to abstain from taking life. Consequently, some Buddhists advocate the development and use of artificial organs. Rather than extending life through heroic measures, increased practice of palliative end-of-life care would be more in keeping with the spirit of Buddhism. The same argument has to be used, however, by those who favor transplants. The body is, after all, transient and ultimately worthless (Masaki, 1993), and the gift of life is the greatest gift an individual can give.

The reluctance for organ transplants also can be traced, in part, to the Chinese notion of filial piety. The opening lines of the *Hsiao Ching* (Classic on Filial Piety), stated, "Filial piety is the basis of virtue and the source of our teachings. We receive our body, our hair, and [our] skin from our parents, and we dare not destroy them" (St. John's University Press, 1961/1975, p. 4). The Chinese referred to this passage to argue against their sons and daughters shaving their hair when entering the Buddhist order. Thus, a person should be buried with every part of his or her body, and this implies that the donation of one's organs is the most unfilial act a child can perform.

These Buddhist/Confucianist concepts have presented a barrier to organ transplants in Japan, as has the heart-based criterion of death. However, after 30 years of debate, the Japanese Parliament passed a law in 1997 that allows a person whose brain has stopped functioning to be defined as dead. In cases where a patient has agreed to this definition of death, the person can donate his or her heart and lungs for transplants. The bill does not provide a legal definition of death, and current Japanese law still defines death as the moment the heart stops beating. It does, nonetheless, allow the brain death standard to be used for willing donors of hearts and lungs. There is one catch: The donor does not have the absolute right to ask physicians to decide whether he or she is considered brain dead. Rather, the donor's family has the ultimate right to veto the doctors' diagnosis of brain death and the patient's wishes. (By contrast, in the United States, brain death is defined by law and physicians do not need the patient's or family's permission to declare an individual brain dead.) In February 1999, 21 months after the approval of the transplant law, Japanese doctors performed their first heart transplant.

The difference regarding the importance of individual autonomy differentiates the U.S. and Japanese approaches to organ transplants. As already noted, in Japan an individual does not have an absolute right to self-determination; the Japanese Parliament allows the family to void any prior directive that a brain dead individual might have made concerning the disposition of his or her organs. The Japanese approach to brain death reflects the manner in which a Buddhist would approach the problem. In an interdependent world where our lives are intertwined with countless others, individuals do not have exclusive claims on their lives. We might have separate lives, but we live in resonance with others.

End-of-Life Decision Making

The Buddha acknowledged the need to accommodate the wishes of others. He did not prescribe rigid rules but proposed general guides from which his devotees could draw lessons in their encounters with suffering and death. The Buddha displayed his flexibility adjudicating the precept against the taking of life. The early narratives relate the predicaments of two very ill monks who wished to commit suicide. In one narrative, the Buddha affirmed the reverence for life by admonishing his disciples for encouraging death, but in the second, the Buddha supported a monk's suicide based on the monk's selfless concern for others and objective evaluation of his own prospects for living. Within the confines of these two sketches, the Buddha clearly did not approach these two cases of willful self-induced euthanasia with some preconceived notion of right and wrong. More correctly, the Buddha considered each case within its immediate context. In Buddhism, a request for euthanasia represents a conflict between the respect for life and the compassion to end continued suffering. Despite the prohibition against ending one's life, there can be occasions when the continuation of life might not be the best alternative. Within the context of a vision of mutuality and interdependence, a Buddhist would seek to accommodate an individual's wish for a gentle death with the physician's duty to do no harm and societal desire to preserve life. An interdependent world strives for a balance of dignity, needs, duties, and responsibilities between and among individuals. All elements of suffering must be considered (Nakasone, 1990).

To aid in decision making, the Buddha outlined a four-step method in the *Samantapāsādikā*, a 5th-century commentary on the Buddhist precepts. This method asks the devotee to consult the Buddha, his disciples, and other experts. The Buddha charged his followers to use their own judgment if these authorities fail to provide adequate answers (Sanghabhadra, 1970). This method allows one to challenge time-honored convictions and prescribed rules of conduct.

My experience with Buddhist families supports the practice that end-of-life decisions usually are done by family deliberation and by consensus. The family, however, usually looks to the eldest member of the family for leadership. Individuals and families also might seek advice from the deceased. They approach the family altar and the memorial tablet of an honored elder for counsel. The Chinese and, to a lesser extent, the Japanese believe that the spirit of the individual resides in the memorial tablet. This practice reflects the continuing relationship of the living with the dead.

Every family and situation is unique. As a minister, I did not offer a definitive answer or prescribed rule that should be followed. Rather, I always tried to provide alternatives to help an individual or family members to reach a decision with which they felt most comfortable. In many ways, the task of the Buddhist priest is easy. Devotees understand death to be a part of life because change and suffering are endemic to life, and death is not to be feared. However, the difficulty lies in aiding the individual and/or family to a personal understanding of death and life. For devoted Buddhists, grief is deep and narrow, not a prolonged brooding search for answers.

The Buddhist attitude toward death also might appear among Asian American Christians. Recently, an esteemed colleague passed away, and when

I called to express my condolences to his wife, she was matter-of-fact about his passing. Although he had suffered a congenital heart condition that he had inherited from his parents, she expressed gratitude for the fact that he had outlived them by 10 years. When I mentioned the wife's attitude to a Chinese Confucian friend who happens to be an ordained Lutheran cleric, he was not surprised. "Asians," he said, "see life from the perspective of death" (E. Yee, personal communication, May 15, 1997). Traditionally, Okinawans, who comprise approximately 14% of the collective Japanese population in Hawaii, also share this attitude toward life. When a man proposes marriage, he asks a woman whether she will enter his family crypt, and a couple promises to be faithful by saying, "Until we enter the crypt."

■ CONCLUSION

The advances in medical science and technology have provoked Buddhist cultures to reenvision their doctrines and practices. Japanese Buddhism in Hawaii and the continental United States faces the challenges of cultural diffusion and modernization. Jōdoshinshū Buddhist clerics and lay leaders struggle to strike a balance between the desire to preserve the traditional teachings and the need to adapt to a religiously pluralistic society. For too long, the Buddhist faith interpreted questions related to its doctrine and culture in deference to the language and values of the West. Today, Jōdoshin Buddhism, as with other peripheral cultures, is in a position to shape new paradigms for its faith and ritual and to offer a different insight to questions generated by the advances of science and medicine. In my opinion, Buddhism has much to offer. Its vision of an interdependent world supports work of environmentalists. Deep ecology and global security, current buzzwords, echo the Buddha's original insight. Its mortuary rituals reinforce family solidarity and individual identity as well as a sense of gratitude for all ancestors of the past, present, and future. Likewise, it is hoped that the Obon festival, the public expression of gratitude of our indebtedness to others, will diffuse throughout the world and be a reminder that we are responsible for each other's well-being.

■ REFERENCES

Buddhaghosa. (1956). *Path of purification (Visuddhimagga)* (B. Nanamoli, Trans.). Colombo, Sri Lanka: R. Semage. (Original work appeared ca. 450 C.E.)

Buddhist Churches of America. (1997). *1996 annual report*. San Francisco: Author.

Ching, J. (1993). *Chinese religions*. Maryknoll, NY: Orbis.

Conze, E. (1962). *Buddhist thought in India: Three phases of Buddhist philosophy*. London: Allen and Unwin.

Hirakawa, A. (1990). *A history of Indian Buddhism, from Sakyamuni to early Mahayana* (P. Groner, Trans.). Honolulu: University of Hawaii Press. (Original work published 1974)

Honpa Hongwanji Mission of Hawaii. (1997). *The 85th legislative assembly annual reports*. Honolulu, HI: Author.

Masaki, H. (1993). Tōyō tetsugaku to seimei rinri [Eastern philosophy and bioethics]. *Seimei Rinri* [Bioethics], 1(3), 49-52.

Nakasone, R. Y. (1990). *Ethics of enlightenment*. Fremont, CA: Dharma Cloud Publishers.

Reischauer, E. O. (1977). *The Japanese*. Cambridge, MA: Harvard University Press.

Robinson, R. H., & Johnson, W. L. (1982). *The Buddhist religion: A historical introduction* (3rd ed.). Belmont, CA: Wadsworth.

Sanghabhadra. (1970). *Shan-Chien-P'i-P'o-Sha: A Chinese version by Sanghabhadra of Samantapāsādikā* (P. V. Bapat & A. Hirakawa, Trans.). Poona, India: Bhandarkar Oriental Research Institute. (Original work appeared in 489 C.E.)

Shinran. (1962). *Tanni shō [Notes lamenting differences] (R. Fujiwara, Trans.). Kyoto, Japan: Ryukoku University. (Original work appeared in late 13th century)*

St. John's University Press. (1975). *The Hsaio-Ching* [Classic on filiality] (M. L. Makra, Trans.). New York: Author. (Original work appeared ca. 200 C.E.; originally published in 1961)

Sugimoto, E. I. (1966). *A daughter of the samurai*. Rutland, VT: Tuttle.

Thompson, L. G. (1996). *Chinese religion: An introduction* (5th ed.). Belmont, CA: Wadsworth.

Part 4

End-of-Life Issues in Institutional Cultures and for Special Populations

*W*hereas people's end-of-life choices can be influenced by their cultural and religious traditions, their choices also are affected by the institutions with which they interact and other groups to which they belong. This section of the book presents chapters about end-of-life considerations within two institutional cultures (the hospital/nursing home and the military) and for two groups of individuals facing illness and disability (people living with AIDS and people living with disabilities).

Questions addressed in this section include the following:

- How does the culture of the hospital, especially in the emergency room and intensive care unit, affect whether or not someone's advance directive is honored?
- What elements of the hospital culture keep us from improving care to dying people?

- What practices and ceremonies have evolved in the military to prepare its members whose job description might include going off to war, killing, and perhaps dying themselves?
- Why is there growing support for euthanasia and assisted suicide among some people living with AIDS?
- What fears about liberalized euthanasia laws face some people living with disabilities?
- How does the Netherlands manage requests for euthanasia and assisted suicide?
- What safeguards and supports are in place in the Netherlands to keep people from seeking euthanasia and assisted suicide for financial reasons?

These four chapters were written by individuals who work within these communities and have intimate knowledge of these cultures. They show how an expanded definition of culture is needed to truly understand the varying factors that affect an individual's preferences and options at the end of life.

Chapter 15

Issues in End-of-Life Decision Making in the Hospital and Nursing Home Culture

CHARON A. PIERSON

Hospitals and long-term care (LTC) facilities (nursing homes) are complex organizations with distinct and sometimes conflicting cultures. They are staffed by a variety of professionals and other personnel who provide care and treatment to patients who are temporary or permanent residents of the institutions. The patients, their families, and a variety of third-party insurers pay for this care and treatment and have expectations of the institutions and their staffs. Many factors influence these expectations such as the patients' previous experiences with hospitals and illnesses, the types of illness the patients have, sociocultural influences on the patients and their families, financial factors, political mandates, and the history of health care professions in this country.

According to postmodern theorists, institutional cultures are created and sustained by many discourses. Discourses are defined by Wicks (1995) as "ways of constituting knowledge, social practices, and forms of subjectivity" (p. 123). At the risk of being overly simplistic, one could argue that there are two primary and competing discourses that constitute the culture of hospitals and LTC facilities: the discourse of curing and the discourse of comforting. The balance between cure and comfort has varied both historically and currently according to many factors. The profession of medicine, for example, claims "curing illness" as its province, whereas the profession of nursing claims "comforting and caring" as its roles (Morse, Bottorff, Anderson, O'Brien, & Solberg, 1992). Whether or not a cure is seen as a viable option for the hospitalized patient greatly affects the way in which end-of-life decisions are made by individuals, families, professional groups, and society at large.

This chapter focuses on dying as a social rather than a physiological process. The primary objective is to uncover how the discourses of curing and caring create and sustain the cultures of hospitals and LTC facilities and how those cultures, in turn, affect end-of-life decisions. Using a case study, relevant literature, and personal experience as a clinical nurse and sociologist, I examine the effects of the primacy of the lifesaving ethic and the marginalized ethic of palliative or comfort care on the decisions made by staff, patients, and families at the end of life.

■ HISTORICAL PERSPECTIVE

Starr (1982) argued that physicians claim cultural authority over disease as members of a community of professionals with a history of legitimate and validated science related to illness and treatment. This authority allows medicine to define illness, and by extension health, and to give advice on the proper treatment of all illnesses and the appropriate health promotion activities of individuals and communities. The cultural authority of medicine privileges a discourse that defines the reality of illness, the value of certain signs and symptoms in the diagnosis of illness, and the validity of specific treatments in the tradition of the medical model of disease, that is, a biophysical model. In modern health care settings, this dominant medical discourse institutionalizes the devotion to technology and the primacy of curing, and it marginalizes the alternative discourses of caring and palliation. Throughout history, this was not always the case.

Premodern medicine had its roots in religion, not in science. It was thought that evil spirits caused disease and that cure was effected by divine intervention. Priests, rather than physicians, often ministered to the sick, and in fact there was little a physician could offer in the way of effective treatments.

Scientific advances led to impressive changes, such as hospital antisepsis, surgical anesthesia, and infection prophylaxis and treatments, that fostered a shift in the class of diseases treated by the modern physician during the early 1900s. No longer were the majority of patients dying of acute infectious or traumatic conditions because medicine now had new science to treat and cure such problems. What remained were the chronic illnesses for which the modern hospital emerged as the focal point of health care systems in the modern world (Turner, 1987).

A number of social, economic, and political factors influenced the evolution of the modern hospital and the rise in professional authority of physicians (Starr, 1982). Foremost among them was the industrial revolution that transformed modern society from a rural agricultural base to an urban industrial base. From a productivity perspective, it made sense to locate sick patients in one place, a hospital, where they could be cared for by professional caregivers such as nurses and an expert physician could visit several patients in one stop. Hospitalization allowed family members to continue working in factories and businesses rather than caring for sick patients at home, and travel times and expenses for physicians were reduced significantly by not having to make several home visits. Not only was financial productivity for physicians enhanced, but professional productivity and enrichment of medical knowledge developed under the "clinical gaze" (Foucault, 1975). For Foucault (1975), the clinical gaze could evolve only in a hospital-based practice where patients could be examined, treated, and used as examples with which to teach apprentice physicians the body of knowledge called clinical medicine.

As technology advanced and clinical medicine developed new ways of diagnosing and treating disease, the biophysical medical discourse assumed primacy and medical specialists increasingly saw death as failure. In the tradition of reductionism, with enough objective evidence from scientific tests and procedures, medicine should be able to devise cures for all disease, from cancer to the common cold. There is no alternative to cure in this medical model. Even dying presents an opportunity to learn from the clinical gaze of repeated testing, attempts at treatments no matter how small the benefit, and the final clinical gaze—autopsy. Taken to its extreme, the clinical gaze does not allow death to occur without scientific observation or intervention, nor does it promote palliation or comfort. In the historical development of clinical medicine, the primacy of the discourse of curing has marginalized the discourses of comforting and caring as well as other alternative discourses that define the cultures of hospitals and LTC facilities.

■ THE DO-NOT-RESUSCITATE OR NO-CODE ORDER

The dramatic scenes of dying patients being brought back to life are known to the general public through television shows such as *Dr. Kildare, St. Elsewhere, Chicago Hope,* and *ER.* There are a number of terms for cardiopulmonary emergencies such as "code," "code blue," "Dr. Stat," "Code 9," and many other signals hospitals use when publicly paging for emergency assistance over the loudspeaker system. All of these terms mean that a patient has had a cardiac arrest and requires cardiopulmonary resuscitation (CPR), which is performed by a team of specialists, sometimes referred to as the "code team." In most hospitals, "calling a code" activates an emergency response team composed of physicians, respiratory therapists, anesthesiologists, and intensive care unit (ICU) nurses who are prepared to go to the site of the emergency and perform CPR, even though they do not know the patient or the circumstances of the emergency. There usually is a code team on call 24 hours a day in every hospital, even though there is no way in which to predict when or where the need for CPR will arise. This is further evidence of the primacy of the lifesaving ethic in modern hospitals.

The purpose of using secret signals for CPR in public is to keep "death work" out of public view (Sudnow, 1967). Because the public is aware of the fact that CPR does occur and that patients sometimes are "brought back from the dead," these secret signals do not actually fool most people. The general public has little understanding of what actually occurs during a code, but most people expect that "everything" will be done in emergency situations and that miraculous things can happen in modern hospitals. This lifesaving ethic or mandate is not written anywhere; it is just part of the dominant discourse in the culture of the hospital. In fact, this ethic of curing and lifesaving is so routine that to do otherwise requires a special order, that is, the "do-not-resuscitate" (DNR) or "no-code" order.

Although a patient might have an advance directive specifying a desire not to be resuscitated under futile conditions, the medical personnel take their direction from the DNR order. The DNR order is a formalized statement in the medical record that confirms the medical opinion that attempts at CPR would be futile because of the patient's prognosis. This decision usually is made collaboratively with the patient, the patient's family, and other caregivers such as nursing and respiratory therapy. A DNR order might be found in the patient's chart, on a sign near the patient's bed or door, or on a bulletin board at the nurses' station. There often is an accompanying order for "comfort care only." To comply with licensing regulations and mandates from Medicare and Medicaid, there also must be documentation in the progress notes that the decision to post a DNR order was reached in collaboration with the family, the patient, and other staff. The attending physician and resident, nurses, social workers, and (occasionally) consultants such as psychiatrists and psychologists write this documentation in notes.

In the ideal situation, the decision is reached in a multidisciplinary care conference attended by all of these parties. Once the decision is reached, however, it is important that the information be transmitted to everyone who cares for the patient. Thus, it is necessary to display in some way, preferably in a not so obvious way, that the patient has a DNR order, for it usually is the nurse or nursing assistant on the unit who finds the patient dead. It has been my experience in LTC facilities that families react in a very negative way to "DNR" or "no code" being posted on a sign over the patient's bed. Consequently, some facilities use something less obvious such as a pink star or banner with the words "comfort care please." The difficulty families have with the concept of DNR is their belief that "DNR" means "do not do anything." It is important that families understand that patients will not be abandoned by health care workers and that lifesaving or resuscitation is not the same thing as caring or comfort measures.

When there is no DNR order on the chart, nurses have other ways of implementing DNR practices. The most common of these practices is a "slow code." To nurses, a slow code means that the discovery of the body and the emergency page for a code should take long enough that those who respond to the emergency will quickly see that resuscitation is futile because the patient has been dead too long. This is a practical, commonsense way of getting around the lifesaving mandate when it is clear to the nurses that CPR would be futile or even cruel.

In many LTC facilities, there is no code team, and the need for CPR will initiate a chain of events designed to circumvent that problem. The nurse must call 9-1-1 to activate the community emergency medical system, which will then transfer the patient to the nearest emergency room (ER) by ambulance. The response will not be as immediate as with a hospital-based code team; thus, nurses who are not accustomed to performing emergency CPR might be called on to participate in the code. Such emergencies are time-consuming, are emotionally draining, and create havoc with the normal routines of the facility. Because LTC facilities have fewer professional staff, the nurses will try to anticipate the patient's downward trajectory and transfer the patient to the hospital before the actual need for a code occurs. That way, the need for CPR will occur in a hospital where a code team is available for emergency CPR.

■ THE DYING TRAJECTORY

Glaser and Strauss (1968) use the term "dying trajectory" to describe the social process of dying. This social process of dying is interactionally constructed by the dying patient, the family, and the health care providers involved in the case within the culture of the institution in which the dying occurs. Within a general hospital setting, three types of dying trajectories are common: (a) a lingering trajectory leading to an expected death, (b) a swift trajectory leading to an expected death, and (c) a sudden trajectory leading to an unexpected death. Patients in certain areas of the general hospital (e.g., the ER) are more likely to experience unexpected deaths, whereas most patients in LTC facilities experience the lingering trajectory leading to expected deaths.

In the ER: Save Life First, Ask Questions Later

In an ER, the culture is organized around the primacy of the lifesaving ethic, and because of the rapidity with which emergent conditions evolve, little time is spent on deliberating end-of-life decisions. It is only after an ER patient has been stabilized and the family has been told all the details that the deliberations can begin. It is not uncommon for ER staff to perform painful and invasive lifesaving procedures on patients whose identities are unknown to the staff. Any advance directives are not discussed, or even considered, until the emergency is over. This is congruent with the mission of the ER to treat anyone with trauma or sudden onset of a critical incident such as a heart attack.

The assumption is made that anyone who presents to the ER does so for lifesaving treatment, an assumption that creates problems in cases such as the one involving Lillian, described in subsequent subsections. Although the case of Lillian is a hypothetical one, I have based the incidents on situations I have encountered in more than 25 years as a clinical nurse in a variety of settings including the ICU, the postanesthesia unit, medical and surgical wards, LTC facilities, and primary care settings. In my own professional experience and in talking with my colleagues, the incidents I describe occur quite frequently.

The Case of Lillian

Lillian was a 59-year-old woman with advanced breast cancer who lived at home with her 67-year-old husband, Marvin. Lillian had advance directives clarifying that she did not want to live on life-support equipment, and she had told Marvin that she was ready to die after fighting cancer for many years. Late one evening, Lillian developed severe chest pain and shortness of breath, and both she and Marvin panicked. Marvin called 9-1-1, and Lillian was taken via ambulance to the local ER, where she was treated for a myocardial infarction (heart attack). While in the ER, Lillian suffered cardiac arrest twice; the staff performed CPR, and Lillian was successfully resuscitated each time. When Marvin next saw his wife, she was unconscious, intubated, and hooked up to the life-support equipment that she previously had stated she did not want.

Marvin was then left to make the decision to maintain or remove the life support in a culture where the ER doctors and nurses, who did not know about her living will or advanced breast cancer, had worked for hours to save Lillian's life. When Lillian's heart stopped beating in the ER, there was no time to ask her husband about her wishes or to search the record room for her advance directives. To successfully resuscitate a victim of cardiac arrest, the ER staff has to move quickly, and their bias always is toward saving the life and asking questions later.

In the ICU

Patients usually are transferred out of the ER rather quickly to a location in the hospital where they will spend their days recovering. For the critically ill and medically unstable patients, that place will be the ICU (Benoliel & Degner, 1995). Here, the staff-to-patient ratio is high, and the physical layout of the unit is structured so that doctors and nurses can monitor patients closely and intervene quickly to prevent death. As a result, the technological work takes precedence over patient privacy, family visiting, and interior comfort and design. Lifesaving technology and the dominant medical discourse reign supreme in the ICU; comfort often is a secondary consideration.

The Continuing Case of Lillian

Returning to our case study, Lillian was transferred to the ICU, still intubated and on life support, while Marvin waited outside the unit in the visiting area reserved for families of ICU patients. Lillian's prognosis at this point still was uncertain, but the immediate danger was over. Marvin, who was beginning to wonder whether he had done the right thing in calling 9-1-1, decided to call the couple's children who lived out of state. Sometime later, the ICU nurse and the doctor assigned to care for Lillian came out to the waiting room to talk with

Marvin. It was only then that any of the hospital staff finally got the information that Lillian had end-stage breast cancer and a living will and that additional family members would be arriving within 24 hours.

Armed with this new information about Lillian and her family, the ICU staff had to discuss her care plan. The first item for discussion was the patient's prognosis, which was clouded by the fact that she had three serious problems: a history of breast cancer, a recent myocardial infarction, and a potential problem of brain damage during the cardiac arrests. Terminal breast cancer can have a lingering dying trajectory, and without an oncology consultation, the ICU staff were reluctant to make prognostications. The prognosis for Lillian's recovery from the myocardial infarction, however, was quite good. After laboratory tests and careful analysis of her cardiograms, the staff determined that the damage to Lillian's heart had been relatively minor. With only the cardiac data to go by, the physicians proposed an aggressive plan to treat Lillian's slightly damaged heart. What remained unclear, however, was the question of permanent brain damage due to hypoxia during the cardiac arrest. Only further testing and time would answer that question, and on the orders of the physicians, Lillian would remain on life support until all the data could be gathered.

The nurses agreed with the physicians to keep Lillian alive, but for different reasons; they wanted Lillian's children to have a chance to see their mother before she died. In general, nurses value opportunities for closure between patients and their families and view this final interaction as comforting to both parties. The ICU nurses knew that they could keep Lillian alive long enough for the family to arrive. After the family was together, another negotiation would ensue about the benefit of keeping Lillian alive for further attempts at treatment. By that time, an oncology consult would be completed and old records would be obtained and reviewed. Meanwhile, Lillian, who had specified in her living will that she be allowed to die without extraordinary life support and who might even have envisioned herself dying in her comfortable bedroom at home, remained in the ICU in a coma, attached to a respirator, a cardiac monitor, and several intravenous (IV) lines. Treatment decisions now were out of her hands and resided with her family and the staff of the ICU. Her only possible contribution to the discussion was her advance directives in her chart.

After 4 days in the ICU, Lillian was weaned off the respirator but remained unconscious; her only treatment was the IV fluids to keep her hydrated. Her living will was in the chart, but the ICU physicians had refused to write a DNR order for her because they could not come to consensus on her prognosis relative to the condition that had kept her in the ICU—the question of irreversible brain damage. The neurology consult had not been completed, so the diagnosis of irreversible brain damage could not yet be made with certainty. Consequently, the physicians were unwilling to declare that Lillian was in an irreversible coma or a persistent vegetative state, a declaration prerequisite to implementing her advance directives.

The consulting oncologist had confirmed her terminal breast cancer condition but could not say for certain that she had less than 6 months to live, thus precluding hospice services. Hospice services generally are recognized by third-party payers as legitimate palliative care services; however, eligibility criteria include a predicted death within 6 months of entering the program. A diagnosis of cancer is not a criterion for hospice care, but the use of hospice services for other terminal conditions is not as prevalent. Lillian's husband and children had visited her, and all had said that she was "never going to be the same as she was before this happened." In their close contact with Lillian and her family, the nurses also recognized that the situation was contrary to everything the family and patient had wanted or expected at the end of Lillian's life. But Lillian remained in the ICU because the nurses' assessments and the family's views were not valued in the determination of Lillian's prognosis.

In making their determination of Lillian's prognosis, the nurses had used what Anspach (1987) called "interactive cues," that is, information they learned from interacting 24 hours every day with the patient and the family. The physicians, on the other hand, relied on "technological and perceptual cues," that is, information arising out of diagnostic technology and direct physical examination; their interactions with Lillian and her family amounted to minutes every day, not hours as in the case of the nurses. As Anspach observed, technological and perceptual cues assume a "superior epistemological status" in cultures such as the ICU (p. 219). Other studies have shown that living wills, advance directives, and family and patient preferences do not exert much influence on treatment decisions, particularly in teaching hospitals (Prigerson, 1992). The dominant medical discourse instead relies on objective, scientific, technological findings such as blood tests, cardiograms, CT scans, and the expert opinions of specialist consultants in making treatment decisions.

In the case of patients such as Lillian, who was unable to make a verbal request for a DNR order, the end-of-life decisions always are problematic. The family members must make a determination based on their own knowledge of the patient and the patient's life up to that point. This is not the same as hearing the patient actually say, "Please let me die!" But even if Lillian had awakened from her coma and made such a request, it would not have been granted so easily. Almost universally, the physicians and nurses would have considered Lillian to be depressed because one of the clinical signs of depression is a feeling that life is not worth living. Thus, the staff would have at least recommended a psychiatric consultation to rule out depression, and perhaps even a trial of antidepressants would have been instituted. The "normal" patient in the ICU is not supposed to want to die.

Patients on Lingering Dying Trajectories

Often, it is the nurses who first conclude that a patient is on a lingering dying trajectory and will not recover. Patients who are expected to die lingering deaths do not belong in an ICU for several reasons. Dying patients are, in fact, evidence of a failure of medical technology and contradict the dominant discourse of the ICU. The focus in the ICU is high-tech, and staff quickly lose interest in patients who require comfort or custodial care only. There often is a sentiment among the ICU staff that another patient who really needs the ICU bed will not get it because the bed is occupied by a dying patient, one who does not require the skills of the staff and the capabilities of the high-tech equipment. Nurses also recognize that patients who primarily need comfort care do not receive much comfort in the sterile and often noisy environment of an ICU where visitors are more restricted and the routines of technological care (e.g., attending to machines, IV lines, monitor alarms) disrupt patients' sleep and rest.

The administrative department of a hospital or an LTC facility also is involved in the assignment of beds and the determination of the level of care for patients through organizational procedures such as utilization review. The assignment of level of care to patients determines staffing ratios, reimbursement rates, transfer of patients within the hospital, and discharge planning. As a business, hospitals have a financial interest in the best use of institutional resources, including staff and services. Care plans for a patient must be appropriate and realistic for the patient's diagnosis and prognosis; otherwise, third-party payers can refuse to pay for services. In short, it is not cost-effective to keep someone in the ICU who does not need life-support technology and constant supervision by highly trained and costly staff. Once patients are determined to be on the lingering trajectory toward death, they move into the marginalized discourse of palliative care (Wicks, 1995). They must physically be moved out of the temple of technology, the ICU.

The Continuing Case of Lillian

When hospice is ruled out and the ICU no longer is the appropriate location for dying patients, they will be moved to a chronic medical unit or an LTC facility, as happened in Lillian's case. Following her stay in the ICU, Lillian was taken to a licensed LTC facility. At this time, there is a DNR order in her chart because the consulting neurologist determined, after extensive testing, that Lillian would not recover and declared her to be in a persistent vegetative state. It now has been a month since her admission to the ER, and she has been off the respirator for 3 weeks. She is unconscious, is incontinent, and has several decubitus ulcers (bed sores) on her lower back, hips, and both heels. Her only treatments are IV fluids and dressings to her skin ulcers.

Negotiating Dying: Facing Decisions About
Artificial Nutrition and Hydration

The process of negotiating the social aspects of dying have given rise to what some call "the right to die" or "death with dignity" movements. At the forefront of this movement are those who advocate legalizing euthanasia or physician aid in dying. Equally vocal are those who advocate for broader applications of the principles of palliative care and hospice as well as greater attention to the issue of pain control as alternative solutions to the right to die. Even when everyone is in agreement to remove life support in the form of respirators and cardiac monitors, the issue of artificial nutrition and hydration remains.

Food and fluids are essential to life. Humans can exist without food for more than a month, but without adequate hydration, a person will die within 3 days. Artificial nutrition and hydration are controversial issues, and many states require specific statements in advance directives related to whether or not an individual wants parenteral tube feeding. This can be a requirement apart from directive-based statements related to CPR and life-support technology. The primary issue for discussion seems to be whether or not nutrition and hydration are essential for the comfort of the patient.

This issue of nutrition and hydration is, in my experience, one of the most controversial ones in LTC. Staff often complain among themselves, some of them going so far as to say that doctors and families are starving patients to death. The problem is not that nurses want to avoid these deaths; rather, they are concerned about the patients' comfort. Food is so basic to life and has such strong connections with nurturing, comforting, and caring that caregivers, either family members or professionals, feel a strong need to provide sustenance. Many of the daily rituals in LTC revolve around food and feeding (Diamond, 1992). Patients are weighed on a regular basis to monitor the effects of feeding, social events occur accompanied by food, and the quantity and quality of food served in LTC facilities are strictly monitored by licensing and regulatory agencies. With such attention to nutrition, patients who do not eat or who lose weight are a cause for concern. Feeding patients makes visible the proces of caring. When patients cannot eat, they still can be fed enough food parenterally so that they maintain their body weight and their skin ulcers heal—all signs of "good" care.

Despite advance directives to the contrary, feeding tubes often are inserted as a temporary measure in patients who have suffered a stroke until the prognosis is clear. One of the greatest dangers following a stroke is aspiration of food into the lungs, which causes pneumonia and death. So, until a determination can be made that the patient will not recover the ability to swallow, a feeding tube is inserted. Once the tube is in place, caregivers and families might have more difficulty in agreeing to the withdrawal of the tube than they had in agreeing to the original idea of inserting it after the stroke. Stopping food and fluids often is more difficult than making the decision not to tube-feed initially because feeding is seen not as a medical intervention but rather as evidence of care and comfort.

Given the current system of medical insurance, which is governed by the primacy of the discourse of cure rather than comfort or care, it is not surprising that patients and families opt for more interventions. Particularly in LTC facilities, families pay more for "custodial services" than for rehabilitative services. A good example of this is the problem of feeding patients in LTC. To feed a patient by mouth can take as long as an hour, yet a patient who requires individual feeding is not considered in need of "skilled care," so the reimbursement rate paid by the insurer could be for "unskilled care." To feed a patient through a feeding tube takes only minutes but qualifies that patient for skilled care. The bias that skilled care is the equivalent of technological care and that it is valued more highly than alternative types of care is structurally embedded in modern health care systems. Changing this bias will be difficult because it arises out of the dominant discourse of curing.

Denk, Benson, Fletcher, and Reigel (1997), in a survey of public attitudes about end-of-life decision making, made the following statement: "The general public may not have a very realistic picture of what advance directives can and cannot do and [may] treat them as an easy 'technical fix' for much more complex issues" (p. 113). The strongest correlation to attitudes in their study was with patient choice and the benefit to the patient's length and quality of life. The presence of pain, dementia, incontinence, and the loss of mobility are almost universally regarded as indicators of poor quality of life by both professionals and the general public. The inability to eat or drink is not as clearly related to quality of life, and the use of parenteral feeding seems to alleviate the fear that patients are being starved to death. Rosseau (1992) commented, however, that terminal dehydration reduces pulmonary secretions, nausea, vomiting, and urination and that it produces a natural anesthetic effect from the associated electrolyte imbalance, all of which are beneficial to the dying patient.

The Continuing Case of Lillian

The nurses in the LTC facility are becoming very frustrated trying to deal with the bed sores that will not heal because Lillian is not getting adequate nutrition and her skin is constantly moist from her urinary incontinence, which increases her chances of further skin breakdown. It is true that skin regeneration requires adequate nutrition and specific vitamins and minerals and that urine is an irritant to skin and creates an environment that fosters infection. With Lillian receiving only a sugar and water solution for hydration, she is lacking in the nutrients that would help to heal her skin. The only way in which to give adequate nutrition to someone who is not eating is through a tube directly into the stomach, something that Lillian did not want. Conversely, Lillian continues to be incontinent of urine because she is getting enough fluid through the intravenous to allow her kidneys to function.

The Death Watch

Sudnow (1967) observed that, at some point, a patient makes the transition from being a living patient to being a dying patient. The reasons for this transition are not always evident to the casual observer. In fact, many nurses pride themselves on their ability to predict an approaching death very accurately. Although Sudnow did not elaborate on the interactions that occur when such predictions are being made, there seems to be some element of negotiation that occurs. This is evident in our continuing case study of Lillian.

The Continuing Case of Lillian

During an evening shift, the charge nurse went into Lillian's room to talk to Marvin and check on Lillian. Marvin told the nurse that he thought his wife was in some pain because she had moaned when the nursing assistants changed her diaper a short time before. The nurse assessed Lillian and found her pulse weak and slightly irregular, her respiration rapid and irregular, and her fingers and toes looking dusky—all signs of a failing cardiorespiratory system. The nurse decided that Lillian was dying. There was an order for oxygen for comfort and pain medication, both of which the nurse promptly gave. Then, she stopped all treatments, including the IV. She also notified the nursing supervisor and the physician in charge of the facility. Because there was a DNR order, there was nothing to do but notify the proper people—usually family, supervisor, and physician—and wait. This is what Sudnow (1967) called "a death watch." It might be a very subtle change in a patient's condition that causes a nurse to predict that a patient is dying, but most experienced nurses who have seen a lot of patients die can make that prediction quite accurately.

The death watch that Sudnow (1967) described has many unique characteristics, depending on the type of hospital and unit involved. In LTC facilities, it has been my experience that the nurses will stop all medications except pain medication, stop all treatments, including IV fluids, and stop trying to feed the patient food or fluids except for wetting dry lips to provide comfort. Usually, they will draw the curtain around the patient's bed and dim the lights in the room. Arrangements are made for family members to be at the bedside at all times if the family requests it. When the shift changes, staff who are leaving often predict that the patient will be "gone" by the time they return for their next shift. It also is common for the same staff to check the dying patient's room when they return on their next shift to verify that the death did indeed occur (Diamond, 1992; Sudnow, 1967).

Nurses will continue to talk to the dying patient in a soft voice and frequently say things such as "It's okay to die now" and "Your family is here with you, and they want you to be at peace." Family members seem to do little talking at this time, particularly while the nurse is in the room. Often, family members will leave the room to stand in the hall or go to the nurses station to ask for something. When the dying takes a long time, some nurses will suggest that family members speak aloud giving the patient permission to die. Physicians rarely attend a death unless they are actively involved in trying to stop or hasten it ("It's Over, Debbie," 1988), whereas nurses often act as midwives, guiding patients and supporting families through the death. Even when families are not involved, a nurse might be present at the death, particularly when the patient is well liked by staff. But many deaths in both hospitals and LTC facilities go unattended. If the patient has been a long-term resident on the unit, then staff will even go into the room after the patient has died and say good-bye to the already dead person.

■ CONCLUSION AND RECOMMENDATIONS

I summarize my insights about hospital culture presented in this chapter by relating back to three critical points in the case study of Lillian. The first critical incident occurred when Lillian and Marvin activated the emergency medical system for a health problem for which they were unprepared. Most patients do not understand what dying is all about and never have even seen a dead body. In a rural agrarian society, families experienced births and deaths in their own homes and communities, and children were not shielded from the events that happened during the dying process. The modern hospital has removed death from the family home, hidden it behind the closed curtains and doors of institutions, and constrained the talk about dying so that people do not know what to expect.

As a result of this institutionalization of death, it takes a great deal of education, support, and planning to allow people to die comfortably at home today. Unfortunately, payment for family education, support, and assistive care in the home is underfunded and underused. In the case of Lillian, who perhaps wanted to die in her own home, those efforts were not made. She and Marvin had no one to call other than 9-1-1 when something happened that they did not know how to handle. If home hospice services or a home health agency had been available to them, they would have had an alternative plan for emergencies. By activating the emergency response system, Lillian and Marvin were caught in the culture of curing and lifesaving that is the primary mission of such systems.

There is a movement to provide terminally ill patients with DNR bracelets, much like the medical alert bracelets worn by people with chronic medical conditions. When a patient is wearing a DNR bracelet, paramedics responding to a 9-1-1 emergency call would be allowed to provide comfort care only such as pain medication and oxygen. Providing bracelets is only one part of making such a change; what also has to occur is the embracing of the palliative discourse as a legitimate role for paramedics. This will take time.

The second critical incident relates to the completion and implementation of advance directives. There is a growing body of literature indicating that patients do not have a clear understanding of what advance directives are and what they can do (Denk et al., 1997) or of how they are implemented or ignored in the clinical setting (Prigerson, 1992; SUPPORT Principal Investigators, 1995). Even when patients have advance directives that clearly state their opposition to extraordinary measures, as was the case with Lillian, they might end up on life support while decisions are made among doctors, nurses, administrators, third-party payers, and family members.

Advance directives do not address all the possible issues that might occur during an illness or a hospitalization. There is no way in which to predict every eventuality, nor is there any way in which to write directives for every contingency. At some point, decisions are out of the patient's control and reside in the interactions that constitute the culture of the institution. In hospital settings, that culture is biased toward the dominant medical discourse. In the case of Lillian, that happened several times, even though she had family members who were verbalizing her previously stated wishes. There was, for example, difficulty in achieving consensus on her prognosis, and until her prognosis was terminal, her advance directives could not be implemented.

A third critical issue relates to artificial hydration and nutrition. There is no clear consensus among ethicists and medical professionals as to whether or not feeding terminally ill patients is a comfort measure or an unnecessary means of prolonging life (Jansson & Norberg, 1989). Arguments are persuasive either way, and in the case of comatose patients, there is no way in which to verify whether or not terminal dehydration is beneficial. In the case study of Lillian, the feeding was only fluids, but it could just as easily have been a tube directly into the stomach. Even if feeding is not a comfort issue for the dying patient, the act of providing food and fluids often is a comfort to the caregivers; the determination as to what purposes the feeding serves can be difficult to make.

In summary, this chapter discussed the ways in which powerful norms within the institutional cultures of hospitals and LTC facilities affect decisions related to death and dying. Health care providers, patients, families, and the general public are not always aware of these norms and the ways in which they affect health care decisions. In addition to powerful institutional norms, many of the cultural and religious norms mentioned in other chapters of this volume can complicate an already difficult situation. There is a need for more palliative and social support for those who choose comfort over cure so that they do not become trapped in the institutions where the bias is toward high-tech interventions and cure. Patient and family education is essential to clarify misconceptions about advance directives, nutrition and hydration, and probable outcomes of common interventions such as CPR, radical or palliative surgery, artificial ventilation, parenteral feeding, and medication side effects. Rational decisions about treatments cannot be made when patients and families are not fully informed. Similarly, health care providers cannot help to clarify misconceptions if they have not examined their own biases in these same areas.

The greatest error is to assume that we are independent of or unaffected by the powerful discourses that create and sustain ethnic, religious, and institutional cultures.

■ REFERENCES

Anspach, R. (1987). Prognostic conflict in life-and-death decisions: The organization as an ecology of knowledge. *Journal of Health and Social Behavior, 28,* 215-231.

Benoliel, J. Q., & Degner, L. F. (1995). Institutional dying: A convergence of cultural values, technology, and social organization. In H. Wass & R. A. Neimeyer (Eds.), *Dying: Facing the Facts* (pp. 117-141). Washington, DC: Taylor & Francis.

Denk, C. E., Benson, C. B., Fletcher, J. C., & Reigel, T. M. (1997). How do Americans want to die? A factorial vignette survey of public attitudes about end-of-life decision-making. *Social Science Research, 26,* 95-120.

Diamond, T. (1992). *Making gray gold.* Chicago: University of Chicago Press.

Glaser, B. G., & Strauss, A. L. (1968). *Time for dying.* Chicago: Aldine.

Foucault, M. (1975). *The birth of the clinic.* New York: Random House.

It's over, Debbie. (1988). *Journal of the American Medical Association, 259,* 272.

Jansson, L., & Norberg, A. (1989). Ethical reasoning concerning the feeding of terminally ill cancer patients. *Cancer Nursing, 12,* 352-358.

Morse, J. M., Bottorff, J., Anderson, G., O'Brien, B., & Solberg, S. (1992). Beyond empathy: Expanding expressions of caring. *Journal of Advanced Nursing, 17,* 809-821.

Prigerson, H. G. (1992). Socialization to dying: Social determinants of death acknowledgment and treatment among terminally ill geriatric patients. *Journal of Health and Social Behavior, 33,* 378-395.

Rousseau, P. (1992). Why give IV fluids to the dying? *Patient Care, 26*(12), 71-74.

Starr, P. (1982). *The social transformation of American medicine.* New York: Basic Books.

Sudnow, D. (1967). *Passing on.* Englewood Cliffs, NJ: Prentice Hall.

SUPPORT Principal Investigators. (1995). A controlled trial to improve care for seriously ill hospitalized patients. *Journal of the American Medical Association, 274,* 1591-1598.

Turner, B. S. (1987). *Medical power and social knowledge.* London: Sage.

Wicks, D. (1995). Nurses and doctors and discourses of healing. *Australia and New Zealand Journal of Sociology, 31*(2), 122-139.

Chapter 16

End-of-Life Issues in the Military Culture

PATRICIA W. NISHIMOTO
ROSS E. NEWMANN

*Old soldiers never die, but [99] soldiers in [100] are pitiably
young, and they die in the millions, without beginning to
guess why it is that life asks that of them.*

—Keegan and Holmes (1985, p. 283)

The U.S. military has many proud traditions that transcend ethnic, religious, and traditional cultural boundaries. Those not associated with the military often are unaware of the rich culture of the military, nor are they aware of how those in the military approach death. Although the military in peacetime has a lower overall mortality rate than does the civilian sector (Bartone & Ender, 1994), the idea of death is omnipresent in the minds of those in the military and is ingrained in every facet of daily military life. This fact has led to the development of a number of structures and rituals associated with death. It is due to this expectation of and readiness for death that Bartone and Ender (1994) suggested that the military may serve as a template for other organizations in helping their members to deal with death.

This chapter reviews military views and traditions regarding death and dying with the assumption that the military cul-

AUTHORS' NOTE: The views expressed in this chapter are those of the authors and do not reflect the official policy or position of the Department of the Army, the Department of Defense, or the U.S. government.

ture is unique in its approach. It is important to note that five subcultures exist within the military culture: those of the Army, Navy, Coast Guard, Marine Corps, and Air Force. Whereas each subculture has its own subset of customs, this chapter does not delve into each. Rather, it presents generalized information about the military as a whole. In addition to presenting findings from a review of the literature, this chapter reflects our experiences as nurses, one in the U.S. Army Reserve with 10 years of active duty service and the other a former Air Force service member, both employed at Tripler Army Medical Center, a large military hospital in Honolulu serving Hawaii and the Pacific that is expandable to 1,000 beds in wartime.

■ TRADITIONAL NORMS AND PRACTICES

Even for those not closely associated with the military, there is an awareness of some of the traditional norms and practices of military-associated deaths. The American public is audience to military deaths via the news media as well as via movies such as *Gardens of Stone, Top Gun,* and *Courage Under Fire.* On the Fourth of July, there are 50-gun salutes to the Union. On Veterans Day and Memorial Day, military graveyards are decorated with American flags, and speeches are made and editorials are written to remind us of the meaning of these holidays. Special services are held on those days to commemorate those who have died in the service of their country. But there are other death-related norms and rituals that are not well known. This chapter presents information about the new recruit's introduction to the culture, reminders of death on the job, family notification of a soldier's death, the military funeral, cemeteries and memorials, and advance planning.

Recruitment and Basic Training

The introduction to the culture of the military begins with the recruitment process. Patriotism, courage, heroism, and membership in an elite group are the images that are intertwined with inspiring music in multimedia advertisements and recruiting office posters. The idea of serving in the armed forces to protect America is romanticized, offering promises of seeing the world. Service to one's country and the possibility of making the ultimate sacrifice of one's life are accepted, if not implicitly glorified, as part of the challenge and risk associated with military service (Keegan & Holmes, 1985).

Each recruit attends basic training, where he or she is suddenly assaulted with the very real possibility of injury or death. Recruits are inoculated with dozens of vaccinations to protect them from a variety of deadly diseases endemic to far-off theaters of operations or in the event that an enemy launches an attack of biological weapons. Once past the induction phase, recruits enter active training, including familiarization with and firing of weapons. Concurrent with learning techniques to take life, recruits are taught first aid to save the lives of their comrades and themselves.

Because chemical and biological warfare agents are inexpensive to manufacture and relatively easy to deliver, they have become an ever-present possible threat. Recruits are trained to don heavy and hot uniforms, called "MOPP" (mission-oriented protective posture) gear, designed to save their lives and protect them from the risk of chemical warfare. To make real the idea of death from a tasteless, odorless, invisible agent, young recruits are not only trained to fire their weapons from foxholes under battlefield conditions but also to sleep in the full gear and gas mask (Moore, 1997).

Beyond training with specialized equipment, recruits are constantly reminded of the possibilities of death. They must carry personal chemical warfare agent inoculation kits, which are accompanied by graphic information and training on how they will die if they do not use the kit properly after exposure. This chemical warfare training is not limited to basic training; rather, it continues throughout the military member's career, with constant reminders emphasizing the point to never give the kit to a comrade because it is the responsibility of each individual member of the military to ensure his or her own survival.

Throughout basic training, there is constant repetition of responding to orders, donning gas masks, firing weapons, and training in battlefield activities, all designed to ensure that recruits react automatically to life-threatening situations and are able to survive the shock of battle (Keegan & Holmes, 1985). Military badges, such as the Sharpshooter Badge or the Expert Field Medical Badge, are given to recognize service members for accomplishments and represent to others goals to be attained. Cognizant of the fact that military personnel have families, recruits are provided instruction regarding the need for preparing wills and power of attorney forms and for making provisions for their survivors by buying inexpensive government-subsidized life insurance called Servicemen's Group Life Insurance.

To counterbalance the sense of isolation and inordinate focus on the possibility of personal injury or death, conscious efforts are undertaken to enhance the development of esprit de corps and a sense of membership on a team. Team-building activities, such as cadence songs and "jody calls," are used in morning five-mile runs and other training situations (Dunnigan, 1997). Although these jody calls contain words about dying a heroic death, when sung or shouted loudly as a group, they help to instill a "fighting spirit" that Keegan and Holmes (1985) asserted is necessary for troops to continue to fight despite the wounds, death, and suffering of war. Jody call lyrics include the following (Dunnigan, 1997):

> If I die in a combat zone,
> Pack me up and ship me home.
> Pin my medals on my chest
> And tell my mom I did my best.

Because the Marines are those sent first into battle, this military subgroup often has the highest death rate. New recruits learn the words to the Marine Hymn, which reflects this reality while ascribing pride and honor to the thought of dying for one's country:

> Here's to health to you and to our corps,
> Which we are proud to serve;
> In many a strife we've fought for life
> And never lost our nerve.
> If the Army and the Navy
> Ever look on heaven's scenes,
> They will find the streets are guarded
> By the United States Marines.

Perhaps one of the most sobering parts of basic training is DNA testing. Recruits are instructed that this mandatory testing of their saliva and blood provides data useful for identifying them if their bodies are damaged beyond recognition. Confirmed identification is especially important to a soldier's family members, who want to be certain that the remains they have buried indeed are those of their loved one. The identification of those who have died in battle has been a concern of the military dating back to the Civil War, when dog tags were used to identify bodies left on the battlefield. In Vietnam, fingerprints were used to identify 90% of the dead. The Gulf War introduced the use of DNA to help ensure that no deceased service member would be unidentified (Lane, 1992).

The acculturation of service members to the subculture of death in the military begins subliminally with the individual's initial recruitment and becomes more overt during basic training. Further acculturation occurs on the job.

On the Job

From the very start of one's career, death is a premise of the military. It can be death of the enemy, of the soldier, or of his or her comrades in arms. In the civilian world, death is something that can happen. In the military, death is something that *will* happen and could be more likely to happen sooner than later. Because of this reality, the military always has had to maintain procedures relating to death (e.g., how to remove or bury the potentially disease-ridden remains of the enemy, how to transport the remains of fallen comrades back home). Commanders must ensure that personnel know how to order body bags, register graves, evacuate bodies, and notify families of death (Hasenauer, 1997).

It is due to this sudden and unexpected nature of death in the military that unique associations have been formed to deal with war-inflicted casualties. General George Armstrong Custer and his men left hundreds of widows and fatherless children. It was during this time that the Army Mutual Aid Association (now the Army/Air Force Mutual Aid Association) was formed to help family members complete the multitude of forms incumbent with the death of a loved one in the military and to request needed services. To ensure that military members who are severely wounded are retired in a timely fashion so that they and their families can receive full benefits, the Physical Examination Board Liaison Office was established.

War-Related Triage and Death

Triage in a wartime scenario differs from what is seen in a civilian disaster. This difference is because the goal of wartime triage is to return the service member to battle as quickly as possible, for if the battle is lost, then it could mean the deaths of all individuals in that unit. Thus, in wartime triage, the least wounded member is treated first and the most severely wounded member is treated last if he cannot be immediately evacuated. If the injuries are so severe that the service member would require too many resources, then he is placed in the expectant category (Xenakis, Brooks, & Balson, 1985). An example would be a service member requiring multiple blood transfusions when only a small amount of blood is available. To give him all of the blood available when he still would not be able to return to battle would not be acceptable practice and would deprive the minimally wounded of the opportunity of recovering and returning to the battlefield to help comrades fight. War-related deaths have decreased over the years, however, primarily due to improved medical technology and increased ability to stabilize and move wounded service members to appropriate treatment facilities.

Despite these improvements, death during combat is what troops are trained to expect, and a number of rituals have evolved to try to avoid death in battle, as shown in Table 16.1. Some rituals have to do with bringing oneself good luck or protection (e.g., wearing a St. Christopher's medal, tapping one's gun with rosary beads, not washing one's socks). Others have to do with safety (e.g., not lighting three smokes on a single match given that having "three on a match" would give the enemy enough time to get a fix on the light, aim, and shoot). Similarly, saluting officers in the field would reveal them to the enemy, who might then target the officers in hopes that their troops would surrender if they became leaderless.

The military also has developed its own slang related to death, examples of which are shown in Table 16.2. To help face battle, soldiers down some "Dutch courage." Those in the Air Force today do not have to worry about assignment to a "flying coffin" but still might die as a "tail-gunner Charlie" or a "lawn dart." To say someone "bought the farm" or "canceled Christmas" means that he or she died. Despite jody calls and anthems to the contrary, members of the military can be heard to refer to death as the "old lie."

In addition, each branch of service has developed a different expertise in recovering its dead based on differences in battle situations. For example, the Navy has the ability to store bodies onboard a ship, the Air Force has to retrieve its dead from the wreckage of a plane crash, and the Army and Marine Corps have to retrieve bodies from the field of battle. Those in the Air Force are taught that caring for the dead is the final service they can perform for their fellow airmen (Giles, 1993). By seeing or participating in efforts to recover remains, service members realize that if they are killed in action, the same efforts will be expended for them. During the heat of battle, there is no time for "grief work." Yet, to have a functioning unit, morale must be maintained, and these roles and traditions guide activity and give meaning to death (Bartone & Ender, 1994).

Peacetime Deaths

Whereas the military trains for death in battle, death in the military more often occurs in peacetime than in wartime. Although perhaps not as dramatic as death during combat, peacetime death in the military can come with an unexpected swiftness that often has a deep and profound impact on the military community. Helmkamp and Kennedy (1996) compiled a summary of causes of

TABLE 16.1. Rituals Used to Avoid Death

Avoid lighting three smokes on a single match.
Wear a St. Christopher's medal.
Do not wash your socks.
Avoid people whose time left in the war zone is short.
Tap your gun with rosary beads.
Do not salute officers in the field.

TABLE 16.2. Military Slang and Terms Pertaining to Death

Lawn dart	Air force term referring to crashed airplane
Bought the farm	If a military plane crashed in a field, then the government had to pay the farmer for the loss
Dope on a rope	Rappelling from a chopper in which a person is an easy target
Flying coffins	Nickname for B-17 airplanes in World War II
Gardens of stone	Slang for graveyards during the Vietnam era
Tail-gunner Charlie	The last airplane in a formation, which is more likely to draw fire
The walk	The path of the sentry as he walks across the mat in front of the tomb of the four unknown soldiers in Arlington, Virginia
Cancel Christmas	A term relating to death used by marines
Old lie	The notions that a soldier's death is "dulce and decorum" (or sweet and fitting)
Dutch courage	Refers to "square-faced gin" given to Dutch soldiers before battle so that they could face the possibility of death

death in the military that occurred between 1980 and 1993. Only 2% of military deaths during that period occurred during combat. The leading cause of death for both males and females was from unintentional injuries. Death from diseases was the second leading cause of death, accounting for 20% of the deaths. Death from suicide was the third leading cause of death for males, accounting for 13% of the deaths, and was the fourth leading cause of death for females, accounting for 12% of the deaths (homicide was the third cause for females, accounting for 14% of the deaths). Although this sounds high, the incidence of suicide in the U.S. military is about half that found in the general population, with the risk for males being about twice that for females (Helm-kamp, 1995). Similarly low rates of suicide in the military compared to those in the civilian population were identified in Finland by Schroderus and Lonnqvist (1992).

Training accidents are not an uncommon occurrence. They include things such as parachuting accidents, aircraft crashes, and vehicular and equipment accidents (e.g., tank-related accidents when soldiers' heads protrude outside of the hatch and the turret suddenly is rotated (Hasenauer, 1997; Tyler & Gifford, 1991). In 1996, 571 soldiers were injured in field training exercises, and 11 were killed or permanently disabled (Hasenauer, 1997). These deaths include those incurred during "live firing" in which battle situations are enacted. For example, live ammunition might be used by sleep-deprived troops, and despite strict safety rules, accidents resulting in death can occur (Moore, 1996). Media scrutiny of the military has kept such peacetime deaths in the public awareness.

Even in peacetime, military troops are active. For example, between 1990 and 1997, the army had 25 major deployments involving more than 35,000 soldiers in more than 70 countries. In 1996 alone, active duty troops were deployed an average of 138 days (Grange & Telander, 1997). Deaths that occur during peacekeeping missions often are among the more visible of military noncombat deaths and have had a profound and lasting impact on the military as well as on the nation as a whole. For example, in 1983, 283 Marines were killed in Beirut in a suicide bombing of their barracks. In 1985, an air charter carrying 248 soldiers home from a peacekeeping mission crashed in Newfoundland, killing all those aboard. Other peacetime casualties occurred in 1989 with the deaths of 47 seamen on the *USS Iowa* and the deaths of 37 seamen in the bombing of the *USS Stark* (Giles, 1993). In each of these mass casualty incidents, service members were called on to piece together the bodies of their comrades for purposes of identification, a further reminder that death is an ever-present reality of military life even during peacetime (McCarroll, Ursano, & Fullerton, 1993, 1995; McCarroll, Ursano, Wright, & Fullerton, 1993).

Family Notification of Death

The plights and exploits of war have long been romanticized in legends and stories. But changes in communication technology have increased its coverage and immediacy. During the early days of the United States, print media and telegrams brought the action of war closer to home. Later, radio offered a way in which to hear the latest word from the front lines. During World War II, the public would see theater newsreels of battle scenes before the main features. Vietnam, however, brought television coverage of blood, carnage, and death into the living rooms of American families. Suddenly, war lost much of the romance it had held when depicted in the movies. Because the television networks now were providing almost instant reports of battlefield action, families could watch the evening news, only to see loved ones killed before their eyes.

Seeing a loved one killed on the 6 o'clock news is one way of providing notification of the death of a military member, but obviously, such a callous and uncaring process is not acceptable. Due to advances in technology, the process of notifying the next of kin of a military member's death has changed over time. During World War II and the Korean War, families were not told of deaths until weeks later, and even then, they were informed by telegram with no opportunity to learn details of how the deaths occurred.

After the Korean War, the notification procedure was changed to include having a military representative personally visit the family's home after the telegram notification. During the Vietnam War, the procedure was changed to a personal visit by the military to the home of the family with a confirmation telegram following the visit. The procedure carefully prescribed that the visiting military member must be of the correct rank, wear a specific uniform, visit between the hours of 6 a.m. and 10 p.m., and convey a prepared statement. For example, casualty affairs officers assigned to provide notification of the death of an Army soldier are instructed to repeat to the next of kin the following message:

> The Secretary of the Army has asked me to express his deep regret that your (relationship) (died/was killed in action) in (country/state) on (date). (State the circumstances of the deceased military member's death.) You will be further advised as additional information is received. The Secretary extends his deepest sympathy to you and your family in your tragic loss. (Department of the Army, 1994, p. 32)

Although these words might sound harsh on first reading, they are well thought out and experienced based. The words convey reassurance to the next of kin that the dead service member will be treated with respect and in the military tradition and that the death was an honorable one. As noted by Bartone and Ender (1994), families tend to cope better if they believe that the death of a service member was for a noble or good cause.

The Military Funeral

The precision in honoring a military member's death extends to the funeral service. For example, military regulations dictate exactly where each family member is to be seated and what is to be said to the next of kin. When the American flag is handed to the next of kin, the Army official says, "On behalf of the president of the United States and the people of a grateful nation, may I present this flag as a token of appreciation for the honorable and faithful service your loved one rendered this nation" or "This flag is presented on behalf of a grateful nation as a token of appreciation for the honorable and faithful service rendered by your loved one" (Department of the Army, 1994, p. 46).

There are specific honors and rituals associated with honoring deceased members of the military. In 1872, General George Washington established the Badge of Military Merit for those who were wounded or killed in battle. That award is now called the Purple Heart and symbolizes to the family that the sacrifice of their loved one was valued and appreciated by the nation. The American flag is placed over the casket of each dead service member, a tradition that first began during the American Revolution to symbolize the obligation of the nation to care for those who were ordered to guard it (Keegan & Holmes, 1985). When the flag-draped casket of a deceased military member is moved, uniformed personnel render honors by saluting if outdoors or by standing at attention if indoors. Such rendering of honors has been seen on television with the return of bodies from Vietnam.

The military funeral allows a "quiet finality" that acknowledges the loss and helps to bring closure to a death that might have occurred overseas, far from family and home (Keegan & Holmes, 1985). A tradition often observed at military funerals is the roll call. Historically, the roll would be called at the conclusion of each battle to ensure the safety and welfare of soldiers in the unit. The use of the roll call in funeral ceremonies dates back to the Civil War battle of New Market, when it was used to honor a group of cadets from Virginia Military Institute who were killed or injured in the battle (Wise, 1978). The use of the roll call in funerals and other military ceremonies continues to the present day. For example, at a memorial service, a military member might call out the names of a unit's members. As his or her name is called, each member stands in full uniform and announces, in a loud voice, "Here, sir." Then, the deceased's name is called. It is called three times. The emptiness of the absent reply signifies the gap that now exists because of the death.

A striking part of the funeral procession is the presence of a riderless horse with boots placed backward in the stirrups to signify that the military member no longer is able to serve his or her country. Planes may fly overhead in the traditional missing man formation. Most Americans are familiar with the 21-gun salute in which 7 rifles are fired in unison three times to honor the deceased. The three volleys have roots in ancient Roman times; when earth was thrown three times into the sepulchre, the family members would call the name of the dead three times, and as they left the grave site, they would say *vale* (farewell) three times (Lovette, 1939). To acknowledge the shame of killing during war and as a symbol of reverence, the position of the guns is reversed from the manner in which they typically are held (Lovette, 1939). A bugler will sound taps as a body is buried or as it is lowered from the ship. Taps is a song of "truce to pain" and is used not only to end the military day but also to mark the end of life for a military member (Keegan & Holmes, 1985).

The military keeps those missing or killed in action in the forefront of thought through rituals not directly connected with death. At a formal military dinner known as "Dining In," a lone table is placed at the front of the room. At this unoccupied table is a rose with a yellow ribbon (to not forget), a glass of water, boots backward with dog tags draped over them, and a single candle lighted in memory of those who died in the service of their country. A toast is made to "our fallen comrades," and a spirit of solemnness permeates the room.

The close-knit nature of the extended family that exists in the military creates grieving issues that might not be present in the civilian sector. These grieving issues become evident with the death of a comrade, be it from sickness, accident, or suicide. Such deaths are felt deeply by members of the unit, and debriefings and counseling sessions are held to assist and comfort those left behind (Budd, 1997). In the culture of the military, it is not just immediate family but also "buddies" and close friends who can experience intense grief. The funeral and memorial rituals help families, friends, and comrades to cope with their losses.

Cemeteries and Memorials

Tourists frequently plan their trips around visits to national cemeteries such as Punchbowl in Hawaii and the National Cemetery in Arlington, Virginia. It is at these national cemeteries that visitors silently look on row after row of neatly aligned white tombstones that serve as a reminder of the sacrifices made (Ealons, 1997b). The tombstones are identical and have simple notations on them listing only the name, rank, awards, and dates of birth and death (Table 16.3).

TABLE 16.3. Example of Gravestone Marker

KENICHI
NISHIMOTO
LTC
US ARMY
WORLD WAR II
KOREA
VIETNAM
SEPT 1 1913
APR 2 1990
PURPLE HEART

In addition to military cemeteries, war memorials placed throughout the community at large are poignant reminders visited by thousands of visitors yearly. For example, a World War II monument in Charleston, South Carolina, honors 374 officers and 3,131 men from 52 submarines who are missing in action and refers to them as still on patrol. Civilian corporations have begun to contribute to these memorials. In 1995, IBM paid for a permanent computer at the Korean War Memorial in Washington, D.C. The computer allows visitors to print the service records of soldiers in the Korean War and also prints pictures of the soldiers in their uniforms ("News Notes," 1997).

Even anonymity in death has special meaning in the military. The Tomb of the Unknown Soldier in Arlington National Cemetery holds the body of an unknown soldier who died in 1921 and was buried there in 1931. The unknown soldier's tomb inscription reads "Here rests in honored glory an American soldier known but to God" (Ealons, 1997a). It is this tomb that has been given a special military honor, with honor guards at the tomb 24 hours a day, 365 days a year.

Advance Planning

There are three additional death-related issues that should be addressed: organ donation, physician-assisted death, and advance directives. Health care professionals not associated with the military might question whether these issues are addressed differently in the military from how they are in the civilian sector—and if so, then how.

The issue of organ donation in a military setting is identical to that in the civilian sector. Military health care professionals work closely with their civilian counterparts to coordinate organ donation when appropriate. In fact, military patients are routinely given an opportunity to express their wishes regarding organ donation. The only time that organ donation in the military differs from that in the civilian sector is during a wartime scenario when harvesting of organs is not possible. The second death-related issue, physician-assisted death, does not differ from that in the civilian sector. Health care professionals in the military follow American Medical Association guidelines regarding this issue. However, on advance directives, the military differs somewhat from the civilian sector. As mentioned earlier, members must complete wills and power of attorney forms and must make arrangements for dependent and family members in the event that the military members are shipped out. In cases where both parents are active duty, the family needs to ensure that grandparents or other adults are available to care for children if the parents are activated at the same time. The military medical community fully supports the use of advance directives related to health care as mandated by the Patient Self-Determination Act of 1991. This stays in effect even during a wartime situation for all beneficiaries of military medical care who are in non-war zones. For active duty personnel in war zones, wartime triage procedures are employed.

Changes to These Traditions

The traditions of the military are so ingrained and so much a part of military life that they have changed very little over the past 200 years. The endurance of these traditions is what provides such a great amount of support to service members and their families. The familiar phrases and behaviors help to provide a sense of stability in the face of crisis and turmoil. The traditions help to build the esprit de corps needed to perform dangerous missions.

As downsizing of the military continues, resulting in fewer and fewer full-time military personnel, traditions might be at risk of being lost in the future (Foster, 1997). In fact, this already has begun to occur, as commanders are being forced to refuse requests for burial honors due to downsizing (DeCrane, 1998). What used to be a 30-year career for recruits coming into the military has now become, for many, a brief introduction to the military before returning to civilian life, leaving fewer "experienced" service members to carry on the traditions and to pass them on to new, younger members. This could put military members at a distinct disadvantage in dealing with the death and dying that comprise such a large component of military life.

■ RECOMMENDATIONS

As the military continues to dramatically downsize, reserve components will be used more frequently. Frequent activation of reserve units will have a direct impact on the civilian community. Following 3- to 6-month periods of active duty, reservists will return to civilian life, to be attended by civilian providers. To be able to fully support these so-called "weekend warriors," providers will need to have some awareness of military life and traditions. A mental health professional who works with young adults who never have faced the reality of death might not be able to accurately assess a reservist of the same age group who is comfortable with the topic of death. Knowledge of military culture allows providers to draw on the strengths of traditional practice, particularly if it is something in which the client takes comfort. As with the cultural background of any client, it is vital that providers conduct an assessment of values, beliefs, and desires.

■ REFERENCES

Bartone, P. T., & Ender, M. G. (1994). Organizational responses to death in the military. *Death Studies, 18,* 25-39.

Budd, F. (1997). Helping the helpers after the bombing in Dhahran: Critical-incident stress services for an air rescue squadron. *Military Medicine, 162,* 515-520.

DeCrane, P. (1998). Military burial honors. *The Retired Officer, 54*(3), 25-26.

Department of the Army. (1994). Army Regulation 600-8-1. In *Army casualty operations/assistance/insurance* (pp. 32, 46). Washington, DC: Author.

Dunnigan, T. P. (1997). *Modern military cadence.* Alexandria, VA: Byrrd Enterprises.

Ealons, C. A. (1997a). Honor never rests. *Soldiers, 52*(5), 13-15.

Ealons, C. A. (1997b). In honored glory. *Soldiers, 52*(2), 30.

Foster, R. (1997). The sound of tradition. *Soldiers, 52*(12), 28-30.

Giles, K. (1993). Educating air force mortuary officers: Confronting death anxiety. *Death Studies, 17,* 85-91.

Grange, D. L., & Telander, P. D. (1997). Reserve components, active partners. *Soldiers, 52*(6), 2-3.

Hasenauer, H. (1997). Staying alive in the field. *Soldiers, 52*(6), 23-25.

Helmkamp, J. C. (1995). Suicides in the military: 1980-1992. *Military Medicine, 160,* 45-50.

Helmkamp, J. C., & Kennedy, R. D. (1996). Causes of death among U.S. military personnel: A 14-year summary, 1980-1993. *Military Medicine, 161,* 311-317.

Keegan, J., & Holmes, R. (1985). *Soldiers: An illustrated history of men in battle.* New York: Konecky & Konecky.

Lane, L. (1992). No more unknowns: Identifying the dead through DNA. *Soldiers, 47*(7), 24-25.

Lovette, L. P. (1939). *Naval customs: Traditions and usage.* Annapolis, MD: U.S. Naval Institute.

McCarroll, J. E., Ursano, R. J., & Fullerton, C. S. (1993). Symptoms of posttraumatic stress disorder following recovery of war dead. *American Journal of Psychiatry, 150,* 1875-1877.

McCarroll, J. E., Ursano, R. J., & Fullerton, C. S. (1995). Symptoms of PTSD following recovery of war dead: 13-15 month follow-up. *American Journal of Psychiatry, 152,* 939-941.

McCarroll, J. E., Ursano, R. J., Wright, K. M., & Fullerton, C. S. (1993). Handling bodies after violent death: Strategies for coping. *American Journal of Orthopsychiatry, 63,* 209-214.

Moore, A. (1996). Sleep to survive. *Soldiers, 51*(8), 31-33.

Moore, A. (1997). Biological detection agents. *Soldiers, 52*(7), 38.

News Notes. (1997, July). *The Retired Officer Magazine,* p. 25.

Schroderus, M., & Lonnqvist, J. K. (1992). Trends in suicide rates among military conscripts. *Acta Psychiatrica Scandinavica, 86,* 233-235.

Tyler, M. P., & Gifford, R. K. (1991). Fatal training accidents: The military unit as a recovery context. *Journal of Traumatic Stress, 4,* 233-248.

Wise, H. A. (1978). *Drawing out the man: The VMI story.* Charlottesville: University Press of Virginia.

Xenakis, S. N., Brooks, F. R., & Balson, P. M. (1985). A triage and emergency treatment model for combat medics on the chemical battlefield. *Military Medicine, 150,* 411-415.

Chapter 17

End-of-Life Issues in the HIV/AIDS *Community*

RUSSEL OGDEN

The thought of suicide is a great consolation; by means of it, one gets successfully through many a bad night.

—Nietzsche (1886/1973, p. 103)

*I*n his acclaimed book, *How We Die,* Nuland (1993) said, "There has never been a disease as devastating as AIDS. . . . Medical science has never before confronted a microbe that destroys the very cells of the immune system whose job it is to coordinate the body's resistance to it" (p. 172). As the epidemic of HIV approaches the end of its second decade, rates of infection continue to rise in much of the world, and more people are falling ill with the catastrophic symptoms that lead to AIDS. Indeed, although recent medical discoveries hold out hope for AIDS sufferers, HIV disease has only very recently surrendered the distinction of being the leading cause of death for persons between 25 and 44 years of age in the United States (Russell, 1997). Nonetheless, given that science has failed to cure viruses of much lesser sophistication, the epidemic is far from over. This chapter addresses end-of-life decision making in the context of AIDS.

Death by HIV disease often involves severe suffering for the patient. Wasting syndrome, Kaposi's sarcoma, dementia, progressive multifocal leucoencephalopathy, and a host of other opportunistic infections are widespread at the end stages of the disease. A diagnosis of HIV/AIDS often catapults young people into a consciousness of old age, and the trajectory of dying is prolonged over several years. It is not surprising that because persons with AIDS (PWAs) are uniquely positioned to contemplate their mortality with profound awareness, consideration often is given to euthanasia and/or assisted suicide (EU/AS).

The circumstances associated with AIDS and awareness of death also force questions about preparing for death and trying to control its timing. Modern technologies mean that controlled dying is managed on a continuum, beginning with the articulation of treatment instructions that address symptoms of suffering and progressing to decisions regarding the precise timing, location, and manner of death. Typical of the younger generation of health care consumers, intellectual and influential PWAs generally seek an egalitarian role in their treatment and in their experience with death. Characteristic assertiveness and sense of community are catalysts in affirming the classic American values of individual autonomy and self-determination.

Attitudes toward death and dying are subject to a variety of influences, but for PWAs the context of such attitudes is more immediate. An impending death from HIV disease amplifies the urgency with which one might consider assisted death because, by its very nature, AIDS is predictably cruel and progressively deteriorative. Yarnell and Battin (1988) argued that AIDS is *the* disease that makes the case for euthanasia because for many PWAs it is not a matter of choosing between life and death; rather, it is a matter of choosing between dying now or dying later in perhaps an even more difficult way.

A request for EU/AS presents perhaps the most troubling moral and ethical dilemma for people who care for PWAs. This chapter presents a general overview of the relationship of AIDS to the right-to-die movement, recent policy and legal developments, and a summary of the research dealing with AIDS-related suicide and assisted death. In addition, the chapter explores the phenomenon of "back-street" or "coathanger" euthanasia and discusses some of the implications that such practices hold for the future.

Definitions

There is considerable controversy regarding the terms used to define the act of ending a person's life. Here, euthanasia is defined as an act or treatment that is *intended* to end the life of a terminally ill patient at the *request* of the patient, for example, death by lethal injection. Assisted suicide is distinguished from euthanasia in that the patient is the one who takes his or her own life with the assistance of another individual. For example, a physician might prescribe a lethal dose of drugs that the patient would self-administer. Both euthanasia and assisted suicide are encompassed under the term *physician-assisted death*.

Overview of the Legal Climate

EU/AS are illegal acts in most parts of the world, and the penalties are severe for those who break the law. In many U.S. states, assisted suicide is punishable with a mandatory jail sentence of variable duration. Euthanasia generally is interpreted as murder, resulting in a life sentence and, in some jurisdictions, the death penalty. A paradox of the criminal law is that there is no legal distinction between the consensual killing of a dying person and the senseless murder of someone who wishes to live. For this reason, advocates in the right-to-die movement have for nearly two decades lobbied legislatures and courts to decriminalize EU/AS.

In the Netherlands, EU/AS are illegal, but the practices have existed openly for more than a decade; provided that physicians meet specific requirements, they will not be prosecuted. The most recent data available from the Netherlands indicate that about 2.3% of all deaths occur by euthanasia and a further 0.4% by assisted suicide (van der Maas et al., 1996). The five legal requirements are cumulative: The request for EU/AS must be *voluntary and durable,* it must be established that the patient's wish to die is *well considered and persistent,* the physician must discuss the matter of EU/AS *repeatedly* with the patient to establish that the patient experiences the suffering as *unbearable and hopeless,* and there must be *consultation* with an independent physician before EU/AS can be performed (Dillmann & Legemaate, 1994; van der Maas et al., 1996).

In the United States, the right-to-die issue appears to be taking on a social and legal significance equivalent to that of the landmark abortion decision in *Roe v. Wade* (1973) that effectively gave women the right of access to abortion. Drawing in part on arguments supporting the right to abortion, two 1996 appeals court decisions declared laws prohibiting assisted suicide to be unconstitutional (*Compassion in Dying v. State of Washington,* 1996; *Quill v. Vacco,* 1996). On appeal, the U.S. Supreme Court overturned the decisions and declared that there is no constitutional right to assisted suicide. Nevertheless, although the nine judges were unanimous in refusing to recognize such a right, five of the judges expressed the opinion that they did not reject such a right in principle and that the court would be open to future cases regarding the right to assistance in suicide (*Vacco v. Quill,* 1997; *Washington v. Glucksberg,* 1997).

In addition, the court confirmed that individual states could pass legislation permitting assisted suicide.

This is illustrated by Oregon's 1997 vote in support of its Measure 16, a citizen's initiative ballot that in 1994 legalized medical acts of assisted suicide for terminally ill persons diagnosed as having fewer than 6 months to live. Although this signifies a victory for proponents for allowing assisted suicide, the law has some problems. For example, to ensure patient voluntariness, it specifically prohibits injections and requires that the patient self-administer lethal drugs, more or less requiring oral consumption. Unfortunately, oral self-administration of lethal drugs, even under the supervision of a physician, offers no guarantee that death will proceed as expected. Indeed, literature from the Netherlands suggests that oral euthanatics are subject to various risks—vomiting, coma, de-cerebration, slow and distressed dying—and that lethal injection always should be available as a backup (Kimsma, 1996; van der Maas, van Delden, Pijnenborg, & Looman, 1992). Given that the Oregon law precludes injections as a backup in the event that self-administered drugs fail, an amendment eventually will have to be made to allow euthanasia in addition to assisted suicide if the law is to be deemed socially responsible to the patients who use it.

Litigation can be a powerful means to effecting social change, and AIDS patients have figured prominently in this policy arena. In the landmark U.S. Supreme Court cases of *Washington v. Glucksberg* (1997) and *Vacco v. Quill* (1997), PWAs and their physicians were among the plaintiffs. America's oldest and largest nonprofit AIDS organization, the Gay Men's Health Crisis and Lambda Legal Defense and Education Fund (1996), filed an amicus brief arguing that the Constitution protects the right of individuals to control their deaths with assisted suicide if necessary. When the Supreme Court declared that there was no such constitutional protection, the nation's foremost AIDS advocacy organization, AIDS Action (representing more than 1,400 community groups), issued a statement to the media:

> AIDS Action is deeply disappointed by the U.S. Supreme Court's decision today against physician-assisted suicide. Essentially, the Supreme Court has ruled against empowering people with terminal diseases, including HIV disease, to exercise their fundamental right to make individual decisions about how they live with their disease, including their right to freely choose in a dignified and humane way the manner and time of their death. AIDS Action believes that the federal government should not interfere with an individual's exercise of the fundamental right to make his/her own decisions about life

and death, decisions that should be made with the assistance of [his/her] physicians and other health care professionals. (AIDS Action, 1997, p. 1)

Following the U.S. Supreme Court decisions, the Florida Supreme Court was asked to hear an application from Charles Hall and his physician, Cecil McIver, for a judgment that the Florida statute prohibiting assisted suicide contravened the Privacy Clause of the Florida Constitution. Hall, who suffered from AIDS, argued that his physician should be permitted to prescribe a lethal dose of medication that he could self-administer. Like the U.S. Supreme Court, the Florida Supreme Court denied Hall the right to an assisted suicide but also left the door open for legislative change by stating that a statute authorizing assisted suicide would not necessarily be unconstitutional (*Krischner v. McIver,* 1997).

Although legal challenges asserting the rights of autonomy and self-determination have figured prominently during recent years, the notion that individuals have the right to make deeply personal decisions about their bodies was entrenched in American legal culture nearly a century ago. In 1914, the distinguished Justice Benjamin Cardozo ruled, "Every human being of adult years and sound mind has a right to determine what shall be done with his body" (*Schloendorf v. Society of New York Hospital,* 1914, p. 93). Since then, the concept of consent has received increasing attention in the courts and in medical ethics, reflecting the shift from a paternalistic physician-patient relationship to a participatory model. Today, informed consent is at the core of the physician-patient relationship and governs treatment and nontreatment decisions. It is a fundamental right that individuals are free from unwanted physical interference, and this right is increasingly being interpreted as one that should extend to the right to be free from having the law prevent a terminal or incurably ill individual's wish to die.

■ AIDS AND SUICIDE

Since the beginning of the AIDS epidemic, it has been suspected that an HIV diagnosis presented an increased risk of suicide, but early accounts were mostly anecdotal or clinical. One of the first studies to measure suicide risk and AIDS found that the relative risk of suicide was 36 times higher for New York men with AIDS than for those without AIDS diagnoses (Marzuk et al., 1988). Marzuk et al.'s (1988) study was based on 1985 data, when most therapies were

ineffective against HIV infection. A later study by Cote, Biggar, and Dannenburg (1992) used national data and concluded that males with AIDS have a risk
of suicide 7.4 times greater than that of demographically similar men in the
general population. It was theorized at the time that therapeutic advances and a
possible reduction in social stigma for AIDS had contributed to a reduced suicide rate among PWAs.

Establishing the extent of suicidal behavior is difficult, and it is likely that
the number of AIDS-related deaths due to suicide is underreported (Cote et al.,
1992; Marzuk et al., 1988). In some cases, the coroner might not know the HIV
status of suicide victims. Some physicians might unwittingly register suicides
as AIDS-related deaths simply because the suicides were unsuspected or carefully concealed. In other cases, suicides might not be documented at the request of family or friends or to protect insurance benefits (Slome, Moulton,
Huffine, Gorter, & Abrams, 1992).

To determine factors influencing suicidal intent, Schneider, Taylor,
Hammen, Kemeny, and Dudley (1991) compared suicidal ideation in large
samples of bisexual and gay HIV-negative men to that in HIV-positive men.
They found that "among HIV-positive [suicide] indicators, AIDS-related
death and illness events predicted suicidal intent but not current distress symptoms. Some suicidal ideation in response to AIDS-related events may be an effort to cope rather than a manifestation of psychological distress" (p. 776).
Whereas in the general population suicidal ideation has been strongly associated with depression and hopelessness, in HIV-positive men suicidal ideation
was associated with mood disturbance, loneliness, and lack of perceived control over AIDS risk and AIDS-related life events. Schneider et al. theorized
that "in view of the severe, uncontrollable, future threat posed by AIDS, suicidal thoughts may serve the function of cognitive mastery" (p. 785). That is, for
asymptomatic persons with HIV, consideration of suicide might be helpful for
the individual to face an unknown future with AIDS with a greater sense of
control. An example of such coping is illustrated with the following response
of an HIV-positive individual:

> My suicidal thoughts were centered around what I would do if I developed
> AIDS. Suicide would be an option. A close friend of 32 years (he is now 35) is
> dying of KS [Kaposi's sarcoma]. I try to imagine what I would do in his cir-
> cumstances. This leads me to suicidal thoughts. . . . I guess I would do it if
> there was no other option and I was in a lot of pain. . . . I think that thinking
> about suicide alternatives is a way for me to cope, or deal with the "what I
> would do" question, if I were to develop AIDS. (p. 785)

It was further reported that suicidal ideation as an adaptive or coping function has been relatively unexplored and demands further attention from researchers. Indeed, if suicidal ideation is a coping mechanism during the asymptomatic period of HIV infection, then the act of self-killing when one is well along in the dying process could well be seen as a means, albeit a final one, of coping with incurable and terminal illness.

■ ORGANIZATIONAL SUPPORT FOR ASSISTED DEATH FOR THOSE WITH AIDS

PWAs represent a diverse group in the United States. The majority come from socially stigmatized groups in society—gay men, intravenous drug users, women of low socioeconomic status, immigrants, and other minority groups. Some members of these groups have achieved a degree of power and privilege, whereas the majority remain disenfranchised and disadvantaged when it comes to accessing medical care and palliative services. On the one hand, it is argued that social disenfranchisement can contribute to a state of despair, and inadequate access to quality health care can precipitate requests for assisted death (Passik, McDonald, Rosenfeld, & Breitbart, 1996). On the other hand, advocacy organizations such as AIDS Action have been instrumental in organizing and providing a voice for PWAs from various subgroups and in promoting significant improvements in treatment for HIV disease.

Recent years have witnessed a growing policy culture among AIDS organizations in Western nations to support the concepts of voluntary euthanasia and assisted suicide. The Canadian AIDS Society (1991) was one of the first to endorse the notion that PWAs should be allowed to "choose death as their next form of treatment" and that death could be seen as "the ultimate form of healing when those whose bodies are exhausted and racked with pain are able to achieve peace and closure in their lives" (p. 2). The British Columbia Persons With AIDS Society (1994) published a position statement calling for "safe access to medically assisted euthanasia." Similarly, the AIDS Committee of Toronto (1995) has a position statement supporting assisted suicide. In Australia, the AIDS Council of New South Wales has produced a widely circulated booklet, *Choosing to Die: A Booklet for People Thinking About Euthanasia and for Those Asked to Assist* (van Reyk, 1995).

AIDS organizations in the United States have been slower to adopt official positions on assisted death issues. This is paradoxical given that the American

AIDS movement and the right-to-die movement share similar chronological origins and common values on self-determination (Friess, 1996). Perhaps because a primary emphasis of the AIDS movement always has been *living* with AIDS, there has been a reluctance to give official endorsement of the right to die because that might be seen as defeatist. Nevertheless, the right to choose death was placed on the global AIDS agenda at the 1997 International Summit on Promoting Standards of Care for People Living With HIV/AIDS About End-of-Life Issues. The summit produced a position statement identifying universally fundamental issues that arise at the end of life for persons with HIV disease, including "the involvement of persons with HIV and AIDS in the discussion and debate concerning end-of-life decisions" and "the right to make deeply personal decisions concerning our bodies, including decisions regarding the manner and timing of death" (see Appendix).

That the AIDS movement is supporting policy concerning the right to choose death as a treatment option should come as no surprise. It is a policy issue that has arrived because of increasing technological intervention on the human body. Although PWAs want to live as best as they can with the disease and seek to maximize treatment opportunities while minimizing coexisting stigma and discrimination, the problem of impending death never is far away. The cultural force of death denial is less integrated into the fabric of the HIV community because experiences of the nearly two-decade-long AIDS epidemic have shed a realistic light on what it means to be mortal. Hence, AIDS activists deal with two questions on opposing sides of the same coin: "What more can be done to live with HIV?" and "When is enough, enough?" For PWAs, death has been on the private agenda since the beginning of the epidemic, and now it is on the public agenda, forcing the attention of medical professionals and state legislators. For example, the film *It's My Party* (Kleizer, 1996) and the New York theater production *A Question of Mercy* (Hughes & Rabe, 1997) both feature gay men with AIDS who plan assisted suicides. When mainstream film and theater begin to address the social taboos of euthanasia, gay sexuality, and AIDS simultaneously, assisted death truly has emerged from the closet.

■ ATTITUDES AND PRACTICES REGARDING EU/AS AMONG HEALTH PROFESSIONALS

Across Western countries, physician support for legalization of voluntary euthanasia and assisted suicide varies between 35% and 62% (Bachman et al., 1996; Baume & O'Malley, 1994; Cohen, Fihn, Boyko, Johnson, & Wood,

1994; Kuhse & Singer, 1988; Lee et al., 1996; Verhoef & Kinsella, 1996). Some of the disparities might be due to cultural differences, question wording, and distinctions made between voluntary euthanasia and assisted suicide. Nonetheless, nearly all professional medical and nursing organizations are fundamentally opposed to EU/AS as an option (American Medical Association, 1996).

United States

Some recent surveys of U.S. physicians offer indirect measures of the number of requests and rate of compliance with acts of EU/AS. Back, Wallace, Starks, and Pearlman (1996) reported that 12% of Washington state physicians had received requests for assistance in dying within the previous 12 months: "Of the 156 patients who requested physician-assisted suicide[s], 38 (24%) received prescriptions, and 21 of these died as a result" (p. 919). In another study of Oregon physicians, Lee et al. (1996) reported that 21% of the respondents had been asked to provide aid in dying and that 7% had complied.

There is a growing body of literature advancing the notion that suicide should be evaluated on the basis of the *reasons* for the act, not the act itself. Given the progressive, deteriorative, and incurable nature of HIV disease, Werth (1995) argued, "AIDS may provide an impetus to change the traditional absolutist approach of suicide intervention and prevention into a contextual approach in which the intensity of suicide intervention required is viewed as varying along a continuum" (p. 65). The argument is that the suicidal behavior of an informed, mentally competent, terminally ill person can be viewed from a different perspective from that of someone who is reacting to emotionally traumatic but treatable events.

Several studies have given specific attention to investigating attitudes regarding assisted death in the context of AIDS. Slome, Mitchell, Charlebois, Moulton-Benevedes, and Abrams (1997) studied San Francisco Bay area physicians who provide HIV care and compared survey data from 1990 and 1995. They found that the number of physicians willing to grant assistance in suicide to AIDS patients increased from 28% in 1990 to 48% in 1995. A majority (53%) of the respondents in the 1995 survey reported that they had assisted the suicides of patients suffering from AIDS at least once, with a mean number of 4.2 times. Studies of other physician populations not specializing in HIV care indicate that between 7% and 9% have provided assistance in suicide to terminally ill patients (Fried, Stein, O'Sullivan, Brock, & Novack, 1993; Lee et al., 1996).

The profession of nursing has not been the subject of much investigation regarding EU/AS, although nurses do spend much more time with terminally ill patients than do physicians. Leiser et al. (1996) surveyed 214 California nurses working with AIDS patients. The majority (54%) reported having been asked indirectly, and 38% reported being asked directly, to assist in patient sui-cides. In addition, 7% reported assisting the suicides of AIDS patients in the workplace, and 10% reported assisting them outside the workplace. When asked whether they would help a patient obtain a lethal dose, 59% responded positively, and 14% reported that they also would be willing to administer a lethal dose.

Canada

A survey of Canadian physicians found that 41% of the 199 physicians with large AIDS-related practices would consider honoring requests for physician-assisted suicide if it were legal, whereas only 27% of the 589 family practitioners surveyed held the same view. This increased support was associated with a stable physician-patient relationship *and* with experience in providing palliative care in end-stage HIV disease (Hogg et al., 1997). In a study of Canadian nurses in AIDS care, Young and Ogden (1998) reported that 22% had received requests for euthanasia and that 42% would be prepared to administer euthanasia in "carefully defined circumstances." In a sample of 527 Canadian social workers, Ogden and Young (1998) found that more than 80% felt that social workers should be involved in social policy development for EU/AS and that 70% believed that they should share in the decision process with clients if such acts were to be legalized. This study also demonstrated that EU/AS decision making sometimes goes beyond the physician-patient relationship, with 21% of social workers reporting that clients had consulted them about EU/AS.

The Netherlands

In the Netherlands, many PWAs choose death hastening as an option. Early estimates suggested that between 10% and 20% of Dutch AIDS patients died by EU/AS (van der Maas et al., 1992). More recently, researchers have calculated that in Amsterdam, where about 55% of Holland's AIDS population reside, more than one in four PWAs die by EU/AS (Bindels et al., 1996; Laane, 1995). For example, Bindels et al. (1996) studied clinical data to determine the mode of death for PWAs, and comparisons were made between those who died naturally and those who died by EU/AS. They found that 29 men (22%) were assisted in their deaths and that, for another 17 men (13%), a decision had been made to withhold or withdraw life-extending treatment or to increase their dosage of narcotics with the knowledge that this action would shorten life.

Bindels et al. (1996) were able to employ a competing risks model that permitted a direct comparison of the incidence of EU/AS with natural dying as a function of time. To establish how much EU/AS actually shortened life, the mean values of variables critical to the function of the immune system were computed over the final 2 years of life for all the participants. In examining these data, the treating physician estimated that none of the PWAs who chose EU/AS would have lived beyond an additional 3 months and that, in 72% of the cases, life was not shortened by more than 1 month. Interestingly, the median survival time after diagnosis of AIDS for the natural death group was 13 months, whereas it was 22 months for the EU/AS group. The implication is that the "relative importance of dying by EU/AS increases with increasing survival time since AIDS diagnosis" (p. 502). That is, the longer one lives with AIDS, the greater the probability that EU/AS will be chosen.

■ THE UNDERGROUND PRACTICE OF EU/AS

Researching the taboo topic of assisted death imposes serious methodological constraints on researchers, and legal implications must be given consideration. Those who illegally assist in the deaths of others are at considerable personal risk in revealing such acts to researchers. Indeed, all reported studies on the actual frequency of EU/AS have been conducted in the Netherlands. This is possible because the subject is discussed openly in Dutch society and it is understood that scientific data gathered on euthanasia will not be used by the state against those who participate in the research. In North America, researchers do not enjoy such support, and in recent years Canadian and American courts have issued subpoenas seeking confidential data from scientists conducting investigations into various forms of illegal behavior (*Inquest of Unknown Female,* 1994; Leo, 1995; Scarce, 1995).

Social controls exercised by the legal and medical professions have proven insufficient to prevent terminally ill persons from seeking assisted deaths. Although there is little investigation into the actual phenomenon of

EU/AS, research that has been done tends to focus on EU/AS within the context of AIDS. Indeed, for many men with HIV disease, EU/AS appear to be a form of death control and body control, similar to the way in which industrialized cultures have come to conceptualize birth control and abortion, as illustrated by interviews with gay men:

> For me, the question [of voluntary euthanasia] is inseparable from other issues that have affected me in my life; homosexuality is one of them. I can't imagine, as a gay man, telling someone else what they can and cannot do with their body in the way that I have been told in various ways in my life. Abortion is the same thing. Do I think that abortion is a wonderful thing? Absolutely not. Would I prevent someone from having one? No. How could I do that? I can't sustain that sort of "It's okay for me but it's not okay for you" attitude.
> (unpublished interview by Ogden, 1998)

There are gender, cultural, economic, and social determinants that would influence agreement with the preceding viewpoint. Tindall, Forde, Carr, Barker, and Cooper (1993) found that more than 90% of gay white Australian men with HIV disease would support the option of euthanasia. Conversely, Breitbart, Rosenfeld, and Passik (1996) found that only 63% of HIV-infected patients in New York City supported physician-assisted suicide. The disparity in the findings of the two studies might be due to racial and cultural differences concerning physician-assisted suicide. Only 38% of the total sample in the Breitbart et al. (1996) study were Caucasian, and only 20% identified themselves as gay white men; significantly lower rates of support for physician-assisted suicide were found among minority respondents compared to gay white male respondents.

To obtain a measure of actual acts of EU/AS, Ogden (1994a, 1994b) conducted a criminological investigation into the underground phenomenon of EU/AS in the AIDS population. A total of 34 assisted deaths were documented, 29 of which took place in the Canadian province of British Columbia. This yielded evidence that at least 2.7% of all AIDS deaths in that province were the result of EU/AS. Given the methodological limitations imposed by the snowball sampling method used to identify the interview participants as well as the extreme sensitivity of the research topic, Ogden proposed that the actual rate of assisted death in the AIDS population could be as high as 10% to 20%, somewhat lower than statistics later reported in Dutch studies (Bindels et al., 1996; Laane, 1995).

An alarming finding of Ogden's (1994a) research was that about half of all the underground assisted deaths were "botched." EU/AS acts that were not medically supervised were likened to back-street abortions and have given rise to the term "coat-hanger euthanasia" (Farnsworth, 1994). One respondent reported, "There is nothing worse than, in the process of trying to alleviate suffering, to see that you are causing more" (quoted on p. 89). The following case example illustrates the horrific misadventure that can take place in assisted suicide.

The Case of William

William (a pseudonym) has HIV and plans to have an assisted suicide when he becomes unable to do the things that give him enjoyment. His story involves the assisted suicide of his roommate who had AIDS. William had a pact to assist his roommate to die. But because his roommate appeared relatively healthy and a physician had indicated a willingness to assist, the plan never was seriously organized. When his roommate's condition deteriorated quite suddenly, the roommate was hospitalized. The medical team scheduled a series of tests—chemotherapy and invasive procedures—something that the roommate always had rejected. After 2 days in the hospital, the roommate discharged himself and returned home. He announced to William that he had come home to die. He was in considerable pain and was taking liquid morphine.

The roommate abruptly announced, 2 days later, that he was going to die that afternoon. He had spoken with his physician and was convinced that the doctor was going to administer a lethal dose later that afternoon. Elated and relieved, the roommate began calling all his friends to say good-bye. To clarify the euthanasia plan, William telephoned the doctor:

> The doctor told me that it would be illegal for him to give a lethal injection but said, "I will give him something that will make him really comfortable." The way he said it, I thought he was going to prescribe a combination of drugs that I could give and inform us that if we mixed A, B, and C, it could be lethal.

When the doctor did arrive, he left only liquid morphine and no euthanasic. Later that evening, the roommate announced that he was ready to die. William was prepared to help but lacked the confidence to do so. He had consulted on the telephone with a member of a right-to-die society earlier that day and had received instructions regarding the use of plastic bags:

> Even after reading *Final Exit,* I was not very conversant. The roommate did not have any barbiturates. . . . He had maybe two seconals. But he had so many

pain killers, tranquilizers, sleeping pills, [and] one-half liter of morphine. . . .
I fed him about 30 pills with some vodka, and he threw it up. He said, "Go
away, leave me alone for a few minutes." In the meantime, these two guys
phone; they are in the neighborhood and want to stop by. One had been
around earlier. I explained what was going on, and they agreed to come over.

A short while later, the roommate announced that he was ready to try
again. This time, he refused alcohol, blaming it for causing the earlier vomiting. Instead, the pills were mixed with yogurt and morphine. As he began to
lose consciousness, he asked, "Have you got the plastic bag ready?"

> We thought we would basically poison him. We thought the morphine would
> be enough to stop his heart. After 20 minutes, he lost consciousness, and we
> monitored his breathing. For a while, the other two didn't want to touch
> [him], [or] touch the bag, [or] help prop his head. . . . They did not want to be
> directly involved. . . . So, we got the bag on and thought this was all going per-
> fect. The guy at [the right-to-die organization] had said it would all be over in
> one-half [hour] to an hour. . . . An hour later, he's not dead. So, we thought
> about it, and another half-hour later, he is still breathing. I thought, "Maybe
> there's a hole in the bag" . . . so we double-bagged him. I had set an egg timer
> just to keep in touch with reality, and the timer went "ding," underneath my
> pillow, and oh God, like here's [the roommate] laying in bed, right—he sat
> up! He had heard the bell, and then he quickly plopped himself down! It was
> just some sort of automatic reflex. One of the others became concerned about
> the length of time it was taking and that it was not fair to [the roommate], and
> he suggested the cushions. So, basically what we did was smother him, and
> that took about 10 minutes, to smother him. . . . I'm really glad we took a pro-
> active stance. It would have been very sad to have revived him. (Ogden,
> 1994a, pp. 81-83)

■ CONCLUSION

For many people, a diagnosis of AIDS is the equivalent of a death sentence
but without the certainty of an execution date. For PWAs, the prolonged trajectory of dying and the increased medicalization of care often mean the adoption
of the role of "professional patient." After nearly two decades of the HIV epidemic, many PWAs have been exposed to a cumulative experience of suffering
and education. They have watched their peers die from HIV disease, gained a
sophisticated knowledge and awareness of HIV pathology, and developed an
awareness about the EU/AS underground. All this contributes to a face-to-face

confrontation with mortality that most healthy people never will experience. Although the law continues to uphold the concept of the "sanctity of life," it would appear that the concept—at least for a good number of PWAs—does not mean that life never can be taken; death from disease need not be the only legitimate way in which to die. Indeed, opinion polls, survey data, and increasing accounts of actual cases of EU/AS suggest that the current prohibition against EU/AS is inconsistent with the values of significant segments of society.

There are several explanations for the apparently high level of support for EU/AS in the AIDS population. Advances in technology and medical innovations prolong and postpone death. AIDS is a diagnosis that leads to virtually certain death, and the process of dying can be particularly protracted with great suffering. In addition, many PWAs have witnessed AIDS-related death among their peer group and possess high levels of awareness about the disease and the dying process. Many members of the AIDS movement are active in promoting their right to take control of their health care, and for some, deliberately assisted death is part of the continuum of health care decision making. Finally, many PWAs have learned to resist suggestions from others regarding what constitutes the morally correct way in which to use one's own body.

The current underground practices of EU/AS have far-reaching implications. In a historical sense, they mirror the events that led to the decriminalization of contraception and abortion. Millions of copies of books and pamphlets about methods of self-deliverance (Docker & Smith, 1993; Humphry, 1991; Right to Die Society of Canada, 1997) are being distributed globally, but their dissemination is uniformly opposed by the medical profession and has been subjected to censorship. Nevertheless, historians of the birth control movement know that similar literature about contraceptive methods once was branded as immoral, corrupting, and a violation of the sanctity of life. Indeed, it was not until 1937 that the American Medical Association finally gave guarded endorsement to modern birth control; today, the practice has almost universal societal approval.

Management of death by EU/AS appears to have begun as an isolated phenomenon and a reaction to a desperate situation. Death-seeking behavior that currently is subjected to legal temperance and defined as a social taboo is steadily becoming an internalized normative behavior in the AIDS population and possibly other groups. It might well be that today's clandestine forms of death management someday will mirror the history of the contraception movement and ultimately materialize as a social virtue.

■ APPENDIX

Position Statement: International Summit on Promoting Standards of Care for People Living with HIV and AIDS About End-of-Life Decisions (Madrid, June 13-15, 1997)

Preamble

The International Summit on Promoting Standards of Care for People Living With HIV and AIDS About End-of-Life Decisions is a consortium of persons with HIV, care providers, activists, and academics with a diversity of experiences with HIV disease.

We have given careful reflection to our experiences and have identified fundamental common grounds concerning the many issues that arise at the end of life for persons with HIV disease.

The dying experiences for persons with AIDS vary significantly both within and across cultures. In some cultural settings, the dying person may be surrounded by high levels of professional and technical care; others will be distinguished by the provision of human, nonprofessional, and nontechnical care. Furthermore, there are some settings, irrespective of cultural norms and economic resources, where a person with AIDS will experience a dying process that is divorced from any human, professional, or technological care.

We do not take a position on whether one manner of dying is intrinsically better than another. We do, however, strongly oppose the taking of a person's life against her or his consent. We also agree that when a person dies in a manner that might be acceptable to others but is inconsistent with the dying person's values, it is an affront to human dignity. Regardless of one's sociocultural setting and economic circumstance, we believe that the dying process for all persons with HIV can be improved.

Resolution

Therefore, we resolve to encourage, promote, and improve standards of care at the end of life. Areas of attention are [as follows]:

1. The notion that decisions regarding the dying process are as important as decisions concerning living (after all, dying is an integral part of living);
2. The development and dissemination of information concerning end-of-life options for those infected and affected by HIV and AIDS;
3. Early consideration regarding end-of-life care and treatment decisions;
4. The psychosocial well-being of the dying person;
5. Improved management of symptoms, both physical and mental, that are associated with HIV and dying;
6. The right to make deeply personal decisions concerning our bodies, including decisions regarding the manner and timing of death;
7. The involvement of persons with HIV and AIDS in the discussion and debate concerning end-of-life decisions; and
8. Legislative reform and policy development to protect the rights of persons with HIV and AIDS.

■ REFERENCES

AIDS Action. (1997, June 26). *AIDS Action disappointed by Supreme Court decision against assisted suicide* [press release]. Washington, DC: Author.

AIDS Committee of Toronto. (1995). *Position statement on assisted suicide.* Toronto: Author.

American Medical Association. (1996). *Brief of the American Medical Association, the American Nurses Association, and the American Psychiatric Association, et al. as amici curiae in support of petitioners in* Vacco v. Quill. Washington, DC: Author.

Bachman, J. G., Alcser, K. H., Doukas, D. J., Lichtenstein, R. L., Corning, A. D., & Brody, H. M. (1996). Attitudes of Michigan physicians and the public toward legalizing physician-assisted suicide and voluntary euthanasia. *New England Journal of Medicine, 334,* 303-309.

Back, A. L., Wallace, J. I., Starks, H. E., & Pearlman, R. A. (1996). Physician-assisted suicide and euthanasia in Washington State: Patient requests and physician responses. *Journal of the American Medical Association, 275,* 919-925.

Baume, P., & O'Malley, E. (1994). Euthanasia: Attitudes and practice of medical practitioners. *Medical Journal of Australia, 161,* 137-144.

Bindels, P. J. E., Krol, A., van Ameijden, E., Mulder-Folkers, D. K. F., van den Hoek, J. A. R., van Griensven, G. P. J., & Coutinho, R. A. (1996). Euthanasia and physician-assisted suicide in homosexual men with AIDS. *Lancet, 347,* 499-504.

Breitbart, W., Rosenfeld, B. D., & Passik, S. D. (1996). Interest in physician-assisted suicide among ambulatory HIV-infected patients. *American Journal of Psychiatry, 153,* 238-242.

British Columbia Persons With AIDS Society. (1994). *Choices: A position statement on euthanasia.* Vancouver, British Columbia: Author.

Canadian AIDS Society. (1991, November 21). *The right to choose.* Ottawa: Author.

Cohen, J. S., Fihn, S. D., Boyko, E. J., Johnson, A. R., & Wood, R. W. (1994). Attitudes toward assisted suicide and euthanasia among physicians in Washington State. *New England Journal of Medicine, 331,* 89-94.

Cote, T. R., Biggar, R. J., & Dannenburg, A. L. (1992). Risk of suicide among persons with AIDS. *Journal of the American Medical Association, 268,* 2066-2068.

Dillmann, R. J. M., & Legemaate, J. (1994). Euthanasia in the Netherlands: The state of the debate. *European Journal of Health Law, 1,* 81-87.

Docker, C. G., & Smith, C. K. (1993). *Departing drugs: An international guidebook to self-deliverance for the terminally ill.* Victoria: Right to Die Society of Canada.

Farnsworth, C. (1994, June 14). Vancouver AIDS suicides botched. *The New York Times,* p. C12.

Fried, T., Stein, M., O'Sullivan, P., Brock, D., & Novack, D. (1993). Limits of patient autonomy: Physician attitudes and practices regarding life-sustaining treatments and euthanasia. *Archives of Internal Medicine, 153,* 722-728.

Friess, S. (1996, March 5). Uneasy alliance. *The Advocate,* pp. 46-48.

Gay Men's Health Crisis and Lambda Legal Defense and Education Fund. (1996). *Brief for the amici curiae in support of the respondents in* State of Washington v. Glucksberg *and* Vacco v. Quill. New York: Author.

Hogg, R. S., Heath, K. V., Bally, G., Cornelisse, P. G. A., Yip, B., & O'Shaughnessy, M. V. (1997, June). *Attitudes of Canadian physicians toward legalizing physician-assisted suicide for persons with HIV disease.* Paper presented at the Third International Conference on AIDS Impact: Biopsychosocial Aspects of HIV Infection, Melbourne, Australia.

Hughes, D. (Director), & Rabe, D. (Writer). (1997). *A question of mercy* [play]. New York: New York Theater Workshop.

Humphry, D. (1991). *Final exit.* Eugene, OR: Hemlock.

Kimsma, G. K. (1996). Euthanasia and euthanizing drugs in the Netherlands. In M. P. Battin & A. G. Lipman (Eds.), *Drug use in assisted suicide and euthanasia* (pp. 193-210). New York: Pharmaceutical Products Press.

Kleizer, R. (Director). (1996). *It's my party* [film]. Santa Monica, CA: United Artists.

Kuhse, H., & Singer, P. (1988). Doctors' practices and attitudes regarding voluntary euthanasia. *Medical Journal of Australia, 148,* 623-627.

Laane, H. M. (1995). Euthanasia, assisted suicide, and AIDS. *AIDS Care, 7*(Suppl. 2), S163-S167.

Lee, M. A., Nelson, H. D., Tilden, V. P., Ganzini, L., Schmidt, T. A., & Tolle, S. W. (1996). Legalizing assisted suicide: Views of physicians in Oregon. *New England Journal of Medicine, 334,* 310-315.

Leiser, R., Mitchell, T. F., Hahn, J., Mandel, N., Slome, L., Townley, D., & Abrams, D. I. (1996, July). *Nurses' attitudes toward assisted suicide in AIDS.* Poster session presented at the 11th International AIDS Conference, Vancouver, British Columbia.

Leo, R. A. (1995). Trial and tribulations: Courts, ethnography, and the need for an evidentiary privilege for academic researchers. *American Sociologist, 26,* 113-134.

Marzuk, P. M., Tierney, H., Tardiff, K., Gross, E. M., Morgan, E. B., Hsu, M., & Mann, J. J. (1988). Increased risk of suicide in persons with AIDS. *Journal of the American Medical Association, 259,* 1333-1337.

Nietzsche, F. (1973). *Beyond good and evil* (R. J. Hollingdale, Trans.). London: Penguin Books. (Original work published 1886)

Nuland, S. B. (1993). *How we die: Reflections on life's final chapter.* New York: Vintage Books.

Ogden, R. D. (1994a). *Euthanasia, assisted suicide, and AIDS.* New Westminster, British Columbia: Peroglyphics.

Ogden, R. D. (1994b). Palliative care and euthanasia: A continuum of care? *Journal of Palliative Care, 10*(2), 82-85.

Ogden, R. D., & Young, M. G. (1998). Euthanasia and assisted suicide: A survey of social workers in British Columbia. *British Journal of Social Work, 28,* 161-175.

Passik, S. D., McDonald, M. V., Rosenfeld, B. D., & Breitbart, W. S. (1996). End of life issues in patients with AIDS: Clinical and research considerations. In M. P. Battin & A. G. Lipman (Eds.), *Drug use in assisted suicide and euthanasia* (pp. 91-111). New York: Pharmaceutical Products Press.

Right to Die Society of Canada. (1997). *The art and science of suicide.* Victoria, British Columbia: Author. Available: http://www.rights.org/deathnet

Russell, S. (1997, September 12). AIDS death rates fall among adults 25 to 44. *San Francisco Chronicle,* p. A1.

Scarce, R. (1995). Scholarly ethics and courtroom antics: Where researchers stand in the eyes of the law. *American Sociologist, 26,* 87-112.

Schneider, S. G., Taylor, S. E., Hammen, C., Kemeny, M. E., & Dudley, J. (1991). Factors influencing suicide intent in gay and bisexual suicide ideators: Differing models for men with and without human immunodeficiency virus. *Journal of Personality and Social Psychology, 61,* 776-788.

Slome, L. R., Mitchell, T. F., Charlebois, E., Moulton-Benevedes, J., & Abrams, D. I. (1997). Physician-assisted suicide and patients with human immunodeficiency virus disease. *New England Journal of Medicine, 336,* 417-421.

Slome, L. R., Moulton, J., Huffine, C., Gorter, R., & Abrams, D. I. (1992). Physicians' attitudes toward assisted suicide in AIDS. *Journal of Acquired Immune Deficiency Syndrome, 5,* 712-718.

Tindall, B., Forde, S., Carr, A., Barker, S., & Cooper, D. A. (1993). Attitudes to euthanasia and assisted suicide in a group of homosexual men with advanced HIV disease [letter to the editor]. *Journal of Acquired Immune Deficiency Syndrome, 6,* 1069-1070.

van der Maas, P. J., van Delden, J. J. M., Pijnenborg, L., & Looman, C. W. N. (1992). Euthanasia and other medical decisions concerning the end of life. *Health Policy, 22*(1/2), 1-262.

van der Maas, P. J., van der Wal, G., Haverkate, I., de Graaff, C., Kester, J. G. C., Onwuteaka-Philipsen, B. D., van der Heide, A., Bosma, J. M., & Willems, D. L. (1996). Euthanasia, physician-assisted suicide, and other medical practices involving the end of life in the Netherlands, 1990-1995. *New England Journal of Medicine, 335,* 1699-1705.

van Reyk, P. (1995). *Choosing to die: A booklet for people thinking about euthanasia and for those asked to assist.* Sydney, Australia: AIDS Council of New South Wales.

Verhoef, M. J., & Kinsella, T. D. (1996). Alberta euthanasia survey: 3-year follow-up. *Canadian Medical Association Journal, 155,* 885-890.

Werth, J. (1995). Rational suicide reconsidered: AIDS as an impetus for change. *Death Studies, 19*(1), 65-80.

Yarnell, S. K., & Battin, M. P. (1988). AIDS, psychiatry, and euthanasia. *Psychiatric Annals, 18,* 598-603.

Young, M. G., & Ogden, R. D. (1998). End of life issues: A survey of English speaking Canadian nurses in AIDS care. *Journal of the Association of Nurses in AIDS Care, 9*(2), 18-25.

Cases and Legislation Cited

Compassion in Dying v. State of Washington, 79 F.3d 790 (9th Circuit) (1996).

Inquest of unknown female. (1994, October 20). Oral reasons for judgment of the Honorable L. W. Campbell, 91-240-0838, Burnaby, British Columbia.

Krischner v. McIver, No. 89837 (Florida) (1997).

Quill v. Vacco, 80 F.3d 716 (2nd Circuit) (1996).

Roe v. Wade, 410 U.S. 113 (1973).

Schloendorf v. Society of New York Hospital, 211 N.Y. 125, 105 N.E. 92 (1914).

Vacco v. Quill, Westlaw 348037 (1997).

Washington v. Glucksberg, Westlaw 348094 (1997).

Chapter 18

End-of-Life Issues: A Disabilities Perspective

TOM KOCH

*D*uring an international polio epidemic in the early 1950s, the use of iron lungs encasing patients from foot to chin were employed to maintain the lives of those who otherwise certainly would have died of respiratory failure caused by bulbar poliomyelitis (Wackers, 1994). The salvation of thousands of persons, mostly children, through a cumbersome process of mechanical ventilation was seen as a major triumph in both medical circles and society at large. For years, *Reader's Digest* and other popular magazines detailed the triumphs of those who became bridge masters and honor students despite the restrictions of a clumsy encasement. It allowed them to live intellectually and socially active lives despite their physical restrictions.

During the 1990s, however, a different spirit has emerged. The possibility of a physically restricted life maintained through medical technology no longer is a cause for celebration. During the age of euthanasia, it is an argument for assisted suicide. Patients with multiple sclerosis, Lou Gehrig's disease, AIDS, and a host of other potentially limiting diseases seek the right to assisted suicide, not assistance in living with disability. These are not terminally ill patients or those for whom treatment options have been exhausted in the final days of acute illnesses. More typically, they are chronically ill patients rejecting the possibility of a physically restricted life. What euthanasia proponents seek is not just control of one's own death but also social assistance and approval in the ending of one's life before physical death is imminent.

Who we are, what we do, and how we choose to live all influence our thinking about end-of-life issues. In this, I am no exception. I am a bioethicist and a writer with a long-standing interest in this area. Research for this chapter comes from a variety of sources, including personal interviews conducted with proponents and opponents of physician-assisted death in the Netherlands, Canada, and the United States. My perspective also is informed, however, by the lessons learned while caring for my chronically ill father for 5 years, until his death, and from my own experience of being visually impaired. For me, the issue must be, first and foremost, one of living with dignity despite restrictions, not "death with dignity."

■ EUTHANASIA IN THE NETHERLANDS

In 40 years, we have gone from celebrating the survival of polio patients (although in a physically restricted state) to advocating the assisted deaths of fragile persons who face physical limits. Why has the potential for life with dignity despite restrictions turned into a call to assist disabled persons to untimely deaths? Both advocates and proponents of assisted suicide seek answers in the Netherlands, where physicians are allowed to practice euthanasia. This chapter begins with the realities of Dutch euthanasia and then attempts to interpret the North American debate over assisted suicide in light of that experience.

This is the netherworld of social ethics, an area of uncertainty in which diverse but passionate opinions are held by different peoples. There are no easy answers or clear solutions. What appears certain to some is that a movement that began as a way in which to end unbearable physical suffering has become something else. Dutch courts have approved the deaths of a 50-year-old woman with chronic depression and of an infant with Down syndrome. Those two deaths provide us with a starting point as we seek an understanding of the realities of physician-assisted suicide and socially approved, physician-induced death.

Voluntary Euthanasia: The Case of Nettie Boomsma

Nettie Boomsma was a sane, 50-year-old social worker suffering from acute depression. She repeatedly told her doctor and friends that she had lived for her children, and now both were dead. One son committed suicide in 1986, and the second died of a malignant tumor in May 1991. Separated from her husband and an unhappy marriage in 1988, the divorce became final the year in which her second son died. She began hoarding prescription pills after her first son's suicide and used them in a failed suicide attempt after her second son's death. She refused bereavement therapy, intensive counseling, and psychiatric hospitalization. Instead, she began looking for someone who would help her to die. She talked about dying with her family doctor, a psychologist, a social worker at Groninger Hospital, volunteers at a euthanasia information center, and friends (Chabot/OMII Dossier, 1993).

Boomsma was a member of the Dutch Voluntary Euthanasia Society, an organization advancing assisted suicide as a moral right. She called the organization for help. In August 1991, the organization referred her to psychiatrist Boudewijn Chabot, a society member. The doctor and patient met 30 times during a 2-month period for a total of 24 hours of counseling. During that period, she did not waiver in her insistence that she had nothing left to live for or in her refusal of more intensive therapy. On September 28 of that year, Chabot came to Boomsma's house prepared to help her die. In her youngest son's former bedroom, and with witnesses present, he handed her a lethal dose of 20 sleeping pills diluted in some liquid and told her that she could use them as she wished. She drank it without difficulty, and 45 minutes later Chabot pronounced her dead (Chabot/OMII Dossier, 1993).

We know so much about this case because, for the next several years, Boomsma's euthanasia/suicide became a test case that stretched the bounds of Holland's liberalized policies on physician-assisted suicide. After Boomsma's death, Chabot made a full report to the local coroner, as required under Dutch law in all cases of physician-assisted suicide. The coroner, in turn, notified local prosecutors, who brought charges against Chabot.

Two things kept Chabot's actions before the court. This was the first case in which a clinically depressed patient committed suicide with the knowing assistance of a licensed physician. Second, there was Chabot's unfortunate lapse in procedure. Before giving his patient her lethal dose, he failed to obtain the legally required second opinion of a medical colleague asserting that the patient's suffering was intolerable and without hope of improvement. Expert testimony that was admitted to the court, however, did the job after the fact. Physicians reviewing the case concluded that Boomsma's lack of an "intimate part-ner relationship" lessened hope of her recovery without intensive treatment, which she refused (Chabot/OMII Dossier, 1993). In 1994, the Netherlands Su-preme Court found Chabot guilty of assisting in Boomsma's suicide but ruled that he should not be punished.

Not everyone was pleased. "A Bridge Too Far," declared headlines in the country's largest daily newspaper, *De Telegraaf* ("Dutch Woman's Aided Death," 1994, p. A1). The writers argued that euthanasia in the case of painful, terminal disease is one thing, but killing a recently bereaved, severely de-pressed woman is quite another. This, they said, was an act beyond both the law and the strong Dutch sense of necessary care and propriety. Not at all, replied Justice Ministry spokesperson Victor Holtus, who told reporters that the coun-try's policy on euthanasia and physician-assisted suicide underlines a person's right to choose death, even if he or she is free of physical pain or terminal illness.

"This is a classic example of the slippery slope," said Karl Gunning, head of the Dutch Physician's Union, which has opposed liberalizing euthana-sia ("Dutch Woman's Aided Death," 1994, p. A1). Gunning added that Boomsma's death, or the death of anyone like her, was an inevitable result of liberalizing euthanasia. "We have always predicted that once you start looking at killing as a means to solve problems," Gunning told reporters, "you'll find more and more problems where killing can be the solution" (p. A1).

Voluntary Euthanasia Society

Chabot and Boomsma were introduced to each other by members of the Dutch Voluntary Euthanasia Society, which actively works to liberalize Hol-land's already liberal policies regarding assisted suicide. Its history typifies that of the movement at large. The society began in 1973 after Truus Postma-Van Boven euthanized her mother, an elderly woman dying a painful death from metastastic end-stage cancer. Postma-Van Boven then turned herself in and, although convicted, was given a suspended sentence. With that judgment began the Dutch movement to end irremediable pain and suffering in terminal illness through physician-assisted euthanasia. Over the years, however, its mandate has expanded to one advocating death on demand. As former U.S. Surgeon General C. Everett Koop put it, "Euthanasia and assisted suicide used to be discussed in reference to intractable pain; now, it is more dissatisfaction with the human condition" (Koop, 1993, p. 57).

Martine Cornelisse-Claussen, a psychologist and staff member at the Voluntary Euthanasia Society, explained the following to me in a 1994 interview:

> The first thing is what a person wants himself [or herself]. We are an association which has strong roots in self-determination. We even think [that] if a person could still have a lot of treatments, if the doctor says "Well, you know, I still see all kinds of chances for you," if that person doesn't want to go through it, he [or she] should have the possibility to do this in his [or her] own way.

Despite the liberalization of the nation's laws, the Dutch Voluntary Euthanasia Society believes that the current laws still are too strict. Under the 1993 legal compromise allowing euthanasia, physician-assisted suicide remains a criminal act. But when at least two physicians agree that a competent adult patient who repeatedly requests death does so because of chronic and incurable suffering, then no criminal charges will be filed if the patient is helped to die.

The key word is *suffering*. In these and other cases, the concept has come to be defined ever more broadly to include existential angst and emotional distress. To members of the Dutch Voluntary Euthanasia Society and to euthanasia advocates generally, the issue is not the reason why someone wishes to die but rather what they see as a person's right to make that decision unilaterally. This is voluntary euthanasia, a decision by people who can make a choice for and participate in their own deaths. Cornelisse-Clausen assured me that involuntary euthanasia, or the killing of people unable to state their preferences, is not what the Dutch policy is about. "Our society is only talking about people who can utter their will. We are not talking about little babies or babies who were born disabled."

Involuntary Euthanasia: The Case of Baby Ross

Yet, involuntary euthanasia has been supported by the Dutch Voluntary Euthanasia Society and sanctioned by the Dutch courts. There was, for example, the 1987 case of Baby Ross, a child facing neither untreatable pain nor long-term physical suffering. The Down syndrome newborn would have lived if only the pediatrician had operated to repair an atresia, an opening in its intestine. This is a fairly common birth defect, and its repair is relatively straightforward.

The Ross parents refused the operation on the advice of their doctor, a professor of pediatric surgery, who argued that the child's long-term quality of life would be unacceptable. Officials wanted to insist on the operation, but the child's parents argued that it was their choice and not the state's, an issue of self-determination by parental proxy. Baby Ross died, and a court case began that expanded the playing field on which physician-assisted suicide can be exercised. The crucial court testimony, all agree, came from a colleague of the defendant, another professor of pediatric surgery. He argued as an expert witness that, had the operation been performed, Baby Ross's quality of life would have been unacceptable and Baby Ross would have suffered because of the Down syndrome complex.

The Dutch Supreme Court vindication of the physician, however, did not end the debate. The involuntary euthanasia of an infant troubled many who otherwise supported liberalized euthanasia policies. They did not like the fact that the euthanasia movement, which began as a way in which to end unbearable physical suffering, had been expanded to allow the death of Down syndrome infants. Critics were quick to point out that hundreds of similarly afflicted children had survived handily in the past.

The Baby Ross case now is a legal precedent sanctioned by the Dutch Pediatric Society. In 1993, it issued a set of guidelines to assist members in determining whether a newborn's future would be "non-livable." These include the ability to communicate with others and look after oneself in later life, potential life expectancy, and the "degree of suffering now and in the future" (Van Leeuwen & Kimsma, 1993). But *suffering,* like *quality of life,* is a subjective term. It means whatever an expert or advocate decides it means. One's degree of suffering might be as dependent on the family one is born into as are the deficits one is born with. Quality of life might grow as much from the level of community support a person and family receives as from the underlying genetic imprint. Yet, both quality of life and suffering now are accepted as rationales for voluntary and involuntary euthanasia in Holland.

Assisted Death Among Older Adults

By 1994, more and more euthanized deaths were occurring in Holland in individuals whose illnesses had not reached terminal stages and for whom palliative care (i.e., care focused on physical comfort and pain relief rather than on cure) was not yet needed. "Many patients don't want to wait until the end stage comes," Cornelisse-Clausen told me in the 1994 interview. "They have a very open communication about this with their doctors, and some of them choose to die before the end stage starts." This was especially true, she added, among seniors over 70 years of age. This is a major change from 1990, when statistics showed relatively few elderly using euthanasia as a means of escaping the restrictions that aging can bring. Now, the Dutch Voluntary Euthanasia Society is fielding more and more requests for information from seniors who want to be ready "just in case," she said. Seniors are afraid of the lack of autonomy and dignity that accompany diseases such as Alzheimer's and Parkinson's. According to Cornelisse-Clausen, older adults are saying to their doctors, "I saw my mother suffer terribly. If it starts with me, I'll come to you and ask for pills to end my own life." When reminded that many patients live full lives through the early stages of most diseases, including those that affect the elderly, Cornelisse-Clausen shrugged and indicated that it was the patients' choice.

Euthanasia and AIDS

The use of physician-assisted suicide to avoid even early, nonterminal phases of debilitating illness also is increasing rapidly in Holland's AIDS community. Like seniors afraid of the lack of autonomy and dignity that accompany illnesses such as Parkinson's or Alzheimer's, AIDS patients who fear the course of their disease are considering early euthanasia. "For them," said Cornelisse-Clausen, "it is a comforting idea." Thus, it is no surprise that after the liberalization of euthanasia laws, physician-assisted death increased markedly as a cause of death in the Dutch AIDS community ("Euthanasie bij groot deel," 1993).

Holland's Safeguards Against Abuse

Although assisted death is being used in a growing variety of situations—pain, dementia, AIDS, depression, Down syndrome—essential safeguards interwoven into Dutch society have prevented the wholesale "moral holocaust" predicted by some opponents of liberalizing euthanasia. They are, first, the country's strong tradition of personalized family medicine and, second, the cradle-to-grave, complete health care coverage that all Dutch citizens automatically receive as a birthright.

Family physicians in Holland do not have hospital privileges. Nor do most want them. They are mediators between the greater establishment of medical specialists and the broad needs of their patients. Their forte is diagnosis, that is, determining what a problem is and knowing where to go for help in its treatment. They make frequent house calls and are trained to talk with and listen to their patients and to build long-term relationships based on mutual trust and knowledge. Thus, a physician whose patient says "I can't take this" might respond personally as well as professionally by saying "Try these things first. We'll work it out. With a specialist's help, we can make this better."

As important, "free choice" in Holland means equal choice irrespective of cost. Home care, support, expensive medications, machines to support life, and hospice and hospital treatment all are paid for by the country's program of universal health coverage. Dutch physician Gerrit Kimsma explained in a 1994 interview,

> The Netherlands has an extensive primary care system with universal access, with a nursing support that covers 24-hour care for terminal patients. Since there is universal insurance coverage, there are no financial reasons to stop treatment. There is also an extensive system of homes for the elderly and nursing homes that are financed by taxes.

This means that Boomsma did not have to worry that psychiatric treatment would bankrupt her finances. The Ross parents had no worry that future care of their Down syndrome child would mean an inability to pay for another child's education. The elderly can get the home care they need. Patients with Lou Gehrig's disease may receive ventilator support and home care if they choose to live past the disease's paralyzing respiratory crisis. Multiple sclerosis patients are assured of wheelchairs and other assisting devices if they are needed.

Kimsma, a practicing family physician and an expert on euthanasia who also teaches at the Free University of Amsterdam, believes that this level of support is an essential safeguard preventing euthanasia from becoming a holocaust. The choice for assisted suicide, according to Kimsma, must be unencumbered by economic fears. Otherwise, it becomes something else, something potentially nasty and ugly. Offering euthanasia without full care can be like asking the fragile among us to play Russian roulette with a nearly fully loaded gun.

There is surprising unanimity on this point in Holland. The Dutch are concerned that countries attempting to copy their experiment in euthanasia will do so without also ensuring complete medical coverage that gives individuals real freedom of choice. Cornelisse-Claussen said in the interview,

> Everyone here is able to get good health care. I think only in this context can a law like we have be passed. If the socioeconomic circumstances in a country are different, and if there are lots of financial problems with getting good care, then people should be very, very, very careful about introducing these possibilities.

■ EUTHANASIA IN NORTH AMERICA

Requests for Assisted Suicide
by Disabled Adults

The U.S. courts are prone to accepting requests for euthanasia by people with disabilities. In the case of 31-year-old quadriplegic Kenneth Bergstedt of Las Vegas, Nevada, the courts ruled that giving him a lethal dose of sedatives was not suicide, assisted suicide, or murder. It was, instead, a means for him to regulate his own medical care. Bergstedt asked the courts for euthanasia when his father, who cared for him, became ill (Johnson, 1990). Without his father, he would have no companions and nobody to care for him. There would be, simply, no way in which to live and nobody to live for.

In such cases, according to psychologist Carol Gill in a court affidavit, a self-determined desire for euthanasia is not necessarily free choice. Rather, it might be the inevitable result of society's failure to provide the type of support the Dutch offer to everyone. She noted that, in most cases where a severely ill or disabled person asks for help to die, there is a problem in the support system. Unfortunately, the disabled person often is surrounded by people who agree with the person's desire to die because living in that condition is something that they themselves would find difficult (*Gamble v. Baptist Hospital,* 1990).

Another U.S. case, *Bouvia v. Superior Court* (1986), underlines that conclusion. Elizabeth Bouvia, a quadriplegic with cerebral palsy and arthritis, told the court that she wanted to die because being a disabled person was so difficult. The judge, in his concluding opinion, thought that this was reasonable. "Can anyone blame her if she wants to fold her cards and say 'I am out'?" the judge asked. "I believe she has an absolute right to effectuate that decision [to die]" (quoted in Miller, 1993, p. 58). Interestingly, once granted the right to die, Bouvia chose instead to live. It was as if the support and recognition of her hardships gave her the will to go on living.

Larry McAfee also petitioned the court for the right to die because he found life on a respirator too difficult to continue. He had been injured in a motorcycle accident and asked the court for permission to disconnect his breathing apparatus (*State v. McAfee,* 1989). His suicide wish was encouraged and supported by his father, a newspaper columnist, and by a lawyer (Kemp, 1993).

Alerted to this case, members of the California disabled community met with McAfee. People such as Stanford University professor Paul Longmore, who also uses a respirator, convinced McAfee that there was indeed life—not merely existence—after paralysis. In the end, McAfee decided to live. But it took a publicized court fight for euthanasia to bring him counseling and to marshal the resources for him not only to survive but also to triumph in the face of disability.

Paul Steven Miller, the U.S. director of disability outreach for the White House Office of Presidential Personnel, has amassed a growing file of cases like McAfee's in which lack of financial and social support have led to suicide or to court petitions for euthanasia. His conclusion is an indictment of the assumption that "self-determination" is sufficient reason for the death of a person who is ill: "Those who advocate the right to assisted suicide work to support the right of self-elimination rather than the elimination of the barriers in society prohibiting persons with disabilities from achieving independent lives with dignity" (Miller, 1993, p. 56).

Support for the ill and disabled in Canada, although more comprehensive than that provided in the United States, still is limited. Provincial health care programs often are reluctant to pay the cost for lifesaving medications because they are too expensive. Margaret Somerville, a McGill University ethicist, summarized the situation: "We're faced with what might be called a world of competing sorrows, full of tragic and difficult choices" (quoted in Mickelburgh, 1992, p. A17). This "world of competing sorrows" is one of cost efficiency in the face of disease. Unlike the Netherlands, Canada does not provide comprehensive services for its disabled citizens. In Toronto, for example, the Wheeltrans system for handicapped users is chronically oversubscribed and underfunded. Without it, severely challenged residents cannot get out unless they have the money for specially equipped private transportation.

Society at large also provides minimal assistance to those caring at home for disabled family members. Denis Warner, the pseudonym of a Toronto lawyer whose wife has advanced multiple sclerosis, sold the family home and refinanced his mother's home to pay for his wife's home care (Koch, 1994b). The problem, simply, is that "government does not have very much assistance for people who want to look after people at home" (p. 44).

Involuntary Euthanasia: The Case of Baby Doe

Similar to the case of Baby Ross in Holland was the case of Baby Doe, an Indiana infant who died in 1982. The parents of newborn Baby Doe worried that their Down syndrome child would suffer an unacceptable quality of life (Kemp, 1993). Despite offers from at least 10 couples to adopt him, the parents received permission from the Indiana courts to let the infant die. Many in the Down syndrome community argued angrily that, had Baby Doe been allowed to live, his quality of life would have been more than sufficient. Among the critics was syndicated U.S. news columnist George Will, whose son, Jonathan, has Down syndrome. According to Will, Jonathan is the best whiffle-ball hitter in his part of the state (Maryland), and his only suffering is due to anxiety surrounding the poor start of the Baltimore Orioles. Will wrote in a syndicated column. "He is doing nicely, thank you. . . . He can do without people like [Baby] Doe's parents, and courts like Indiana's, asserting that people like him are less than fully human" (quoted in Kemp, 1993, p. 76).

Assisted Death and AIDS

Fear of end-stage AIDS also is a driving force behind the euthanasia movement in North America. Many AIDS activists in Canada and the United States have coupled their concern for appropriate treatment with an advocacy of euthanasia policies. See Ogden's chapter in this volume (Chapter 17) on the response of the HIV/AIDS community.

I believe that there is a sad irony here. The AIDS pandemic has been a crucial force driving the movement for recognition of homosexuals in North American society. It has brought together formerly disparate groups into a movement based not simply on sexual preference but, more important, on the way in which mutual support and human need allow all of us to face adversity, especially terminal illness and debilitating disease. The famous AIDS quilt, with individual panels that name and remember victims of the disease, symbolizes the human face that members of the AIDS community have given to bereavement. In hospital and hospice rooms where patients lie sick, members of those patients' communities gather both to comfort the ill and each other, irrespective of sexual preference.

Faced with a devastating illness ravaging their community, AIDS activists have made of palliative care a celebration of life, transforming our bereavement rituals in the process. Columbia University's Richard Neugebauer, who has studied this phenomenon, found in the AIDS community little of the paralyzing depression that death typically brings to the rest of us. Instead, he discovered resilience, solidarity, reconnection, and engagement stemming from the process of people facing debilitating illness as a community (Horn, 1993). In the process, members of a patient's disparate communities—work acquaintances, former lovers, church members, family members (often estranged), friends—come together.

For more than 20 years, palliative care experts from Elisabeth Kübler-Ross, whose writings helped define the field, to cancer specialist Bernie Siegal have written about living while dying, about the stages the patient and family pass through when facing terminal illness, and the things they learn along the way (Kübler-Ross, 1981; Siegal, 1990). Kübler-Ross pioneered work on end-of-life changes, that is, on how people come to face and accept death resulting from progressive illness. Nobody knows how much time they have, Siegal tells audiences around the world, but illness teaches us how to live today. A cancer specialist turned writer and lecturer, Siegal moved from the aggressive treatment of individual patients to the equally challenging role of helping people to accept their mortality while living life to the fullest despite a potentially fatal illness. Albeit in slightly different ways, both writers advocate what the AIDS community has demonstrated, that is, an ability to live with uncertainty and to make of life an affirmation, however much longer one might have.

One understands the temptation to die early and to use euthanasia as a means of avoiding the multiple afflictions that are part of this disease's often long and downward course. With that, however, also might be lost the lessons learned through facing illness together (Koch, 1994a, 1998)—a loss to society and perhaps also to the individual who, while still relatively healthy, decides to drink a lethal cocktail and say good-bye to the world.

■ THE BIAS AGAINST LIVING A RESTRICTED LIFE

In addition to not providing full support for people living with disability, there are other societal biases that work against living with disability. When a disabled person requests help to die, we do not ask whether that death wish would be dampened by social support providing the tools that can make a disabled life meaningful and rich. We do not ask whether the death is necessary.

With the best of intentions, North American lawyers, jurists, and journalists grease the slide down euthanasia's slope with the assumption that suicide makes sense when someone is disabled or chronically ill. Along the way, they have redefined chronic illness as necessarily terminal and painful, even where treatment is possible. "One of the things which has happened is that chronic illnesses that are potentially treatable and maintainable have been sliding down a slippery slope," said palliative care physician Bill McArthur, a former chief coroner of British Columbia. "Mrs. Rodriguez's case is an excellent example. She suffered from amyotrophic lateral sclerosis (ALS), or Lou

Gehrig's disease, which by no means is a terminal illness" (personal communication, May 28, 1994).

Sue Rodriguez's fight for the right to assisted suicide was followed closely by euthanasia advocates from Holland to San Francisco (Vienneau, 1993). From the start, her supporters and her lawyer, Chris Considine, insisted that she was terminally ill. Speed in judgment, Considine argued to the courts, was simply a human necessity. Almost without exception, news reporters followed his lead in describing Rodriguez as "terminally ill" and "dying." That she must be in great pain was assumed, almost taken for granted.

Terminal illnesses are conditions for which there is no treatment, adaptation, or assistance that will prolong a person's life. End-stage cancer is an example. Late-stage congestive heart failure is another. Many ALS patients, however, can continue to live with the use of mechanical aids. Nor is this a "vegetative" existence. Stanford professor Longmore, physicist Stephen Hawking, *Providence Journal-Bulletin* columnist Brian Dickinson, and others all live productive and interesting lives despite having suffered ALS's virtually complete paralysis (Graves, 1997). Yet, without debate or question, the Canadian Supreme Court accepted Rodriguez's claim that she was terminally and painfully ill. The assumption of her pain was so widespread that her doctor called a news conference after her assisted suicide to state clearly that she was not suffering physically in her final days and hours.

To be fair, many physicians have assisted in redefining chronic illnesses as terminal conditions. Most do not encourage patients with ALS to accept life on a respirator because, like Baby Ross's pediatrician, they believe that the resulting quality of life will be unacceptable. We know this from the reports of patients and their families who have fought their doctors for the right to live. When ALS patient Justice Sam Filer of the Ontario court was facing the disease's respiratory crisis, doctors urged his wife, Toni, to let him die. She recalled, "They encouraged me, eight of them surrounding me, to let him die and let him die with dignity. I said, 'I'll take care of his quality of life, thank you very much; you take care of saving his life' " (quoted in Bindman, 1993, p. A1).

Bindman's (1993) story ran under the headline "Judge Stays on Bench to Fight His Disease's 'Death Sentence'," but the text made clear that Filer chose to live for other reasons entirely: "I love the law. I am proud to be able to serve my community in my present capacity, which in no way impinges on my ability to see, to hear, to think, to read, to reason, and to remember" (quoted on p. A1). There was no death sentence. Filer endured as a lawyer and as a man to serve his community, the law, and his family. "My decision was made somewhat easier when Toni reiterated, time and again, that she would rather have me on a ventilator than not at all" (quoted on p. A1).

■ A RESTRICTED LIFE

An extraordinary series of recent advances in communication and mobility technologies have made it possible for people such as Hawking and Filer not merely to exist but to thrive. For the first time, even those completely paralyzed can communicate through computer interfaces responding to eye movements, head-held pointers, or minute muscular twitches. Hawking's most recent books were written in this way, as was Filer's most recent memos.

This, perhaps, is the final irony. Just as opportunities appear for the severely disabled to live among us as full members of society if only we would offer them our support, euthanasia reclassifies their conditions as terminal and rationally deserving of death. Perhaps we assume that this is appropriate because of our own fear and ignorance or our own inability to confront disease. In the words of Miller (1993),

> Too often, third parties such as health care professionals, lawyers, judges, and others are quick to assume that a request for suicide is due to the disability and thus rational.... The potential for abuse is therefore very great.... The simple fact is that society's response to an individual who expresses the desire to commit suicide should be no different for a disabled person than for an able-bodied person. Before considering whether assisted suicide should be a right ... we should first attempt to create the option of a dignified life. (pp. 61-62)

This is what neither Canada nor the United States has made a priority. Neither country provides sufficient home support, respite for family caregivers, expensive computer communication systems, state-of-the-art electric wheelchairs, and/or sufficient counseling or vocation retraining for everyone who needs them. Then, despite this lack of support, we argue that people seeking death because of miserable lives are exercising their self-determination. Even the Dutch Voluntary Euthanasia Society would reject this. Without complete support, the organization insists, the deck is stacked against free choice and self-determination.

■ WHO DECIDES?

If there is anything that this long history teaches us, it is that judges and physicians are not good arbiters in complex moral situations such as this. It was the justices of Canada's Supreme Court and the British Columbia Court of Appeals who accepted, without question, a lawyer's assertion that Rodriguez was terminally ill. Supreme Court justices in the Netherlands defined Boomsma's and Baby Ross's deaths as acceptable. During the 1920s, the Supreme Courts of both the United States and Germany approved the involuntary sterilization of disadvantaged women as just, right, and proper. The record of the lower courts is even worse.

Nor should the requirement of physician certification lay anyone's fears to rest. During the 1980s, Hawking told the story of being diagnosed with ALS and then being virtually abandoned by his attending physician. Eight physicians surrounded Toni Filer, attempting to convince her to let her husband die instead of living a restricted life. In Holland, doctors have redefined "quality of life" to necessarily exclude infants such as Baby Ross. Others have made clinical depression after the death of one's child(ren) into a terminal condition. From this perspective, physician certification, even with the necessity of a judicial review, is no safeguard at all.

■ CONCLUSION

In my opinion, arguing for a right to die is foolish. Death is not a right; it is an inevitability. Nor do the freedoms of a democratic society necessarily guarantee individuals the right to choose the moments of their deaths. That is what the U.S. Supreme Court ruled in its 1997 decisions on euthanasia in cases such as *Washington v. Glucksberg* (1997) and *Vacco v. Quill* (1997). There is perhaps a situation in which assisted suicide makes sense, and that is in the case of terminal illness and unbearable and untreatable pain.

Today, however, medicine has the capability to keep us free from pain through the judicious use of drugs such as morphine and heroin if they are given in adequate doses (Somerville, 1993). A judicious mix of modern technology and social assistance can support even the most restricted individual in a life that has the potential for communication, relation, and meaning. Yet, across the euthanasia debates, these potentials too often are ignored in the rush to insist on an individual's right to hasten death rather than face a life already foreshortened by illness or limited by a physical condition.

If we were honest with ourselves, then the death certificates of those who died because they could not face physical restrictions would read "death by pride" or perhaps "cause of death: hubris." The death certificates of those whose desire for death was caused by untreated pain would read "death by malpractice." And the death certificates of those who died rather than face restricted lives in which they lacked the tools and assistance required by their illnesses would read simply "death caused by social indifference."

As I prepared to leave the offices of the Dutch Voluntary Euthanasia Society, Cornelise-Claussen asked me what I thought about euthanasia and her group's program. What I said in response is, perhaps, a fitting end to this chapter.

Holland's health care system is the best we can conceive of today. In that context, euthanasia probably is the best policy of its kind imaginable. It represents, however, the end stage of an adolescent and immature philosophy that I suspect soon will be perceived as antiquated, outmoded, and medieval. It states autonomy and self-determination as absolutes, but as our society matures, a more communal perspective surely will dominate. We need the pesky, irascible, implacable voices of people like Sue Rodriguez in our lives. Perhaps in time, we will come to understand this and to see that death because of disability is murder by pride, a waste and not a triumph. A mature society would insist that disability is no barrier to participation and that physical or emotional problems are no reason for state-assisted suicide. Hawking is no less a man for his ALS. Sam Filer is no less a jurist. Down syndrome need not have prevented Baby Ross from living a life in Holland.

A right to die with dignity is less important than a right to live with dignity within the community of one's choice. To promise the former and ignore the latter is, well, medieval. When we accept that both as individuals and as a community, legalized euthanasia will become a figment of history, like witchcraft trials and public hangings. People then will look back and ask, "How could our grandparents have been so silly?"

■ REFERENCES

Bindman, S. (1993, January 11). Judge stays on bench to fight his disease's "death sentence." *Toronto Star,* p. A1.

Dutch woman's aided death rekindles euthanasia debate. (1994, June 23). *Toronto Star,* p. A1.

Euthanasie bij groot deel van terminale aidspatienten. (1993, July 10). *NRC Handlesblad,* p. 9.

Graves, F. G. (1997). Writing for his life. *American Journalism Review, 17*(2), 24-31.

Horn, M. (1993, June 14). Grief re-examined. *U.S. News and World Report,* pp. 81-84.

Johnson, M. (1990, September-October). Unanswered questions. *Disability Rag,* pp. 1, 16.

Kemp, E. J. (1993). Paternalism, disability, and the right to die. *Issues in Law & Medicine, 9*(1), 73-76.

Koch, T. (1994a). *A place in time: Caregivers for their elderly.* New York: Praeger.

Koch, T. (1994b). *Watersheds: Crises and resolution in our everyday life.* Toronto: Lester Publishing.

Koch, T. (1998). *Second chances: Crisis and renewal in our everyday lives.* Toronto: Turnerbooks.

Koop, C. E. (1993). On the ministry of medicine. *Making the Rounds, 1*(2), 57.

Kübler-Ross, E. (1981). *Living with death and dying.* New York: Collier Books.

Mickelburgh, R. (1992, January 21). Drawing the lines on the cost of sustaining life. *Globe and Mail,* p. A17.

Miller, P. S. (1993). The impact of assisted suicide on persons with disabilities: Is it a right without freedom? *Issues in Law and Medicine, 9*(1), 46-62.

Siegal, B. (1990). *Love, medicine, and miracles: Lessons learned about self-healing from a surgeon's experience with exceptional patients.* New York: HarperCollins.

Somerville, M. (1993). The song of death: The lyrics of euthanasia. *Journal of Contemporary Health Law and Policy, 9,* 1-76.

Van Leeuwen, E., & Kimsma, G. K. (1993). Acting or letting go: Medical decision making in neonatology in the Netherlands. *Cambridge Quarterly of Healthcare Ethics, 2,* 265-269.

Vienneau, D. (1993, October 1). Right-to-die decision now up to parliament. *Toronto Star,* p. A12.

Wackers, G. L. (1994). *Constructivist medicine.* Maastricht, Netherlands: Universitaire per Maastricht.

Cases and Legislation Cited

Bouvia v. Superior Court, 225 Cal. Rptr. 297 (CTAPP) (1986).

Chabot/OMII Dossier, 045.0374-tv, CME 93-46A, Docket No. 478-1993 (E. Schweiger, Trans.) (1993).

Gamble v. Baptist Hospital, No. 90-10211-III (Tenn., Ch. Ct) (1990).

State v. McAfee. 259 Ga. 579, 385 S.E. 2d (1989).

Vacco v. Quill, 117 S. Ct. 2293 (1997).

Washington v. Glucksberg, 117 S. Ct. 2258 (1997).

Implications

Chapter 19

Talking to Patients About Death and Dying: Improving Communication Across Cultures

SHARI L. KOGAN
PATRICIA L. BLANCHETTE
KAMAL MASAKI

eath is inevitable and universal, yet many individuals and families are uncomfortable with the dying process or end-of-life discussions. Cure is of utmost concern. Yet, when it is not possible, it is incumbent on practitioners to acknowledge the dying process and to help patients and their families through it. Although health professionals are in a unique position to help people through this intense period, they are not exempt from the difficulties of dealing with death and dying. This is understandable given that health care professionals come from the same death-avoiding society as their patients and often are uncomfortable with the topic themselves (Feifel, 1990). Health care training programs focus on diagnosis and treatment rather than on palliation, and they emphasize the physical body over the social, psychological, and spiritual aspects of a person.

305

Developing skills in working with terminally ill patients is crucial, however, as the population ages and more people suffer prolonged deaths from chronic diseases. In addition, practitioners must realize that medicine is undergoing a critical shift from its paternalistic tradition to more patient-directed and patient-centered care models that require a holistic view of health.

Previous chapters have dealt with medical, legal, cultural, and religious issues affecting how individuals face the dying process. This chapter aims to help the clinician incorporate that information and put it to practical use in the context of caring for a dying person. Whereas we provide some references to the literature, much of the chapter's content and all of the illustrative cases are presented from our experiences as practicing physicians and faculty in the Geriatric Medicine Fellowship Program of the University of Hawaii at Manoa.

■ DISCUSSING DEATH

Who Should Be Involved in Discussions?

The Primary Care Practitioner

Patients often find themselves in unfamiliar circumstances at the ends of their lives. They might have recently been told of a frightening diagnosis and might have been referred to multiple subspecialists. They might be admitted to a health care facility in which health care workers, although skilled, lack the familiarity and long-earned respect of the patient.

Therefore, in discussions of death and dying, it is preferable that the primary care physician take responsibility for these discussions, although others on the health care team can play important contributing roles. The primary care or attending physician usually is the person selected to take the lead because he or she has an ultimate responsibility for the patient's care and most likely has established a meaningful relationship with the patient over time. The primary physician has been trusted with confidential personal information, might have seen the patient though prior illness and recovery, and is likely to be familiar with the patient's values and family dynamics.

Because some patients might wait until they are in the late stages of disease before going to the doctor or could be assigned to a new doctor when moved from one facility to another, providers might find themselves caring for dying patients who are complete strangers to them. In these cases, it is imperative that the practitioner spend some time getting to know the new patient and his or her family, as illustrated by the case of Mr. W (Case 19.1).

CASE 19.1. Mr. W

Mr. W was a 70-year-old Hawaiian man with advanced dementia who had been non-verbal and bed-bound in a nursing home for 5 years. He was admitted to the hospital with pneumonia when I was assigned the case as a 1st-year geriatric fellow. From the minute I saw him, I realized that the prognosis was not good. The patient had no living will or durable power of attorney for health care. His wife JoAnn, who was devoted to him and visited him every day at the nursing home, wanted him to be a full code. She seemed somewhat suspicious that the hospital would push her to let him die or have him return prematurely to the nursing home. Despite intravenous antibiotics, his condition continued to deteriorate over the next 2 weeks. Because JoAnn was at his bedside much of the time every day, I spent some time with her every day talking about his condition and her feelings, and we began to develop a good relationship. Gradually, she came to realize and even accept that her husband's care was futile. Then, 3 weeks into the hospitalization, Mr. W developed an empyema, which would require drainage with a chest tube. After discussing the situation, JoAnn realized that this was futile care. A mutual decision was made to forgo the chest tube and allow Mr. W to die. Although we had developed a warm rapport, I worried that she would hate me forever and blame me for her husband's death. I was astonished and pleased when, after he passed away, she asked me to become her personal physician.

Family and Loved Ones

If it has not occurred before, then the period of a terminal illness is the time to involve family and loved ones in accordance with the wishes of the patient. It is important to understand that a patient might be part of a nontraditional family and for practitioners to ask the patient whom he or she wishes to have included in discussions about the patient's care. For purposes of this chapter, the term *family* includes both people who are related to the patient and others who the patient considers family. If acceptable to the patient, then conferences involving the patient, family, and other loved ones often are the most efficient way in which to disseminate information, answer questions, and arrive at consensus for end-of-life planning.

Patients often worry more about the people they leave behind than about themselves, and they appreciate efforts to ease their families' anxieties. Involving family members early and often, even allowing them to witness the compassionate interactions between practitioners and patients, can do much to alleviate tension. Conferences also provide an opportunity for patients to reiterate their wishes for their care and, thereby, solidify consensus with regard to limits of treatment. Family members also can relate stories about situations involving the patient that reflect lifelong values and preferences. This can be especially helpful when patients are unable to communicate their wishes themselves.

Sometimes, a patient will have appointed a surrogate decision maker through a durable power of attorney for health care (DPOA-HC), and this individual must be included in discussions. Often, a patient who has not taken legal steps to appoint a surrogate has one in mind, and the patient should be encouraged to make this expectation known to family and friends as well as to the health care staff. Research suggests that fewer than half of terminally ill patients have discussed end-of-life issues with surrogates (legal or otherwise), but in cases where detailed discussions have taken place, surrogates are able to make accurate substituted judgments (Sulmasy, Terry, & Weisman, 1998).

Other Health Care Professionals

Most legal and ethical problems that occur at the end of life happen when patients no longer are able to communicate for themselves and there is disagreement among family members and close personal friends. In these cases, care conferences can be critically important to avoid strife, arguments, unnecessary and unwanted medical interventions, and subsequent litigation. Social workers, counselors, and clergy can be very helpful, especially when consensus is difficult to achieve.

What Issues Should Be Discussed?

Putting Advance Directives in Perspective

The earlier phases of the dying process are an excellent time to clarify certain issues. Of critical importance are discussions about available and appropriate technology; as much as possible, consensus should be sought on when and how to limit treatment. The living will and the DPOA-HC are two advance directive documents that can help to guide end-of-life treatment decisions and must be drafted while patients are able to understand them. However, although these can be important and useful legal documents, we feel strongly that they should be the result of, and not a substitute for, in-depth discussions with patients and families. Inadequate communication among doctors, patients, and families is one of the most common reasons for referr

as illustrated by the case of Mr. S (Case 19.2).

CASE 19.2. Mr. S

I became involved with Mr. S, a Caucasian man, when his atte_____ physician presented his case to the hospital ethics committee. Mr. S had three children from his first
marriage to Audrey. Although they now were adults, it was obvious that they still felt
resentment about their parents' divorce 25 years ago and toward Claire, the second
wife of 15 years. Now, Mr. S had advanced Alzheimer's disease and had stopped eating. The issue before the ethics committee was whether or not Mr. S should be started
on tube feeding. He had a living will that specified that he would not want tube feeding
if he ever was in an irreversible condition. He also had a durable power of attorney for
health care in which he appointed his second wife, Claire, to make decisions for him.
Both wives and all three children were present at the ethics committee meeting, and
the children were arguing in favor of inserting a feeding tube. They were very angry
with Claire and accused her of selfish motives. On further discussion, it became clear
that they felt left out of the decision-making process, had not known that their father
had completed these advance directives, and had not had time to come to grips with
their father's choices. They were even more surprised to find out that their own
mother, Audrey, had a living will as well that she never had discussed with them.
Eventually, they came to understand what a living will meant, that their father had
written his himself when still alert, and that his decisions would result in reduced suffering. Over the ensuing week, the family was able to come to a consensus with the attending physician that tube feeding would not be initiated. Mr. S died shortly
thereafter.

Even if a patient already has an advance directive, he or she might want to
modify it. In addition, living wills do not cover every eventuality that can confront a patient in the course of his or her dying. Thus, it is very likely that new
decisions will be made while old decisions are reworked throughout the dying
process. When given verbal directives by patients on these issues, practitioners
should carefully document the decisions and the reasons for them as stated by
the patient. When a clear decision has been made, practitioners should document the patient's instructions, especially as they affect code status and surrogate decision making. They should make sure that copies of advance directives
are given to all physicians involved in the patient's care in case another physician, such as the patient's oncologist or surgeon, admits the patient at some
point.

Because living wills cannot cover every possible variation of situations
that arise in the dying process, practitioners will be better prepared to carry out
a patient's wishes if they understand the patient's values and significant life ex-

eriences. Patients and families who feel that they have had a chance to share their stories, concerns, and hopes will be more likely to trust the practitioners and to feel comfortable with the advice and guidance offered. Patients and families who feel rushed, left out, or silenced are more likely to be distrusting of the system and the motives of practitioners who suggest limits to treatment.

Physical Aspects of Dying

At the end of life, practitioners need to effectively relay information that is honest, compassionate, and timely regarding diagnosis, prognosis, and options. The patient and his or her family need to know that, if a cure is not possible, the focus of treatment will shift from prolongation of life to relief of pain and enhanced quality of life. The practitioner also should realize that the patient might hold unrealistic beliefs and myths about the dying process. To elicit any misconceptions and consequent anxieties that these beliefs and myths might provoke, the patient can be asked, "Is there anything you wish to know about how the end may come?" Discussion of possible respiratory distress; nausea; loss of ability to eat, speak, or sit up, as well as how these situations can be managed, helps the patient and family to prepare for death. Acknowledgment, reassurance, and comfort are vital goals of the communication process, and at this time of life, they might be the most important treatments.

Fears and Concerns

Dying can be a frightening process. Practitioners should address the patient's fears and concerns, both rational and irrational, both spoken and unspoken. Anxiety can be reduced by directly addressing these issues.

Dying patients and their families often fear pain, loss of autonomy, and isolation. Regarding pain, it is not an inevitable part of dying, and patients never should be allowed to die in pain. The practitioner should inform the patient and family that, in most cases, the pain can be controlled to keep the patient comfortable. The practitioner then should do everything in his or her power to keep that promise. In terms of autonomy, some loss of independence is likely to occur, and the practitioner should acknowledge and be empathic to the fact that the patient might experience functional changes and trouble adjusting to them and to changes in body image. Acknowledgment of this fear and open, mutual discussions about the course of dying can help to alleviate some anxiety about loss of dignity and self-determination. Fears about isolation and abandonment often surface when curative treatments are suspended.

Health care workers should assure the patient that, despite limiting life-prolonging treatments, the patient still will be receiving treatment (in this case, palliative treatment) and that the practitioner will remain vigilant in overseeing this care. Regularly scheduled visits by the physician should be continued, with a focus on emotional support as well as on palliation.

Other fears also might be revealed to the practitioner. For example, a patient worrying that his or her disease is contagious or hereditary might feel guilty about the possibility of spreading it to family members. Another patient might fear afterlife consequences of wrongs committed during his or her life. Whatever the patient's concerns, the simple act of recognizing and acknowledging these fears often is appreciated. Social workers and clergy who have worked with terminally ill patients and hospice-trained personnel also will be of great help. If there is no evidence of a social work visit in the medical record, then the physician should call for one. The physician also can encourage the patient and his or her family to discuss concerns with their minister or refer them to a hospital chaplain.

It is usual for patients to have legal, financial, and interpersonal issues that are unresolved. By involving patients and families in end-of-life discussions and plans, practitioners can optimize patients' ability to manage their limited remaining productive days to address these concerns. Although Mr. E was well prepared, his case illustrates the importance of giving the patient and family as much control as possible over the dying process (Case 19.3).

CASE 19.3. Mr. E

Mr. E was a young, intelligent African American man with a promising military career. When we began to investigate why he was losing so much weight, we never expected to find what we did—extensive, inoperable, terminal colon cancer. With amazing poise and levelheadedness, Mr. E handled the news and informed his wife and children. Because the military requires its members to have made arrangements about what to do in the case of their deaths, it did not take Mr. E long to put his affairs in order. We scheduled regular visits to follow his progress and handle his symptoms. Within a few months, he clearly was getting close to death. We discussed whether he would like to stay home with hospice or be admitted to the hospital. He was concerned that it would be too emotionally and physically taxing for his wife and kids if he remained at home. We admitted him when he needed to have better pain control than he could manage at home. He began to get lethargic, but during his lucid moments we would visit and hold hands. He was grateful that he could have visitors without requiring his wife to behave as a hostess. His family was at the hospital most of the day and was with him when he expired peacefully.

The Meaning of Life

In old age and during the dying process, it is common for people to reflect on the meanings of their lives. The concepts of "legacy" and "life review" are of prominent interest at this time. For some, discussions about one's children and grandchildren predominate, whereas for others, thoughts about one's life work or the ability to give substantially to others are important. Other patients might be motivated to arrange gifts to charities, universities, or health care institutions. Becoming satisfied with the meaning of one's life, and the good that one can do even in death, can be both fulfilling and comforting.

Timing the Discussion

Ideally, it is best to begin discussing end-of-life issues long before patients become terminal and their deaths are imminent. It might be difficult for patients to imagine what they would want for themselves in hypothetical situations far into the future. However, these early discussions can reveal consistent life values that will persist when patients reach the ends of their lives, as illustrated in the case of Mr. Q (Case 19.4).

For some patients, dying might be obvious because it is occurring within the context of an acute illness. However, death often occurs secondarily to prolonged illness and disability (e.g., that caused by dementia or stroke) that involve more subtle shifts from the chronic phase to the terminal phase of the illness. Hence, in many patients, the process of dying consists of a step-by-step, gradual decline. In these cases, it might be difficult to perceive when the patient has entered a terminal phase.

Nevertheless, it is important for practitioners to be aware of when to change from the "curing" to the "caring" mode. This is, no doubt, an ongoing process of observation, assessment, and diagnosis on the part of practitioners. But when practitioners become aware of a shift from curing to caring in their own thinking, discussions should be initiated with the patients and families. The patients and families might already have sensed that the patients are dying and are awaiting confirmation. Some might be shocked and angry to discover that modern medical knowledge and technology are incapable of providing a cure. In most cases, people will need time to accept, reflect, plan, and prepare for the dying and palliative care processes to begin.

CASE 19.4. Mr. Q

Into his 90s, Mr. Q maintained a reputation as a sophisticated, eloquent, and sought-after lawyer. He was of Eastern European descent and was raised with the Jewish faith. He was a voracious reader and an avid traveler, and he was fluent in several languages. His routine, even after being widowed, included going into his office every day and frequenting cultural events with friends. But prostate cancer and several falls were taking their toll on his ability to get around by himself. He had discussed with me his values about life, and during his most recent decline, we reviewed his wishes regarding end-of-life care. He was fiercely independent and proud, and he said that he never would want to be dependent on others. Although his daughters lived several hours away by plane, they were close to their father and were aware of this desire to remain independent. During a visit from one of the daughters, I received a call at home. Mr. Q was having a terrible headache and was weak on one side. In the emergency room, a CT scan confirmed a large hemorrhagic stroke, and Mr. Q quickly lost the ability to speak. A neurosurgeon was consulted, and he felt that he could save Mr. Q's life but did not think that Mr. Q ever would regain the ability to walk, talk, or care for himself. I knew that this was not the way in which he wanted to live, but if surgery were declined, then he most likely would die. Now, his daughters were faced with making this life-and-death decision. Although it was painful to let go, we knew that his wish would be to die rather than be kept alive in a highly dependent state. He passed away the next day. I made a small presentation at his memorial service, which was a celebration of his life. A few months later, when his daughters returned to organize his estate, we got together for dinner and remembered him together.

When patients suffer greatly before death, it usually is because there has been no decision to begin "comfort measures only," and attempts at futile curative treatment are continued to the end. As mentioned earlier, it is important to stress that palliative care does not mean "no treatment." In addition to the provision of pain-relieving medication, patients, families, and practitioners may agree to the curing of minor intervening illnesses (e.g., infections that cause discomfort) while agreeing with an overall plan of comfort measures.

After Death

Communication can continue with the family after the patient passes away. Maintaining a rapport with the family can be accomplished with a phone call or note of condolence and often is greatly appreciated to help establish closure, as illustrated in the case of Mrs. M (Case 19.5). In some cultures, it is hoped that health care providers who were particularly close to the patient and/or family will attend the funeral or memorial service.

CASE 19.5. Mrs. M

Mrs. M was a vibrant, funny Hispanic grandmother and a terrific cook. Although she
had no written living will, she had discussed many times with her daughter, Anna, and
with me about her trust in God's plan for her life and her wishes to "go naturally"
when it was her time to leave this earth. During a series of strokes, Mrs. M lost more
and more function. When she no longer was able to swallow, we realized that the end
of her life was near. Although Anna abided by Mrs. M's wishes to go naturally, I
sensed that she was struggling with her own feelings of helplessness and guilt. After
Mrs. M passed away, I sent a note of condolence to Anna. I told her that by expressing
her wishes so clearly, Mrs. M had tried to save her daughter from having to make difficult end-of-life decisions for her. Also, Mrs. M was ensuring that her life would end in
a way that was consistent with her values, regardless of who was caring for her. I tried
to let her know that these choices were not ours to make. Mrs. M's daughter wrote
back a long, beautiful, and emotionally cathartic letter. She described how she had felt
guilt over what she perceived as her decision to allow her mother to die. She thanked
me for helping her to understand and to begin to process her feelings of guilt and grief.

■ APPROACHES TO RELATING

Building Rapport

Practitioners communicate with patients during the death and dying process for the same reasons as they communicate during all patient encounters.
However, these contacts often take on more urgency and importance for the
terminally ill. Good communication builds rapport, respect, and participation.
These positive perceptions of the relationships act to enhance patient satisfaction, improve care and outcomes, and (probably) reduce suffering and cost by
allowing treatment to be tailored to patients' needs, feelings, and expectations.
Many families believe that terminal care could be improved by better physician communication. Families praise physicians who are "open, communica-
tive, and collaborative" and criticize those who are "impersonal or take death
as a matter-of-fact thing" (Hanson, Danis, & Garrett, 1997, p. 1341).

Throughout these interactions, practitioners should try to find ways in
which to continue to build rapport with patients. However, the practitioner-
patient relationship is not a friendship that is intended to be mutually satisfy-
ing. Practitioners should avoid trying to get their emotional support from patients. But a discussion of shared interests, such as music, sports, or literature,
can help to humanize the interaction and deepen the sense of connection that is
necessary for the medical therapeutic alliance (Zinn, 1993). The appropriate

use of humor might help to ease tension, especially if it has been an important part of the practitioner-patient relationship in the past (Coulombe, 1995). As Peabody (1927) stated so eloquently nearly three quarters of a century ago,

> The practice of medicine in its broadest sense includes the whole relationship of the physician with his [or her] patient. Time, sympathy, and understanding must be lavishly dispensed, but the reward is to be found in that personal bond which forms the greatest satisfaction of the practice of medicine. (p. 877)

Listening

Practitioners must attentively receive information from their patients, as each patient's death is a process specific and unique to him or her. A health care provider never should make assumptions about the patient's understanding of the diagnosis and what it means to him or her. Asking the patient open-ended questions can elicit this information and put the practitioner-patient relationship on solid ground (Table 19.1). Useful questions include "Tell me what you know about your medical condition," "What does this mean to you?," and "How do you think all this is going to turn out?" When a patient acknowledges that he or she is dying, a good follow-up question is "What runs through your head when you think about that?" This opens the conversation to how this experience feels and its connection with the rest of the person's life (Smith, 1996; Smith & Harris, 1993). Practitioners who take the time to do this often are surprised at the differing beliefs and attitudes people have regarding death and dying (Coulombe, 1995).

To listen well, one must silence distracting internal voices. It is important to actively listen and to avoid the natural impulse to formulate the next question or the solutions to the problems raised. Illness leads to a sense of isolation and can raise many negative emotions. Just listening and reflecting in an open and empathic manner and allowing the patient to voice his or her concerns might be the most helpful and therapeutic prescription. These interactions can be very brief yet highly effective (Branch & Malik, 1993).

A simple way in which to facilitate communication with empathy is to help the patient to name the emotion that is underlying the content of the practitioner's talk. Often, patients are confused about their own emotions in these difficult times, and labeling the emotion helps them to sort out their feelings and confront them (Zinn, 1993). This naming can take the form of "You seem frustrated that it took so long" or "You must have been scared when you heard

TABLE 19.1. Using Open-Ended Questions

Purpose	Examples
To assess how much the patient knows about his or her condition and what this means	Tell me what you know about your condition. What does this mean to you? How do you think this is going to turn out?
To surface beliefs and myths about the dying process	Is there anything you wish to know about how the end might come? What runs through your head when you think about this?
To learn more about decision-making patterns and preferences	How much do you want told to your family about your condition? Who else would you like to have involved in discussions about your care?
To identify and give permission to express fears and concerns	You seem frustrated that it took so long. Some people might be afraid to receive this news. I would be sad and angry if it happened to me.

the news." Rephrasing and repeating what the patient has said can help to avoid misunderstandings and affirm to the patient that the practitioner is attentive.

For patients who are denying an affect that is obvious to practitioners or for those who are superimposing their anger onto practitioners, the "permission-giving" or "justification" style of interviewing can be highly effective. This allows the patients to express fears and concerns that might seem embarrassing or unacceptable to them. In this style, practitioners would make statements such as "Some patients may worry that something they have done wrong in the past may have caused this disease" and "For many people, such a terrible diagnosis would be painful; I would be very sad and angry if it happened to me." This technique builds a welcoming environment in which to raise difficult issues; it also reassures patients that practitioners are nonjudgmental about these concerns.

Nonverbal Communication: Remembering Your Body Language

Sitting at the bedside takes no longer than standing by the bed, but this in itself speaks eloquently of the practitioner's intention to focus on the patient. Sitting announces that the practitioner is not on his or her way to something more important but rather is there to listen attentively. Sitting also puts the patient and practitioner on the same physical level and, therefore, is more comfortable for the patient and imparts an unspoken sense of equanimity. It actually can save time in encounters by eliminating some of the patient's anxiety and, therefore, making the interchange more efficient.

Nonverbal communication is an important part of every conversation. Practitioners should take clues from hand gestures, facial expressions, and agitation or physical withdrawal. The process of dying is new to every patient. He or she might not have had time to develop ease with discussions or an adequate vocabulary to be fluent with questions or responses. Hand-holding, touching, and a physical presence in the room are silent but effective ways in which providers can convey reassurance and support to patients or families.

Verbal Communication

Take Your Time

Patients probably will have unspoken fears/concerns or medical problems clouding their ability to absorb information and formulate responses. Some patients might be overwhelmed if presented with a lot of complicated facts all at once. For these patients, it might be more productive to discuss a few issues at a time. It often is necessary to repeat information on different visits to confirm or further mutual understanding. A practitioner should reassure the patient that, although he or she is dying, the relationship between patient and practitioner is not over and that regular contact and ongoing interaction will continue.

Practitioners should not try to deal with important issues when there is not enough time. This will only result in inefficiency and a decay of trust. Acknowledging the concern and setting up a follow-up appointment for a more thorough discussion conveys both a caring attitude and a professional manner.

Beware of Jargon

Discussions of end-of-life issues should be tailored to the level of understanding of the patient. The practitioner might need to find simpler terms that can adequately convey the message, especially when more technically correct terms might cause confusion. For example, the words *blood-thinner, breathing machine,* and *electric shock* might be more familiar than the words *anticoagulant, ventilator,* and *cardioversion.* Also, some terms are more psychologically loaded than others. For example, the word *tumor* might be more acceptable than the word *cancer.* For many, a tumor represents something concrete, specific, and manageable, whereas cancer represents a hopeless state of decay. Again, the answer comes from listening; use the word that the patient favors in his or her questions. But remember that people who lack medical training might misuse technical phrases. Asking "What does that mean to you?" often can be quite revealing, as illustrated by the case of Mr. B (Case 19.6).

CASE 19.6. Mr. B

I was covering for the weekend and was called to visit Mr. B, an elderly gentleman who was a recent immigrant from Southeast Asia. He had critical aortic stenosis that three surgeons had called inoperable, but his family wanted him to be a full code. As his condition continued to deteriorate, I knew that it would be pointless and painful to attempt to resuscitate him. I called a family conference and, through the grandson (who was the only English-speaking member of the family), talked about Mr. B's condition. The family members realized that he was dying and seemed to be accepting of this so long as he was kept comfortable, but they were insisting that he be placed on a ventilator. It finally occurred to me to ask whether they knew what a ventilator was. They answered that it was the mask over his face that gives him oxygen. I explained that a ventilator was a tube that goes into the windpipe through the mouth that is attached to a machine that would force him to keep breathing when he could not breathe by himself. The family members quickly responded that this was not at all what they wanted for him. We had been in agreement all along but were using the medical terms to mean different things. Mr. B survived the weekend but died comfortably on Monday with his family at his bedside.

Because practitioners easily slip into the use of medical jargon, and because patients might smile and nod just to be polite, it is practical to ask the patient to repeat in his or her own words what the physician has said. This will help to confirm that true communication has occurred. George Bernard Shaw said, "The greatest problem with communication is the illusion that it has occurred" (quoted in Hallenbeck, Goldstein, & Mebane, 1996, p. 397).

Communicate on the Patient's Level

The key to successful communication is finding the level at which both the patient and the practitioner can comfortably relate to each other. The patient brings his or her own life experiences, cultural expectations, educational backgrounds, and personality traits to these discussions, influencing the characteristic tone of the information shared. It is the responsibility of the practitioner to meet the patient at his or her level and to let the patient lead the discussion to the extent possible.

Letting Them See It in Writing

Some patients and families may benefit from educational materials that relate to their conditions. These are available from national nonprofit organizations, such as the American Cancer Society and the Alzheimer's Association, that often have local offices. There also is a wealth of health education materials available through the Internet. Written materials help patients to learn more about their conditions and provide a resource that they can refer back to as they allow themselves to assimilate the information.

It is increasingly common for families to ask to see the patients' medical records. If the patients agree or if the families have legal authority, then this should be permitted, but with guidance and interpretation from the practitioners. For example, a family member affiliated with our program was offended by reading the word *noncontributory* under the family history section, thinking that this referred to the family not making a monetary contribution to the hospital. After reading the record, the spouse became suspicious of the health care providers. Fortunately, a brief discussion of the record turned up this surprising misinterpretation so that the issue could be clarified.

■ CROSS-CULTURAL CONSIDERATIONS

How Much to Tell

During the past few decades in the United States, it has become the ethical norm (backed by law) to give full and truthful disclosure of diagnoses and prognoses to patients. This is particularly important for terminal patients who need to make plans for themselves and for their families. Practitioners should be aware, however, that in some cultures it is common practice to withhold information from patients, especially for diagnoses such as cancer that are felt to deprive patients of all hope. One should remain sensitive to the fact that, although patients have the right to know, they also may choose to exercise their equal right not to know certain details of their conditions (Hallenbeck et al., 1996). Asking patients "What questions do you have?" and "How much do you

CASE 19.7. Mrs. Y

Mrs. Y's case was referred to the ethics committee by a hospital staff person who was concerned about a violation of her autonomy. In reviewing the case, it was revealed that Mrs. Y was an alert, 83-year-old Japanese woman who was admitted to the hospital for shortness of breath. During the evaluation of this symptom, she was found to have an advanced case of lung cancer. Her physician informed her oldest son and her husband, both of whom told the physician that they did not want Mrs. Y to be informed about the diagnosis. They told the physician that, in the Japanese culture, cancer is felt to be a diagnosis that robs the patient of hope. The U.S.-trained hospital staff person, however, felt that by not telling Mrs. Y her diagnosis, she would be robbed of the power to make decisions for herself. A member of the ethics committee recommended that the physician directly ask Mrs. Y whether she would like to be told of her diagnosis when it was discovered and whether she would like to make decisions about her treatment. When asked these questions, Mrs. Y clearly answered, "No, you ask my son and my husband."

want to know about your condition?" will help practitioners to make these assessments, as illustrated in the case of Mrs. Y (Case 19.7).

Who Makes Decisions

In the United States, patient autonomy or self-determination has become the foremost legal and ethical principle guiding medical decision making. Practitioners are required to allow patients to make informed decisions regarding the nature and extent of their own personal medical care. As stated earlier, practitioners should provide as much data as the patients need and want to make knowledgeable choices. Because current practices emphasize individual autonomy, practitioners might overlook family members or purposefully exclude them from discussions.

We believe, however, that families should not be excluded out of hand. First, a patient whose traditional culture is more collectivist might seek guidance from the oldest child, the entire family, or a respected community leader or spiritual guide (McLaughlin & Braun, 1998), as illustrated by the case of Mrs. Y (Case 19.7). Even in individualist cultures, however, the family is the closest emotional-social circle of the patient. Family members often act as caregivers and can offer valuable perspectives to both the practitioner and the patient. Finally, research suggests that the vast majority of dying patients choose family members as surrogates (Hanson et al., 1997; Sulmasy et al., 1998). Thus, although it is important to be knowledgeable about and sensitive

CASE 19.8. Mrs. C

Mrs. C was an 85-year-old, Chinese nursing home resident. For many years, she had been bed-bound and nonverbal, but her devoted family visited regularly. Although she had a responsible son, Bennett, and although her daughter, Susan, was the oldest child, it actually was her youngest child, Elaine, who was the primary family decision maker for Mrs. C. Elaine was the one who knew her mother the best and came daily to help feed her, groom her, and tidy up her cozy room. After a bout of aspiration pneumonia, Mrs. C no longer would open her mouth to eat. When she did, she would leave the food on her tongue without even attempting to chew or swallow it. I called a family conference to decide on a plan of care. Bennett and Susan felt that, if it were up to them, they would have me insert a feeding tube. However, because Elaine was the closest and knew her mother best (even though she was not the son, nor the oldest, nor the most educated of the children), they respectfully bowed to her decision to not insert a feeding tube, which allowed their mother to pass away within the week.

to the cultural backgrounds of patients, it is equally important not to assign cultural stereotypes to patients. Individual personalities, experiences, and situations often have more influence on behavior and choice than does native culture or religion (Hallenbeck et al., 1996), as illustrated by the case of Mrs. C (Case 19.8). In all cases, it is important to let the patient be the guide. The practitioner can begin to find out the patient's preferences by asking "How much do you want told to your family about your condition?" and "Who do you want to involve in decisions about your care?"

Language

Language barriers are common in our multicultural society. It is worth seeking out competent interpreters, especially those who can act as cultural guides as well as translators. Most health care facilities maintain lists of interpreters willing to facilitate patient-practitioner communication.

■ COMMON OBSTRUCTIONS TO COMMUNICATION

Anticipating the obstacles in the road to communication will help the practitioner to navigate past them.

Cognitive Dysfunction

Some dying patients will have cognitive dysfunction from delirium, sedation, or underlying dementia. Unless it increases patient discomfort, sedating medications may be withheld before visits to improve the potential for meaningful conversation. Identifying and treating the causes of delirium can provide comfort. Involving patients to the greatest extent possible is desirable. But in many cases, the physician will need to rely on family and advanced directives for guidance and on the patient's nonverbal communication for assessing patient comfort.

Sensory Impairments

Many patients will have sensory impairments such as visual or hearing deficits. To maximize the patient's ability to participate, create a quiet, well-lit, comfortable space that enhances communication. Inexpensive headset hearing amplifiers often can improve the interaction.

Depression

It is helpful to expect that depression might occur. Treating depression will improve the patient's mood, provide great comfort to the patient and family, and help the patient to take a more active role in his or her care. The existence of depression, however, should not limit discussions. Research suggests that depressed patients are able to make decisions regarding resuscitation, are not adversely affected by discussing their death, and do not request more aggressive interventions after recovering from depression (Cotton, 1993).

■ PRACTITIONERS AS A PART OF THE SOLUTION OR THE PROBLEM

Major barriers to good communication might be the discomfort and inexperience of practitioners themselves. These barriers must be overcome if effective therapeutic relationships are to occur. Practitioners should honestly examine their own prejudices that might interfere with open communication and/or cause them to avoid talking with patients.

TABLE 19.2. Techniques to Improve Patient-Practitioner Communication

---

Use communication to build rapport.

- Discuss shared interests outside of the patient's condition.
- Ask open-ended questions.
- Communicate at the patient's level.
- Show that you are listening by repeating back what you hear or feel from the patient.

When visiting the patient and/or family, sit down.

Avoid jargon.

Assess for and remedy, if possible, conditions that might obstruct communication.

- Depression
- Cognitive dysfunction
- Sensory impairment
- Discomfort on the part of the provider

Use competent language interpreters as needed.

Facilitate patient/family access to additional help.

- Call for a social work consult.
- Ask whether the patient and/or family members would like to talk to their minister or the hospital chaplain.
- See what printed material might be available.

It is not easy for anyone to tell a person that he or she is dying. Added to this, however, health care providers might harbor feelings of failure or disappointment with themselves in being unable to save their patients. They might fear that they will be seen as failures by patients or families. They might worry that their patients will become depressed or give up if they are told bad news. It also is possible that the experiences of patients might rekindle painful episodes in practitioners' memories. Although it might be uncomfortable for practitioners, uncovering and sharing these commonalities can be a powerful tool for building empathy and rapport. When a true connection occurs between the practitioner and the patient, it can transform the practitioner from the dispassionate bearer of harsh news to a meaningful partner in an alliance that is therapeutic and sustaining for both practitioner and patient.

■ CONCLUSION

Dying is a profound transition for the family and is the ultimate transition for the individual. As health care providers, we become skilled in science and medicine, but the care of a dying person encompasses much more. The practitioner also must understand and help to address the social, emotional, and spiritual needs of the patient. This means being sensitive to both the cultural-religious background of the patient and the personal experiences that have shaped his or her values, beliefs, and attitudes. The practitioner also should assist family and loved ones, who might require as much attention as does the patient to ease their concerns and to allow them to go on with their own lives. The only way in which to meet these needs is for the practitioner to be skilled in communication, a skill that can be learned and honed (Table 19.2). The purpose of this chapter was to help practitioners to expand their abilities so that they might become more adept at empathic and patient-directed communication, a therapeutic tool to be wielded with skill and compassion.

■ REFERENCES

Branch, W. T., & Malik, T. K. (1993). Using "windows of opportunities" in brief interviews to understand patients' concerns. *Journal of the American Medical Association, 269,* 1667-1668.

Cotton, P. (1993). Talk to people about dying: They can handle it, say geriatricians and patients. *Journal of the American Medical Association, 269,* 321-322.

Coulombe, L. (1995). Talking with patients: Is it different when they are dying? *Canada Family Physician, 41,* 423-437.

Feifel, H. (1990). Psychology and death: Meaningful rediscovery. *American Psychologist, 45,* 537-543.

Hallenbeck, J., Goldstein, M. K., & Mebane, E. W. (1996). Cultural considerations of death and dying in the United States. *Clinics of Geriatric Medicine, 12,* 393-406.

Hanson, L. C., Danis, M., & Garrett, J. (1997). What is wrong with end-of-life care? Opinions of bereaved family members. *Journal of the American Geriatrics Society, 45,* 1339-1344.

McLaughlin, L. A., & Braun, K. L. (1998). Asian and Pacific Islander cultural values: Considerations for health care decision-making. *Health & Social Work, 23,* 116-126.

Peabody, F. W. (1927). The care of the patient. *Journal of the American Medical Association, 88,* 877.

Smith, D. (1996). Ethics in the doctor-patient relationship. *Critical Care Practitioner, 12,* 179-197.

Smith, D., & Harris, S. (1993). Communication and case-based ethics: Issues in medical training and practice. In E. Berlin-Ray (Ed.), *Case studies in health communication* (pp. 31-46). Hillsdale, NJ: Lawrence Erlbaum.

Sulmasy, D., Terry, P., & Weisman, C. (1998). The accuracy of substituted judgments in patients with terminal diagnoses. *Annals of Internal Medicine, 128,* 621-629.

Zinn, W. (1993). The empathic physician. *Archives of Internal Medicine, 153,* 306-312.

■ SUGGESTED READING

Armstrong, D. (1987). Silence and truth in death and dying. *Social Science & Medicine, 24,* 651-657.

Council on Scientific Affairs. (1993). Physicians and family caregivers: A model for partnership. *Journal of the American Medical Association, 269,* 1282-1284.

Delbanco, T. L. (1992). Enriching the doctor-patient relationship by inviting the patient's perspective. *Annals of Internal Medicine, 116,* 414-418.

Feinberg, A. W. (1997). The care of dying patients. *Annals of Internal Medicine, 126,* 164-165.

Jeret, J. S. (1989). Discussing dying: Changing attitudes among patients, physicians, and medical students. *Pharos, 52*(1), 15-20.

Koenig, B. A., & Gates-Williams, J. (1995). Understanding cultural difference in caring for dying patients. *Western Journal of Medicine, 163,* 244-249.

Krigger, K. W., McNeely, J. D., & Lippmann, S. B. (1997). Dying, death, and grief: Helping patients and their families through the process. *Postgraduate Medicine, 101,* 263-270.

Lynn, J., Teno, J. M., Phillips, R. S., Wu, A. W., Desbiens, N., Harrold, J., Claessens, M. T., Wenger, N., Kreling, B., & Connors, A. F., Jr. (1997). Perceptions by family members of the dying experience of older and seriously ill patients. *Annals of Internal Medicine, 126,* 97-106.

Matthews, D. A., Suchman, A. L., & Branch, W. T. (1993). Making "connexions": Enhancing the therapeutic potential of patient-practitioner relationships. *Annals of Internal Medicine, 118,* 973-977.

McCormick, T. R., & Conley, B. J. (1995). Patients' perspectives on dying and on the care of dying patients. *Western Journal of Medicine, 163,* 236-243.

Miyaji, N. T. (1993). The power of compassion: Truth-telling among American doctors in the care of dying patients. *Social Science of Medicine, 36,* 249-264.

Muncie, H. L., Magaziner, J., Hebel, R., & Warren, J. W. (1997). Proxies' decisions about clinical research participation for their charges. *Journal of the American Geriatrics Society, 45,* 929-933.

Platt, F. W., & Keller, V. F. (1994). Empathic communication: A teachable and learnable skill. *Journal of General Internal Medicine, 9,* 222-226.

Sorenson, J. H. (1987). The character of love to guide re-humanizing dying. *Journal of the American Geriatrics Society, 35,* 262-263.

Still, A., & Todd, C. (1986). Differences between terminally ill patients who know, and those who do not know, that they are dying. *Journal of Clinical Psychology, 42,* 287-296.

Stollerman, G. H. (1986). Lovable decisions: Re-humanizing dying. *Journal of the American Geriatrics Society, 34,* 172-174.

Streim, J. E., & Marshall, J. R. (1988). The dying elderly patient. *American Family Physician, 38,* 175-183.

Suchman, A. L., Markakis, K., Beckman, H. B., & Frankel, R. (1997). A model of empathic communication in the medical interview. *Journal of the American Medical Association, 277,* 678-682.

Author Index

Ablon, J., 121, 123
Abrams, D. I., 270, 273, 282, 283
Ackerman, T. F., 57, 65
Address, R. F., 184, 187, 193, 196, 197
Adelstein, S. J., 13, 22
Aggarwal, G., 14, 16, 19, 22
Akhter, J., 211
Alcser, K. H., 79, 81, 272, 281
Alexander, Marc R., 162, 165-179, 329
Alfonso, I., 29, 33
Allen, A., 89, 90, 93, 99
Alston, R. L., 24, 35
Alva, M. E., 96, 100
Alzola, C., 48, 53
Amadeo, M., 27, 36
Anderson, G., 232, 247
Anderson, T., 151, 162
Angel, J. L., 85, 98
Angel, R. J., 85, 98
Angus-Lepan, H., 27, 28, 36
Anspach, R., 239, 247
Appelbaum-Maizel, M., 57, 67
Applewhite, S. R., 85, 99
Aquinas, Thomas (Saint), 155, 163
Arenberg, D., 25, 35
Armstrong, D., 325
Arnold, A., 24, 35
Asai, A., 56, 65
Asch, D. A., 65
Ashley, B., 168, 172, 178
Athar, S., 208, 211
Augustine (Saint), 155, 162
Awad, C. A., 24, 33
Awad, I. A., 24, 33

Azen, S., 88, 89, 90, 93, 98, 99, 115, 117, 125, 123, 135, 139, 141, 143

Bachman, J. G., 79, 81, 272, 281
Back, A. L., 273, 281
Bajwa, K., 56, 65
Bally, G., 274, 282
Balson, P. M., 253, 263
Bapat, P. V., 228
Barbano, H. E., 26, 34
Baril, A., 148, 162
Barker, S., 276, 283
Bartlett, E. T., 62, 67
Bartone, P. T., 249, 254, 257, 262
Bartus, R. T., 26, 34
Bass, S. A., 98
Bastida, E., 85, 98
Battin, M. P., 162, 266, 282, 283
Bauer, R. L., 55, 67
Bauman, A., 166, 178
Baume, P., 166, 178, 272, 281
Bayley, N., 25, 34
Beck, S. A., 18, 22
Beckman, H. B., 325
Beers, M. H., 66
Beinert, W., 167, 178
Bennett, L., 72, 73, 80
Benoliel, J. Q., 237, 247
Benson, C. B., 242, 246, 247
Berlin-Ray, E., 324
Berman, N. G., 34
Bernal, G., 85, 98
Bernat, J. L., 19, 22

Biggar, R. J., 270, 281
Bindels, P. J., E., 275, 281
Bindman, S., 297, 300
Blackhall, L. J., 88, 90, 93, 98, 99, 115, 117,
    123, 125, 135, 143, 139, 141
Blanchette, Patricia L., 1-9, 33, 34, 49, 97, 305,
    329
Bleich, J. D., 185, 188, 189, 191, 192, 193, 196
Boero, J. F., 62, 67
Bookman, T. A., 187, 196
Boone, K. B., 24, 34
Borowitz, E., 187, 196
Bosma, J. M., 267, 283
Bottorff, J., 232, 247
Boyko, E. J., 272, 281
Boyle, P., 167, 178
Branch, W. T., 315, 324, 325
Braun, K. L., 1-9, 37-53, 83-100, 108, 109,
    110, 111, 112, 113, 114, 115, 118, 119,
    120, 123, 320, 324, 330
Breitbart, W. S., 271, 276, 281, 282
Brennan, F. T., 65
Brierly, P., 148, 162
Brigham, J. C., 56, 65
Brink, S., 57, 65
Brislin, R., 2, 7, 9
Brock, D., 274, 282
Brody, H. M., 24, 34, 65, 272, 281
Brokenleg, M., 127, 134, 137, 140, 142
Brooks, F. R., 253, 263
Brown, J. K., 17, 22
Bryan, N., 24, 35
Buchwald, D., 140, 142
Budd, F., 259, 262
Buddhaghosa, 218, 227
Burera, E., 17, 22
Burhansstipanov, L., 133, 142
Burke, G. L., 24, 35
Burnam, M. A., 91, 100
Busby-Whitehead, J., 34

Cafferty, P. S. J., 98
Cain, K. C., 57, 67
Calhoun, M. A., 118, 123
Callahan, D., 159, 162
Callaway, R., 80, 81
Camicioli, R., 25, 34
Campbell, J. L., 65
Caralis, P. V., 77, 78, 79, 81, 89, 90, 91, 93, 98
Carley, M. M., 50, 51, 52, 53
Carman, M. D., 25, 34
Carr, A., 276, 283
Carrese, J. A., 127, 135, 142
Carter, B. S., 136, 142
Cary, R., 24, 33

Cases, D., 96, 100
Cassel, C. K., 13, 22, 57, 58, 65, 66, 98
Cassem, E. H., 13, 22
Chambers, C. V., 78, 81
Chapman, C. R., 14-15, 17, 20, 21, 22
Charlebois, E., 273, 283
Charles, G., 77, 82
Chatters, L. M., 75, 81
Chesney, M., 77, 82
Chin, A. E., 65
Chin, S-Y., 107, 115, 123, 124, 125
Ching, J., 214, 228
Choudhry, N. K., 65
Christensen, H., 25, 35
Chung, C., 118, 119, 125
Churchill, L. R., 77, 81
Chye, R., 14, 16, 19, 22
Claessens, M. T., 14, 16, 18, 22, 58, 66, 325
Clark, J., 66
Clarnette, R. M., 166, 179
Cleary, P. D., 81
Cohen, C. B., 155, 162
Cohen, G. D., 25, 26, 34
Cohen, J. S., 272, 281
Cole, D. R., 75, 82
Collins, J. J., 65
Conley, B. J., 325
Connors, A. F., 14, 16, 18, 22
Connors, A. F., Jr. 48, 53, 58, 62, 66, 325
Connors, J. A. F., Jr., 48, 53
Considine, Chris, 297
Conze, E., 215, 216, 228
Cooper, D. A., 276, 283
Cornelisse, P. G. A., 274, 282
Corning, A. D., 79, 81, 272, 281
Cornoni-Huntley, J., 26, 34
Corsellis, J. A. N., 24, 35
Costa, P. T., Jr., 25, 26, 34, 35
Cote, T. R., 270, 281
Cotton, P., 322, 324
Coulombe, L., 315, 324
Counts, D. A., 143
Counts, D. R., 143
Coutinho, R. A., 275, 281
Crain, M., 108, 109, 123
Cranford, E. H., 13, 22
Crook, T., 26, 34
Cross, A. W., 77, 81
Cuellar, J. B., 85, 93, 94, 95, 98
Culig, K. M., 24, 34
Cullen, R. F., 29, 33
Curiel, H., 98, 99

Daar, J. F., 60, 65
Daly, B., 62, 67

Daniels, R., 112, 115, 124
Danis, M., 48, 53, 77, 82, 314, 320, 324
Dannenburg, A. L., 270, 281
Davidson, B., 109, 125
Davis, A., 108, 109, 110, 125
Davis, B., 77, 78, 79, 81, 89, 90, 91, 93, 98
Davis, K. A., 34
Davis, M., 77, 81
Davis, R. B., 62, 66
de Graaff, C., 267, 283
Dean, M. C., 17, 22
DeCarli, C., 25, 35
DeCrane, P., 261, 262
Deer Smith, M. H., 129, 130, 13, 143
Degner, L. F., 237, 247
Delbanco, T. L., 325
DeLeon, M. J., 24, 25, 35
Denk, C. E., 242, 246, 247
Deptula, D., 27, 34
Der-McLeod, Doreen, 108, 109, 110, 123
Derse, A. R., 166, 179
Desbiens, N., 14, 16, 18, 22, 48, 53, 58, 62, 66, 325
Desmond, B., 108, 109, 124
DeSpelder, L. A., 1-2, 6, 9
Diamond, J. J., 78, 81
Diamond, J., 7, 9
Diamond, T., 242, 244, 247
Dickinson, Brian, 297
Dillmann, R. J. M., 267, 282
Doak, C. C., 96, 98
Doak, L. G., 96, 98
Docker, C. G., 279, 282
Doerflinger, Richard, 165
Donius, M., 50, 51, 52, 53
Donne, J., 156, 162
Donnelly, S., 14, 18, 22
Dorff, E., 188, 189, 190, 192, 196, 197
Dossey, L., 195, 196
Dougherty, C., 160, 163
Dougherty, J. H., 28, 34
Doukas, D. J., 50, 51, 53, 79, 81, 95, 98, 272, 281
Doyle, D., 20, 22
Dresser, C. M., 133, 142
Dresser, R., 57, 65
Duclos, C. W., 132, 142
Dudley, J., 270, 283
Duenas, D., 29, 33
Dull, V. T., 50, 51, 52, 53
Dunn, P. M., 50, 51, 52, 53
Dunnigan, T. P., 252, 262

Ealons, C. A., 259, 260, 262
Eaton, T. A., 49, 53

Edge, R. S., 38, 53
Edinger, W., 127, 142
Edmonds, M., 107, 125
Egbert, C. B., 77, 78, 81, 89, 98
Egbert, J. R., 77, 78, 81, 89, 98
Eisenberg, L., 98
Eleazer, G. P., 77, 78, 81, 89, 98
Ellison, C. G., 74, 81
Ender, M. G., 249, 254, 257, 262
Eng, C., 77, 78, 81, 89, 98
Enright, P. L., 24, 35
Epstein, A. M., 76, 78, 81, 82
Espino, D. V., 86, 87, 95, 99
Evans, A. T., 62, 67, 77, 82
Evans, L. K., 60, 66

Faber-Langendoen, K., 55, 65
Farberow, N. L., 144
Farnsworth, C., 277, 282
Fazekas, F., 24, 34
Federman, D., 13, 22
Feifel, H., 305, 324
Feinberg, A. W., 325
Ferris, S. H., 24, 25, 26, 34, 35
Fialkow, M. F., 78, 82, 89, 99
Field, D., 26, 34
Field, M. J., 98
Fihn, S. D., 272, 281
Filley, C. M., 24, 34
Fins, J. F., 48, 53
Fischer, P., 28, 34
Fisher, J. B., 26, 28, 34
Flemming, D. W., 65
Fletcher, J. C., 242, 246, 247
Fletcher, J., 156, 160, 163
Flicker, C., 25, 34
Fogel, B. S., 34
Folstein, M. F., 27-28, 32, 33, 34
Folstein, S. E., 28, 32, 33, 34
Forde, S., 276, 283
Foreman, W. B., 19, 22
Forquera, R. A., 132, 142
Foster, M. G., 38, 53
Foster, R., 261, 262
Foucault, M., 233, 247
Fowkes, W., 104, 124
Fowler, F. J., Jr., 81
Francesca, G., 140, 142
Frank, G., 88, 89, 90, 93, 98, 99, 115, 117, 123, 125, 139, 141
Frankel, R., 127, 135, 136, 141, 144, 325
Franks, J., 115, 123, 124
Fransen, P., 166, 178
Freehof, S., 188, 190, 196
French, J., 134, 137, 141, 142

Fried, L., 24, 35
Fried, T., 274, 282
Fried, T. R., 57, 65
Friedland, R. P., 25, 35
Friess, S., 272, 282
Fukuhara, S., 56, 65
Fulkerson, W. J., 48, 53
Fullerton, C. S., 256, 263

Galanti, G. A., 137, 141, 142
Galbraith, A., 77, 82
Gallego, D., 85, 98
Gallo, J. J., 34
Gamble, V. N., 76, 81
Ganzini, L., 273, 274, 282
Gardner, P., 74, 81, 84, 86
Garrett, J., 314, 320, 324
Garrett, J. M., 77, 81, 82
Gates, Pat, 165
Gates-Williams, J., 25
Gatsonis, C., 81
Gavrin, J., 14-15, 17, 20, 21, 22
George, A. E., 24, 25, 35
Gerber, D. R., 65
Gerdner, P., 98
Gershon, S., 26, 34
Gert, B., 19, 22
Gevers, S., 65
Giambra, L. M., 25, 35
Gibson, P. H., 24, 35
Gifford, R. K., 256, 263
Gigliotti, L. K., 175, 178
Giles, K., 254, 256, 262
Gillick, M. R., 57, 65
Gilligan, T., 66
Giordano, J., 98
Glantz, L., 66
Glaser, B. G., 236, 247
Goldberg, J., 81
Goldberg, M. A., 34
Golding, J. M., 91, 93, 100
Goldstein, M. K., 104, 124, 318, 319, 321, 324
Goldstein, R. M., 76, 78, 81
Goldstein, S., 182, 196
Golomb, J., 24, 25, 35
Gomez, Celina, 83-100, 88, 90, 93, 96, 99, 330
Gonwa, T. A., 76, 78, 81
Gonzalez, G., 84, 98
Good, B. J., 95, 98
Good, J. J., 95, 98
Goodman, R. A., 124
Gordon, A. K., 78, 81
Gordon, H., 187, 196
Gordon, M., 55, 66
Gordon, S. F., 142

Gorter, R., 270, 283
Gottlieb, M., 166, 179
Gould-Martin, K., 110, 124
Grange, D. L., 256, 262
Graves, F. G., 297, 300
Gregory, W. D., 173, 178
Grisso, J. A., 60, 66
Gross, E. M., 269, 270, 282
Grossman, D. C., 127, 132, 142
Groves, J. R., 38, 53
Gu, N., 111, 115, 125
Gula, R. M., 153, 154, 159, 160, 163, 167, 172, 178

Haas, J. S., 81
Hachinski, V. C., 24, 35
Haffner, L., 140, 142
Hahn, J., 274, 282
Hai, H. A., 199-211, 330
Hall, Charles, 269
Hall, E., 5, 9
Hallenbeck, J., 104, 124, 318, 319, 321, 324
Hallikainen, M., 35
Halperin, M., 189, 196
Hammen, C., 270, 283
Handelman, L., 122, 124
Hänninen, T., 25, 26, 35
Hanson, J., 17, 22
Hanson, L. C., 48, 53, 314, 320, 324
Harding, C. G., 96, 99
Hardt, E. J., 140, 142
Haring, B., 159, 163
Harjo, S., 129, 130, 142
Harper, M. S., 98
Harrell, L. E., 80, 81
Harris, R. P., 77, 81
Harris, S., 315, 324
Harrold, J., 14, 16, 18, 22, 58, 66, 325
Hasenauer, H., 253, 256, 262
Hauerwas, S., 176, 178
Haverkate, I., 267, 283
Haxby, J. V., 5, 35
Hazuda, H. P., 55, 67, 91, 92, 93, 94, 99
Heath, K. V., 274, 282
Heaton, R. K., 24, 34
Hebel, R., 325
Hébert, R., 27, 35
Hedberg, K., 65
Hedgepeth, J., 77, 78, 81, 89, 98
Helmkamp, J. C., 254, 256, 262
Henderson, G., 24, 35
Hendrix, L., 107, 125
Hepburn, K., 127, 136, 140, 141, 142
Hesse, K. A., 66
Higginson, G. K., 65

Hikoyeda, Nancy, 101-125, 107, 223, 330-331
Hill-Gutierrez, E., 34
Himmelman, R. B., 17, 22
Hirakawa, A., 215, 228
Hirayama, K. K., 114, 124
Hirschfeld, M., 109, 125
Hodak, J. A., 24, 33
Hoebel, E. A., 134, 142, 144
Hofmann, J. C., 62, 66
Hogg, R. S., 274, 282
Holm, L. A., 25, 35
Holmes, R., 249, 250, 251, 252, 258, 259, 262
Holmes, S. B., 80, 82
Hook, E. W., 13, 22
Hooyman, N. R., 23, 35
Horn, M., 295, 300
Hornung, C. A., 77, 78, 81, 89, 98
Hough, R. L., 91, 100
Howieson, D. B., 25, 35
Howieson, J., 25, 35
Hsu, M., 269, 270, 282
Hudson, B. L., 74, 81, 84, 86, 98
Hudson, L. D., 57, 67
Huffine, C., 270, 283
Hughes, D., 272, 282
Humphry, D., 279, 282
Husain, Asad, 199-211, 200, 331
Husain, I., 200, 211
Husberg, B. S., 76, 78, 81
Inge, W. R., 156, 163

Inui, T. S., 127, 142
Irish, D. P., 100, 142
Iserson, K. V., 22, 62, 66

Jacob, W., 188, 196
Jacobs, D., 25, 36
Jakobovits, I., 188, 189, 191, 196
James, D. F., 187, 196, 197
Janssens, L., 168, 170, 178
Jansson, L., 246, 247
Javitt, J., 76, 78, 82
Jecker, N. S., 57, 67
Jenkins Nelsen, V., 100
Jeret, J. S., 325
Jex, S. A., 76, 82
John Paul II (Pope), 150, 160, 163, 167, 173,
     174, 175, 176, 177, 178
John, R., 129, 132, 142
Johnson, A., 132, 143
Johnson, A. R., 272, 281
Johnson, C. J., 1, 9
Johnson, M., 293, 300
Johnson, M. S., 75, 82

Johnson, W. L., 215, 228
Jonsen, A. R., 30, 36
Jorm, A. F., 25, 35
Josephy, A. M., Jr., 129, 130, 143
Juknialis, B. W., 62, 67
Jump, B., 109, 124
Jungries, C. A., 24, 35

Kahn, Y. H., 187, 196
Kalish, R. A., 75, 81, 112, 114, 124
Kapp, Marshall B., 55-68, 66, 196, 331
Karno, M., 91, 100
Katz, J., 76, 78, 82
Katzman, R., 25, 35
Kaufert, J. M., 134, 140, 143
Kaufman, S. R., 3, 9
Kavesh, William, 181-197, 183, 184, 187, 191,
     192, 194, 196, 331-332
Kawas, C., 25, 35
Kaye, J., 25, 34
Kaye, J. A., 25, 35
Keegan, J., 249, 250, 251, 252, 258, 259, 262
Kelkala, E., 25, 26, 35
Kellehear, A., 166, 179
Keller, V. F., 325
Kelly, J., 24, 34
Kemeny, M. E., 270, 283
Kemp, E. J., 293, 294, 295, 300
Kenedy, P. J. (and Sons), 165, 179
Kennedy, R. D., 254, 262
Kern, D., 66
Kester, J. G. C., 267, 283
Khan, F. A., 208, 211
Kiloh, L. C., 27, 35
Kim, S. S., 112, 124
Kimsma, G. K., 268, 282, 290, 292, 301
King, A., 121, 124
Kinsella, D. T., 166, 179
Kinsella, T. D., 273, 283
Kipman, A. G., 282
Kirk, K., 155, 163
Kitano, H. H. L., 112, 115, 124
Kiyak, H. A., 23, 35
Kjellstrand, C. M., 56, 65, 76, 78, 81
Klein, I., 188, 196
Kleinert, G., 24, 34
Kleinert, R., 24, 34
Kleinman, A., 98
Kleizer, R., 272, 282
Klessig, J., 104, 109, 112, 115, 124
Klintmalm, G. B., 76, 78, 81
Kluckhohn, C., 134, 143
Kluckhorn, F., 6, 9
Kluger, A., 24, 25, 35
Knaus, W. A., 48, 53

Koch, Tom, 285-301, 294, 296, 300, 332
Koehler, K. M., 89, 90, 93, 99
Koenig, B., 4, 9, 88, 98, 102, 108, 110, 124, 125, 325
Koenig, H. G., 175, 178
Koepp, R., 47, 53, 96, 99
Kogan, Shari L., 49, 97, 305, 332
Koivisto, K., 25, 26, 35
Koop, C. E., 288, 301
Korte, A. O., 86, 87, 99
Korten, A. E., 25, 35
Koss, E., 25, 35
Kral, V. A., 26, 35
Kramer, B. J., 131, 143
Kravitz, S. L., 85, 98
Kreling, B., 14, 16, 18, 22, 58, 66, 325
Krieger, J. W., 132, 142
Krigger, K. W., 325
Krol, A., 275, 281
Krotki, K. P., 60, 66
Kübler-Ross, E., 296, 301
Kuehn, N., 17, 22
Kuhse, H., 273, 282
Küng, H., 156, 157, 159, 163
Kutza, E. A., 98

Laakso, M., 25, 26, 35
Laane, H. M., 275, 282
Laaskso, M. P., 35
Lamberton, V., 66
Landerfeld, C. S., 62, 67
Lane, G. A., 153, 163
Lane, L., 252, 263
Lang, L. T., 122, 123, 124
Lanting, W. A., 29, 33
LaPann, K., 60, 66
Larrabee, G. J., 26, 35
Larson, E. J., 49, 53
Lasch, L. A., 78, 81
Lauri, S., 109, 125
Lawler, W. R., 86, 87, 95, 99
Layson, R. T., 66
Lechner, H., 24, 34
Lee, L., 31, 36
Lee, M. A., 273, 274, 282
Legemaate, J., 267, 282
Leighton, D., 134, 143
Leiser, R., 274, 282
Leo, R. A., 275, 282
Lesser, I. M., 24, 34,
Levy, D. E., 28, 34
Levy, D. R., 76, 78, 81
Lewis, B., 202, 211
Lewis, R., 127, 133, 134, 137, 140, 143
Lew-Ting, C., 91, 100

Lichtenstein, R. L., 79, 81, 272, 281
Lickiss, J. N., 14, 16, 19, 22
Licks, S., 48, 53
Lin, J. Y., 109, 125
Lincoln, C. E., 74, 76, 81
Lindeman, R. D., 89, 90, 93, 99
Lindsay, J., 27, 35
Lipman, A. G., 282
Lippmann, S. B., 325
Lo, B., 13, 22, 56, 65, 78, 82, 89, 99
Locke, B. Z., 26, 34
Locke, D. C., 3, 9
Logan, G. M., 76, 78, 81
Lombardi, F., 133, 143
Lombardi, G. S., 133, 143
Longmore, Paul, 293, 297
Longstreth, T., 24, 35
Lonnqvist, J. K., 256, 263
Looman, C. W. N., 268, 274, 283
Loustaunau, M. O., 3-4, 7, 9
Lovette, L. P., 259, 263
Lowenstein, B., 57, 67
Luce, J. M., 66
Lundquist, K. F., 100, 142
Lynn, Joanne, 14, 16, 18, 22, 48, 53, 58, 62, 66, 325, 332

Ma, J., 65
MacDonald, N., 17, 18, 19, 22
MacDonald, R. N., 17, 22
Mackinnon, A. J., 25, 35
Macmillan, K., 17, 22, 184, 196
Magaziner, J., 325
Mai, M. L., 76, 78, 81
Maislin, G. M., 60, 66
Makadon, H. J., 81
Makra, M. L., 228
Malik, T. K., 315, 324
Mamiya, L. H., 74, 76, 82
Mandel, N., 274, 282
Mann, J. J., 269, 270, 282
Manolio, T. A., 24, 35
Manson, S. M., 128, 132, 142, 143
Marcial, E., 77, 78, 79, 81, 89, 90, 91, 93, 98
Marder, K., 25, 36
Marjorie, A. M., 140, 142
Markakis, K., 325
Markides, K. S., 85, 98, 142, 143
Markson, L., 66
Marshall, J. R., 325
Martino, Ronald A., 21, 23-33, 332-333
Marzuk, P. M., 269, 270, 282
Masaki, H., 224, 228
Masaki, Kamal, 49, 97, 305, 333
Massagli, M. P., 81

Matocha, L., 108, 124
Matthews, D. A., 325
May, P. A., 132, 143, 144
McAdoo, H. P., 142
McAfee, Larry, 293
McArthur, Bill, 296
McBride, M., 107, 125
McBride, M. R., 111, 112, 124
McCabe, M., 134, 137, 139, 143
McCann, R., 77, 78, 81, 89, 98
McCarroll, J. E., 256, 263
McClellan, M. A., 85, 98
McConnell, T., 66
McCormick, T. R., 57, 67, 325
McCrae, R. R., 26, 34
McCready, W. C., 85, 98
McCue, J. D., 13, 22
McCullough, L. B., 50, 51, 53, 95, 98
McCullough, P. K., 27, 35
McDonald, M. V., 271, 282
McEntee, W. J., 26, 35
McGann, J. R., 173, 178
McGee, M. G., 1, 9
McHugh, P. R., 28, 32, 33, 34
McIver, Cecil, 269
McIver-Gibson, J., 51, 53, 95, 98
McKinley, E. D., 77, 82
McLaughlin, L., 6, 9
McLaughlin, L. A., 320, 324
McManus, D. Q., 24, 35
McNabney, M. K., 66
McNeely, J. D., 325
McQuay, J. E., 92, 99
Mebane, E., 104, 124
Mebane, E. W., 318, 319, 321, 324
Mehringer, C. M., 24, 34
Meier, D. E., 57, 58, 66, 78, 82
Melendy, H. B., 115, 124
Mellon, J., 72, 73, 82
Mersky, H., 24, 35
Mertz, K. R., 78, 82
Mezey, M., 57, 66
Michel, M., 88, 89, 90, 93, 98, 99, 115, 117, 123, 125, 135, 139, 141, 143
Mickelburgh, R., 301
Middleton, D., 127, 134, 137, 140, 142
Miles, S. H., 47, 53, 96, 99
Miller, A. K. H., 24, 35
Miller, B. L., 24, 34
Miller, P. S., 293, 294, 298, 301
Miller-Perrin, C., 57, 67
Millsap, R. E., 26, 34
Mintz, S., 72, 82
Miranda, B. F., 111, 112, 124
Miranda, M. R., 142, 143
Mishal, A. A., 208, 211

Mitchell, T. F., 273, 274, 282, 283
Mitty, E., 57, 66
Miyaji, N. T., 325
Moertel, C. G., 13, 22
Mogielnicki, R. P., 19, 22
Mokuau, N., 5, 9
Monzaemon, Chikamatsu, 220
Moore, A., 251, 256, 263
Moore, C. L., Jr., 79, 82
Mor, V., 77, 82
Moreno, J. D., 56, 66
More, Thomas, 155, 163
Morgan, E. B., 269, 270, 282
Morgan, W., 134, 143
Mori, G., 148, 162
Morris, C. A., 76, 78, 81
Morris, J. C., 24, 35
Morrison, R. S., 57, 58, 66, 78, 82
Morse, J. M., 232, 247
Moulton, J., 270, 283
Moulton-Benevedes, J., 273, 283
Mouton, Charles P., 71-82, 75, 77, 82, 333
Muecke, M. A., 118, 124
Mulder-Folkers, D. K. F., 275, 281
Muller, J., 108, 109, 124
Mulligan, H. D., 18, 22
Muncie, H. L., 325
Murphy, D. P., 48, 53
Murphy, J., 34
Murphy, S. T., 88, 89, 90, 93, 98, 99, 115, 117, 123, 125, 135, 143, 139, 141
Mykkänen, L., 25, 26, 35

Nakasone, Ronald Y., 30, 213-230, 225, 228, 333
Necker, N. S., 30, 36
Neimeyer, R. A., 247
Nelsen, V. J., 142
Nelson, H. D., 273, 274, 282
Neugebauer, Richard, 295
Newman, L. E., 191, 195, 197
Newmann, Ross E., 249-263, 333-334
Ng, W. L., 123, 124
Ngin, C., 110, 124
Nichols, R., 108, 110, 111, 112, 113, 114, 115, 118, 119, 120, 123
Nichter, M., 127, 135, 136, 141, 144
Nietzsche, F., 265, 282
Nishimoto, Patricia W., 249-263, 334
Nishimura, M., 114, 115, 125
Norberg, A., 109, 125, 246, 247
Norburn, J. K., 77, 81
Novack, D., 274, 282
Nowak, T. T., 118, 119, 125
Nu'man, F. H., 201, 211

Nuland, S. B., 66, 265, 282

O'Boyle, M., 27, 36
O'Brien, B., 232, 247
O'Brien, L. A., 60, 66
O'Connor, M. A., 48, 53
O'Connor, P., 91, 99
O'Leary, D., 24, 35
O'Malley, E., 272, 281
O'Neil, J. D., 134, 140, 143
O'Neill, O., 159, 163
O'Rourke, K., 165, 167, 168, 172, 173, 178
O'Shaughnesy, M. V., 274, 282
O'Sullivan, P., 274, 282
O'Toole, E. E., 62, 67
Oden, M. H., 25, 34
Offenbacher, H., 24
Ogden, R. D., 274, 276, 278, 282, 283
Ogden, Russel, 265-283, 334
Ogle, K. S., 65
Ohnuki-Tierney, E., 36
Oken, B. S., 25, 35
Olsen, E., 78, 82
Onwuteaka-Philipsen, B. D., 267, 283
Orona, C., 108, 110, 125
Osako, M., 115, 125
Osborne, K. B., 179
Ostheimer, J. M., 79, 82

Palmer, J. M., 89, 90, 99, 117, 125, 135, 143
Panagiota, V. C., 140, 142
Paniagua, F. A., 140, 143
Panzer, V. P., 25, 34
Papazian, O., 29, 33
Parry, J. K., 124, 125
Partanen, K., 35
Passik, S. D., 271, 276, 281, 282
Patrick, D. L., 57, 67, 77, 81
Patterson Fago, Julie A., 13-22, 330
Patterson, D. R., 57, 67
Pattison, E. M., 20, 22
Paulanka, B. J., 124, 125
Pawling-Kaplan, M., 91, 99
Payer, F., 24, 34
Payne, K., 67
Peabody, F. W., 315, 324
Pearce, J. K., 98
Pearlman, R. A., 57, 67, 273, 281
Pearman, W. A., 38, 53
Pelaez, M. B., 85, 98
Pellegrino, E. D., 171, 174, 175, 176, 177, 179
Perkel, R. L., 78, 81
Perkins, H. S., 55, 67, 91, 92, 93, 94, 99
Perrin, K. O., 57, 67

Pfeifer, J. E., 56, 65
Pfeifer, M. P., 62, 67
Phan, P. C., 179
Philip, J., 14, 16, 19, 22
Phillips, L., 109, 125
Phillips, R. S., 14, 16, 18, 22, 48, 53, 58, 66, 325
Pierson, Charon A., 231-247, 334-335
Pietsch, James H., 1-9, 31, 33, 34, 36, 37-53, 335
Piette, J., 77, 82
Pijnenborg, L., 268, 274, 283
Pittman, E., 109, 125
Pius XII (Pope), 153, 163
Platt, F. W., 325
Plum, F., 28, 29, 30, 34, 36
Pomara, N., 27, 34
Poppe, P. R., 96, 100
Posner, J. B., 29, 30, 36
Potter, P., 24, 35
Powell, T., 57, 67
Power, B. M., 30, 36
Powers, R., 80, 81
Preston, R. J., 134, 143
Preston, S. C., 134, 143
Prigerson, H. G., 239, 245, 247
Printz, L. A., 17, 19, 22, 67
Purnell, L. D., 124, 125
Putsch, R. W., 127, 142
Putsch, R. W., III, 140, 142
Pyörälä, K., 25, 26, 35

Quigley, H. A., 76, 78, 82

Rabe, D., 272, 282
Rabins, P. V., 34
Rachels, James, 67, 154, 163
Radner, H., 24, 34
Rael, R., 86, 87, 99
Raffin, T. A., 66
Rahman, F., 208, 211
Ramakrishna, J., 115, 125
Ramsey, G., 57, 66
Ramsey, P., 154, 163
Randolph, S., 85, 91, 93, 99
Rao, P. V. V., 79, 82
Rao, V. N., 79, 82
Raphael, S. P., 186, 197
Rapoport, S. I., 25, 35
Rashdell, H., 156, 163
Rasooly, I., 65
Rawlinson, D. G., 28, 34
Reed, R., 127, 135, 136, 140, 141, 142, 144
Regnard, C., 17, 22

Reines, A. J., 19, 187, 197
Reinikainen, K. J., 25, 26, 35
Reisberg, B., 25, 34
Reischauer, E. O., 220, 228
Reisner, A. I., 188, 189, 190, 192, 194, 197
Reynolds, D. K., 75, 81, 112, 114, 124
Rhoades, E. R., 129, 130, 131, 143
Rhodes, L. A., 127, 135, 142
Riegel, T. M., 242, 246, 247
Riekkinen, P. J., 25, 26, 35
Riekkinen, P. J., Sr., 35
Robinson, R. H., 215, 228
Rockwood, K., 27, 35
Rodriguez, P., 27, 28, 36
Rodriguez, Sue, 297, 298
Romero, L. J., 89, 90, 93, 99
Root, J. H., 96, 98
Rosenfeld, B. D., 271, 276, 281, 282
Rosner, F., 184, 190, 194, 197
Rothman, M. B., 85, 98
Rousseau, P., 243, 247
Rowell, Mary, 147-163, 335
Royall, R. M., 76, 78, 82
Rubin, S. M., 78, 82, 89, 99
Rudick, M. 162
Rudin, A. J., 187, 197
Russell, S., 265, 283
Rybicki, L., 14, 18, 22

Sachdev, P. S., 27, 28, 36
Sachs, G. A., 67
Saeger, R. H., 200, 211
Safar, P., 13, 22
Safer, L. A., 96, 99
Salon, J. E., 67
Salthouse, T. A., 25, 36
Samuelson, N., 184, 197
Sanchez-Ayendez, M., 84, 85, 99
Sandling, J., 136, 142
Sanghabhadra, 226, 228
Sano, M., 25, 36
Sapir, M., 77, 78, 81, 89, 98
Satcher, D., 78, 82
Savitt, T., 80, 82
Scarce, R., 275, 282
Schaie, K. W., 25, 36
Schapiro, M. B., 25, 35
Scherzinger, A. L., 24, 34
Schiffer, R. B., 34
Schmader, K., 175, 178
Schmidt, R., 24, 34
Schmidt, T. A., 50, 51, 52, 53, 273, 274, 282
Schmitz, S. P., 24, 34
Schneider, S. G., 270, 283
Schneiderman, L. J., 30, 36

Schofield, P. W., 25, 36
Schoolfield, J. D., 55, 67
Schroderus, M., 256, 263
Schwartz, D. R., 134, 137, 141, 142
Scofield, G., 67
Scott, E., 65
Scott, R., 25, 35
Seage, G. R., III, 81
Secundy, Marian, 75
Sehgal, A., 77, 82
Seldin, R., 182, 196, 197
Self, D., 27, 36
Seltzer, S., 187, 197
Semage, R., 227
Settle, M. B., 62, 67
Shapiro, E., 85, 98
Shapiro, R. S., 166, 179
Sheehan, D. C., 19, 22
Sheiman, S. L., 67
Sherkat, S. E., 74, 81
Shimizu, D., 5, 9
Shinran, 219, 228
Shoenfeld, P., 77, 82
Shope, J. T., 80, 82
Siala, M. E., 211
Siaw, L. K., 166, 179
Sidorov, J. E., 62, 67
Siebens, H., 66
Siegal, B., 296, 301
Siegel, R., 196
Siegert, E. A., 60, 66
Silliman, R., 34
Simeone, W. E., 134, 143
Singer, D., 182, 196, 197
Singer, P., 273, 282
Singer, P. A., 55, 65, 66
Singer, Peter, 154
Singh, B. K., 79, 82
Singh, R., 27, 34
Skeels, A., 14, 16, 19, 22
Slome, L., 274, 282
Slome, L. R., 270, 273, 283
Slomka, J., 67
Smith, A. C., 62, 67
Smith, C. K., 279, 282
Smith, D., 315, 324
Smith, J. S., 27, 28, 36
Smucker, D. R., 127, 142
Sobo, E. J., 3-4, 7, 9
Soininen, H., 35
Solberg, S., 232, 247
Soloveitchik, J. B., 184, 197
Somerville, M., 294, 299, 301
Sommer, A., 76, 78, 82
Sonsino, R., 186, 197
Sorenson, J. H., 325

Sotomayor, M., 85, 91, 93, 98, 99
Spangler, Z., 111, 112, 124
Spetzler, R. F., 24, 33
Starks, H. E., 57, 67 273, 281
Starr, E. R., 129, 133, 141, 143
Starr, P., 232, 233, 247
Staten, F., 79, 82
Stears, J. C., 24, 34
Stein, M., 274, 282
Stern, Y., 25, 36
Still, A., 325
Stocking, C., 67
Stollerman, G., 66
Stollerman, G. H., 325
Stone, C. L., 200, 211
Strassfeld, M., 196
Strassfeld, S., 196
Strauss, A. L., 236, 247
Streim, J. E., 325
Strickland, A. L., 1-2, 6, 9
Strodtbeck, F., 6, 9
Strothers, H., 77, 78, 81, 89, 98
Strull, W. M., 78, 82, 99
Suchman, A. L., 325
Sudarsky, L., 25, 36
Sudnow, D., 234, 243, 244, 247
Sugarman, J. R., 132, 142
Sugimoto, E. I., 222, 228
Sullivan, F. A., 167, 179
Sulmasy, D., 308, 320, 324
Supik, J. D., 91, 92, 93, 94, 99
Syme, D., 186, 197
Szabo, E., 56, 65

Ta, M., 118, 119, 125
Taishi, Shotoku, 220
Talamantes, Melissa A., 83-100, 85, 86, 87, 88,
    90, 93, 95, 96, 99, 335
Talbert, C. H., 152, 163
Tan, S. Y., 166, 179
Tardiff, K., 269, 270, 282
Tarshish, C., 24, 25, 35
Taylor, A., 132, 143
Taylor, R. J., 67, 75, 81
Taylor, S. E., 270, 283
Telander, P. D., 256, 262
Tendler, M. D., 190, 191, 193, 194, 197
Teno, J., 62, 66, 77, 82
Teno, J. M., 14, 16, 18, 22, 48, 53, 58, 66, 325
Terry, P., 308, 320, 324
Terry, R., 25, 35
Thomas, C. L., 24, 36
Thomasma, D. C., 171, 174, 176, 177, 179
Thompson, L. G., 222, 228
Tielsch, J. M., 76, 78, 82

Tierney, H., 269, 270, 282
Tilden, V. P., 273, 274, 282
Tindall, B., 276, 283
Tisdale, M. J., 18, 22
Todd, C., 325
Tolle, S. W., 273, 274, 282
Tomlinson, B. E., 24, 35
Torres-Gil, F. M., 98
Townley, D., 274, 282
Treviño, M. C., 91, 93, 99
Trigger, B. G., 134, 143
Trimble, J. E., 128, 143
Truog, R. D., 137, 143
Tulsky, J. A., 48, 53
Turner, B. S., 233, 247
Turner, K., 14, 16, 19, 22
Turner-Weeden, P., 127, 133, 143
Tyler, M. P., 256, 263

Uhlmann, R. F. 57, 67
Ursano, R. J., 256, 263

Valente, T. W., 96, 100
van Ameijden, E., 275, 281
van Delden, J. J. M., 268, 274, 283
van den Hoek, J. A. R., 275, 281
van der Heide, A., 267, 283
van der Maas, P. J., 267, 268, 274, 283
van der Wal, G., 267, 283
van Griensven, G. P. J., 275, 281
Van Heerden, P., 30, 36
Van Leeuwen, D., 290, 301
van Reyk, P., 271, 283
Van Winkle, N. W., 132, 144
VanderLaan, R., 109, 125
Veatch, R., 67
Ventres, W., 127, 135, 136, 141, 144
Vera de Briceno, R., 96, 100
Verhoef, M. J., 166, 179, 273, 283
Vienneau, D., 297, 301
Villa, R. F., 86, 87, 100
Vladeck, B. C., 65
Vorgrimler, H., 179

Wackers, G. L., 285, 301
Waddell, C., 166, 179
Wallace, E., 134, 144
Wallace, J. I., 273, 281
Wallace, S. P., 91, 100
Walsh, D., 14, 18, 22
Wanzer, D. H., 13, 22
Warren, J. W., 325

Wass, H., 247
Webb, J. P., 134, 144
Weber, E. P., 47, 53, 96, 99
Wei, M., 77, 78, 81, 89, 98
Weinstein, M. A., 50, 51, 52, 53
Weisbard, A. J., 192, 194, 197
Weisman, C., 308, 320, 324
Weiss, M. G., 115, 125
Weiss, S. J., 78, 82, 89, 99
Weissman, J. S., 81
Wells, C. E., 27, 36
Wells, K. B., 91, 93, 100
Wenger, N., 14, 16, 18, 22, 48, 53, 58, 62, 66, 325
Wennecker, M. B., 76, 78, 82
Werth, J., 283
Westlake Van Winkle, Nancy, 127-146, 355-356
Wheeler, S. E., 160, 163
Whitehouse, P., 26, 34
Wicks, D., 231, 240, 247
Wijdicks, E. F. M., 30, 36
Wildman-Hanlon, D., 175, 178
Will, George, 295
Willard, W., 134, 144
Willems, D. L., 267, 283
Williams, A., 152, 163
Williams, R. M., 3-4, 9
Wilson, M., 77, 78, 81, 89, 98
Wise, H. A., 258, 263
Wood, F., 79, 82

Wood, R. W., 272, 281
Woods, J. E., 211
Wright, K., 77, 78, 79, 81, 89, 90, 91, 93, 98
Wright, K. M., 256, 263
Wu, A. U., 58, 66
Wu, A. W., 14, 16, 18, 22, 325

Xenakis, S. N., 253, 263

Yamamato, S., 123, 124
Yarnell, S. K., 266, 283
Yasmeen, M. N., 208, 211
Yee, E., 227
Yeo, Gwen, 101-125, 107, 108, 109, 114, 115, 122, 124, 125, 223, 336
Yip, B., 274, 282
Young, E. W., 76, 82
Young, J. J., 111, 115, 125
Young, M. G., 274, 282, 283
Youngner, S. J., 62, 67
Younoszai, B., 86, 100

Zerwekl, J. V., 13, 16, 20, 21, 22
Zinn, W., 314, 315, 324
Ziv, L., 109, 125
Zlotowicz, B., 187, 197
Zohar, N., 188, 195, 197
Zonderman, A. B., 25, 26, 34, 35

Subject Index

Abraham, 186, 202
Acculturated, 4
Active euthanasia, 56, 59
Acupuncture, 16
Adam, 202
Advance directives:
    African Americans and, 78-79
    American Indians and, 140
    Asian/Pacific Islanders and, 103
    Chinese Americans and, 109
    defined, 41
    discussing with patients, 308-311
    follow-through with, 48
    health care professional training on, 97
    Hispanic Americans and, 89-90
    inclusiveness of, 246
    on Internet, 43
    Judaism and, 192-194
    Korean Americans, 117-118
    living wills, 41-42
    military and, 260-261
    modifying, 309
    patients' understanding of, 245
    portability of, 47-48
    PSDA and, 40-43
    strengthening, 49-52
    values history and, 50-51
    when to complete, 49
    who completes?, 47
    who knows about?, 47
Advanced interventions, 52
African Americans:
    advance directives and, 78-79
    autopsy and, 80

communication with patients, 76-77
cultural and religious issues, 71-82
death rates, 74
end-of-life preferences, 75-80
euthanasia and, 79
historical background, 72-74
"magical thinking," 75
organ donation and, 79-80
patient autonomy and, 88
physician-assisted suicide and, 79
racism and, 75-76
religious beliefs, 74-75
treatment preferences, 77
Afterlife:
    Muslim belief in, 203-205
    Navajo belief in, 133-134
    See also Eternal life
Age-associated memory impairment (AAMI), 26
Aging of brain:
    anatomical changes and, 24
    cognitive changes and, 25. *See also* Cognitive functioning
    neurological changes and, 24-25
    personality and, 25-26
Agitation, as symptom of dying, 19
AIDS:
    advance directives and, 47
    African Americans with, 76
    appetite stimulants for, 19
    assisted death and, 271-272, 295-296
    EU/AS and, 266-269
    Kaposi's sarcoma and, 270
    suicide and, 269-271

See also HIV/AIDS; Persons with AIDS
AIDS Action, 268
Alaska Natives. *See* American Indians
Alcoholism, American Indians and, 132
ALS. *See* Amyotrophic lateral sclerosis (ALS)
Alzheimer's disease, 27, 31, 77
American Bar Association:
    Commission on Legal problems of the Elderly, 43
    PSDA and, 49
    Web site, 43
American Indians:
    background on, 128-133
    end-of-life decision making, 135-138
    health care delivery and health status, 131-133
    recommendations for dealing with, 138-141
    views on death and dying, 133-134
American Medical Association, 49
Amino acid supplementation, 19
Amyotrophic lateral sclerosis (ALS), 296-297.
    See also Lou Gehrig's disease
Anorexia, 18
Anti-Semitism, 183
APIA. *See* Asian/Pacific Islanders
Apnea, 20
Appetite stimulants, 19
Army/Air Force Mutual Aid Association, 253
Artificial nutrition, 172, 241-243
Artificial hydration, 172, 246
Asoka, 215
Asian Americans:
    end-of-life decisions and, 101-125
    See also Asian/Pacific Islanders (APIA)
Asian Indian Americans, 107, 116-117
Asian/Pacific Islanders (APIA):
    advance directives and, 103
    autopsy and, 104
    cautionary notes about, 102
    family *vs.* individual decision making, 103
    hospice care and, 105
    life support and, 104
    organ donation and, 104
    potential conflicts with, 103-105
    subgroup beliefs, 105-123. *See also* specific subgroups
    terminal illness disclosure and, 103
    time-of-death traditions, 104-105
    See also Asian Americans
Assisted death:
    AIDS and, 295-296
    among older adults, 290-291
    See also Euthanasia; Physician-assisted death; Assisted suicide
Assisted suicide:
    Catholicism and, 171-176

Christianity and, 155-157, 157-161
    defined, 266
    Judaism and, 187-188
    requests by disabled adults, 293-296
    See also Assisted death; Euthanasia; Physician-assisted suicide
Authority:
    Catholic, 166-168
    of health care professionals, 232
Autonomy, 46
    American Indians and, 135-138
    as absolute, 300
    Christianity and, 158-160
    individual, 3
    Judaism and, 187-188, 192-193
    See also Patient autonomy; Self-determination
Autopsy:
    African Americans and, 80
    American Indians and, 138-139
    Asian/Pacific Islanders and, 104
    Hispanic Americans and, 91-92
    Islam and, 208
Ayurvedic medicine, 116

Baby Doe case, 294-295
Baby Ross case, 289-290
Bergstedt, Kenneth, 293
Bible:
    eternal life in, 151
    Jewish life description in, 182
    prohibition of killing in, 150
    suffering and, 151-152
    suicide accounts in, 155
Bicultural society, 4
Bioethics:
    autonomy and, 158-160
    health care professional training on, 97
    See also Ethical considerations
Boomsma, Nettie, 287-289, 292
Bouvia, Elizabeth, 293
Bouvia v. Superior Court, 293, 301
Brain:
    aging of, 23. *See also* Aging of brain
    medulla, 30
Brain death, 29-31, 223-225
Bronchodilators, 17
Buddhism:
    beliefs and doctrine, 216-219
    birth as rebirth, 122
    brain death and organ transplants, 223-225
    Confucianism and, 219-223
    differing traditions in, 102
    end-of-life decision making, 213-230

four noble truths, 217-218
in United States, 214
Japanese Americans and, 113-115
karma and, 118, 122, 217, 221, 224
Korean Americans, 117
Obon, 222-223
origin and spread of, 214-216
transference of merit, 218-219

Cachexia, 18-19
Calvin, John, 155
Cambodian Americans, 122-123
Canada:
    EU/AS and AIDS in, 274
    religion in, 148
Canadian AIDS Society, 271
Cancer:
    advance directives and terminal, 47
    African Americans and, 74
    American Indians and, 133
    appetite stimulants for, 19
    breast, 239
    Hispanic Americans and, 86
    infiltrating, 17
    pain and, 15
Capacity, 31-33, 45
Cardiopulmonary resuscitation (CPR), 44, 50,
    234, 241
Cardozo, Benjamin (Justice), 269
Casey, Joseph (Bishop), 153
Catholicism:
    Anointing of the Sick, 171
    beliefs about life, 173-174
    Catholic authority, 166-168
    dimensions of human person, 168-170
    end-of-life teachings, 171-177
    euthanasia and, 171-173, 175
    Filipino Americans and, 111
    helping poor and, 175-176
    love and true mercy, 174-175
    percent of Christians, 148
    percent of U.S. population, 165
    suffering and, 176-177
    Vietnamese Americans, 118
    withholding and withdrawal of treatment
        and, 153
Centers for Disease Control and Prevention, 74
Chabot, Boudewijn, 287-289
Chabot/OMII Dossier, 301
Cheynes-Stokes respiration, 17, 20
Chinese Americans, 105-106, 108-111
Christ. *See* Jesus Christ
Christianity:
    American Indians and Alaska Natives, 129
    autonomy and, 158-160

background considerations, 149-150
beliefs about life, 157-158
Christian community, 148-149
common concerns and shared perceptions,
    161
compassion and, 160-161
debate on end-of-life issues, 153-157
end-of-life decisions and, 147
Korean Americans, 117
Native Hawaiians, 120
scriptural roots, 150-153
suffering and, 151-153
suicide and, 155-157
withholding and withdrawal of treatment,
    153-155
Chronic obstructive pulmonary disease
    (COPD), 14, 86, 132
"Clinical gaze," 233
Cognitive dysfunction, as communication bar-
    rier, 322
Cognitive functioning:
    delirium and, 28
    dementia and, 26-27
    pseudodementia and, 27-28
Coma, 29, 172. *See also* Persistent vegetative
    state
Comfort-care-only order, 41, 44-45, 51, 235,
    313
Communication:
    African American patients and, 76-77
    after death (with family), 313
    American Indian style of, 140
    approaches, 314-319
    cross-cultural, 305-325
    decision maker and, 320-321
    health care practitioner and, 322-323
    language barriers and, 321
    listening and, 315-316
    nonverbal, 316-317
    obstructions to, 321-322
    patient's level and, 318-319
    rapport building and, 314-315
    techniques to improve, 323
    timing and, 312-313
    verbal, 317-318
Compassion:
    Christianity and, 160-161
    hospice programs and, 174-175
Compassion in Dying v. State of Washington,
    267, 283
Competency, 31-33, 45
Confucianism:
    Buddhism and, 219-223
    family and, 103
    Nikkei Japanese and, 113
    organ donation and, 110

Vietnamese Americans, 118
Confucius, 219
Congestive heart failure, 14, 16
Consent, 38-39. *See also* Informed consent
Considine, Chris, 297
Cornelisse-Clausen, Martine, 289-292, 300
Courts:
    avoiding litigation in, 62-64
    end-of-life decision making and, 60-62
    See also U.S. Supreme Court
CPR. *See* Cardiopulmonary resuscitation
Cross-cultural communication, 305-325
Cruzan v. Director, Missouri Department of
    Health (1990), 39, 53, 61-62, 67
Cruzan, Nancy, 39-40
Cuban Americans, 85, 89. *See also* Hispanic
    Americans
Cultural competency, 8
Cultural relativism, 7
Culture:
    commonalities across, 6
    communicating across, 305-325
    defined, 2
    dominant, end-of-life care and, 3-4
    hospital and nursing home, 231-247
    influence at life's end, 4-5
    pluralism and, 2-3
    U.S. *See* U.S. culture
    why study?, 5-7
    See also Ethnic perspectives *and names of*
    specific cultures
Custer, George Armstrong (General), 253
"Custodial services," 242

Dawes General Allotment Act of 1887, 130
Death:
    average age, ix
    brain, 29-31, 223-225
    clinical, 21
    communication after, 313
    health care training on, 96-97
    institutionalization of, 245
    life after. *See* Afterlife; Eternal life
    postponing, 13
    punishment and, 186
    talking to patients about, 305-325
    war-related, 253-254
    See also Dying
Death with dignity, 241
Death rates, African American, 74
Death rattle, 17
Death songs, American Indian, 137
Death watch, 243-244
Decision making:
    autonomous vs. collective, 5-6

surrogate. *See* Surrogate decision making
    See also End-of-life decision making
Dehydration, 17, 19
Dementia, 26-27
    quality of life and, 243
    vascular, 27
Depression, 322
Diabetes, 132
Dialysis patients, 77
Dickinson, Brian, 297
Disabilities perspective:
    end-of-life decisions, 285-301
    euthanasia in the Netherlands, 286-292
    euthanasia in the U.S., 293-296
    restricted life, 296-298
Disproportionate burden, 173
"Divine rescue," 74
DNA testing, military and, 252
Doctors. *See* Health care professionals
Do-not-resuscitate (DNR) order, 44-45
    bracelet with, 245
    defined, 41
    hospitals and, 234
    Islam and, 207
Down syndrome, 289-290, 294-295
DPOA-HC. *See* Durable power of attorney for
    health care
Durable power of attorney for health care
    (DPOA-HC), 37, 40, 63-64
    African Americans and, 78
    as advance directive, 42-43, 308
    defined, 41
    Hispanic Americans and, 89-90
    surrogate decision maker and, 46, 308
Dutch Voluntary Euthanasia Society, 288, 300
Dying:
    Christian euphemisms for, 149
    common symptoms, 14-19
    negotiating, 241-243
    physical aspects of, discussing, 13-22, 310
    process of, 13-14
    signs of, 20-21
    See also Death
Dying trajectory, 236-244
    artificial nutrition and hydration, 241-243
    death watch, 243-244
    emergency room and, 236-237
    intensive care unit and, 237-240
    lingering, 240-241
Dysesthesias, 15
Dyspnea, 16-17

Eastern Orthodox religion, 148
Emergency room (ER), 235, 236-237
Emphysema, 17

End-of-life decisions:
    African Americans, 71-82
    AIDS/HIV Position Statement, 280
    American Indians and Alaska Natives, 127-146
    Asians and Pacific Islanders, 101-125
    Buddhism, 213-230
    Christianity, 147
    cognitive changes and, 23-36
    courts and, 60-64
    culture and, 1-9
    disabilities and, 285-301
    ethical considerations and, 55-68
    ethnic perspectives, 69-144
    Hispanic Americans, 83-100
    HIV/AIDS community, 265-283
    hospital and nursing home culture, 231-247
    influences on, 6
    Judaism, 181-197
    military culture, 249-263
    Muslims, 199-211
    religious perspectives, 145-228
Eternal life:
    Catholic belief in, 171
    See also Afterlife; Bible, eternal life in
Ethical considerations, 55-68
    American Indians and, 136-137
    courts and, 60-64
    definitions, 56
    ethical consensus, 56-58
    ethical disputes, 59-60
    euthanasia and, 286
    Judaism and, 186
    See also Bioethics; Social ethics
Ethnic perspectives:
    African American, 71-82
    American Indian/Alaska Native, 127-146
    Asian/Pacific Islander, 101-125
    Hispanic American, 83-100
    See also Culture
EU/AS. *See* Euthanasia and/or assisted suicide
European Americans:
    advance directives and, 89
    autopsies and, 91-92
    patient autonomy and, 88
Euthanasia:
    African Americans and, 79
    AIDS and, 271-272, 291
    Catholicism and, 171-173, 175
    Christianity and, 155-156, 157-161
    defined, 56, 266
    Hispanic Americans and, 91
    involuntary, 56, 289-290, 294-295
    Judaism and, 188, 190-192
    legalizing, 241
    Netherlands and, 286-292
    North America and, 292-296
    passive, 173, 190-192
    per se, 172
    voluntary, 56, 287-289
    See also Active euthanasia; Assisted death; Assisted suicide; Euthanasia and/or assisted suicide; Physician-assisted death; Physician-assisted suicide
Euthanasia and/or assisted suicide (EU/AS)
    health professionals attitudes and practices and, 272-275
    legal climate and, 267-269
    underground practices of, 275-278
    See also Euthanasia

Family:
    American Indians and, 140
    Asian Indian Americans and, 116
    Asian/Pacific Islanders and, 103
    Buddhism and, 226. *See also* Filial piety
    communication with, 307-308, 313
    filial piety and. *See* Filial piety
    Hawaiian values of, 120
    Hispanic Americans and, 85, 93
    hospitalization and, 233
    Japanese Americans and, 113
    Korean Americans and, 117-118
    military, notification of death, 256-257
    request for medical records by, 319
Family consent statutes, 46, 63
Farrakhan, Louis, 201
Fatigue, 18
Fears, discussing, 310-311
Feeding tube, 52, 242
Fe, 87
Feinstein, Moshe, 191
Filer, Sam (Justice), 297-298, 300
Filer, Toni, 299
Filial piety:
    Asian/Pacific Islanders and, 103
    Buddhism and, 219, 221, 224
    Japanese Americans and, 113
    Korean Americans and, 117-118
    Filipino Americans, 106, 111-112
Full treatment/resuscitation, 52
Funerals:
    Cambodian American, 123
    military, 258-259
    New Orleans, 73
    Samoan American, 121
    See also Memorial rituals
Futile treatment, 173

Gamble v. Baptist Hospital, 293, 301

Gastrostasis, 19
Gautama, Siddhãrtha, 214-217
Ghulam Ahmad, Mirza, 201
Gill, Carol, 293
Glover, Jonathan, 154
Gunning, Karl, 288

haNasi, Judah, 190
Hawaiians. *See* Native Hawaiians
Hawking, Stephen, 297-299
Healing circles, Judaism and, 194-195
Health care professionals:
  communication and, 305-325. *See also*
    Communication
  cultural understanding of, 139
  end-of-life training for, 96-97
  EU/AS attitudes and practices, 272-275
Heart disease:
  African Americans and, 74
  American Indians and, 131-132
  Hispanic Americans and, 86
Hindus, 116
Hispanic Americans:
  advance directives and, 89-90
  autopsy and, 91-92
  causes of death for, 86
  community education and outreach, 96
  cultural themes, 94
  culture, faith, and religion, 86-87
  diversity of, 84-86
  end-of-life decision making, 83-100
  euthanasia and, 91
  hospice and, 91
  life-prolonging treatment and, 90
  organ donation and, 92
  patient autonomy and, 88
  patient care for, 93-95
  professional education, 96-97
  religion of, 86-87
HIV/AIDS:
  African Americans and, 74
  American Indians and, 132
  end-of-life decisions and, 265-283
  See also AIDS
Holland. *See* Netherlands
Homicide:
  African American males and, 74
  American Indians and, 132
  black-on-black, 71
Hospice care:
  as compassionate, 174-175
  Asian/Pacific Islanders and, 105
  Hispanic Americans and, 91
  Islam and, 207
  Judaism and, 194-195

Hospitals:
  death in, 13
  do-not-resuscitate order and, 234-235
  emergency room, 235-237
  end-of-life decision making and, 231-247
  historical perspective, 232-233
  ICU (intensive care unit), 237-240
Hydration, 172, 241-243, 246
Hypoxia, 16

ICU (intensive care unit), 237-240
In re Quinlan, 61, 67
Incontinence, quality of life and, 243
Indian Health Care Improvement Act of 1976,
  130
Indian Health Service (IHS), 131
Indian Removal Act of 1930, 129
Indian Reorganization Act of 1934, 130
Indian Self-Determination and Education As-
    sistance Act of 1975, 130
Individual autonomy, 3
Infant mortality, American Indians and, 131
Informed consent, 3, 38-40
Inquest of Unknown Female, 275, 283
Institutional cultures:
  disabled, 285-301
  HIV/AIDS community, 265-283
  long-term care (LTC) facilities, 231-247
  military, 249-263
Insurance, life, military, 251
"Interactive cues," 239
Internet, advance directives on, 43
Interventions, aggressive, 60
Intravenous (IV) nutrition:
  American Indians and, 137
  fluids, 52
Involuntary euthanasia, 289-290, 294-295
Isaac, 202
Ishmael, 202
Islam:
  autopsy and, 208
  belief system and practices, 202-204
  end-of-life practices and considerations,
    204-208
  Filipino Americans and, 111
  five pillars of, 203-204
  North American community, 199-201
  organ donation and, 208
  physician-assisted death, 207-208
  social support systems, 209
  suicide and, 207-208
  See also Muslims
Islamic Health and Human Services, 209
Islamic Medical Association (IMA) of North
    America, 207-208

Isserles, Moses, 183, 190, 192

Japan, organ transplantation law, 29
Japanese Americans, 106, 112-116
    death rituals, 221-223
Jesus Christ, 151-152, 166, 168, 171, 174-176,
    202-203
Joint Commission on Accreditation of Health-
    care Organization, 63
Judaism:
    advance directives, 192-194
    American Jewish Community history, 182
    assisted suicide, 187-188
    autonomy, 187-188
    end-of-life decision making, 181-197
    healing circles and hospice, 194-195
    organ transplants, 194
    Orthodoxy, 185, 189, 193
    pain and suffering, 188-189
    passive euthanasia, 190-192
    pre-enlightenment communal structure,
      183-184
    reconstructionism, 184-185
    reform and conservative movements, 184
    Talmud and legal codifications, 182-183
    value of saving life, 185-186
Judgment Day:
    African Americans and, 80
    Islam belief in, 203, 205

Karma, 118, 122, 217, 221, 224
Kevorkian, Dr. Jack, 79, 149
Kimsma, Gerrit, 292
Korean Americans, 88-89, 107, 117-118
Krischner v. McIver, 269, 283

Life:
    as gift of God, 157-158
    discussing meaning of, 312
    sanctity of, 158, 173-174
Life expectancy:
    African American, 74
    African slaves, 72
    American Indians and, 131
Life insurance, military, 251
Life support:
    Asian/Pacific Islanders and, 104
    Buddhism and, 115
    Chinese Americans and, 109
    Hispanic Americans and, 90
    Islam and, 206-207
    technology, 241

Lillian, case of, 236-241, 243-244
Limitation of Medical Care form, 135-136
Limited interventions, 51
Liver disease, American Indians and, 132
Living will, 40, 308
    as advanced directive, 41-42
    defined, 41
    Islam and, 207
    modifying, 309
    patient's values and, 50-51
Livor mortis, 21
Longmore, Paul, 293, 297
Long-term care (LTC) facilities, 231-247
    conclusions and recommendations, 245-247
    do-not-resuscitate or no-code order, 234-
      235
    dying trajectory and, 236
    food and feeding rituals, 242
    historical perspective, 232-233
Lou Gehrig's disease, 292, 296-297
Love, Catholicism and, 174-175
Luther, Martin, 155

McAfee, Larry, 293
McArthur, Bill, 296
Maimonides, 155
Massage, 16
Materialism, 3
Maternal mortality, American Indians and, 131
Mediastinal disease, 17
Medical insurance, LTC facilities and, 242
Medicare/Medicaid:
    American Indians and, 135
    regulations and mandates, 234-235
Medicine:
    Ayurvedic, 116
    for dyspnea, 17
    Judaism and, 188
    pain, 15-16, 299
    premodern, 232
Memorial rituals:
    Buddhist, 222
    See also Funerals
Memory, aging and, 26
Mental capacity. *See* Competency
Mestizo Indio-Hispanic traditions, 85
Mexican Americans, 84, 88-92. *See also*
    Hispanic Americans
Military:
    advance planning and, 260-261
    cemeteries and memorials, 259
    changes in tradition, 261-262
    end-of-life decisions and, 249-263
    family notification of death, 256-257
    funeral, 258-259

on the job death, 253
peacetime death, 254-256
recruitment and basic training, 250-252
rituals to avoid death, 255
slang and terms about death, 255
traditional norms and practices, 250-262
training accidents, 256
war-related triage and death, 253-254
Military Advance Medical Directive Law, 48,
    53
Miller, Paul Steven, 294
Mini-Mental State Examination (MMSE), 23,
    27-28, 33
Mobility, loss of, 243
Mortality rates, American Indians and, 132
Moses, 202
Muhammad, 201-203, 207
Muhammed, Elijah, 201
Muslims:
    Asian Indian Americans as, 116
    See also Islam

National Values History Demonstration Project,
    51
Native American Graves Protection and Repa-
    triation Act of 1990, 130
Native Americans. See American Indians
Native Hawaiians, 107, 119-120
Nausea, 18
Netherlands:
    AIDS in, 274-275
    assisted death safeguards, 291-292
    EU/AS in, 267, 274-275, 286-292
Neugebauer, Richard, 295
Neuropathic pain, 15, 16
"Next of kin," 63
9-1-1, 235
Nirvana, 218
Noah, 202
No-code order, 234-235
No-CPR order, 41
Nonciceptive pain, 15
North America, euthanasia in, 293-296
Nurses:
    conversation with dying patient, 244
    slow code and, 235
    See also Health care professionals
Nursing homes:
    death in, 13
    See also Long-term care (LTC) facilities
Nutrition:
    artificial, 241-243, 246
    Chinese Americans and end-of-life, 109
    dying patients and, 109
    intravenous (IV), 137

Organ donation:
    African Americans and, 79-80
    Asian/Pacific Islanders and, 104
    Buddhism and, 115
    Chinese Americans and, 110
    Filipino Americans and, 112
    Hispanic Americans and, 92
    Islam and, 208
    military and, 260-261
    Native Hawaiians and, 120
    Vietnamese Americans and, 119
    See also Organ transplants
Organ transplants:
    brain death and, 30
    Buddhism and, 223-225
    Japanese law on, 29
    Judaism and, 194
    See also Organ donation
Orthodox Jews, 185, 189, 193
Out-of-hospital DNR order, 41, 44

Pacific Islanders:
    end-of-life decisions and, 101-125
    See also Asian/Pacific Islanders (APIA)
Pain:
    control of, 14, 16
    Judaism and, 188-189
    medicine for, 299
    quality of life and, 243
    symptom of dying, 14-16
    types of, 15
Palliative care, 8, 58, 97, 154, 295-296
Parens patriae, 45
Parkinson's disease, 27
Passive euthanasia, 56, 173, 190-192
"Paternalism by permission," 77
Patient autonomy, 38-39
    African Americans and, 88
    American Indians and, 139
    decision making and, 320-321
    Hispanic Americans and, 88
    Korean Americans and, 117
    See also Autonomy
Patient Self-Determination Act (PSDA), 37-38,
    54, 63, 68
    advance directives and, 40-43
    African Americans and, 76
    American Indians and, 127
    defined, 41
    limitations, 46-49
    Mexican Americans and, 90
    military and, 261
    Navajo perspective on, 138
Patient's Bill of Rights, 38

Perinatal conditions, African Americans and, 74
Persistent vegetative state (PVS), 28-29. *See also* Coma
Persons with AIDS (PWAs), 266
    suicide rate among, 270
    See also AIDS; HIV/AIDS
Peyote, 129
Physician Orders for Life-Sustaining Treatment (POLST) document, 51-52
Physician-assisted death, 59
    euthanasia and assisted suicide as, 267
    military and, 260-261
    See also Assisted death; Euthanasia; Physician-assisted suicide
Physician-assisted suicide, 155
    AIDS Action on, 268
    African Americans and, 79
    Islam and, 207-208
    legalizing, 241
Physicians. *See* Health care professionals
Pluralism, culture and, 2-3
Postma-Van Boven, Truus, 288
Pot, Pol, 122
Program for All-inclusive Care of the Elderly (PACE), 89
Protestantism, 148
PSDA. *See* Patient Self-Determination Act
Puerto Ricans, 84. *See also* Hispanic Americans
PWAs. *See* Persons with AIDS

Quality of life, 243
Questions, open-ended, 316
Quill v. Vacco, 267, 283
Quinlan, Karen Ann, 153
Qur'aan, 203-208

Rachels, James, 154
Racism, African Americans and, 75-76
Rapid Identification Documents, 54
Reincarnation. *See* Successive rebirth
Religions:
    African American, 74-75
    American Indian and Alaska Native, 129
    Buddhism, 213-230
    Christianity, 147-163
    end-of-life decisions and, 145-228
    Hispanic American, 86-87
    Islam, 199-211
    Judaism, 181-197
    premodern medicine and, 232
    See also names of specific religions
Respiratory secretions, 17

Restlessness, as symptom of dying, 19
Restricted life, 296-298
"Right to die," 241
Right to Die Society of Canada, 279
Right-to-die movement, 267
Rigor mortis, 21
Rivera, Diego, 86
Rodriguez, Sue, 296-297
Roe v. Wade, 267, 283
Roman Catholicism. *See* Catholicism
Ronald McDonald Houses, 140

Samoan Americans, 121
Schloendorf v. Society of New York Hospital, 269, 283
Secularism, 3
Self-determination, 38, 56
    as absolute, 300
    American Indians and, 135-138
    decision making and, 320-321
    See also Autonomy
Servicemen's Group Life Insurance, 251
Shaw, George Bernard, 318
Singer, Peter, 154
"Skilled care" vs. "unskilled care," 242
Slaves, African, 72
"Slow code," 235
"Social disengagement," 20
Social ethics, 286. *See also* Ethical considerations
Soul:
    after-death beliefs about, 92. *See also* Afterlife; Eternal life
    rebirth of, 115
Spirit possession, Cambodian Americans and, 122
Spirits, malevolent, 223
Spirituality, *Fe*, 87
State v. McAfee, 293, 301
Stereotypes, 8
Stroke:
    African Americans and, 74
    dementia caused by, 27
    Hispanic Americans and, 86
Subcultures, 4
    Asian/Pacific Islander, 105-123
    Hispanic, 84
Substituted judgment concept, 57
Successive rebirth, 221
Suffering:
    Buddhism and, 218
    Catholicism and, 176-177
    Christianity and, 151-153
    Judaism and, 188-189
    subjectivity of, 290

Suicide:
  AIDS and, 269-271
  American Indians and, 132
  facilitated, 59
  Islam and, 207-208
  military and, 255
  physician-assisted. *See* Assisted suicide;
    Physician-assisted suicide
SUPPORT Principal Investigators, 48, 49, 57,
  245
Surrogate decision maker, 45-56
  defined, 41
  DPOA-HC and, 308
  Native Hawaiians and, 120

Talmud, 183
Ten Commandments, 150
Terminal illness:
  Cambodian Americans and, 122
  informing Japanese Americans about, 114
Torah, 182
Transmigration, 221
Treatment, withholding and withdrawal of,
  153-155
Triage, 253-254
Tribal Self-Governance Program of 1992, 130
Tuskegee Syphilis Study, 76

U.S. Constitution:
  due process clause, 39
  Fourteenth Amendment, 39
U.S. culture:
  as melting pot, 2-3

dominant, 3-4
U.S. Supreme Court:
  on assisted suicide, 267-269
  on euthanasia, 299
  on physician-assisted death, 59-60
Uniform Durable Power of Attorney Act (Hawaii), 43-44, 54
Uniform Health Care Decisions Act, 40-41
Uniform Health Care Decisions Act (Hawaii),
  43, 46
United States, EU/AS and AIDS in, 273-274

Vacco v. Quill, 59, 68, 268, 283, 299, 301
Values history:
  advance directives and, 50-51
  Hispanic Americans and, 95
Vascular dementia, 27
Vietnamese Americans, 107, 118-119
Violence, urban, 71
Voluntary Euthanasia Society, 288-289, 300
Vomiting, 18

Washington, George, 258
Washington v. Glucksberg, 59, 68, 267-268,
  299, 301
Web site:
  American Bar Association, 43
  Council on Islamic Education, 209
Webb, Alexander Russell, 200
Will, George, 295
William, case of, 277-278

About the Contributors

Marc R. Alexander, S.T.D., is Theologian for the Diocese of Honolulu and founding Executive Director of the Hawaii Catholic Conference, the public policy arm for the Roman Catholic Church in the state of Hawaii. He holds degrees in philosophy and theology, including an M.A. and a licentiate in sacred theology (summa cum laude) from the Catholic University of Louvain as well as a doctorate in sacred theology from the Gregorian University in Rome. He has published in both the United States and Europe. He is a fellow of the St. Francis International Center for Healthcare Ethics and serves as a governor's appointee to state-sponsored committees on decision making in Hawaii.

Patricia L. Blanchette, M.D., M.P.H., is Professor of Medicine and Public Health at the John A. Burns School of Medicine and School of Public Health at the University of Hawaii at Manoa. She is director of the medical school's cross-departmental Geriatric Medicine Program and Geriatric Medicine Fellowship Program, the Pacific Islands Geriatric Education Center, and the John A. Hartford Foundation–Kuakini Medical Center's Center of Excellence in Geriatric Medicine. After graduating with concurrent M.D. and M.P.H. degrees from the University of Hawaii at Manoa, she completed an internal medicine internship and residency at the Dartmouth-Hitchcock Medical Center and a fellowship in geriatric medicine at Harvard Medical School. She is board certified in internal medicine and geriatric medicine. She has won numerous awards and honors, including an Excellence in Teaching Award, Distinguished Alumni, Best Doctors in America, and the Soroptimist's Women of Distinction Award.

Kathryn L. Braun, Dr.P.H., is Director of the University of Hawaii Center on Aging and Associate Professor at the University of Hawaii School of Public Health. Her research focuses on Asian and Pacific Islander aging, with publications exploring ethnic differences in life expectancy and mortality as well as cultural variations in disease perceptions and health practices. She is author of the study and faculty guides associated with the telecourse, "Growing Old in a New Age." She is a fellow in the Gerontological Society of America and the Association for Gerontology in Higher Education. She received a Board of Regent's Medal for Excellence in Teaching from the University of Hawaii in 1998.

Julie A. Patterson Fago, M.D., is Assistant Professor of Medicine and Director of Clinical Geriatric Programs at the Center for the Aging at Dartmouth Medical School. She also is the geriatric consultant to Dartmouth Hitchcock Medical Center's End-of-Life Project.

Celina Gomez, M.D., is a family physician and a faculty member with the Department of Family Medicine at the Universidad Autonoma de Nuevo Leon, Monterrey, Mexico. She completed a fellowship in bioethics at the University of Texas Health Science Center in San Antonio in 1997. While in San Antonio, she worked with Melissa Talamantes on a study of advance health planning among Mexican Americans. They are replicating their San Antonio study in Monterrey and are particularly interested in issues of acculturation.

Hamid Abdul Hai, M.D., is a cardiologist who trained at the Peter Bent Brigham Hospital, the Harvard Medical School, and the Harvard School of Public Health. He is Associate Professor of Cardiology at Northwestern University and practices cardiology in Chicago. He also is an Islamic scholar, popular speaker, writer, and *Khateeb* (sermon giver). He is a vice-chairman of the Council of the Parliament of the World's Religions and is chairman of the Islamic group of that organization. He serves on the board of directors of the American Islamic College and is a fellow of the American College of Cardiology.

Nancy Hikoyeda, M.P.H., teaches in the gerontology program at San Jose State University and is an associate faculty member at the Stanford Geriatric Education Center. She received a B.A. in education from the University of Utah and her M.P.H. and certificate in applied social gerontology from San Jose State. Her research and publications are in the areas of health, aging, and ethnicity, particularly long-term care utilization and policy. She also is a doctoral candidate at the University of California at Los Angeles School of Public Health and is a recipient of a predoctoral fellowship from the UCLA/ VA/RAND Medtep Research Center for Asian/Pacific Islanders to study the role of ethnicity in the quality of life of institutionalized Japanese American women.

Asad Husain, Ph.D., is Professor of Political Science and Director of the Summer Institute of Islamic Studies at Northeastern Illinois University. He also is president of the American Islamic College in Chicago. He received his M.A. degree in journalism and international relations, and later his Ph.D., from the University of Minnesota. He is the author of several books and many articles. He established the Institute of Muslim Minority Affairs at King Abdul Aziz University at Jeddah, Saudi Arabia, in 1975. For his work on Muslim minorities, he received a Professional Advancement and Merit award in 1995. He is one of the founders of the Muslim Community Center of Chicago and is affiliated with many other Islamic organizations, including the International Strategy and Policy Institute. In 1996, the Vatican presented him with the Order of Merit of the Knights and Ladies of the Equestrian Order of the Holy Sepulcher of Jerusalem.

Marshall B. Kapp, J.D., M.P.H., received his B.A. from Johns Hopkins University, after which he completed a J.D. with honors from George Washington University and an M.P.H. from the Harvard University School of Public Health. He serves as Director of Geriatric Medicine at Wright State University and holds an adjunct faculty appointment at the University of Dayton School of Law, teaching courses on legal and ethical aspects of health care. As founding editor of the *Journal of Ethics, Law, and Aging,* he also has served as consultant to a wide range of government and private agencies. He also is the recipient of numerous awards, including the *Journal of Healthcare Risk Management* Award for Writing Excellence as Author of the Year from the American Society for Healthcare Risk Management.

William Kavesh, M.D., M.P.H., is Medical Director of Primary Care Geriatrics at the Philadelphia Veterans Administration Medical Center. He also is a clinical assistant professor of medicine and fellow of the Institute on Aging at the University of Pennsylvania Health System as well as an adjunct assistant professor of public health at the Boston University School of Public Health. Educated at the Massachusetts Institute of Technology, Albert Einstein College of Medicine, and Harvard School of Public Health, he also is a member of the American Geriatrics Society and the Gerontological Society of America. He has been writing about Jewish medical ethics and related issues for more than 20 years and is a member of the editorial board of the *Journal of Ethics, Law, and Aging.*

Tom Koch, M.S., is a writer/researcher specializing in issues surrounding the care of the fragile. The author of eight books, including *The Limits of Principle: Who Lives and What Dies,* he also is a research associate in bioethics at the Hospital for Sick Children in Toronto and a forum associate for the David Lam Center at Simon Fraser University. He is the director of Information Outreach, a Toronto-based research organization.

Shari L. Kogan, M.D., is Director of Geriatric Services for the Queen's Medical Center in Honolulu, Hawaii. She studied medicine at the Mount Sinai School of Medicine and then taught geriatrics and ethics while on active duty in the U.S. Air Force. Following this, she was an assistant professor of geriatric medicine at the John A. Burns School of Medicine in Honolulu, teaching in both the medical school and the geriatric medicine fellowship programs.

Joanne Lynn, M.D., M.A., M.S., is Professor of Health Care Sciences and Medicine and Director of the Center to Improve Care of the Dying at the George Washington University Medical Center. As a geriatrician and former medical director of the Washington Home and Hospice of Washington, she was elected to the Institute of Medicine in 1996. She also has been on the board of directors of Concern for Dying, the American Bar Association's Commission on Legal Problems of the Elderly, and the Hastings Center Task Force that wrote the Guidelines for the Termination of Treatment and the Care of the Dying. She also served as project director of the President's Commission for the Study of Ethical Problems in Medicine and Biomedical and Behavioral Research and as co-director of SUPPORT (Study to Understand Prognoses and Preferences for Outcomes and Risks of Treatments).

Ronald A. Martino, M.D., graduated from Rutgers University in 1971. After receiving his M.D. from Tufts University School of Medicine in 1975, he completed residencies in both neurology and psychiatry at Mount Sinai Hospital in New York City in 1980. He is board certified in both specialties and has a private practice in Fairbanks, Alaska. He is a member of the Phi Beta Kappa and Alpha Omega Alpha honor societies, and he continues to serve in the army reserves as commander of the 1984th U.S. Army Hospital with the rank of colonel.

Kamal Masaki, M.D., is a board-certified internist and geriatrician as well as Associate Professor in the Geriatric Medicine Program and Associate Program Director of the Geriatric Medicine Fellowship Program in the John A. Burns School of Medicine at the University of Hawaii. She is involved in several research programs and is the clinical director for the Honolulu Heart Program, the Honolulu-Asia Aging Study, and the Hawaii Center for the Women's Health Initiative, among others. She has an interest in ethical issues and has been a member of the ethics committee at the Kuakini Medical Center since 1990.

Charles P. Mouton, M.D., M.S., is Assistant Professor in the Division of Community Geriatrics, Department of Family Practice, at the University of Texas Health Science Center at San Antonio as well as Assistant Clinical Professor at the University of Medicine and Dentistry of New Jersey. He received his M.D. from Howard University and his M.S. in clinical epidemiology from the Harvard University School of Public Health. After completing his residency in family practice at Prince George's Hospital Center in Cheverly, Maryland, he received his geriatrics fellowship at the George Washington University Medical Center. He is a member of the Gerontological Society of America, the American Geriatrics Society, the Society of Teachers of Family Medicine, and the National Medical Association.

Ronald Y. Nakasone, Ph.D., teaches Buddhist thought, ethics, and aesthetics at the Graduate Theological Union at Berkeley, California. An ordained Buddhist priest, he studied Buddhism at the University of Hawaii at Manoa, Ryukoku University in Kyoto, Japan, and Harvard University. He received his doctorate in Buddhist studies from the University of Wisconsin–Madison. He is an affiliate faculty member of the Stanford Geriatric Education Center at Stanford University and a founding member of the Elder Ministry (formerly the Institute of Spirituality and Aging), a grassroots organization dedicated to educating and serving the spiritual needs of elders and their caregivers. He is the author of *Ethics of Enlightenment, Sermons and Essays in Search of a Buddhist Ethic,* and numerous articles that give a Buddhist perspective on bioethics.

Ross E. Newmann, M.S., R.N., F.N.P.-C., A.C.R.N., is based at the Community Medicine Clinic and HIV Clinic at the Tripler Army Medical Center of

Hawaii. He also serves as Clinical Assistant Professor of Nursing at the University of Hawaii at Manoa, Instructor of Nursing at Hawaii Pacific University, and Family Nurse/HIV Practitioner at Tripler Army Medical Center. He received his M.S. from the University of Hawaii at Manoa in 1995 and is a member of the American Academy of Nurse Practitioners, Association of Nurses in AIDS Care, and Sigma Theta Tau International Honor Society of Nursing.

Patricia W. Nishimoto, B.S.N., M.P.H., D.N.S., is lieutenant colonel in the U.S. Army Reserves, Nursing Corps. After receiving a scholarship during the Vietnam War to attend the Walter Reed Army Institute of Nursing, she served 10 years of active duty followed by 18 years of reserve experience. Dividing her time between serving as an associate professor at the University of Hawaii at Manoa, chief nurse at the 1984th General Hospital, and oncological clinical nurse specialist at Tripler Army Medical Center, she also is a member of various military and civilian organizations. These include the Association of Military Surgeons of the United States, Reserve Officer Association, Order of Military Medical Merit, Association of Nurses in AIDS Care, Oncology Nursing Society, Sigma Theta Tau Honor Society of Nursing, and Association of Death Educators and Counselors.

Russel Ogden, B.G.S., B.S.W. (R.S.W.), M.A., received his M.A. in criminology at Simon Fraser University in 1994. He was awarded the university's Sterling Prize in Support of Controversy for his research and his principled protection of the confidentiality of research participants. He took up Ph.D. studies at the University of Exeter in England, where his cross-national research into the underground phenomenon of assisted death again has become the subject of controversy and is the topic of a senate academic inquiry. He recently returned to Canada, where he is an independent researcher working on end-of-life and academic freedom topics. He is a member of the British Columbia Association of Social Workers and the British Columbia Civil Liberties Association. He also has published survey research on assisted death issues regarding social workers and nurses.

Charon A. Pierson, R.N., M.S., G.N.P., Ph.D., is Associate Professor of Nursing at the University of Hawaii at Manoa. She has been in clinical practice as a gerontological nurse practitioner for 16 years and has taught nurse practitioners since 1986. As a part of her doctoral work in medical sociology, she researched and published on issues related to end-of-life decision making. Her other academic interests include ethnomethodology and conversation analysis within the context of multidisciplinary collaborative hospital rounds. She is active in many professional nursing organizations and is president of the Hawaii chapter of Sigma Theta Tau, the National Nursing Honor Society.

James H. Pietsch, J.D., is Director of the University of Hawaii Elder Law Program, Associate Professor at the William S. Richardson School of Law, and Clinical Adjunct Professor at the John A. Burns School of Medicine. He received his B.A. from Georgetown University and his J.D. from the Catholic University of America. He is a member of numerous bar associations, including the Hawaii State Bar Association, National Academy of Elder Law Attorneys, and Bar of the Supreme Court of the United States. Within the community, he serves on various committees focusing on ethics and health care, including the Governor's Blue Ribbon Committee on Living and Dying With Dignity and the Queen's Medical Center Ethics Committee. In 1990, he was the recipient of the fifth annual Paul Lichterman Memorial Award for contributions to the advancement of law and aging.

Mary Rowell, R.N., M.A., is Bioethicist at the Hospital for Sick Children and the University of Toronto Joint Centre for Bioethics. She is a registered nurse in the United Kingdom and Canada, and she has worked extensively in health care education in the field of ophthalmology and blindness prevention in Southeast Asia, China, the Indian subcontinent, and Eastern Europe. She is a graduate of the University of London in philosophy, medical ethics, and medical law. She is undertaking further graduate studies in theology at the University of Toronto.

Melissa A. Talamantes, M.S.G., is Assistant Professor at the University of Texas, teaching in the areas of gerontology and community medicine. Before joining the faculty at the University of Texas Health Science Center, she worked several years as a case manager and counselor for older adults and family caregivers in community-based programs in California, New Mexico, and Texas. She also has served as a hospice volunteer. She is a board member for the American Society on Aging as well as an officer for the Association for Anthropology and Gerontology. She is a board member for community-based organizations, including the South Central Chapter of the Alzheimer's Association, Sister's Care of San Antonio, and Benetia Family Center.

Nancy Westlake Van Winkle, Ph.D., is Associate Professor of Behavioral Sciences in the College of Osteopathic Medicine at Oklahoma State University. After receiving a double B.A. in sociology and anthropology from Pennsylvania State University, she received her M.A. in sociology from the University of New Mexico and her Ph.D. in sociology from the University of Kentucky. She also is a member of the gerontology faculty and an adjunct associate professor in the Department of Sociology at Oklahoma State. She serves as a member of various professional associations, including the American Sociological Association, Gerontological Society of America, and Association of Gerontology in Higher Education.

Gwen Yeo, Ph.D., is an educational gerontologist who has been active in the field for 25 years. With experience as a social worker and teacher of sociology at colleges in Texas and California, she completed her doctoral program in education with a research emphasis in gerontology at Stanford University. Since 1975, she has taught and developed gerontology and geriatric curriculum at Chabot College and Stanford University. She is the founding director of the Stanford Geriatric Education Center, which has helped to develop the field of ethnogeriatrics (health care for elders from diverse ethnic backgrounds). Her research interests include ethnicity and long-term care. In addition to numerous other local and national board appointments, she serves on the editorial board of the *Journal of Gerontology: Psychological Sciences* and on the ethnogeriatrics advisory committee of the American Geriatrics Society.